LITERARY STUDIES IN ACTION

Literary Studies in Action

The aim of the INTERFACE series is to build bridges between the traditionally divided disciplines of language studies and literary studies. A major task in bridge-building is surveying and preparing the land on either side. In *Literary Studies in Action* Durant and Fabb are doing exactly this.

Literary Studies in Action is a new kind of textbook: a combination of workbook and handbook. Instead of just telling you about the discipline of literary studies, *Literary Studies in Action* helps you to answer questions about its history and current practice: about what to do and how to do it, and why literature has been and can be studied. In doing so, it attempts to develop an informed view of where the object of our study in 'literary studies' fits into larger patterns of knowledge and thought.

The numerous examples chosen for analysis range over the last thousand years of writing in English throughout the world, and include a variety of different kinds of texts. *Literary Studies in Action* also contains over a hundred activities for you to carry out yourself, to develop practical analytical skills and to structure your theoretical work.

This is a textbook for the times, which addresses itself brilliantly to the twin phenomena of expanding horizons and diminishing resources of English studies.
— *David Lodge*

The Authors

Alan Durant and Nigel Fabb were involved in setting up Strathclyde University's Programme in Literary Linguistics, where Alan Durant is director and Nigel Fabb is lecturer. In 1986 they co-organised the international conference 'The Linguistics of Writing' and co-edited the proceedings as *The Linguistics of Writing: Arguments between Language and Literature* (Manchester University Press/Methuen, Inc, 1987). Alan Durant is also the author of *Ezra Pound: Identity in Crisis* (Harvester/Barnes & Noble, 1981), and *Conditions of Music* (Macmillan/SUNY, 1984).

The INTERFACE Series
A linguist deaf to the poetic function of language and
a literary scholar indifferent to linguistic problems and
unconversant with linguistic methods, are equally
flagrant anachronisms. – Roman Jakobson
This statement, made over twenty-five years ago, is no
less relevant today, and 'flagrant anachronisms' still
abound. The aim of the INTERFACE series is to examine
topics at the 'interface' of language studies and literary
criticism and in so doing to build bridges between these
traditionally divided disciplines.

Already published in the series

NARRATIVE A Critical Linguistic Introduction
Michael J. Toolan
LANGUAGE, LITERATURE AND CRITICAL
PRACTICE Ways of Analysing Text
David Birch

The Series Editor
Ronald Carter is Professor of Modern English Language
at the University of Nottingham. He is National Co-
ordinator of the LINC (Language in the National
Curriculum) Project 1989–1992.

LITERARY STUDIES IN ACTION

ALAN DURANT AND NIGEL FABB

London and New York

First published 1990
by Routledge
11 New Fetter Lane, London EC4P 4EE
Simultaneously published in the USA and Canada
by Routledge
a division of Routledge, Chapman and Hall, Inc.
29 West 35th Street, New York, NY 10001

Reprinted in 1992

Typeset by Scarborough Typesetting Services
Printed in England by
Clays Ltd, St Ives plc

British Library Cataloguing in Publication Data

Durant, Alan
    Literary studies in action. – (Interface).
    1. English literature. Criticism – Manuals
    I. Title.   II. Fabb, Nigel.   III. Series
    820.9

    ISBN 0–415–03931–2
    ISBN 0–415–02945–7 pbk

Library of Congress Cataloging in Publication Data

Durant, Alan.
    Literary studies in action.
    (The Interface series)
    Bibliography: p.
    Includes index.
    1. English literature – Study and teaching.
I. Fabb, Nigel.   II. Title.   III. Series: Interface (London,
England)
PR33.D87   1989   820'.7   89–10465
ISBN 0–415–03931–2
ISBN 0–415–02945–7 (pbk.)

Contents

vi   Contents

Series editor's introduction to the Interface series

There have been many books published this century which have been devoted to the interface of language and literary studies. This is the first series of books devoted to this area commissioned by a major international publisher; it is the first time a group of writers have addressed themselves to issues at the interface of language and literature; and it is the first time an international professional association has worked closely with a publisher to establish such a venture. It is the purpose of this general introduction to the series to outline some of the main guiding principles underlying the books in the series.

The first principle adopted is one of not foreclosing on the many possibilities for the integration of language and literature studies. There are many ways in which the study of language and literature can be combined and many different theoretical, practical and curricular objectives to be realized. Obviously, a close relationship with the aims and methods of descriptive linguistics will play a prominent part, so readers will encounter some detailed analysis of language in places. In keeping with a goal of much work in this field, writers will try to make their analysis sufficiently replicable for other analysts to see how they have arrived at the interpretive decisions they have reached and to allow others to reproduce their methods on the same or on other texts. But linguistic science does not have a monopoly in methodology and description any more than linguists can have sole possession of insights into language and its workings. Some contributors to the series adopt quite rigorous linguistic procedures; others proceed less rigorously but no less revealingly. All are, however, united by a belief that detailed scrutiny of the role of language in literary texts can be mutually enriching to language and literary studies.

Series of books are usually written to an overall formula or design. In the case of the Interface series this was considered to be not entirely appropriate. This is for the reasons given above, but also because, as the first series of its kind, it would be wrong to suggest that there are formulaic modes by which integration can be achieved. The fact that all the books address themselves to the integration of language and literature in any case imparts a natural and organic unity to the series. Thus, some of the books in this series will provide descriptive overviews, others will offer detailed case studies of a particular topic, others will involve single author studies, and some will be more pedagogically oriented.

This variety of design and procedure means that a wide variety of audiences is envisaged for the series as a whole, though, of course, individual books are necessarily quite specifically targeted. The general level of exposition presumes quite advanced students of language and literature. Approximately, this level covers students of English language and literature (though not exclusively English) at senior high-school/upper sixth form level to university students in their first or second year of study. Many of the books in the series are designed to be used by students. Some may serve as course books – these will normally contain exercises and suggestions for further work as well as glossaries and graded bibliographies which point the student towards further reading. Some books are also designed to be used by teachers for their own reading and updating, and to supplement courses; in some cases, specific questions of pedagogic theory, teaching procedure and methodology at the interface of language and literature are addressed.

From a pedagogic point of view it is the case in many parts of the world that students focus on literary texts, especially in the mother tongue, before undertaking any formal study of the language. With this fact in mind, contributors to the series have attempted to gloss all new technical terms and to assume on the part of their readers little or no previous knowledge of linguistics or formal language studies. They see no merit in not being detailed and explicit about what they describe in the linguistic properties of texts; but they recognize that formal language study can seem forbidding if it is not properly introduced.

A further characteristic of the series is that the authors engage in a direct relationship with their readers. The overall style of writing is informal and there is above all an attempt to lighten the usual style of academic discourse. In some cases this extends to the way in which notes and guidance for further work are presented. In all cases, the style adopted by authors is judged to be that most appropriate to the mediation of their chosen subject matter.

We now come to two major points of principle which underlie the conceptual scheme for the series. One is that the term 'literature' cannot be defined in isolation from an expression of ideology. In fact, no academic study, and certainly no description of the language of texts, can be neutral and objective, for the sociocultural positioning of the analyst will mean that the description is unavoidably political. Contributors to the series recognize and, in so far as this accords with the aims of each book, attempt to explore the role of ideology at the interface of language and literature. Secondly, most writers also prefer the term 'literatures' to a singular notion of literature. Some replace 'literature' altogether with the neutral term 'text'. It is for this reason that readers will not find exclusive discussions of the literary language of canonical literary texts; instead the linguistic heterogeneity of literature and the permeation of many discourses with what is conventionally thought of as poetic or literary language will be a focus. This means that in places as much space can be devoted to examples of word play in jokes, newspaper editorials, advertisements, historical writing or a popular thriller as to a sonnet by Shakespeare or a passage from Jane Austen. It is also important to stress how the term 'literature' itself is historically variable and how different social and cultural assumptions can condition what is regarded as literature. In this respect the role of linguistic and literary theory is vital. It is an aim of the series to be constantly alert to new developments in the description and theory of texts.

Finally, as series editor, I have to underline the partnership and cooperation of the whole enterprise of the Interface series and acknowledge the advice and assistance received at many stages from the PALA Committee and from Wendy Morris at Routledge. In turn, we are all fortunate to have the benefit of three associate editors with considerable collective depth of experience in this field in diffferent parts of the world: Professor Roger Fowler, Professor Mary Louise Pratt, Professor Michael Halliday. In spite of their own individual orientations, I am sure that all concerned with the series would want to endorse the statement by Roman Jakobson made over twenty-five years ago but which is no less relevant today:

> A linguist deaf to the poetic function of language and a literary scholar indifferent to linguistic problems and unconversant with linguistic methods, are equally flagrant anachronisms.

Literary Studies in Action by Alan Durant and Nigel Fabb offers a unique contribution to the Interface series in that the authors have combined a wide-ranging introduction to many recent developments and analytical techniques in literary studies with approaches to the classroom study of such texts which, collectively, offer a radically different pedagogic design. The book shows above all, however, how the different perspectives from which texts are read or the subject of literary studies conceived are rooted in different literary and cultural theories. As the authors themselves put it on p. 2, in this way they 'follow theory' throughout providing as they do a guide to exciting and newly developing theories of literature which are beginning to have a profound impact on departments of English throughout the world. But the book is also radical in the way it challenges 'armchair' approaches to text study; instead Durant and Fabb provide a prodigious range of activity-based, student-centred projects which at all times foster both active involvement with the texts studied as well as productive interaction with fellow students and with tutors. The pedagogic strategy of the whole book offers something excitingly new and different in the study of literature. David Lodge puts it aptly in his endorsement of the book when he says this is a textbook for the times.

Ronald Carter

List of Activities

Suggestions for using this book

This book consists of three main types of material:

(a) descriptions and explanations (exposition);
(b) questions (in some cases with answers provided);
(c) activities.

Literary Studies in Action is intended as a book to be worked with as well as read. For this reason its interactive parts – particularly the activities – are probably its most important element. Much of the benefit to be gained from the book is to be had from working through the activities it contains, rather than just by reading the connecting text. To make this easier, we have left space in the text for you to write into it; in this way the final contents of the book will be provided as much by you as by us. We think that working through problems and issues is the only way of bringing into the book the elements of individual intervention and active learning which are the traditional foundation of literary studies.

Some activities are presented simply as a way for you to check that you have understood items of terminology or how to do specific operations with a piece of text. Others ask questions which have specific correct answers. Where we think this is the case, we list those answers at the back of the book (we have added a note in the activities indicating that answers are provided). In most cases, however, we do not provide correct answers or recommended solutions to the problems outlined in the activities. Generally this is because there is no single right answer to the questions. In some cases, there may be an answer but we do not know it, and in other cases, we may (think we) know the answer but nevertheless feel that you need to work it out for yourself (if the activity is to be of any use to you). In some cases, the instructions in the activity do not enable you to reach a final conclusion. Here it is up to you (if you wish) to pursue the implications further; we hope you will have gained enough 'momentum' while doing the activity to enable you to extend its investigations into new areas. In general, what you gain from the activities will come from your experience of *doing* them and reflecting on your results, not from sitting back and guessing a 'hidden answer we are really looking for'.

Each activity is annotated with a suggested time, to give you some sense of the scale of commitment we feel it is likely to require. Estimated times are given on the assumption of an individual working alone. There are, however, advantages in working with other people; and in this case activities may take slightly longer, because of the time it will take you to get organised (though a group is less likely than an individual to get stuck and so lose time). If you are likely to be working in self-run groups you may find it helpful to look at the section entitled 'Suggestions for teaching a course with this book'.

What to do if you get stuck

Stop and do something else.

Go back and read the passage in question again, or read more slowly.

Use the index and table of contents to remind you of the context of what you are reading.

Stop reading this book and follow up suggested and further reading.

Look in a guide to literary terms, or a companion to literature, or a dictionary, or Brewer's *Dictionary of Phrase and Fable*, *The Oxford Companion to the Mind*, *The Encyclopedia Britannica*, etc. Ask a librarian for suggestions if necessary.

Skip to the next section or chapter.

Remember that some of the questions asked in the activities are difficult for anyone to find clear answers to; difficulty in deciding on answers may point to unresolvable problems raised by the questions, rather than to any deficiency in your knowledge or ability.

'Do' an activity by deciding (and writing next to the activity) exactly why you think it cannot be carried out as asked.

Suggestions for teaching a course with this book

The activities in this book have been written in such a way that they can be done by an individual working alone. But if *Literary Studies in Action* is being used as part of a course, they can profitably be done by student groups in a 'workshop' class. Our own experience of using these and similar activities with a class of second-year undergraduates at the University of Strathclyde and elsewhere suggests that the following general procedure works effectively.

A class time of 50 minutes is set aside. Each room has thirty students and one or two co-ordinators, and each student has a copy of the activity. We begin with the general instruction: 'Form groups of four to five; each group should choose a "secretary" to take notes and be responsible for reporting back to the class.' Students spend 30 minutes in the groups working through the activity. The co-ordinator circulates from group to group, provides input as appropriate and helps people get 'unstuck' where necessary. We attempt to be minimally directive in providing answers, on the basis that the process of working through the problem is the main educational goal (the questions which make up the activities, on the other hand, are very directive). After 30 minutes the groups come together as a class. Using some sort of rotation pattern, the co-ordinator collects from each of the group 'secretaries' a response to each question, and lists them on a blackboard. The collected answers are then compared and discussed by everyone. This final stage of the session lasts about 20 minutes.

Many of the activities in this book can be used in this way, although long activities may need to be edited (or used over a longer period of class time, or possibly partly done by you with the whole class). Estimated times given for the activities may be reducible in groupwork situations, because there are more people trying to solve the problems; on the other hand, the more contentious and individual issues may take longer to deal with in a group, because of disagreements.

Workshops of this kind have several things to recommend them. They provide the high student involvement of a seminar while requiring the low teacher-time input of the lecture. Workshops are as open to individual creativity as a written project or homework, but at the same time encourage people to work together, and provide direct experience of collaborative work. They also have at least partly definable end points, so that students know when the activity is finished in a way which is free from the arbitrariness of time simply running out. In our experience, workshops of this kind provide one of the most efficient, challenging and enjoyable ways for students to engage in literary studies.

Alongside this use of the activities as workshop sessions, the descriptive material is also likely to lend itself to use as course material. Some chapters (e.g. Chapter 1) may be more suitable for self-instruction than for class use. Although there may be some benefits in using the chapters in the order in which they appear in the book (our cross-references assume this), other sequences are possible.

Acknowledgements

This book was completed in July 1988. It grows out of our experience of teaching and discussing issues about literary study, especially in the Programme in Literary Linguistics at the University of Strathclyde, Glasgow. Parts of the book develop directly from our work in the Programme in Literary Linguistics; other parts have their origins in courses and seminars given for the British Council and other organisations, not only in Scotland but also in Algeria, Austria, Brazil, Finland, India, Malaysia, Morocco, the Philippines, Spain, Thailand and the United States. We are grateful to everyone who made a contribution during those sessions, and apologise for any unacknowledged ideas we may have borrowed.

The following people commented on the manuscript, in part or whole, and the book has benefited by their comments and criticisms: Sylvia Adamson, Derek Attridge, Jennifer Bradley, Adam England, Janet Fabb, Margaret Fabb, Shridhar Gokhale, Debbie Hodder, Leonard Koussouhon, Vicky Ley, Colin MacCabe, Sara Mills, Martin Montgomery, Mary Louise Pratt, Rebecca Thomas, Shan Wareing, Deirdre Wilson.

Sakina Mrani Alaoui did the drawings on p. 144.

Thanks to Wendy Morris and Alison Barr at Routledge, and to our series editor Ron Carter.

The production of this book was supported by the Programme in Literary Linguistics. We thank Margaret Philips, Administrator of the Programme, for her help in its preparation.

The authors and publishers would like to thank the following for permission to use copyright material:

'Oread' from H.D., *Collected Poems 1922–1944*. Copyright © 1982 by the Estate of Hilda Doolittle. Reprinted by permission of New Directions Publishing Corporation, and by permission of Carcanet Press Limited.
'Home after Three Months Away' from *Life Studies* by Robert Lowell. Copyright © 1956, 1959 by Robert Lowell. Reprinted by permission of Farrar, Straus and Giroux, Inc., and by permission of Faber and Faber Ltd.
Extract from 'The Patriot', from Nissim Ezekiel *Latter Day Psalms* © 1982, reprinted by permission of Oxford University Press.

Introduction

Aims

Literary Studies in Action is a new kind of study guide to literature. It investigates, and helps you to answer, three questions which confront you when you are working in literary studies (and to some extent in the related fields of communication studies, cultural studies and media studies).

What should you do?
How should you do it?
Why should you do it?

Succeeding in a course means being able to do whatever is asked of you. This is where the 'what' and 'how' questions are relevant. A coursebook or workbook should help you acquire the skills you need to achieve established goals in literary studies. *Literary Studies in Action* does this. But coursebooks and textbooks often stop here, handing down a tradition of knowledge and skills from their own secure position on the ladder of history. *Literary Studies in Action* tries not to do this. Instead it seeks to go beyond other textbooks by rejecting the idea that success in an existing course means not asking *why* the course is the way it is. You study literature in a particular place at a particular time, and this book should help you explore how you got there, where you go next, and how the intellectual and social landscapes of the discipline came to surround you in the ways they do. The book works through these problems by asking historical and critical questions about the development of existing frameworks for studying literature (and other related subjects). It also investigates what alternatives exist.

In *Literary Studies in Action* we take a confident, rather than defensive, view of literary studies and their importance: we bring 'what' and 'how' together with 'why'.

We suggest that developing the skills you need to study literature can be combined with reflecting on what that study is for, how it was established, and what sorts of thing it is possible to learn through it.

Many established courses proclaim 'English literature', 'literature in English' or 'English studies' as the exemplary discipline for expressing your own critical opinions and judgements. This book should help you meet the external demands set by such a course, but it should also help you develop an intelligent independence from the views expressed and handed down by others, whether in a course or a work of criticism or theory.

Context

There is a specific context for introducing a new kind of study guide such as *Literary Studies in Action*. We are now surrounded by a vast range of representations of social experience. Yet although new academic disciplines have emerged to focus on the production of this array of representations and information (media studies, communication studies, information science), studying literature is still the most widely engaged-in of these disciplines. Nevertheless, the consensus which this reflects – that there is still some special purpose in studying literature – is not founded on a consensus about what that special purpose is.

History plays an important role in *Literary Studies in Action*. This is because the past imposes shapes and limits on our thoughts about the present. In thinking, we use categories and procedures that we acquire from our social surroundings, and in this sense the past is a valuable resource of knowledge and judgement. But conflicts and contradictions surrounding those categories and procedures also persist into present forms of things, where they can confuse our images of how things are now. Since our activities and beliefs are conditioned by the past in this way, views of the past – no matter how distorted or partisan – retain an active force in the present. This force is very often beneficial. But sometimes it is this same force of history which surfaces to prevent us analysing, altering, or rejecting given states in favour of new or different perceptions and interpretations.

The present is directly connected to the past, as its 'unfinished business'.

Many traditional ways of studying literature have been questioned and undermined, to an extent that it is hard to press on with the old methods and orthodoxies. But critiques of those methods have rarely been accompanied by specific proposals about what to do instead. In many cases, the critiques simply explore, in spiralling depth and detail, the arguments why things shouldn't be done in the old ways – while frequently going on doing in general terms what they did before: business as usual. Where new methodological proposals (such as stylistics) *do* exist, they have tended to develop as specialised minority options within the subject, rather than as revisions to its primary direction or purpose. In the case of literature in English in particular, there have also been *social* changes which significantly alter the context in which people study. The rapid rise of English as an international language – now used in a wide range of different contexts of multilingualism and for a very wide range of different purposes – outpaces concern with its literature as the expression of a narrow Anglo-American high culture. As a result, many people who set out now to study 'literature' in English may see no obvious purpose in doing so. When faced with the spectrum of academic subjects dealing with questions of history, society and communication, they are likely to see studying literature as a remote and apparently confused activity – possibly even as a set of parochial squabbles taking place in a back alley of modern intellectual enquiry. To someone thinking about beginning literary study in this context, our suggestion is this.

To study literature seriously, you need to acquire specialized skills required for the tasks the discipline demands. But to make sense of your study, you also need to develop an informed view on how your study fits into larger patterns of knowledge and thought.

Following theory

In the last thirty years a large body of work has developed which is concerned with analysing the basic principles and procedures of studying literature and other cultural forms. This work has come to be known as 'literary theory' or simply as 'theory'. *Literary Studies in Action* could only have been written in the light of this work, and we refer to it often in the book. Nevertheless we have focused on individual questions and issues, rather than on particular theoretical works and authors, because we hope that *Literary Studies in Action* will 'follow theory' in two particular senses.

First, we hope *Literary Studies in Action* will take up the valuable challenge which 'theory' has signalled, by encouraging you as a reader to analyse the underlying principles and assumptions of your views. We hope our readers will seek to formulate – and constantly re-evaluate and question – systems of analysis and interpretation without becoming mystified by or subservient to systems which have already been developed.

Second, we hope this book will 'follow' theory in another sense. With the expansion of work in literary theory has come a sudden explosion of courses on literary theory *itself*. Sometimes these courses focus on the publications of theoreticians as a new catalogue or 'canon' for study. They take 'theory' as a course *content*, rather than as part of a course *process*. In contrast with these courses, *Literary Studies in Action* hopes to establish that the major way forward from valuable insights of the last thirty years is towards new courses informed by theory – which use theoretical awareness to explore issues and practical concerns in new ways – rather than new courses in theory itself.

This, we suggest, is the real challenge of 'theoretical' work: the lesson of 'theory' is *analytic work* of theory formulation and theory assessment, not learning theories – *any* theories – as dogma.

Using *Literary Studies in Action*

While *Literary Studies in Action* as a book should be self-contained, providing problems to solve *and* space to solve them in, we do not mean this to suggest that it is the only book you will need. Apart from following up problems and lines of argument wherever possible in the various works we refer to in the notes and bibliography, you need to be constantly looking at and thinking about the wide range of texts around you – novels, adverts, songs, television and radio programmes, newspapers, signs, graffiti, dramas, etc.

Only by connecting your thoughts in working through *Literary Studies in Action* with your own changing experience as a reader, listener and viewer will you be making the use of this book that we intend. *Literary Studies in Action* does not aim to be an exhaustive or definitive survey of studying literature in English. We hope simply to provide materials and procedures for working through problems that should lead into other readings and investigations beyond the horizon of *Literary Studies in Action* itself.

1 What are you letting yourself in for when you study 'literature in English'?

When you start on a course of study in an academic subject or discipline you face this problem:

Q. Why should you take up this discipline in particular?

Why not any one of the other subjects you might take up instead? The only way you can decide between different fields of study seems to be by comparing the one you think you *might* study with other disciplines into which the field of knowledge and possible enquiry is divided up.

But this problem is circular when you start. To decide why it is worth working in any given field, you need to know something about what goes on in that field. But to know what goes on in it, you need to get involved, at least to the extent that you can compare it with *other* fields. But if you do that, you have already taken your decision, and started work in one particular field rather than another.

This circularity is not an irrelevant trick or puzzle; it has a practical bearing on your studies. To be able to compare different fields, you appear to need to start out by suspending serious questioning of what you are doing. But the only way of justifying this is to have enough faith that the larger questions will either not matter, or will become clearer later. By the time you know whether either or these is in fact the case, you are likely to be so far into your studies that many of your other options will have disappeared.

This seemingly needed 'suspension' of investigating the foundations and purpose of your studies is our starting point. In *Literary Studies in Action* we do not accept the need for such an act of faith in the purposes and value of studying literature in English. Instead, we begin by investigating your own initial perceptions, intentions and aspirations, to raise issues which the work which follows should then explore in detail.

You almost certainly already have *some* interest in and sense of literary studies, to have got to the point of picking this book up.

1.1 Your personal aims in studying literature in English

We begin by asking some basic questions about the field of literary studies:

What are literary studies in English *for*?
What do you *expect* to encounter when you set out on a course in literary studies in English?
What would you *like* to see in such courses?

As a way of beginning to explore these questions, consider your own intentions and circumstances. If you are on a course in literary studies, or if you are about to start one, why have you decided to work in this field in particular, rather than in any other? What do you hope the course will do *for* you, and what do you hope it will do *to* you?

 Now do Activity 1 on page 4

1.2 How your own motivation relates to public justifications for courses

Your responses to Activity 1 amount to a statement of your motivation, or reasons for *choosing* to work in the discipline. In one sense, you are a **consumer** of an educational package when you pick a course. You choose from a range of course 'products' available to you (hence some of the descriptions used to describe syllabus alternatives and the process of choosing courses: 'course shopping', 'portfolio of courses', 'mini-cafeteria system of options', etc.). You choose – within syllabuses and courses available – a type of study most closely in line with your aims and wishes.

But this idea of being an educational 'consumer' is only part of the story. In making your choice, you also set yourself on course for a particular kind of **participation in the social process**. You will be prepared for and directed towards particular kinds of social role, and not others. As you gradually gain specific types of skill and knowledge, your views of society and your capacity to act within it will be shaped in particular ways.

Q: Does the way you have described your motivation in Activity 1 suggest to you anything more general about your interest in education (e.g. how education relates to personal development, jobs, social outlook, etc.)?

One reason for being interested in questions of purpose or motivation before beginning to work in detail on

Activity 1   *Assessing your own interest in literary studies*
(40 mins)

1. To identify your own motivation, among the many different possibilities that exist, circle the appropriate value on the scale against each item in the list below. (Each item is an actual reason we have heard for choosing a literary studies course.)

    5 = feel strongly
    0 = disagree; don't feel this

The reason I am interested in a course in literature in English is . . .

. . . because it will improve my   5 4 3 2 1 0
communicative skills (e.g. writing,
speaking, etc.).

. . . because it will allow me to experience   5 4 3 2 1 0
the thoughts and feelings of other people,
including people who are no longer alive.

. . . because it will help me in a process of   5 4 3 2 1 0
self-discovery and personal development.

. . . because it will give me a broad base of   5 4 3 2 1 0
ideas for thinking about individual and
social behaviour.

. . . because it is less authoritarian and   5 4 3 2 1 0
structured than other subjects.

. . . because it will be a way of comparing   5 4 3 2 1 0
aspects of my own culture with another
culture.

. . . because it isn't scientific or   5 4 3 2 1 0
technological and it allows more scope for
subjective answers.

. . . because it's the area I have the best   5 4 3 2 1 0
qualifications in.

. . . because I'm not qualified to study in   5 4 3 2 1 0
other, more desirable areas.

. . . because the subject will lead to wider   5 4 3 2 1 0
job opportunities than other subjects I
might consider.

. . . because it is not applied to any   5 4 3 2 1 0
particular problem or goal; it allows for
thought without any particular application
or purpose.

. . . because it will offer insights into past   5 4 3 2 1 0
and present culture and society, and
develop my critical thinking about these
things for the future.

. . .because it will enable me to earn a   5 4 3 2 1 0
living.

Add (and then grade) any other options here that you feel are missing:

....   5 4 3 2 1 0

....   5 4 3 2 1 0

....   5 4 3 2 1 0

2. Now, on a separate sheet of paper, list the options in descending order of the degree to which you agree with them (i.e. with the ones you have scored highest at the top). Rewrite this list as a short essay, stopping when you reach a point somewhere down the list when the reasons no longer appear to have a significant effect on your motivation. Your essay amounts to a brief and informal statement of your current intentions. (Later, you will be able to find established contexts for these ideas in the history of literary studies; and when you finish working with this book, it will be useful to consult this initial place-marker.)

 Now rejoin text on page 3

topics in literary studies is that your reasons for under-taking a course can be completely at odds with those proclaimed by the course itself. You may be trying, for instance, to study very much 'against the grain' of a course's assumptions and professed purposes. Here are some possible ways in which you and the course might be at cross-purposes:

The course's aims	Your aims
to teach you about the relationship between literary works and their historical contexts	to learn about what writers have said on some topic of particular interest to you

The course's aims	Your aims
to teach you about a tradition of great works	to learn about how literature serves as a form of ideology to promote the interests of a ruling class
to prepare you for a role as a citizen in your society	to pass the course with an above average grade

As a way of exploring these and other possible contra-dictions, and of beginning to connect your personal motives with 'stated objectives' of the discipline itself, try the following activity, which involves examining your views about what courses in 'English literature', 'literature in English' or 'English studies' typically *claim* to be for.

☞   *Now do Activity 2*

1.3 Where do your motivations come from?

Any conflicts and contradictions which were shown up by Activity 2, between your own aims in studying and the various kinds of published or proclaimed aims of the field, may well seem unique to you. But are discrepancies of this kind in fact purely individual and idiosyncratic? Or are there common tendencies and patterns within them,

when you compare your own responses with other people's? It is possible, for instance, that 'studying literature' attracts people with particular aptitudes and preferences, which would reveal themselves in decisions made in the activity. It could be that there are larger social patterns as regards such motivation. Without investigation, it is not possible to say. Such investigation might begin by looking at which classes of people (along different lines – social class, gender, race, age, etc.) study literature, and how representative they are of society as a whole. For example, we might ask why it is the case that in literature departments in British universities there are more male teachers than female, and more female students than male, and why in English literature depart-

---

Activity 2   *Aims of literature courses*

(40 mins)

1. Each option below represents a commonly asserted intellectual, moral, or social aspiration of courses on literature in English. Indicate how common or likely you think each statement of aim is, as a published or proclaimed aim of a literature course (e.g. in a course outline, blurb on the back cover of a book, etc.). Do this by circling the appropriate number by each one.

     5 = most likely to be a published aim
     0 = least likely to be a published aim

(Qualify or modify any of the aims below if you wish.)
The aims of a course in English literature are . . .

. . . to familiarise you with a selection of   5 4 3 2 1 0
acknowledged great works.
. . . to develop your descriptive and   5 4 3 2 1 0
analytic skills as a reader of literature.
. . . to help you work out for yourself   5 4 3 2 1 0
which books are important and valuable,
independently of what other people think.
. . . to increase the pleasure you get out of   5 4 3 2 1 0
books.
. . . to make you a more sensitive person.   5 4 3 2 1 0
. . . to make you a morally better person.   5 4 3 2 1 0
. . . to familiarise you with the   5 4 3 2 1 0
development of a national cultural
tradition.
. . . to enable you to get a degree in an   5 4 3 2 1 0
enjoyable way.
. . . to tell you about established critical   5 4 3 2 1 0
views on works in the history of English
literature.
. . . to provide a source of comparison   5 4 3 2 1 0
with another literature with which you are
more familiar.

. . . to encourage creative writing.   5 4 3 2 1 0
. . . to extend your personal experience,   5 4 3 2 1 0
through your reading about the
experiences and imaginary experiences of
others.
. . . to develop awareness that questions   5 4 3 2 1 0
about literature involve social,
psychological, linguistic and political
dimensions.
Add (and then grade) any other major aims you think
should have been included here.

....   5 4 3 2 1 0

....   5 4 3 2 1 0

....   5 4 3 2 1 0

2. Now go through the list again, indicating how closely you think each aim fits with, or is compatible with, what you have identified as your own purposes in Activity 1. Do this by drawing a triangle or a different-colour circle around each one.

     5 = coincides most closely
     0 = coincides least closely

3. On a separate piece of paper, write down your decisions for part 1 and your decisions for part 2 as two vertical lists, one beside the other. In doing so, put each list *in order*, according to the marks you have given them, with the ones you have assigned the highest numbers to at the top. Differences in order between the two lists will show up areas of incompatibility between what you personally are looking for in studying literature and what you think literature courses generally seek to offer.

☞   *Now rejoin text above*

ments in many countries where English is not a first language, there are generally more female teachers than male and there is a more even ratio of men to women students. Or we could look at the black/white classification of people. Around 3–4 per cent of the British population is black, though in the British departments of English literature we have worked in, virtually everyone – except special-category 'overseas students' – is white.

Q: Can you find information here about motivations and the social function of literary studies, or is some other kind of explanation relevant?

☛ *Now do Activity 3*

Activity 3   *Significant social groupings in literary studies*
(40 mins)

The purpose of this activity is to describe the social patterns which exist in your educational situation.
1. The first thing you need to decide is what counts as 'your educational situation'. It might, for example, include everyone involved in the Department of English Literature in your college.
2. Now decide on some terms to describe groupings in the educational situation. Terms which might seem relevant are: students, research students, teachers, undergraduates, postgraduates, administrative staff, senior managers (Dean, Principal, etc.), etc.
    Choose some terms and put a different one at the top of each column (one is done for you).
3. Decide on a simple system of categories which describe social groupings. Categories you might think are *relevant* are: gender, colour, religion, age (e.g. students straight from school, 'mature' students, etc.), and national origin. For each one that you choose, write the category and the terms into the left column in the table above (an example is given).
4. Now match the social groupings with the educational groupings. You can do this by, for example, writing the number of men professors (in your educational situation) on the 'gender: men' line in the 'professors' column.

5. List some possible social explanations for the patterns you identify.

educational groupings → social groupings ↓	prof's				
gender: men gender: women					
....					
....					
....					
....					
....					
....					
....					

☛ *Now rejoin text*

Q: Looking back over the activity, how do you decide which categories will be 'significant' and which will lead to 'false' or 'distracting' patterns? You could, for example, have chosen as a relevant social grouping 'height: people who are tall vs. people who are short'. Did you choose this grouping? If not, would it have been a good idea to have done so?

How to interpret what you have done in the activities

When you look at the responses you have made in Activities 1 and 2, you may have some reservations about the activities. You may be irritated by them. On the

basis of our experience with trial groups, your reservations and irritations may well include the following.

■ The options are so vague that any one of them could be interpreted in a way that would include more or less any of the others.
■ Even if you define them narrowly, the options overlap.
■ If you simply say 'studying literature should do *all* these things', there is no selection left to make.

Have we in fact got anywhere?
We suggest that there *is* a usefulness in working through this type of activity, even if you accept some or all of the above criticisms. One kind of usefulness, for example, is that the activities expose something of the

range of established claims about the aims of courses in 'English literature'. More importantly, though, what should become clear is that these aims are **not all compatible**. You have to choose among them, to pick on certain directions at the expense of others. It is difficult, for instance, simultaneously to accept that there is a set of 'best' books to study whilst at the same time holding that the aim of a course is to develop your own independent judgements about which books are valuable or pleasurable (judgements which will be different for each person involved in the course).

To get an overall sense of what you are doing, and why, you need to work through the complexities which surround these divergent alternatives. Also, for the kind of work you will be doing later in the book, it is useful to have a 'place-marker' on what, at the beginning, you think the 'official' aims of studying literature are, and how these compare with your own aims.

There is another general kind of usefulness too. Your assessment of aims above is unlikely to have proved definitive or conclusive. It is more likely that it will have opened up further questions, in ever-increasing echoes, rather than enabling you to define for yourself one direction of study. We suggest that this moment of doubt, confusion, or simply instability of judgement is itself potentially valuable.

Moments of doubt at the beginning of working with this book may help dislodge the idea that a stable and satisfactory definition of the aim of literary studies exists – always somewhere just over the horizon of your present object of attention.

Definitions of aims for literary studies are always *constructs*, the result either of unquestioned influence or of selections along the lines you have made above.

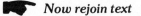   *Now do Activity 4*

Activity 4   *How aspects of study fit together*
(20 mins)

1. Look back to Activity 2. Using abbreviated 'keyword' forms (e.g. 'great works' for 'familiarise you with a selection of acknowledged great works'), write down the options which you felt were important (i.e. scored highly) on a large piece of paper, laying them out in the form of a circle.
2. Now connect the options, by drawing arrows to indicate cause and effect (you might, for example, think that 'developing descriptive skills' leads to 'increase the pleasure that you get out of books'; and so you would

draw an arrow between them to show this).
3. Does your diagram suggest patterns of study that it would be useful to follow? Your answers and thoughts here will inevitably be very provisional. It is one aim of *Literary Studies in Action* to create opportunities for you to reach more considered views on questions of this kind.

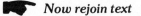   *Now rejoin text*

1.4   What do you expect a course to contain?

Activities 1 and 2 considered the *purpose* of courses in English literature; the activity which follows looks at the *content* of these courses. If, for example, a course is called

ENGLISH LITERATURE, what range of works would you expect it to include? And what range of texts would you want it to include?

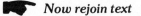   *Now do Activity 5*

Activity 5   *Expected and actual content of a course in English literature*
(60 mins)

The table below lists different *categories of texts* which might be found in a course called 'English literature' (some texts might fit into more than one category). We have left space for you to add further categories if you think they are relevant.
1. How *likely* do you think you would be to encounter

works from each category in a course called 'English literature' in your own academic situation? Use one of three letters, A to C.

   A = very likely to encounter
   C = very unlikely to encounter

An example is done for you; we think we would be very likely to encounter some works written in England in such a course, so we write A in column 1 on the relevant line. If you disagree, change the letter.

2. Now write into column 2 your opinion about how important or central each option *should* be in a course called 'English literature'. Use one of three numbers 1 to 3.

1 = central or important
3 = marginal or unimportant

We have made a suggested answer on the first line; because we think that some works written in England would be central and important in such a course, we have filled in 1. If you disagree, change the number.

	Column 1 the situation you study in	Column 2 the situation you would like to study in
□ *thinking in terms of place . . .*		
Works written in English from:		
England	A	1
Scotland		
Wales		
Northern Ireland		
Eire		
USA		
Canada		
Australia		
New Zealand		
South Africa		
India		
Zimbabwe		
Nigeria		
Kenya		
West Indies		

Add any other countries you think relevant:

....

....

....

□ *thinking in terms of language . . .*
works written in Middle English (e.g. by Chaucer)
translated works written originally in Middle English
works written in Old English (e.g. *Beowulf*)
translated works originally in Old English
works written in Britain in Latin
translated works written in Britain in Latin
works written in Britain in Welsh
translated works originally in Welsh

works translated into English from other languages
Add any other languages you think relevant:

....

....

....

....

□ *thinking in terms of genre and medium . . .*
novels
poems
plays
other written, 'non-literary' texts (e.g. newspapers, diaries, advertisements)
films
radio programmes
television programmes
popular music records
Add any other genres/mediums you think relevant:

....

....

....

....

□ *thinking in terms of value and pleasure . . .*
works which are agreed to be of special value
works which are pleasurable

3. Before you continue, consider whether your selection in column 2 is feasible. Could you actually fit examples of all these works into the course time available to you in your current academic situation?

YES/NO → if 'no' then go back over column 2 and revise it in order to be more selective

4. How closely do the options you have labelled '1' in column 2 correspond with the ones you have labelled 'A' in column 1?

very closely	not closely
↓	↓
what you would like to study and what you expect you will study overlap very closely	your sense of what it is important to study does not fit well with your expectation of what courses in this field generally contain

5. Can you explain the choice of options which you have given 'A' in this activity by looking at your estimate of public justifications for courses in English literature in Activity 2?

6. Can you explain the choice of options which you have given '1' in this activity by looking at your choice of personal aims in Activity 1?

7. Imagine yourself to be in one of these countries (choose one you are not already in). Circle the country you choose.

Ireland	Finland	India
Brazil	Australia	Sierra Leone
Singapore	The United States	Britain

8. In the light of the decision you made in 7, now go through parts 1 and 2 of this activity again. Which options would you number or letter differently, and why?

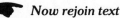 *Now rejoin text*

Like Activity 2 about the purpose of literary study, this activity to do with course content is likely to raise more questions than it can resolve. Its usefulness is that it can draw attention to the *criteria* of inclusion and exclusion that you work with.

1.5 A 'canon'

In the last section, we looked at different possibilities which exist as regards deciding on the content or 'coverage' of courses in literature in English: what you would expect to find, and what you would hope to find. A term which is relevant here is **canon**.

The *Oxford English Dictionary* lists the following as some of the meanings for the word 'canon'.

(a) a law laid down by the (Christian) Church;
(b) a general rule or fundamental principle governing the systematic and scientific treatment of a subject (including canons of criticism, taste, and art); an example of this meaning is the following sentence from 1879: 'We may assume it as a canon of ordinary criticism that a writer intends to be understood.'
(c) the collection or list of books of the Bible accepted by the Christian Church as genuine and inspired; by extension, any set of sacred books.

An extension of meaning (c) is given in Thrall, Hibbard and Holman's *A Handbook to Literature (Revised)* (1960), which suggests that 'canon' can mean 'the

accepted list of books of any author, such as Shakespeare'. In recent decades, the term has come to be extended further, so that Eagleton in *Literary Theory* (1983) refers to 'the so-called "literary canon", the unquestioned "great tradition" of the "national literature" '.[1] It is this latest meaning which we are concerned with here, the notion of the canon as a list of writers and texts which are considered (by someone or by a group of people) to have lasting value and importance.

Q: What is the significance of the definitions of 'canon' given by the *Oxford English Dictionary* for our understanding of the most recent meaning of the term?

A canon is often the basis for the choice of texts in a course in literary studies. But as was probably suggested by the last stage of Activity 5, the criteria for including or excluding works in academic courses change over time, and between different places. This means that even a canon of works – a set of works often chosen for their 'timeless' values – is subject to redefinition, revision and updating. Given this liability of the 'canon' of literature to be revised and altered, one potentially useful way of thinking further about the decisions you have just made is to think about them in the light of a particular selection of texts which *have actually been chosen* to operate as a 'canon' (note incidentally that the term 'canon' would not have been used for the following list at this time).

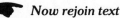 *Now do Activity 6 on page 10*

Activity 6   *Investigating an outline of English literature from 1894* *(60 mins)*

The 'Table of English Literature' below comes from *A Manual of Our Mother Tongue*, a school textbook by H. Marmaduke Hewitt and George Beach, published in 1894. This manual is concerned almost entirely with the English language (and includes a large historical component). The table comes at the end of a section outlining the history of the English language, and is followed by a list of important newspapers and magazines. A footnote to the table says, 'The various types denote the order of importance, as SHAKESPEARE, **Bacon**, *Jonson*, Sackville' (i.e. a text or author in boldface is more important than a text or author in italics, etc.). This list is interesting because it is explicit about which writers and works are in the 'canon' it constructs, and what the relative ranking of these writers and works is. It therefore allows detailed investigation of how an actual canon is constituted: what it includes, what it excludes, and how it ranks texts in order of significance. The particular canon we have chosen is also interesting because it is likely to be representative of (probably conservative) opinion in Britain, at the time when English literature studies was emerging, about what the most valuable and important texts in 'English literature' are. The table is reproduced without additions or deletions, *exactly* as it was printed.

TABLE OF ENGLISH LITERATURE
From 1558 to present time

Authors	Works
Lord Sackville (1536–1608)	The Induction, a poetical preface to the Mirror for Magistrates. Gorboduc, *first regular tragedy in blank verse.*
Sir Walter *Raleigh* (1552–1618)	*History of the World*
Edmund **Spenser** (1553–1599)	**Faery Queen**; and Shepherd's Kalendar (Poetry).
John Lyly (1553–1600)	Euphues, a fantastic romance.
Richard Hooker (1553–1600)	Ecclesiastical Polity; and Sermons.
Sir Philip Sidney (1554–1586)	Arcadia, a euphuistic, prose, heroic romance; Sonnets.
Lord **Bacon** (1561–1626)	**Advancement of Learning; Essays; Novum Organum.**
Michael Drayton (1563–1631)	Polyolbion (Poem of 30,000 lines).
William Shakespeare (1564–1616)	DRAMAS, Poems (Sonnets).
Ben Jonson (1574–1637)	*Dramas*, Songs, English Grammar.
Archbishop Usher (1581–1656)	Annals; Chronologia Sacra (Prose).

Authors	Works
Thomas Hobbes (1588–1679)	Leviathan, and Behemoth, both works on Ethics and Politics.
Izaak Walton (1593–1683)	Compleat Angler (Prose).
George Herbert (1593–1632)	The Temple (Poetry); The Country Parson (Prose).
Edmund Waller (1605–1687)	An Amatory Poet.
Thomas Fuller (1608–1661)	Church History; Worthies of England.
John **Milton** (1608–1674)	Comus, Lycidas, **Paradise Lost**, Sonnets (Poems); Areopagitica (Prose).
Lord Clarendon (1609–1674)	History of the Great Rebellion.
Samuel *Butler* (1612–1680)	*Hudibras*, a mock heroic poem.
Richard Baxter (1615–1691)	Saint's Rest; Call to the Unconverted (Prose).
John **Bunyan** (1628–1688)	**Pilgrim's Progress**, Holy War, Grace Abounding.
John **Dryden** (1631–1700)	Virgil's Georgics and Eneid (Translated); Plays; Absalom and Ahithopel; Hind and Panther (Poetry).
Samuel Pepys (1632–1703)	Diary (Prose).
John *Locke* (1632–1704)	*Essay on the Understanding*; Letter concerning Toleration.
Isaac **Newton** (1642–1727)	**Principia**, Optics, Observations on the Prophecies.
Daniel **De Foe** (1661–1731)	**Robinson Crusoe**; History of the Great Plague.
Richard Bentley (1661–1742)	Dissertation on the Epistles of Phalaris.
Dean *Swift* (1667–1745)	*Gulliver's Travels*; Tale of a Tub; Drapier's Letters (Prose).
Sir Richard *Steele* (1671–1729)	The Conscious Lovers (Drama); Papers in Tatler, **Spectator**, and Guardian.
Joseph **Addison** (1672–1719)	Cato (Drama); Papers in Tatler, **Spectator**, and Guardian.
Edward Young (1681–1765)	Night Thoughts (Poetry).
Bishop Berkeley (1684–1753)	The Minute Philosopher (Metaphysical) (Prose).
Alexander **Pope** **(1688–1744)**	**Translation of Iliad**; Essay on Man; Rape of the Lock (Poems).
Samuel *Richardson* (1689–1761)	Pamela; Clarissa Harlowe, Sir Charles Grandison (Novels).
Bishop Butler (1692–1752)	Analogy of Religion; Sermons.

Authors	Works	Authors	Works
James Thompson (1700–1748)	The Seasons; Castle of Indolence.	Robert Southey (1774–1843)	Thalaba, Roderick, Curse of Kehama (Poems); Life of Nelson (Prose).
Henry *Fielding* (1707–1754)	Joseph Andrews; Tom Jones (Novels).	Charles Lamb (1775–1834)	Essays of Elia.
Dr. **Samuel Johnson** (1709–1784)	**Lives of the Poets, English Dictionary**, Rasselas (Prose); Vanity of Human Wishes (Poetry).	Thomas Campbell (1771–1844)	Pleasures of Hope, Gertrude of Wyoming (Poems); Life of Petrarch (Prose).
David *Hume* (1711–1776)	History of England.	Henry **Hallam** (1778–1859)	**Europe during Middle Ages; Constitutional History of England**.
Laurence Sterne (1713–1768)	Tristam Shandy; Sentimental Journey (Prose).		
Thomas **Gray** (1716–1771)	Odes; **Elegy** in Country Churchyard.	Thomas Moore (1779–1852)	Lalla Rookh; Irish Melodies.
William Collins (1720–1756)	Ode on the Passions.	Thomas De Quincey (1785–1859)	Confessions of an English Opium-Eater (Prose).
Tobias *Smollett* (1721–1771)	Continuation of Hume's History; Roderick Random (Novel).	Sir William Hamilton (1788–1854)	Lectures on Metaphysics and Logics.
Adam **Smith** (1723–1790)	**Wealth of Nations** (Political Economy).	Lord **Byron** (1788–1824)	**Childe Harold**, Corsair, Lara, Don Juan, Manfred, etc. (Poems).
Oliver **Goldsmith** (1728–1774)	The **Traveller, Deserted Village** (Poems); She Stoops to Conquer, Good-natured Man (Plays); Vicar of Wakefield (Prose).	Percy Bysshe *Shelley* (1792–1822)	Queen Mab, Revolt of Islam, Prometheus Unbound, *The Cloud* (Poems).
		Thomas **Carlyle** (1795–1881)	**French Revolution**; Oliver Cromwell; Frederick the Great; **Sartor Resartus**.
Edmund *Burke* (1730–1797)	*French Revolution* (Political); On the Sublime and Beautiful (Philosophical).	John Keats (1796–1820)	Endymion, Hyperion, Eve of St. Agnes, Lamia (Poems).
William *Cowper* (1731–1800)	The *Task*, Olney Hymns, Translations (Poetry).	Thomas *Hood* (1798–1845)	*Song of the Shirt*, and other poems; Up the Rhine (Prose).
Horne Tooke (1736–1812)	Diversions of Purley (On Language).	Lord **Macaulay** (1800–1859)	**History of England; Essays** on Clive, Milton, etc.; **Lays** of Ancient Rome.
Edward *Gibbon* (1737–1794)	*Decline and Fall of the Roman Empire*.	Nathaniel Hawthorne (1804–1864)	Twice Told Tales; History of New York (**American**).
Sir Philip Francis (1740–1818)	Letters of Junius (Political Invectives). Authorship doubtful.	Lord Lytton (1805–1873)	Lady of Lyons (Poem); My Novel; The Caxtons, etc.
William *Paley* (1743–1805)	*Evidences of Christianity; Natural Theology*.	Earl of Beaconsfield (Benjamin Disraeli) (1805–1882)	Henrietta Temple; Coningsby, etc.
Jeremy **Bentham** (1748–1832)	**Theory of Legislation**.	John Stuart **Mill** (1806–1873)	**Political Economy; Logics**.
Thomas Chatterton (1752–1770)	Poems of Rowley.	Henry Wadsworth *Longfellow* (1807–1887)	Golden Legend, Evangeline, Tales of a Wayside Inn (Poems) (American).
Dugald *Stewart* (1753–1828)	Philosophy of Human Mind; Outlines of *Moral Philosophy*.	William Makepeace **Thackeray** (1811–1863)	Colonel Newcombe, Vanity Fair (**Novels**); The Four Georges.
Robert **Burns** (1759–1796)	**Tam o'Shanter**, and other Poems.	Charles *Dickens* (1812–1870)	*Pickwick* Papers, Bleak House, Dombey and Son, etc. (Novels).
Sir James Macintosh (1765–1832)	Progress of Ethical Philosophy; History of England.	Charlotte Brontë (1815–1855)	Villette, Shirley, etc. (*Novels*).
William **Wordsworth** (1770–1850)	Excursion; The Prelude; **Lyrics**.	Mary Evans (**George Eliot**) (1820–1880)	**Adam Bede**, Middlemarch, Mill on the Floss, etc. (Novels).
Sir Walter **Scott** (1771–1832)	*Lay of Last Minstrel*, Marmion, Lady of the Lake, Rokeby (Poems); **Waverly Novels**.		
Samuel Taylor *Coleridge* (1772–1834)	The *Ancient Mariner*, Christabel, Genevieve (Poems); Aids to Reflection, *Lectures on Shakespeare* (Prose).		

The stages of the activity which follow require you to classify the texts and authors from the corpus. If you do not recognise an author or a text, you may have to look him/her/it up in a reference work such as the ones cited in our 'What to do if you get stuck' Section (p. xii). If you find you do not have specific ideas about authors, do not think that the activity is therefore of no use to you. Make a precise note of *why* you think you do not have ideas about these authors, and what course of action, if any, these reasons suggest to you.

1. Classification by texts

What sorts of texts are in this canon, how many are there of each, and how do they fare in the value-ranking? In order to start examining this, complete the table below by adding further relevant genre types and then fill in the numbers under each column.

Type of genre	CAPITALS	**boldface**	*italic*	roman	(total)
		Number of texts in each genre			
poetry	___	___	___	___	___
novels	___	___	___	___	___
plays	___	___	___	___	___
non-fiction	___	___	___	___	___
....	___	___	___	___	___
....	___	___	___	___	___
....	___	___	___	___	___

2. Classification by author

Classify the authors into pairs or groups of relevant, different types, and fill in the numbers. Add further classifications of authors, and compare the types within each classification.

Type of author	CAPITALS	**boldface**	*italic*	roman	(total)
		Number of texts in each genre			
female	___	___	___	___	___
male	___	___	___	___	___
non-English	___	___	___	___	___
English	___	___	___	___	___
....	___	___	___	___	___
....	___	___	___	___	___
....	___	___	___	___	___
....	___	___	___	___	___

3. List some authors writing between 1558 and 1895 whom you would now want to include in a list like this but who are absent.

4. Where authors are included, are there any texts by those authors which are missing, but which you would now want to be included? List the texts.

5. List some authors in the table who you would no longer want to be included in such a corpus.

6. Where you agree with the table's inclusion of an author, but you do not agree that a specific text by that author should be included, write the text below.

7. Your answers to questions 3–6 should reveal the difference between your current evaluations of the corpus and this late-nineteenth-century evaluation of the corpus. Can you explain any of these differences?

8. The counting exercise you have just done becomes more significant when you *compare* the results with some other counts of authors or texts. You might, for example, try to find out about numbers of authors writing and publishing during the period covered (how many men, how many women, etc.) or about numbers of texts written (how many poetry books, how many novels, etc.); a comparison in this case might be quite revealing. Or you might extend your work in questions 3–7 by comparing it with another corpus – such as your own course syllabus or another list like the one above in a more recent textbook. You can use the basic template, or format, of this activity to work through such a comparison.

☛ *Now rejoin text*

One thing you may feel after doing Activity 6 is that there is no fixed domain of 'English literature'. Any domain you choose to call 'English literature' has to be established by making decisions on a range of complicated questions, and the ways these change between different places and different times. And there are other questions besides, about the precise scope of the definition you adopt for the phrase 'English literature'. Consider, for example, these questions.

Does 'English' mean the English *language*, or some definition of 'English' *nationality*, or historical 'English' identity or *character*? If it means the language, then what range of varieties of English counts as the English language?

Does 'literature' mean everything *written* (etymologically the word 'literature' comes from the Latin *litterae* meaning 'letters'), or does it mean whatever forms the *established representations of a culture* take (hence the otherwise odd term 'oral literature' which means literature in the form of speech, rather than writing)? How do some written texts become 'literature' while others remain 'non-literary discourse' (why do some letters, biographies, histories, etc. enter the 'literature' corpus, but not others?)?

The questions multiply as you look closer. And they become more difficult still when you extend them to include issues concerning what you should actually *do* with the texts when you study them. Put in this way, the questions are in fact precisely the issues which lay behind the decisions you made in Activity 1, concerning the aims of studying literature.

So, to connect your work in the later stages of this chapter with your first decisions, carry out the following activity.

☛ *Now do Activity 7 on page 14*

1.6 You, reading and studying literature in English

Time spent disentangling the sorts of question raised above is in our view time usefully spent, even if it leads to unresolved further questions rather than to answers. If you simply avoid questions of this type, it will be unexamined decisions and views about the larger questions which will form the foundations of your local commentaries and interpretations. Besides, you will find that even the provisional answers you formulate to the general questions will be useful as general statements to support more detailed or local arguments when you write accounts of individual texts.

Foundational questions about literary study cannot be made to go away. So it is important to discover how they surround you at any time, to chart your own route deliberately rather than be blown on the wind of whatever book, teacher or supervisor you are exposed to. But it is also necessary – unless you have a particular reason for wanting to do otherwise – to hold the foundational questions sufficiently in check to go on doing *something*. If you don't, you are likely to be driven by the impossibilities of definition and the endless interconnection of arguments into a silent world, where no action or communication is worthwhile or possible. What is important is to question (though not necessarily abandon) your own settled ideas that have been formed on the basis of experience so far; and to step back from acting out, as if they were new and your own, critical views that may have been acquired without critical inspection from a particular history of writing and teaching which you happen to have encountered.

☛ *Now do Activity 8 on page 16*

Activity 7   *A literary studies questionnaire*
(30 mins)

Answer the questions in sequence. Delete YES or NO as appropriate. 'Jump' a question only if instructed to.

■ A SET OF TEXTS?

1. Is the central object of study in your literature course a particular set of texts?

YES/NO (if NO, go to 13)

2. Are you supposed to learn something *about these texts*?

YES/NO (if NO, go to 8)

3. Should you learn historical and factual information about the texts (e.g. about their authors' lives; about who published them; or whether many people read them)?

YES/NO (if NO, go to 5)

4. Make a note of some of the historical and factual information you should learn.

5. Do you learn something about the effect that the texts have on you?

YES/NO (if NO, go to 8)

6. Make a note of some things you might learn about the effect that the texts have on you.

7. If you answered 'yes' to both 3 and 5, try to say how the two interconnect.

8. Are you supposed to learn something which extends beyond the individual texts themselves, as a more general consequence of reading and hearing about them?

YES/NO (if NO, go to 13)

9. Are you studying a *tradition* of books or kinds of writing?

YES/NO (if NO, go to 13)

10. Is this tradition *your own* cultural tradition (which would be a reason for studying it)?

YES/NO (if YES, go to 13)

11. Are you studying a 'foreign' or 'alien' tradition because you wish to extend and enrich your own cultural tradition?

YES/NO (if YES, go to 13)

12. Are you studying a 'foreign' or 'alien' tradition because you wish to *replace* your own cultural tradition?

YES/NO

■ THE LANGUAGE OF LITERATURE

13. Are you studying how language works in literature, investigating particular ways writers have exploited linguistic resources?

YES/NO (if NO, go to 15)

14. Is it possible to analyse how language works in literature without at the same time working on non-literary language, to have something to compare the *literary* language with?

YES/NO

15. Are you studying how the act of reading a text takes place?

YES/NO (if NO, go to 17)

16. Are *literary* texts particularly suited to studying the act of reading?

YES/NO

■ VALUE

17. Are you being encouraged to develop a set of values of your own?

YES/NO (if YES, go to 19)

18. Are you being led towards a set of values others approve and feel it would be good for you to share?

YES/NO (if NO, go to 20)

19. If you answered YES to either 17 or 18, make a note here of how values can be compared, discussed or assessed.

■ PLEASURE

20. Is one goal of a course in literary studies to read books which give pleasure?

YES/NO (if NO, go to 26)

21. Do you (or the course designer) know, in advance of reading particular books, which ones will give you pleasure?
     YES/NO (if NO, go to 23)
22. Make a note here of how the pleasurableness of a book can be predicted.

23. Are the particular books chosen for study just 'case studies', while it is really the general *nature* of pleasure that is in question?
     YES/NO (if NO, go to 26)
24. Is pleasure something relative, differing between different kinds of society, different places and different times?
     YES/NO (if NO, go to 26)
25. If pleasure is relative, how can it be investigated in a general way? Make some notes here.

■ CITIZENSHIP
26. Do you think that literary studies is intended to prepare you for a role in society?
     YES/NO
27. Does your experience of literary studies show that it does prepare you for a role in society?
     YES/NO
28. If you answered NO to both questions 26 and 27, go to 31.

29. Are you being prepared for LEADERSHIP OF SOCIETY/CRITICISM OF SOCIETY/ACCEPTANCE OF SOCIETY/MANAGEMENT OF SOCIETY (e.g. Civil Service)/MEDIATION OF SOCIETY (e.g. advertising, media)/TEACHING? Underline more than one of these options if appropriate, and add any other role here.

30. For each type of role which you underlined in 29, list two ways in which the study of literature prepares you for that role.

31. Make a note of who is paying for your studies (you, someone else, an institution, some combination, etc.).

32. Why are your studies being paid for by yourself/this person/this institution? What exactly is being bought?

33. Look again at your responses to 26, 27 and 29 in the light of your response to 32. Do you see any incompatibilities or problems? Comment here.

Now rejoin text on page 13

Activity 8   *Why do you read, generally, and why do you read in literature courses?*
(30 mins)

This activity helps you explore the question *why* you read.

The activity contains a list of reasons why you might read texts (List A) and a list of selected texts (List B). If you haven't heard of the particular texts we have chosen for this activity, and don't have any idea what they are like, ask friends or look in a library or bookshop. If this fails to yield results, replace the items you don't know in the list with books being read by people you see around you (on trains or buses, at home, in libraries, etc.)

1. Write next to each text in List B the number of the option (or options) from List A which comes closest to describing why you read, have read, or might think about reading it. (The options allow for the possibility that you haven't, won't and wouldn't consider reading the book at all.) Your decisions in this stage of the activity should relate to your current reading habits outside formal academic study.

2. Now write next to each text the number of the reason (or reasons) which describes most closely why you would think the text worth reading in the context of a literature course.

List A   Reasons

(1) Read because the book will give pleasure.

(2) Read because the book will give pleasure if you have the opportunity to study it and work on what it means.

(3) Read less for pleasure than to learn about the past.

(4) Read less for pleasure then to learn about the author.

(5) Read to try to understand why many people think the book is important.

(6) Read out of curiosity to get some idea of what other people are reading.

List B Texts	Column A Private reading	Column B Course reading
Sylvia Plath, *The Bell Jar*		
V. S. Naipaul, *A House for Mr Biswas*		
Germaine Greer, *The Female Eunuch*		
James Joyce *Finnegans Wake*		
M. M. Kaye, *The Far Pavilions*		
Wole Soyinka, *The Interpreters*		

List B Texts	Column A Private reading	Column B Course reading
Tolstoy, *War and Peace*		
Shirley Conran, *Lace*		
Geoffrey Chaucer, *Canterbury Tales*		
Ernest Hemingway, *A Farewell to Arms*		
(The book you have read most recently:)		
....		
(Another book you have read recently:)		
....		
....		

3. The options are to some extent simplistic. It is quite reasonable to think that there is a 'pleasure' in learning about the past or understanding why many people think a book is important. The way to use this activity is to look for discrepancies between your left column and your right column. These indicate significant *differences*, in terms of motivation, between your idea of your general reading habits and the kind of specialised reading you think a course in literature is for.

4. When you have filled in and compared your two columns, draw up a list of the general differences you think exist between your left column and your right column in terms of the rewards you anticipate from reading in each case.

☛ **Now rejoin text**

Exploring assumptions behind courses (as you have been doing in the activities above) is a 'theoretical' activity. But it doesn't necessarily fall neatly into patterns of theoretical work you may be familiar with. Exploring assumptions underlying courses *may* be part of a broader, *deconstructive* activity. In this case, it contributes to destabilising fixed myths and systems of meaning defining what a literature course should be – so undermining them.

Or it may be a *consumerist* activity. In this case, it seeks to make you a more selective and better informed consumer of the course 'package' you are taking – so enabling you to seek better return on your investments of time, energy and money, or to claim a right to have your own interests represented, as an individual or as a member of a particular group (e.g. women, New Zealanders, Catholics).

Or the two types of activity might overlap, or even be the same.

The questions and activities in this book are intended to have an *enabling* function. You have to fit them into your own priorities and longer-term purposes. *Literary Studies in Action* doesn't aim to prescribe judgements on specific issues – though it inevitably imposes a shape on the questioning process in its own layout and terms. The case for pursuing this kind of enquiry is this: any selection of particular texts you study, or any set of methods you adopt to study with, reflect what that study is thought to be for. There is no way of getting at literary works – or at other uses of language – without in practice adopting some (often acknowledged) view on the question *how* interpretations take place and how reliable or unreliable they are. Studying texts as a way of learning a culture, or learning *about* a culture, will always involve questions about whose culture that culture is, and where the images it presents fit into surrounding social relationships and forms of experience. You inherit a different share in a society – and will therefore be likely to see 'society' from a different angle – depending on whether you are a woman or a man, what colour you are, how old you are, whether you are disabled, whether you are gay, what social class you belong to, and so on.

To link your work on the activities above to your own larger directions and priorities, you need to think through the following questions.

■ How far does the 'culture' you are studying serve to represent what you think of as *yourself*: 'your' values, 'your' pleasures, and 'your' history?
■ If you are learning, or learning about, a culture which *doesn't* seem to be 'yours', are you using the experience to broaden your cultural experience and make yourself 'multicultural' (aware of more than one form of culture)?
■ Or are you using your study to *change* yourself culturally, and to move between competing images of 'culture', not all of which you can be part of at the same time?

To deal with issues of this kind, you need to examine how language and images of culture *work*. You also need to locate your interpretations of books and culture in the context of audiences, institutions, and ideas of knowledge, value and pleasure: to mark out where, in any instance, you and the established orthodoxies around you coincide and where you part company.

How has the study of literature tended to see itself?

The decisions you made while working through Chapter 1 – *whatever* they were – are to some extent shaped by a larger, changing history of studying literature. Your ideas do not spring up out of nowhere; although they have something about them which is personal and original, they grow in you from ideas around you which history and society put your way. The ideas you read and are taught have their own history which extends back beyond the particular individuals – authors, teachers, yourself – who express them. One significance of your own thoughts being options within a larger history in this way is that there is no single 'correct' way to study literature in English, which you can just learn. Any one way of seeing your study exists relative to many other ways which exist, or have existed in the past.

Being in the grip of history in this way, however, does not mean that you have no power over the future. You can still make distinctions between alternative approaches; and you can judge their different values or implications. You can develop new directions or views of your own, or argue a case for any existing established view. But doing either of these things relies on escaping the dogma of any one single approach: whatever view you adopt as the 'best' one, the 'right' one, or the 'most appropriate' one can only be justified on the basis of a supporting structure of argument which engages with the other, different views around it.

In this chapter, we look at how ideas you have worked out in Chapter 1 fit into this larger history of the discipline; and how literary studies has tended to see *itself*. To explore these questions, we need to think about *past* forms of the discipline. But where do these begin; and where should we begin our investigation of them? Why not try 'the beginning'?

2.1 Ideas in their contexts

Often **origins** are taken as a way of getting at a real, 'original' or prime meaning for something. In a dispute about the meaning of a word, for example, one person may point to the word from which that word was derived – its root – as the original meaning of the word. But when you look at origins, you simply get one context from which to establish 'meaning', simply the first of many.[1]

Consider, in this context, the modern English word 'black'. If we trace this word back from the complex range of (often politically partisan and/or racist) meanings it has in modern usage, we find that the earliest root or origin for the word 'black' is 'bhelg', in the ancient language Proto-Indo-European. 'Bhelg' meant something like *white* and is also the origin of the Russian 'belo-' meaning *white*, and English 'bald' meaning *having a white shining head*, as well as English 'bleach', meaning *to make white*. If the meaning of a word is its original meaning, then 'black' would mean *white*! We can understand how the word for *white* ('bhelg') became the word 'black' by looking at the history of the word: in Germanic, the word 'blakaz' (related to 'bhelg') meant *to have blazed* (the blaze of a fire was thought of as something white); something which has blazed (such as wood turned to charcoal) is black. Hence **white** is the origin of **black**.

Given this complexity of tracing things back to 'origins', what can we learn by looking for the origins of literary study?

☛ *Now do Activity 9 on page 19*

The choice you made in this activity, and the reservations you may have expressed, are likely to have depended on at least three kinds of decision you needed to make in order to do so.

(i) You had to settle on some definition of *literary study*. This means finding for 'literary study' a particular content that is different from other treatments of written texts.
(ii) You had to settle on some definition of *academic subject*. You need to take a view of what it means for something to be part of education before you are able to judge whether it is an academic subject or not.
(iii) You had to settle on a particular *place*. An academic subject, such as 'literary study', needn't necessarily start in all places at the same time.

We now subject each of these assumptions to closer examination.

(i) What is distinctive about literary study?

Here are some disciplines which have been concerned with the analysis of literary texts.

Activity 9   *When did the study of English literature start?*
(10 mins)

1. Circle one option.

The formal study of literature in English in universities and colleges *(the subject you are now studying)* began . . .

before the fourteenth   in the fourteenth century.
  century.
in the fifteenth century.   in the sixteenth century.
in the seventeenth century.   in the eighteenth century.
in the nineteenth century.   in the twentieth century.

Give an answer to this question, even if you feel reluctant to do so (for example because of difficulties of definition in the question itself). Pick the closest, or the least inappropriate, option if you are not fully happy with any of the suggestions.

2. If you have major reservations about the question, make a note of these here (but still decide on a best, compromise answer).

Now rejoin text on page 18

Discipline	Aim
Theology and hermeneutics	To get at the 'real' meanings of religious and legal texts for urgent social reasons to do with implementing laws or deciding on forms of religious observance.
Rhetoric	To analyse oratory and persuasion: how to improve performance in speaking and writing, by analysing techniques used by great speakers and writers.
Classical poetics	To investigate the styles, effects, and ethical implications of literary works, especially epic poetry and drama.
Philology and textual criticism	To establish accurate versions of texts (especially texts which have been copied badly and many times, re-edited and added to, or partly lost, etc.).
Professional criticism and reviewing	To intervene in contemporary creative work.
Academic criticism	To inform a new 'professional' audience of teachers and students.

To decide when the study of literature begins, you need to decide which of these qualify as literary study.

(ii) What makes a subject *academic*?

When is learning part of 'education'? Ideas of 'academic subjects', and of education more generally, have been looked at in various ways. Needs can be identified and responded to according to different philosophies of education.

Need	Philosophy of education
to know a body of material	Knowledge-centred education can be called **classical humanist**; the educators delineate the body of what you should know, then teach it.
to grow and develop as an individual	Experience-centred education can be called **progressivist**; the aim is to connect with your actual experience and then extend and develop it.
to equip a population with socially needed skills	Society-centred education is based on **social reconstructionist** ideas; educators train people to fill required roles in a society.

From these different ideas about what education is, different methods of education follow.

There will be decisions about:

Who should be educated (what sectors of the population and to what levels? both women and men? which classes or religious groups? and together or separately?).

What is the appropriate environment for education (whether you are to be educated at home, in a monastery, in a school, etc.).

How education should be paid for.

How a 'subject' should be defined and studied (new subjects emerge and old ones disappear: for the Greeks and Romans, there were seven subjects, a **quadrivium**, made up of arithmetic, geometry, astronomy, and music, and a **trivium**, made up of rhetoric, logic and grammar; now there are many different subjects, grouped, for example, as 'arts' and 'sciences', with many sub-divisions and classifications such as 'social sciences', 'business studies', etc.).

To decide when the study of literature begins, you need to decide what kind of activity counts as *study*, in the study of literature.

(iii) Literary study starts in different places at different times

Education and academic work differ in different places; and such geographical or regional differences are made more complicated by the changing historical forms of contact, influence, and direct control which exist between one society and another. Aspirations and procedures are borrowed and adapted by one society from another in many cases; in many other cases, they are imposed by one society on another, irrespective of that society's own wishes. Variation as regards beginnings for the study of literature in English can be traced to a range of differences in social structure.

Aspect of social structure	Effect on educational provision and policy
religion	different religions have contrasting views on who should be educated, how, and for what reasons
political system	different social and political orders construct different roles for study and learning; ideals of 'literacy necessary for democratic participation', for example, contrast with traditions of control through preventing access to skills and knowledge
economic capability	education relies on institutions, facilities and technologies which cost money, and which are therefore available to differing extents in different societies
language	languages in use, attitudes to those languages, and in many cases language-planning policies to modify use and attitudes, lead to different educational priorities.

To decide when the study of literature begins, you need to decide which place you are thinking about.

2.2 Origins for the study of English literature: three case histories

We saw in the last section that tracing something (e.g. the word 'black') back to its origins does not necessarily give the best account of its current meaning. Nevertheless, looking for origins can be a revealing starting point for further investigation. So in this section we look at the emergence of the study of English literature during the nineteenth century in three social contexts chosen to represent different kinds of educational and political circumstances: Britain, the USA, and India. Here we take the study of English literature to mean formal learning principally concerned with studying literature in educational institutions (especially universities). Before the nineteenth century anything identifiable as the study of literature meant either the study of Greek and Latin texts, or supporting work in the study of English language (especially rhetoric and grammar), generally taking the form of occasional, exemplary references to literature and the use of prescribed reading. Generally, before the nineteenth century, reading English literature was regarded in educational institutions more as a recreational pursuit to be carried out by those being educated alongside their formal study, rather than as a subject of formal study itself.

Britain

The literacy of a population (i.e. how many people can read or write) is controlled by its rulers. In Britain in 1807 a bill was defeated which would have brought elementary education to everyone, and so would have turned a still significantly illiterate population into a literate one (it was defeated because 'it would enable them to read seditious pamphlets, vicious books, and publications against Christianity'). Later in the nineteenth century, nevertheless, and surrounded by other liberal reforms (including, for example, the admission of women into state education), the 1870 Education Act was passed. It introduced compulsory elementary education, and so made possible a rapid growth in the literate public. During the 1880s the British education system was expanded, with a significant growth in the number of people (including women) going to university.

In the context of these social changes the school inspector, poet, and critic Matthew Arnold (1822–88) made a number of radical proposals for the reconstruction of British culture, which were to 'give birth' to English literature studies in Britain. Arnold was concerned about a decline in British culture, which he described as follows:

The culture which is supposed to plume itself on a

smattering of Greek and Latin is a culture which is begotten by nothing so intellectual as curiosity; it is valued either out of sheer vanity and ignorance or else as an engine of social and class distinction, separating its holder, like a badge or title, from other people who have not got it. No serious man would call this *culture*, or attach any value to it, as culture, at all. (*Culture and Anarchy*, 1869)

Arnold thought that this weakening of a culture based on Greek and Latin was compounded by a weakening in the force of Christianity (weakened by the influence of Darwin's *Origin of Species*, 1859). He also thought that it could lead to anarchy – a fragmentation of society, coming from the loss of a common fund of cultural reference. To stop this happening, Arnold proposed the formation of a new type of intellectual social class, largely through humanistic education in the arts (shaped by the study of classics but with a major dimension of English literary studies). This new intelligentsia would be made up of 'generalists', in the sense that their education would not prepare them directly for solving particular, administrative or commercial problems (for example, in administering the British Empire). Instead, it would lay *foundations* for such work by providing general skills and moral qualities. Devised along these lines, the new study of English literature was introduced largely as a secular substitute for religious faith to serve as a cultural 'bonding agent'; Arnold wrote, 'The strongest part of our religion today is its unconscious poetry.' English literature was becoming more widely accessible (and, increasingly, more accessible than the Greek and Latin classics) because of the expansion of the literate public. Influenced indirectly by Arnold and by other compatible currents in educational and political thinking, the study of English literature emerged into the twentieth century. Its origins also suggest that it was conceived partly as a subject especially suitable for women, and partly as a subject that might bring together existing scholarly traditions of classical rhetoric and philology (the study of language) with a new, secular concern about ideas of cultural value and traditions.[2]

The USA

In the United States, English literature gained its first professor in 1860 (at Indiana), and its first PhD was awarded in 1875. At first, 'studying English' meant taking courses in composition, pronunciation and general speaking skills. Composition was designed to develop clarity of thought and expression, and training in speaking was often geared towards removing the social stigma of foreign accents and lower-class speech from upwardly mobile Americans. In the 1880s, English literature separated from general education courses and acquired status as a specialised major subject, organised on historical lines and covering a canon of authors divided into historical periods. In this shift, literature acquired the function of providing a common body of cultural assumptions and references, among a relatively heterogeneous class grouping being educated. English literature took over the role of work on a corpus of scriptures and classics as a way of teaching cultural traditions. The practical work of teaching composition was combined with new kinds of more specialist scholarship on literary topics, and enabled language teachers to present themselves as professional academics of equal standing with colleagues in other, more established and self-evidently 'specialised' fields. By the 1890s, heads of English departments appear to have wanted to distinguish English further, especially from science. To do this, they adopted an increasingly explicit anti-scientific emphasis. At the same time, they emphasised the distinction from essay-writing 'composition' classes ('freshman English'), and did so by making writing proficiency increasingly an *entry requirement* rather than a topic in the course of instruction. This enabled 'literature' to some extent to break away from its roots in the development of language skills. Increasingly, the study of literature was praised as a means of gaining access to the higher parts of human nature and the soul, creating taste and artistic discernment, and not just a way of making language skills improvement more interesting. In this way, the study of English literature took on a new intellectual role in opposition to industrialisation and urbanisation, and to a great extent left its roots in language-teaching behind.[3]

India

Whereas English is an indigenous language in Britain, and was almost from the outset the adopted national language of colonisers of North America, the language only acquired a role in India after being deliberately and artificially established. The early forms in which English was introduced in India involved missionary activity, especially from the seventeenth to the early nineteenth centuries; but there was also some agitation by Indians for instruction in English, particularly with a view to studying Western scientific knowledge, partly in replacement of traditional Sanskrit and Arabic studies. In 1835 the essayist, historian and colonial administrator Thomas Macaulay produced his 'Minute on Education', which formed the basis for Lord Hardinge's (1844) public confirmation of a policy giving preference to English-speakers in the selection of government employees in India. The 1854 Education Dispatch established the use of English both as a useful instrument of communication and as a source of 'civilised' cultural values in a concrete programme for higher education. These developments introduced the English *language* to Indian education, not English literature. The study of literature, which was later deeply consolidated as the principal means of teaching the language, was introduced on the basis of specific 'cultural' dimensions of the thinking behind Macaulay's 'Minute'. Macaulay wanted to create 'a class of persons,

Indian in blood and colour, but English in taste, in opinion, in morals and in intellect'. He claimed that 'a shelf of a good European library' is 'worth the whole native literature of India and Arabia', and on this basis, the study of British culture, in the form of English literature, was introduced through the specialised intermediary class of Indian scholars of English language and literature, as a means of familiarising a colonised population with forms of a culture deemed to be superior to their own, and of introducing, indirectly, the framework of Christian ideas latent in English literary texts.

If we now summarise the motivations for the introduction of literary studies outlined in the three schematic expositions above, we see that origins of the subject cannot in themselves account for its current functions or future possible directions.

Country	Reasons for introduction
Britain	as a secular substitute for religious faith and a suitable subject for women; to serve as a cultural 'bonding agent'
USA	as a means of professionalising English language-teaching and a suitable subject for gaining access to the higher parts of human nature and the soul; to provide a single common fund of cultural reference, create taste and cultivate opposition to industrialisation and urbanisation
India	as a means of familiarising a colonised population with forms of a culture deemed to be superior to their own; to provide exemplary models of the English language in use and to illustrate Christian thought

'Meanings' of the discipline are to be found only in a changing network of definitions and redefinitions which come between such origins and the present forms things take: the forms which we inherit and of which we are part.

2.3 Describing ways of studying literature, from beginnings to now

The rest of this chapter is made up of a set of short, 'snapshot' accounts of different theoretical and critical perspectives, with activities which enable you to test your understanding of them.[4] These accounts and activities provide a guide to some of the main views and changes of direction which come between the origins just described and the situation in literary studies around us now. There are, however, problems associated with thinking about critical and theoretical perspectives, and it is important to consider these from the outset.

Problem 1 Theories as things to use and as things to have an attitude about

What follows in this chapter is not a historical survey of literary criticism and literary theory. It is a list of simple, stereotypical representations, coupled with glimpses of what you would probably *do* with texts if you were working in the particular idiom yourself.

Often, theories and critical perspectives are presented *in the past tense*: without commitment on the part of the presenter to them as attempts to understand the world. This separation of past from present can make it difficult to see which particular beliefs actually motivate or drive courses or critical works you're involved with now. The separation of theory from personal belief can emerge as an apparent openness to *all* critical perspectives (e.g. 'there are many different views on this question . . .'), or by the appearance of superiority to even the 'major' critical views being presented (e.g. 'but Derrida is surely wrong to suggest that . . .'). It seems important, therefore, to distinguish between at least the three following *modalities* of working with theories (we have labelled them M1, M2 and M3).

M1 'Here are some ideas associated with the work of X (for 'X' substitute the name of a critic or theorist); we are studying these ideas because X is historically interesting, but we are not suggesting that we agree with X, or that you should agree with X.'
M2 'Here are some ideas associated with the work of X, which we think are correct and which we are suggesting you should adopt.'
M3 'Here are some ideas associated with the work of X, which – even if we don't agree with them – will enable us to make some progress with the questions we suggest you should be interested in.'

In following theories, you need to monitor which of these modalities – or what combination of them – you are operating in at any one time. (In the case of modality 3 in particular, you also need to make sure that the 'questions you're interested in' are made explicit and agreed.)

Problem 2 Theories as things that are too complicated to explain simply

It might be argued that our outlines simplify unacceptably. You might, for example, say that a theoretical position takes form as *theory* only at a certain level of complexity, below which, for example, structuralism just isn't 'structuralism'. This view sees a theoretical position as a *single complex object*, rather than as a set of more simple assumptions, goals, and methods connected together. A similar tendency is to suggest that a theory can be consumed only in some original form: in this view, the only way to learn about deconstruction is to start with Derrida's *Of Grammatology* (which is a **primary source** of the theory, while a book about Derrida is a **secondary** source). We return to problems of this kind about theories in Chapter 8; but it will be useful for you to try to establish your own present view on each of the three following questions (labelled Q1, Q2 and Q3), before going on to the rest of the chapter.

Q1 Does understanding a theory require understanding its history?

Q2 Does a theory have validity outside its history (and its movements from one geographical and social context to another)?

Q3 If every copy of the works of Bakhtin (a theorist) is somehow lost tomorrow, and only commentaries remain, will we need to stop talking about Bakhtin's 'theory'?

Deep and unresolved problems about the relationship between 'theoretical' work and other types of writing lie behind these questions. In practice, however, very many people – including us and almost certainly your teachers – learn many things/most things/everything about theoretical positions from secondary sources (or a combination of primary and secondary sources). This is only an embarrassment to people who *also* hold the view that theories are not 'detachable' from the primary texts in which they occur. But we should nevertheless add that our accounts here are not intended as substitutes for reading either primary or other secondary texts, or as adequate material to use to justify or condemn any particular approach; they are to help you form a mental map of the scope and likely consequences of holding different theoretical viewpoints.

Bearing these considerations in mind, we now present short summaries of a selection of critical and theoretical ideas and movements which have been relevant in the study of English literature. As you read, you may find it helpful to bear the following general notes about our accounts in mind (N1, N2 and N3).

N1 You will not find all ideas and movements represented; this would not be possible and it is not our intention.

N2 Some theories have only one or two proponents, and a small number of primary texts (Arnold's theory of touchstones with which we begin is like this). Other theories are made up of the work of a large number of theorists and have many primary texts; in many cases, they also extend beyond literary studies, into philosophy, psychology, sociology, politics, etc. Most of the theories which we discuss are like this, and the summaries we provide are very selective and would not be acceptable to all proponents of the theory.

N3 If you find it difficult to follow some parts of our descriptions, this does not mean that you will therefore be unable to follow the rest of the book. We suggest you skip passages you have difficulty understanding, and return to them later (some of the relevant issues are discussed again later in the book,

so you will be in a good position to re-read these opening accounts when you have worked through later chapters).

2.3.1 ARNOLD: 'TOUCHSTONES'

In Section 2.2, we noted Arnold's influence on early forms of the academic study of English literature in British universities. Now we will look at one of Arnold's practical suggestions for thinking about literature. In the essay 'The Study of Poetry' (1880), Arnold suggests that in order to be able to judge **quality** in poetry, comparison with a benchmark or unchanging standard offers a valuable practical guideline. He writes:

> Indeed there can be no more useful help for discovering what poetry belongs to the class of the truly excellent, and can therefore do us most good, than to have always in one's mind lines and expressions of the great masters, and to apply them as a touchstone to other poetry. Of course we are not to require this other poetry to resemble them; it may be very dissimilar. But if we have any tact we shall find them, when we have lodged them well in our minds, an infallible touchstone for detecting the presence or absence of high poetic quality, and also the degree of this quality, in all other poetry which we may place beside them. Short passages, even single lines, will serve our turn quite sufficiently.

 Now do Activity 10 on page 24

2.3.2 RICHARDS AND CAMBRIDGE 'NEW CRITICISM'

The study of English literature undergoes a significant change of emphasis with the early work of I. A. Richards, work which is a source of one of the major critical currents of twentieth-century English studies: **New Criticism**. The influence of New Criticism extends through the work of associates and disciples of I. A. Richards, F. R. Leavis and others into the teaching and writing of many teachers of English around the world today. It also shapes the critical viewpoint of various reference works, such as the *Pelican Guide to English Literature*. Richards's work superimposes new perspectives on the existing framework of study provided by Arnold's approach. But in addition to noting this continuity, it is also important to note changes, since in many contemporary accounts of the history of studying English literature (especially ones written from a post-structuralist viewpoint), Arnold and Richards are compressed together into what are referred to simply as 'traditional' approaches.

The First World War (for Britain, 1914–18) provides an impetus to plans for a new English course at Cambridge (by this time, many other British universities already have English departments). Plans for the new course are first discussed in wartime (in 1917), and it is recognised that the substance and ambience of the course will need to

Activity 10   *Choosing and using a 'touchstone'*
(40 mins)

1. Pick a line or phrase you think is particularly good, from any poem. Write it here.
touchstone 1

....

2. Now choose a second, different poem, and read a section from it. Think back to your chosen 'touchstone 1' line. Can your touchstone serve as a suitable yardstick of value, telling you how good or bad the other piece is?

YES   NO
↓   ↓
the idea of touchstones   the idea of touchstones
seems to work   does not seem to work

(It is important actually to compare the two lines or extracts, rather than simply imagining this activity in the abstract, if you are to work through the complexities of using a 'touchstone' fully.)

3. Make a note of what happens, and/or what difficulties arise, when you compare the second poem with your chosen 'touchstone' line.

4. How would you feel about someone else choosing a 'touchstone' line or lines for you? Would this be likely to make the 'touchstone' effect work better or worse?

touchstone 2
   If thou didst ever hold me in thy heart,
   Absent thee from felicity awhile,
   And in this harsh world draw thy breath in pain
   To tell my story. . . .
   (Hamlet's dying request to Horatio, cited by Arnold as a useful touchstone)

Look back to the piece of poetry which you chose in part 2 of this activity. Does touchstone 2 tell you how good or bad the other piece is?

YES   NO

5. Is Arnold's idea of touchstones workable *now*, as a critical tool?

YES   NO
answer question 6   answer question 7

6. How would you describe to someone how 'touchstones' should be used in practice? (a) How should they be chosen? (b) How many will you need? (c) What kinds of comparison show up relative differences in poetic quality best?

7. List some assumptions about poetry, and about value, which lie behind Arnold's formulations.

Write your answer to question 6 or 7 here.

☛ *Now rejoin text on page 23*

reflect a new context for the humanities. There will be a far broader class base of students, following the introduction of compulsory education two generations earlier; there will be an expansion of competitive grammar-school scholarships to university; and there will also be greater demands on social participation and rights for women and young men who have already given up part of their life to national warfare. By a series of developments (which are both 'intellectual' and institutionally 'political'), the field of English is separated from its earlier dimensions of language study. In particular, the study of the history of the language (e.g. the study of Old English/Anglo-Saxon) is abandoned, as is the study of the general processes of language change (**philology**, associated particularly with German scholars – at that time, thought of as enemies in war). The overall result is that English increasingly finds a focus in literary response brought about by close but *non-systematic* reading.

The war separated two generations of academics with typically different backgrounds and experiences, the new generations creating the new forms of literary studies.

Typical characteristics of academics appointed in general 'literature' field

Pre-war	Post-war
Upper-class backgrounds	Lower-middle-class backgrounds
Arthur Quiller-Couch: a knight	*Richards: father a works manager*
A. C. Bradley: Dean of Westminster	*Leavis: father a musical instrument maker*
Few had experience of the war	Many had experience of the war
	Leavis: as a medical orderly
Generally classicists by training	Many came from other fields (*e.g. Leavis, History; Richards, Mental and moral sciences*)

Richards himself characteristically keeps a distance between himself and literary studies. In 1919 he apparently wants to be a mountaineering guide in the Scottish Highlands rather than a Cambridge lecturer; and after about 1930 his interest in literature seems to become subordinate to more general questions of language and rhetoric, as well as to his continuing interest in travel and mountaineering. During this brief period, nevertheless, he writes two influential books: *Principles of Literary Criticism* (1924) and *Practical Criticism* (1929). In his work of this period, Richards is especially known for creating 'practical criticism', an approach to literary texts which became a course component that still exists in many contemporary literature courses.

The book *Practical Criticism* looks at how a particular group of Cambridge undergraduates evaluated and interpreted poems when they did not know who the author

was and were not provided with footnotes (and so could not draw on knowledge about the author's reputation, or received ideas about the work's reputed literary value and importance). In commenting on the students' responses, the book challenges traditional critical deference to established opinion. But at the same time the 'interpretations' produced by Richards's experimental subjects are used in the book to raise psychological questions about reading and misreading: Richards links his interest in notions of reading literature as something *culturally* important with his interest in mechanisms of communication and interpretation.

To hold views consistent with Richards's notion of 'practical criticism' today, you would have to think roughly the following:

---

1. Received opinion about literature obscures actual contact with the text; and the best way to get round this is to strip away context and accumulated opinion: to read closely for yourself.

2. Seeing what happens when such close reading takes place reveals things about 'the state of culture'; about how people read and about what assumptions underlie attributions of value to literary texts.

3. Reading in the 'new critical' way develops *techniques* of reading, by foregrounding the process of reading and enabling discussion of specific aspects of the text, such as irony, paradox, etc.

4. Reading literature is valuable because in literary uses of language, feelings and perceptions are combined in complex, sometimes contradictory ways. These enable us to draw on *all* the resources of language, and also lead to mental processes of combining and resolving contradictions and tensions at 'higher' levels. The personal ability to produce coherence out of such complexity is considered a valuable psychological resource.

5. Reading literature is valuable because it helps us resist an imperilment of 'culture' and protects us, in a changing world, from popular culture and tastes.

Many people who would advocate 'practical criticism' as a method would in fact claim to hold only some, not all, of these beliefs. This is partly because, since 1929, practical criticism has developed in a variety of different directions, each of which takes up a different aspect of the basic idea of close reading without the support (or interference) of background knowledge and the assumptions and received opinions which that knowledge brings. In practice, an activity called 'practical criticism' can take any of these three forms:

(i) a 'dating' exercise or puzzle (working out, from features of style, topic, theme, etc., what period a text or extract was written in – even possibly by whom);

(ii) discussion of impressions and response, based on sensitivity to the style of the text, and leading towards critical evaluation;

(iii) a task of stylistic analysis, examining 'clues' in the style of the text in systematic ways to support – or create – 'readings' or 'interpretations', then comparing these interpretations and exploring the textual evidence for each.

► *Now do Activity 11 on page 27*

2.3.3 'LEAVISISM': READING, TRADITION AND VALUE

Alongside work by Richards, ideas from the work of F. R. Leavis (1895–1979) still provide perhaps the major landmarks for many students and teachers of literature in English. (Although there were very many other 'New Critics' besides Richards and Leavis, the shaping elements of New Criticism passed through into studying literature in English most clearly from the work of these two critics, at least in Britain.)

F. R. Leavis's work places emphasis on sensitive close reading, and on ideas of the value of particular works and traditions of literature in defining alternatives to the mass cultural production of modern industrial societies. These ideas have added the dimension of **active minority opposition** to the critique of prevailing cultural forms offered two generations earlier by Arnold and others.

The early stages of Leavis's professional career, nevertheless, suggest an important qualification to the stereotypical modern image of him as major and 'official' representative of 'Cambridge English'. Returning from service as a medical orderly in the First World War, Leavis resumes his studies at Cambridge, taking up English for the second part of his course rather than history, in which he had done the first part. By 1921 Leavis has become one of Richards's freelance assistants, within the university's system of temporary tutorial employment; and when the faculty becomes fully established within the university in 1926, Leavis is given a five-year lectureship, to expire in 1931. In 1931, however, his contract is not extended, and much of his work after this date is undertaken in opposition to the definitions of scholarship and culture associated with the official university department (an opposition aggravated further by attacks on (his wife) Q. D. Leavis's PhD dissertation as displacing scholarship and facts in literary studies with opinion and response). Following Leavis's loss of his teaching post, the Leavises convene a small group, mainly of junior members of the university, at their home to discuss literary topics – a group sharing a sense of being a minority repressed and institutionally powerless, separated by class and conditions of employment from the

university's centres of academic power and policy-making. From these meetings, the editorial group of the magazine *Scrutiny* emerges, founded by L. C. Knights and Donald Culver in 1932. A generation later, the work of this initially oppositional *Scrutiny* group is accepted as a Cambridge orthodoxy: the redefinition of literary studies brought about by the work of Leavis and his associates is assimilated with little reference to the important intellectual conflicts and disagreement which lay behind it.

The term 'Leavisite', however, is used very vaguely, both in praise and abuse. To be fully 'Leavisite', you would be likely to hold the following ideas, connected and changing in emphasis in Leavis's own work, but combining together to produce a major critique of established notions of culture.

---

1. The experience of reading works of literature, if sensitively carried out, gives access to a special, unique level of perception and emotion, as a result of experiencing language, thought and feeling in action.

---

2. Historically there has been a decline in values (at least in Britain), from a cultural unity experienced in the seventeenth century to a split and culturally diseased modern society.

---

3. This decline is the result particularly of the use of machines, and especially of the industrialisation of society during the Industrial Revolution and the development of modern mass communications.

---

4. In the present only a minority can see the decline in society or alternatives to it.

---

5. There are 'traditions' of work in literature, and in other arts, which stand in opposition to this decline.

---

6. New kinds of study of literature focusing on these traditions can rehumanise people, and act as an important social force against mass vulgarity.

---

7. Techniques of close reading, such as those developed in practical criticism, can serve as spot checks on the quality or value of texts, and function to distinguish texts according to their relative quality.

Many people who might describe themselves as Leavisites hold idea 1 and possibly 7 but not – at least not explicitly – the others. (It is debatable whether this is properly 'Leavisism' or whether it is simply a general faith in the value of literature.) Equally, many people use the term 'Leavisism' as criticism or abuse without identifying any 'crime' more specific than an apparent commitment to 1 and 7. Arguably Leavis's own originality – his particular extension of the Arnoldian framework of

Activity 11   *Practical criticism*
(60 mins)

Here is the first paragraph of a commentary on a poem, William Wordsworth's 'The Solitary Reaper'.

> The fact that this poem is not equally good in all of its parts does not mean that it is unadmirable. Perhaps no poem is perfect or could be; and perhaps an appearance of perfection is the most suspicious appearance a poem can put up. At any rate, here is a famous poem that deserves its fame, and yet each stanza is inferior to the one before it. The first, which is the best, has none before it, and in fact contains or expresses the whole of the impulse that was moving Wordsworth as he wrote. Not as he saw this Highland girl, for he never saw her. He read about her in a prose book of travels, Thomas Wilkinson's TOUR IN SCOTLAND. Wilkinson saw the solitary lass, and wrote a sentence about her which made Wordsworth in effect see her too – made him, that is, see her as a poet. Many great poems have come thus out of books: most commonly, out of prose books. Prose discovers the matter and leaves it clear; after which the poet has only to write his poem as if the matter of it were his own, as indeed it comes to be.

1. Look at the five-point summary of practical criticism and the three-point summary of procedural options for practical criticism, given on pp. 25–6. Using these summaries, list features in the boxes below. (You will find it helpful to consider features which suggest the context in which the commentary was written; the resources drawn on in writing it; and the purposes for which it was written.)

Box 1 *Features which suggest the passage follows the procedures of practical criticism*

Box 2 *Features which suggest that the passage does NOT follow the procedures of practical criticism*

Box 3 *Features which might or might not show that the passage follows the procedures of practical criticism, but you are not sure which*

---

2. How could you confirm your decisions, or reach a decision as regards things you have put in Box 3? Tick one or more of these options. (N.B. Before you decide to tick them all, make sure that they are compatible with one another.)

(a) Refer to Richards's *Practical Criticism*. If he commends the aspects or features in question, or if there are examples of them in the book, then the features can be thought of as 'practical criticism'.

(b) Make a case of your own, arguing either that these aspects of the passage are *compatible* with the main arguments behind 'practical criticism', or, alternatively, that they are *incompatible*.

(c) Claim that 'practical criticism' as an approach is only concerned with *some* aspects of commentary, and that it is therefore consistent with a 'practical criticism' approach to find aspects of a piece of criticism which have little or nothing to do with the defining properties of 'practical criticism' at all.

☞ *Now rejoin text on page 26*

argument – lay in combining a commitment to close reading as a vital experience of language with the idea of cultural decline and its possible revitalisation *by the actions of an energetic and enlightened minority*.

Clearly Leavis has many things in common with Richards. The clearest contrast between the two lies in their different degrees of commitment to systems of formal analysis of language and meaning. Whereas for Richards the study of literature has a lot to learn from its overlap with linguistics, psychology and anthropology, for Leavis the emphasis in literary reading should be on individually developed close reading skills of 'experiencing' language. Modern images of Leavisism tend to stress its apparent conservatism, by emphasising its concern with tradition and with ideas of experience. But there is another, less emphasised side of Leavis's work: the radicalism of a minority programme of fundamental cultural reform through literary education.

Now do Activity 12 on page 29

2.3.4 MARXIST LITERARY CRITICISM

Karl Marx (1819–83) gave his name to Marxism. But Marxism is the developing cumulation of many people's ideas, positions, and practical actions, not all of which are compatible.[5] What is common to Marxist analyses of society and culture is the idea of **interconnection between different levels of society**. Someone who is a Marxist believes in the inseparability between economic structures and relationships, often called the **base** or **infrastructure**, and the means through which those structures and relationships are represented or expressed: the **superstructure**.

Base or infrastructure	Superstructure
what things get made, who works on making them, who owns the land, tools and materials through which production takes place, how the fruits of such production are distributed among people	language, the arts, literature, rituals, religion, ideas, institutions (e.g. police, schools, etc.)

This separation of material practice from ideas runs into some problems, particularly in dealing with science, which is both part of the base (by creating and using technologies) and of the superstructure (as a collection of ideas).

Marxism and social change

Marxists are concerned to promote and carry through **social change**, especially through analysing the processes of social development using critical methods of

dialectical materialism and historical materialism, both of which enable in literary analysis a relating of literary texts to the material basis of a society (whether capitalist, feudal, communist, etc.) and the conditions of production of those texts (e.g. the existence of libraries and copyright laws). By providing a way of assessing the relationship between a text and a society, the methods of materialism can be used to promote social change by distinguishing between progressive and non-progressive texts. **Progressive texts** are those which contribute to social change towards an egalitarian (socialist) society; **non-progressive texts** are those which do not. Working on the basis of a distinction of this sort, Marxists promote progressive texts, and expose, in non-progressive texts, the limits of the particular world-view represented in them.

There has always been disagreement among Marxist critics, nevertheless, about precisely what a progressive work of literature is. Three kinds of text which have been proposed are:

(a) **Socialist realist texts.** These investigate and offer insights into the underlying network of social forces in a society. There are different views on what kind of texts enable this. On one view, these texts must provide an accurate surface description of society. An example is Upton Sinclair's *The Jungle* (1906); its critical representation of the Chicago meat-packing industry contributed to making possible the introduction of progressive food legislation in the USA (and so could be said to have led, through social analysis and critique, to progressive social change). Another view (associated particularly with George Lukács) includes as socialist realism texts by writers who have no overt commitment to social change, but who nevertheless by a profound intuition reveal in their texts the underlying forces in society.

(b) Non-realistic **distancing texts**. These present representations of society to an audience or reader by using 'alienating' devices which *destroy* any illusion of reality; instead, these texts emphasise the represented, 'theatrical' or 'artificial' nature of what is being seen or read. The aim of this 'alienating' technique is to prevent an audience from uncritical emotional engagement ('wallowing') in the represented world, and instead enable the audience to reflect on, and so understand, social forces. Bertolt Brecht (German, 1898–1956) is the major theorist of, and influence on, this kind of work; Dennis Potter's television series and film *Pennies From Heaven* is a recent example.

(c) **Formally experimental texts,** including much modernist work (by Stein, Woolf, Eliot, Joyce, Pound, etc.). Sometimes these texts have been claimed as socialist, though this is controversial among Marxists (historically, the modernist writers were affiliated across the whole political spectrum; Pound, for example, supported the Italian Fascists). The argument for considering these texts as progressive – which is related to the argument in favour of distancing texts – goes like this: work which disturbs orthodox reading processes forces readers into exploring

Activity 12   'Leavisism'
(30 mins)

Here is the beginning of a commentary on a passage from William Wordsworth's 'Advertisement' to the first edition of *Lyrical Ballads* (1798). In the passage which this commentator is discussing, Wordsworth wrote about literary taste, and cited approvingly Joshua Reynolds's view that taste in poetry is best acquired through 'severe thought, and a long continued intercourse with the best models of composition'.

> When Wordsworth wrote that, severe thought and long-continued intercourse with the best models were more widely possible than now. What distractions have come to beset the life of the mind since then! There seems every reason to believe that the average culti-vated person of a century ago was a very much more competent reader than his modern representative. Not only does the modern dissipate himself upon so much more reading of all kinds: the task of acquiring discrimination is much more difficult. A reader who grew up with Wordsworth moved among a limited set of signals (so to speak): the variety was not overwhelm-ing. So he was able to acquire discrimination as he went along. But the modern is exposed to a concourse of signals so bewildering in their variety and number that, unless he is especially gifted or especially favoured, he can hardly begin to discriminate. Here we have the plight of culture in general.

1. Look at the seven-point summary of Leavisite thinking given above. Using this summary, fill in the boxes below. (You will find it helpful to consider features which suggest the context in which the commentary was written; the resources drawn on in writing it; and the purposes for which it was written.)

Box 1 *Features which suggest that the passage is an example of Leavisism*

Box 2 *Features which suggest that the passage is NOT an example of Leavisism*

Box 3 *Features which might or might not show that the passage is an example of Leavisism, but which you are not sure about*

2. How could you confirm your decisions, or make a decision about features listed in Box 3? Tick one or more of these options. (N.B. Before you decide to tick them all, make sure that they are compatible with one another.)

(a) Refer to Leavis's works. If he commends the aspects or features in question, or if there are examples of them in his writing, then the features can be thought of as 'Leavisism'.

(b) Make a case of your own, arguing either that these aspects of the passage are *not incompatible* with the main arguments behind 'Leavisism', or, alternatively, that they are.

(c) Claim that 'Leavisism' as an approach is only con-cerned with *some* aspects of commentary, and that it is therefore consistent with a 'Leavisite' approach to find aspects of a piece of criticism which have little or nothing to do with the defining properties of 'Lea-visism' at all.

☛ *Now rejoin text on page 28*

new and often contradictory kinds of relationship between parts of the text. Reading constructs a set of relations between text, society and reader which are exposed for analysis by experimental texts; and by implication these destabilisations extend into the reader's broader perceptions of social relations.

Non-progressive works are all other texts. A Marxist response to them exposes how they lead to or reinforce non-socialist social structures. Marxist criticism of literature seeks to enable readers to see through literature's chosen images to its connections with the economic and political base. In doing this, Marxist criticism seeks to show that the applauded 'human achievements' of great literary works can often be traced back to a fabric of *inhumane* social relations which produced them, but which they choose not to represent: Walter Benjamin (German, 1892–1940), one of the members of the **Frankfurt School**, asserts that works of culture 'owe their existence not only to the efforts of the great minds and talents who have created them, but also to the anonymous toil of their contemporaries'; and he concludes, 'There is no document of civilization which is not at the same time a document of barbarism' ('Theses on the Philosophy of History', in the collection *Illuminations*, 1955).

Marxism and the study of ideology

Collectively, Marxist approaches to texts are attempts to expose the way ideas, images and beliefs (collectively, **ideology**) function. Ideology is a socially constructed network of ideas and images which functions to represent underlying economic and political forces, and covers up contradictions, inequalities and exploitation in the society by **mystifying** them, or making them seem 'natural'. In an early work, Marx himself, for example, suggests that the religious 'holy family' in Christianity is a socially needed, constructed image which reflects actual, human families – rather than, as Christianity suggests, the other way round. The mystification of social realities silences dissent and makes it possible for existing social relations to remain as they are (to 'reproduce themselves').

How ideology is thought to achieve this varies between different periods and directions within Marxism.

Ideology's connection with the infrastructure

Ideology **reflects** (and is derived from) the economic base.	When the economy of a society changes, there will be a direct effect on the forms of culture of that society. History goes through a sequence of feudal culture, capitalist culture, finally socialist culture. Literary forms correlate with modes of production, and undergo changes which coincide with changes in the economic base (e.g. if the novel and blank verse enter society with capitalism, they should cease or change, when capitalism is superseded).
Ideology involves the **hegemony** of a particular way of seeing the world.	Antonio Gramsci (Italian, 1891–1937) suggests that economic relations are mediated in societies by complex, interlocking representations which collectively produce an overall, controlling balance or 'common sense' (which is nevertheless unstable and changing) in favour of a particular class or alliance of classes; these classes rule through apparent consent made possible by the body of interwoven images and alliance relationships.
Ideology is **determined in the last instance** by the economy.	Louis Althusser (French, b. 1918) suggests that considerable variation and autonomy can exist in ideological forms, but that *finally* they derive from underlying realities of the economy. The superstructure is made up of **repressive state apparatuses** (e.g. the army, the police) and **ideological state apparatuses** (e.g. education, the Church, literary criticism, etc.): RSAs are only used by the state when ISAs fail to do their job of reproducing existing social relations.

In the case of analysing texts which are made of *language* in particular, investigations of ideology face an additional question: whether language is part of the base, or part of the superstructure, or neither. One line of development in recent Marxist criticism (in opposition to, for example, the view of the Soviet leader Josef Stalin (1879–1953), and leading into post-structuralist and psychoanalytic developments), suggests that the material which provides the building blocks of language (the words and possible sentence structures) determines our thoughts and pleasures, and that people are formed ('cut out') from language or 'constructed' by language as language-using beings. Our linguistic existence and behaviour become things which can be analysed from a Marxist materialist perspective.

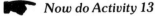 ***Now do Activity 13***

Activity 13   *Trying to distinguish progressive from non-progressive texts*
(60 mins)

Choose a novel you have read or a film you have seen recently. Using the descriptions on pp. 28 and 30, try out a simple Marxist analysis, working through the following tasks.

1. Decide whether the text you have chosen to analyse is 'progressive' or 'non-progressive'. Make a note here of the reasons for your decision.

If you have decided your text is 'progressive', answer question 2; if you have decided it is 'non-progressive' answer question 3.

2. Label your 'progressive' text either (a) socialist realist; (b) distanciating; or (c) formally experimental; then carry out the appropriate task.

   (a) Socialist realist: suggest how it makes it possible to see how society works in a non-egalitarian manner, and how it might contribute to social change.

   (b) Distanciating: describe one distanciating device in the text, and suggest what and how this enables the audience to understand about society.

   (c) Formally experimental: suggest how it destabilises the reader/viewer in such a way as to increase the desire in the reader/viewer for social change in the direction of socialism.

3. For a 'non-progressive' text, suggest one way of analysing your text which reveals its political stance.

Now rejoin text

2.3.5 THE INFLUENCE OF LINGUISTICS: STRUCTURALISM AND STYLISTICS

Twentieth-century linguistics has had two kinds of influence on literary studies. Structuralism takes ideas about analysis developed by linguists for the study of language, and applies these ideas to the study of literary texts (and other cultural phenomena). A different way of using linguistics is stylistics. Stylisticians are concerned with the way that language is used in a text and so are interested more in the findings of linguistics about language than in the methodologies used by linguists. The differences can be summarised as follows:

Structuralism	Stylistics
Interested in the way that a text is *like* a piece of language.	Interested in the way that a text *is* a piece of language.

   One historical difference between the two approaches has been that stylistics tends to be more closely connected with the development of linguistic theories, and the correctness or otherwise of linguistic theories, while structuralism has tended to adopt particular moments from the history of linguistics that seem useful or applicable. Stylisticians often *are* linguists with an interest in literature; structuralists are typically interested in cultural practices and have had some degree of involvement in or contact with linguistics.

Structuralism

The term 'structuralism' could in principle be used to describe any theoretical movement which has an interest in structures. Geologists, for instance, who are interested in the structure of rock formations, might call themselves 'structuralists'. In literary studies, however, 'structuralism' is normally taken to refer to a theoretical approach which studies literary texts as though those texts have *the same sort of structure as language*. A structuralist would say that a text is built out of units which collectively define its properties or function. These units are like the units of speech, and they form a system which is drawn on by a writer or reader in a way similar to the use of the language system.

Structuralists are concerned with:

(a) what the units are;
(b) what combinations the units can exist in;
(c) why the units combine in the way they do and not other ways.

A historical outline of structuralism

Historically, structuralism has travelled widely and developed in many different directions.[6] The following, greatly simplified, schematic diagram of the historical and regional spread of structuralism (including what would generally now be distinguished as 'post-structuralism') may therefore help at least place loosely in time and space some of the developments, and the names you may already associate with them.

Intellectual movement	Topics/areas of study	Some theorists	Sample theoretical texts
Geneva school linguistics Switzerland	Linguistics, which had been interested in how languages change, begins to look at how the parts of a language fit together to form a system. Linguistics may provide a model for studying culture.	de Saussure	*Course in General Linguistics* 1916

Karcevskij studies with Saussure in Geneva, returns to Russia and in 1917 presents Saussure's views to the Moscow Linguistic Circle (who form part of Russian Formalism).

Russian Formalism Moscow and Leningrad 1920s	How language works in literature. How literary texts and literary traditions function as systems.	Eichenbaum ....'The Theory of the Formal Method', 1926 Jakobson ....*The New Russian Poetry*, 1921 Propp ....*Morphology of the Folktale*, 1928 Schklovsky ......'Art as Technique', 1917 Tynjanov ....'On Literary Evolution', 1929

Jakobson emigrates to Prague in 1920 and re-establishes contact with a former Moscow colleague, Troubetskoy.

The Prague Linguistic Circle 1920s and 1930s	The study of sounds **(phonology)**. Further work on the formal analysis of literary texts.	Jakobson ....*Remarks on the Phonological Evolution of Russian Compared With That of the Other Slavic Languages*, 1929 Troubetskoy ....*The Foundations of Phonology*, 1939

Jakobson emigrates from Czechoslovakia in 1939 and arrives in the USA in 1941.

Ecole Libre des Hautes Etudes (New York, early 1940s)	The anthropologist Lévi-Strauss applies to anthropology ideas learned from Jakobson about phonology (they are both teachers at the Ecole)	Jakobson ....*Six Lectures on Sound and Meaning*, 1942–3 (pub. 1976) Lévi-Strauss .....'Structural Analysis in Linguistics and Anthropology', 1945

In 1950, Lévi-Strauss takes up a position as Director of Studies at the Ecole Pratique des Hautes Etudes, Paris.

Parisian structuralism roughly, 1950–70	The attempt to work out grammars or codes for a wide range of cultural forms, taking linguistics as a model.	Althusser..........*Lenin and Philosophy*, 1971 Barthes...........*Mythologies*, 1957 Foucault ....*The Order of Things*, 1966 Lacan ....*Four Fundamental Concepts of Psycho-analysis*, 1964 (pub. 1973) Lévi-Strauss.....*Structural Anthro-pology*, 1958

Emerging interest in the instability of codes in the mid-1960s leads to many structuralists moving away from structuralism.

Post-structural-ism Paris and USA 1970s and 1980s	Critiques of structuralism on philosophical and political grounds, especially concerning the instability of codes. Increasing hostility to linguistics.	Barthes............*S/Z*, 1970 Derrida ....*Of Gram-matology*, 1967 Foucault ....*A History of Sexuality Vol. 1*, 1976 Jameson ....*The Political Unconscious*, 1981 Kristeva ....*Revolution of Poetic Language*, 1974 Said ....*The World, the Text, and the Critic*, 1983

Linguistic origins of structuralism

In this brief history we have emphasised the debt which structuralism owes to linguistics – particularly to the general linguistics of Saussure and the phonological theories (which diverge from Saussure) of Troubetskoy and Jakobson. To understand more about how structuralist theory works, it is important to understand some simple elements of these linguistic theories.

Saussure looked at the collection of words which make up a language. He called a word a **sign**, and suggested that it is the combination of two things – a sound pattern, which is the word as it is pronounced (the **signifier**), and a concept, which is what the word means for a user of the language (the **signified**). Saussure's most important point is that both the signifier and the signified are functional in

a language because each is part of a system (the signifier is like a jigsaw piece in a jigsaw puzzle of language and thought, as is the signified). A particular signifier gets its significance not from what it is but from what it is *not*: that is, from how it differs from all the other signifiers in its particular language system. The same applies to the signified (and hence to the sign as a whole). For example, in the system of English, the signified of the sign 'beef' is what it is (signified = the meat of the dead cow) partly because there is another English sign 'cow' (signified = the living animal). In French, on the other hand, the sign 'boeuf' has as its signified both the living and the dead animal, *because* no other signifier exists to restrict its meaning. So the Saussurean description of language suggests in general terms that a 'language' is a system of conventional contrasts or differences, rather than a list of independent terms with meanings attached to them. That is, what something means, or how it functions, depends on *difference*, or the potential contrasts it can enter into with other terms in the overall system; these potential contrasts define what is technically called the **value** of the word.

Developing this basic idea, Jakobson and Troubetskoy analysed the system of sound contrasts which make up languages. When you pronounce English words, you make some of the sounds by putting your lips together and then pushing air out, opening your lips as you do so. If you were to analyse the exact sounds which are made, you would see that there are quite a lot of objectively different sounds (for example in British English the 'p' of 'pat' is identifiably different from the 'p' of 'lap'). For the purpose of distinguishing one word from another, however, all the possible two-lip ('bilabial') sounds can be grouped into three sound types: /b/ type sounds, /p/ type sounds, and /m/ type sounds. Two different types of 'p' sound will not give you two different words (try pronouncing the /p/ of 'pat' in different ways; you should find that the word retains the same meaning). But 'p', 'b' and 'm' give you three different words: 'pat', 'bat' and 'mat'. The contrasts between these three sounds are **functional** (the contrasts function to differentiate words), and the contrastive status of these three sounds in English makes them **phonemes**. A central property of a phoneme is that when you substitute one phoneme for another you get a word which means something different. For example, if you substitute the phoneme /b/ for the phoneme /p/ in 'pat' you get the different word 'bat'. Substituting a different kind of 'p' instead would not give you a different word, which is why in English the different kinds of 'p' are not different phonemes. **Phonologists** are traditionally interested in what the phonemes of a language are (they are different for different languages). They are also interested in which phonemes are typically found in the same place as which other phonemes, and which phonemes can combine with which other phonemes.[7]

How structuralists adapt linguistics

The anthropologist Lévi-Strauss imitated the idea of the

phoneme as a contrastive and meaningful unit of sound by proposing a **mytheme**, a contrastive and meaningful element of myth (cf. his *Structural Anthropology*, p. 211). His attitude to myths was that they were like sentences of a language, and had meanings which could be found once the basic elements of the myths were identified. The −**eme** ending is used by linguists for other units of language, such as 'morpheme', and has been adapted in, for instance, 'ideologeme' (a contrasting unit in the structure of ideology, cf. Jameson, *The Political Unconscious*, p. 76). One central aim of structuralism is to show that −emes (the atomic contrastive units) combine into systems of 'grammars' or 'codes', and that these codes are the material out of which literary texts, and other cultural things, are made. In this aim, structuralism follows Saussure's proposal for a **semiology** of culture (the study of the sign systems of a culture).

Phonemes are distinguished from each other by two-way or **binary** contrasts. For example, /b/ and /p/ are distinguished by the first being *voiced* (you use your vocal cords in your throat to pronounce it) and the second being *unvoiced* (you do not use your vocal cords); this is the essential difference between the two phonemes and is expressed by saying that /p/ is −*voice* (i.e. unvoiced) and /b/ is +*voice* (i.e. voiced). Structuralists adopt this underlying principle of definition by contrast. Here are some two-way oppositions which a structuralist might say form the basic elements of culture.

nature/culture
reason/madness
left/right
good/bad

Such oppositions can be linked together; for instance, if you think everything which is 'natural' is 'good' and everything which is 'cultural' is 'bad'. In that case, a simple **homology** (or superimposition of oppositions) exists.

nature: culture

good: bad

When you begin to combine oppositions in this way, the resulting patterns can account for complex possibilities of meaning which exist in any culture. Descriptions of large-scale systems of superimposed contrasts can be created for everything from adverts, to themes in novels, to how people decide what to eat and how to eat it. We investigate how binary oppositions work in literary study in more detail in Chapter 5.[8]

   Now do Activity 14 on page 35

Slots and fillers

Many systems of elements in combination will not be made up just of binary oppositions; other methods of description are needed. The following **slot and filler grammar** shows how sentences of English are built by fitting a choice of items ('fillers') into a sequence of slots.

Slots ('axis of combination') →					
1	2	3	4	5	6
The	dog	sat	on	the	carpet
Each	cat	ate		a	mouse
	Mice	lay	near	each	mat

Fillers ('*axis of selection*') ↓

Suggest some more fillers under each slot.

This model (which has elements in common with the American structuralist linguistic approach to language, as well as with British neo-Firthian Linguistics), has been adapted by structuralists for use in cultural and literary analysis. Barthes, for example, builds a slot and filler grammar of clothing in *Elements of Semiology* and *The Fashion System*. Each slot is a part of the body where items of clothing can be worn (top of head, torso, pelvis and legs, lower legs, feet, etc.). The fillers are the different kinds of garment that can be worn in that place. Not only is it possible then to create a system which shows that socks are not worn on the head and that sandals and wellington boots are *alternative* forms of footwear, but also to begin to describe *styles* in clothing, patterns of combination of choices across the various slots. For example, if you choose 'top hat' in the head 'slot', a kind of consistency can be produced by choosing 'tail jacket' in the torso slot that doesn't exist if you choose 'T-shirt.'

Looking back at the first sentence example above, too, it is possible to see that the same possibility of describing stylistic and poetic effect exists there. If you select 'cat' in slot 2, then 'sat' in slot 3, and 'mat' in slot 6, you produce a rhyming pattern (repeated vowel and final consonant sounds in at least two different words). If you choose 'cat' in slot 2, 'crouched' in slot 3 and 'carpet' in slot 6, you produce an alliterative effect (repeated sounds at the beginning of words: we look at these effects in more detail in Chapter 6, p. 116). Roman Jakobson formulated a 'projection principle' to describe this: 'The poetic function projects the principle of equivalence from the axis of selection into the axis of combination' (in Sebeok (ed.), *Style in Language*, p. 358). This means that poetic effects are produced by extending the repetitive relation between fillers (which have to be alike in some respects in order to be eligible for the same slot) to a repetitive relation between the different, successive slots (which don't have to resemble one another, but can be made to show resemblances). This principle accounts for both the rhyme and the alliteration examples above, as well as for

Activity 14   *Investigating by using binary oppositions*

(30 mins)

1. Here are four binary oppositions. Add three more.

(a) constructed   vs.   natural
(b) individual   vs.   social group
                                (i.e. family or
                                community)

(c) good   vs.   evil
(d) female   vs.   male

(e) .... vs. ....

(f) .... vs. ....

(g) .... vs. ....

2. Pick a text. This could be a novel, poem or newspaper article you have recently read or a film or television programme you have recently seen. Write the name of the text here.

....

3. Are any of the seven binary oppositions listed above used in any way in the text – for example, to create a patterning, or to make a particular point, or to create a narrative? Give an example.

4. Make a note here of any other binary oppositions which seem to you to be important in the construction of the text.

.... vs. ....

.... vs. ....

5. Make a note here of seemingly important terms in the text which appear to be part of a binary opposition of which the other term is only *implied*, not actually stated.

6. Are the oppositions you are identifying part of the text itself, or are they something you create for the text, as a reader?

 Now rejoin text on page 34

---

the top-hat-and-tails clothing example and for many others.

From structuralism to post-structuralism

The major part of structuralist work can be thought of as the use of the kind of procedure described above to build 'grammars' or descriptions of the codes of a wide range of cultural forms. Studies of narrative, for example, develop from the idea that stories are made up of slots and possible fillers: not phonemes or words, but events, descriptions, characters, etc. Similarly, some work in psychoanalysis suggests that the human psyche has a 'grammar' that can be described in terms of contrastive oppositions (metaphor/metonymy; imaginary/symbolic, etc.) and possible combinations or permutations of these terms. (We look at how these terms operate in Chapter 7, pp. 161–3.)

The complexity of structuralist work escalates very quickly, however, when these elementary principles of 'code' description are *combined*, in order to describe cultural forms more fully. Barthes and others, for in-

stance, showed how grids of narrative description involving events and other aspects of narrative need to intersect with the 'grammar' of the psyche if we are to explain, for instance, how the pleasure of suspense and then resolution in stories works. As the different descriptions become more complex, and as they interconnect with one another, the problems of justifying *why anyone should accept the descriptions, and what status they are supposed to have* become more difficult to answer. These problems can be seen clearly if we draw up a simple list of the different significances it is possible to attribute to structuralist descriptions.

1. Structuralism's descriptions are simply convenient ways of describing features of texts; the descriptions may or may not relate to structures which have some prior independent existence in the texts themselves.

or

2. Structuralism's descriptions reveal objectively how meanings are created in texts, and amount to a science of how texts work; the structures in the text *determine* reading.

or

3. Structuralism's descriptions enable us to perceive deep-seated patterns of human cognition, showing how the human mind works through showing up common patterns across a wide range of different phenomena.

Post-structuralist work can be thought of as a range of ways of exploring unresolvable issues within structuralism, including issues raised by the three conflicting claims about the significance of structuralism's descriptions described above.

Stylistics

Given simply the broad definition of stylistics as the analysis of language in literary texts, we can find examples of stylistics in classical **rhetoric**, the study (first developed in Greece and Rome, then relayed through mediaeval and Renaissance forms) of how language can be used to create particular, persuasive effects. The recent history of stylistics can be seen by looking back to the historical chart of structuralism, and grafting on a divergent history[9] from about 1950.

Jakobson remains in the USA where he becomes an important influence on the development of **generative linguistics**, particularly on **generative phonology** whose 'classic' text, *The Sound Pattern of English* (by Chomsky and Halle, 1968), is dedicated to him. Another sub-type of generative linguistics called **transformational syntax** forms the basis for a particular kind of stylistics which seeks to show that literary texts are 'transformations' of hidden versions of the same texts, and that these hidden versions are somehow the deeper meanings of the texts. The related field of generative phonology, which investigates how the structure of the mind organises the sounds used in speech, independently forms the basis for analysing sound patterns in literary texts.

Unconnected with his influence on generative linguistics, Jakobson provided an impetus to a different tradition in stylistics with his 'Concluding Statement: Linguistics and Poetics', in which he formulated the projection principle. Jakobson presented the 'Concluding Statement' paper at the Conference on Style at Indiana in 1958, a conference also attended by I. A. Richards. The conference reflects an optimism in the USA at the end of the 1950s about the possibilities of cross-disciplinary work in the humanities, especially between literary criticism, linguistics, psychology, and cultural anthropology.

Transformational linguistics begins to have an influence in Britain in the 1960s, as does British **systemic linguistics** developed primarily by M. A. K. Halliday and part of the neo-Firthian tradition. Halliday's linguistics soon becomes the dominant linguistic force on British stylistics, which develops a substantial body of teaching materials using stylistic approaches to literature.

Increasingly during the 1970s, stylistics develops a new interest in the larger structures of texts, and makes use of the linguistic theories of **discourse analysis**, **sociolinguistics** and **pragmatics**, which seek to relate the form of a text to its use, and to the social contexts in which it is found. A key text is Pratt, *Toward a Speech Act Theory of Literary Discourse*, 1977.

An indication of the different claims which might be made for stylistics can be seen in the following, roughly graded list.

1. Stylistics has a role to play in editorial work; its descriptions of idiosyncratic, 'personal' styles can help in attributing to particular writers works or fragments whose authorship is in doubt.
2. Stylistic descriptions can make already existing intuitions about the meaning of a text easier to write or talk about.
3. Stylistic descriptions can create *new* intuitions about the meaning of a text, as patterns emerge which were not spontaneously noticed.
4. Stylistics can provide a systematic way of describing and then interpreting a text; it forms the beginnings of an objective, scientific process of text interpretation, and can help eliminate impressionism from literary criticism.
5. Stylistics can help develop an interest in linguistic analysis more generally, and so develop awareness of how language functions in *all* its instances of use.

One way in which stylistic analyses have been carried out is this:

1. You produce a linguistic analysis of a text by applying linguistic theory to the text in a predetermined and dispassionate manner.
2. You interpret the resulting linguistic analysis, for example, to show what the text means at some 'deep' or 'ultimate' level.

This approach has been criticised with the claim that the second stage ('interpretation') is very subjective, and that in fact this subjectivity spills over into the supposedly dispassionate or 'objective' first stage of the analysis of the text. (Chapter 6 is concerned with the linguistic analysis of texts. When you work through that chapter, you should bear in mind this criticism of the approach, and consider whether or not it is well-founded.)

► *Now do Activity 15*

Activity 15   *Studying literature and studying style*
(40 mins)

1, As regards studying literature, would you agree with the following statement by F. R. Leavis, from the first page of *The Great Tradition* (1948)?

> I still think, however, that the best way to promote profitable discussion is to be as clear as possible with oneself about what one sees and judges, to try and establish the essential discriminations in the given field of interest, and to state them as clearly as one can (for disagreement, if necessary).

YES/NO

Add comment (e.g. on qualifications to your answer, or difficulties unresolved in the question).

2. In studying literature, does 'establishing the essential discriminations' involve describing individual texts?

YES/NO

Add comment (e.g. on qualifications to your answer, or difficulties unresolved in the question).

3. Are literary texts made of language?

YES/NO

Add comment (e.g. on qualifications to your answer, or difficulties unresolved in the question).

4. Do texts say what they say through using resources of language?

YES/NO

Add comment (e.g. on qualifications to your answer, or difficulties unresolved in the question).

5. Does what the texts say reflect the specific ways in which the language in them is chosen, organised and used?

YES/NO

Add comment (e.g. on qualifications to your answer, or difficulties unresolved in the question).

7. Is 'linguistics' the field in which you would expect the fullest and most accurate descriptions of how language is organised and used to be developed?

YES/NO

Add comment (e.g. on qualifications to your answer, or difficulties unresolved in the question).

6. Is it possible to describe how language is organised and used clearly or systematically?

YES/NO

Add comment (e.g. on qualifications to your answer, or difficulties unresolved in the question).

8. Are descriptive frameworks offered by linguistics helpful in studying literature?

YES/NO

Add comment (e.g. on qualifications to your answer, or difficulties unresolved in the question).

9. Collect together your answers above with the comments you have added. Do these form a general statement about how useful, or lacking in usefulness, stylistic work is likely to be in studying literature?

YES/NO

Add comment (e.g. on qualifications to your answer, or difficulties unresolved in the question).

10. On the basis of your answer to 9, make a note of any limitations or dangers you think are likely to exist in literary study which draws on frameworks developed in linguistics.

Now rejoin text

2.3.6 PSYCHOANALYTIC CRITICISM: FREUD AND LACAN

Freudian criticism

Psychoanalysis is a method of treating particular kinds of mental disturbance, developed at the end of the nineteenth century by Sigmund Freud (1856–1939). The patient is cured by (a) talking freely (free association) to the doctor, reporting all the thoughts which occur, and (b) the analysis or interpretation by the doctor of what the patient says or *does not* say. Freud argued that someone can have thoughts without being aware of them, and these **unconscious** thoughts might determine aspects of behaviour. Unconscious thoughts have been **repressed** by the regulatory mechanisms of the mind (because they might be unacceptable or too upsetting to the person).

Psychoanalytic criticism has a close relation with literary criticism because both are concerned with the analysis of texts. In his earliest work in psychoanalysis, Freud sought to show that the unconscious processes which he had discovered in his patients were also at work in the 'authors' of a range of other cultural phenomena: myths, jokes, religions, slips of the tongue and pen, incidents of forgetting and misremembering – and works of literature. So the beginnings of psychoanalytic criticism are to be found in Freud's broad reference across the sphere of human culture to support his claims about the unconscious; the first works of psychoanalytic criticism of literature are written by Freud himself. In its early forms, psychoanalytic criticism shows how the unconscious thoughts of the writer emerge as 'slips' in his/her text: as unintended meanings which – when combined together – present us with a portrait of the author's psychical formation, and describe deep creative processes shaping the work in question. Although numerous developments have been made subsequently on this basic idea, the notion of charting psychical conflicts at work in a text (worked out in its narrative or themes) remains the defining characteristic of traditional Freudian psychoanalytic criticism.

Alongside his development of psychoanalysis, Freud has had considerable influence on writers and film-makers (e.g. in surrealism). One kind of influence comes from Freud's descriptions of characteristic symbols in which unconscious ideas reach the surface of texts (e.g. a gun = a penis; sweets = sexual enjoyment; pulling out a tooth = castration). Writers have subsequently used these 'Freudian symbols' as a kind of vocabulary of concealed meanings. Psychoanalytic approaches to literature, however, are interested in symbols only to the extent that writers are *unaware* of the meanings (otherwise they would not be unconscious symbols).

Lacanian criticism

More recently, a different emphasis in psychoanalytic criticism has been made, usually associated with the work of the French psychoanalyst Jacques Lacan (1901–81) between the 1950s and the 1970s. Lacan's contribution to psychoanalytic criticism lies in his suggestion that it is not only themes, or features of *content*, which show the trace of psychical conflicts, but also the *forms* in which texts are created. This claim Lacan supports with an account of human psychical development which suggests that psychical development takes place in combination with the acquisition of language. To understand Lacanian approaches to literary study, it is necessary to understand Lacan's description of this combined process of psychical formation and learning to speak, of which a brief summary follows.

A human infant comes to see him/herself as an individual, with a sexed identity and separate from the world and from other people, during the same period as she or he begins to be able to speak. The child's perception of individuality begins when it recognises various absences or things lacking (faeces 'lost' from the body, the mother leaving the room, the traumatic fear of castration). But the sense of identity characteristic of adults is only achieved by passing through moments which establish that these lost objects can never return, and that existence is therefore cut through with absence that can never be restored. Before such experiences, the infant believed itself to exist in a reciprocal, two-way relation with its mother (absent or present; self or other; 'I' or 'you'). But in the process of development it finds itself repeatedly decentred and excluded, for example by the entry of the father into the two-way relationship. The father's entry into this relationship creates a non-reciprocal three-way relation, in which the self can be excluded by the two others relating to each other: the infant no longer occupies in language either the place of 'I' or 'you'; it can also be excluded from a discourse by being 'he' or 'she'. This exclusion is paralleled in the 'entry into language' more generally. As we have seen above, Saussure argued that language is made up only of terms defined by difference and the state of 'not being something else' (cf. our discussion of the English word 'beef', p. 33). Lacan calls the early, self-centred world before sex and language the **imaginary**, and the new world which the child enters the **symbolic**. The symbolic is the unstable world of language, where all meanings, including meanings for the self, have to be created.

Lack and difference, according to Lacan, have to be somehow incorporated into the structure of personality if the infant is to grow up. But human beings negotiate their confrontations with lack and difference in different ways, and so acquire differing psychical formations. In later life, these formations are reflected as symptoms in behaviour, and also in the way people use language. What a person says, or how he/she says it, will indicate things about his/her psychical history, particularly about the extent to which he or she has been able to acknowledge or suppress the traumatic first realisation that language is made of unstable differences rather than of recoverable, full meanings and identities. People construct senses of 'personal identity', with varying degrees of success, by imposing versions of identity (in psychoanalytic terms, **identifications**) across gaps and exclusions left in them by their formation out of original division and difference. Those original gaps and absences Lacan equates with

desire; and as such their return is signalled constantly by marks of desire in what we say. But desire in this sense is not desire for something specific; it is simply part of the formative structure of the human species, and has no ultimate object or goal. It attaches itself to local sexual and other goals and aims, but at a deep level is directed towards an unremediable absence in our earliest formation as human subjects.

How do you do Lacanian criticism?

1. You accept the theses of Lacanian psychoanalysis. Either you accept these because arguments in the theory persuade you, or you are convinced by direct experience of psychoanalysis as a practice.

2. You identify, in a text or group of texts you are analysing, linguistic features (especially metaphors) which indicate the repression of desire, and features which allow desire to surface.

3. When you think you have discovered the existence of such a general psychical tendency, you either investigate connections between these linguistic indicators and their psychical counterparts (the traumatic experiences or blocking mechanisms which shaped the author's entry into the symbolic world), or focus not on what caused the text to be the way it is, but instead consider how you can read it or 'enter' it; you describe the reading processes invited by different types of text and the different structures of pleasure each offers.

Psychoanalysis as a theory and psychoanalysis as a practice

As a source of ideas for literary criticism, psychoanalysis differs from other approaches discussed in this chapter. It is primarily a form of interactive therapy, whose theoretical descriptions and speculations are separated from the practice to form psychoanalytic criticism.[10] Texts are not patients; they cannot be interacted with by the analyst in the same way that patients can. Although some psychoanalytic criticism is done by analysts in parallel with clinical work, the question arises how far it is possible to call work 'psychoanalytic criticism' if it adapts ideas, but not their supporting framework of procedures and methods, from their original psychoanalytic context. Psychoanalysis also suggests that there are structures of psychical, mental activity beyond conscious thought in everyone; this means that anyone doing psychoanalytic criticism has to control or account for the working out of *their own* fixations, obsessions or desires in writing a psychoanalytic commentary.

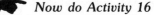 *Now do Activity 16*

Activity 16   *Psychoanalytic reading*
(60 mins)

Consider the following passage from *Macbeth* (V, v, 18–27).

> To-morrow, and to-morrow, and to-morrow,
> Creeps in this petty pace from day to day,
> To the last syllable of recorded time;
> And all our yesterdays have lighted fools
> The way to dusty death. Out, out, brief candle!
> Life's but a walking shadow; a poor player,
> That struts and frets his hour upon the stage,
> And then is heard no more: it is a tale
> Told by an idiot, full of sound and fury,
> Signifying nothing.

At least one critic (Norman Holland, in *The Dynamics of Literary Response*, 1968) has claimed that the passage has, at its core, a fantasy of the psychoanalytic **primal scene**, in which a child either sees, or imagines seeing, its parents in sexual intercourse. (In the plot of the play, the speech occurs as Macbeth is deciding whether he should kill his king, Duncan.)

Some pieces of evidence used by Holland to justify reading the passage as a fantasy of the primal scene are:

(i) The 'tomorrows' and 'yesterdays' of the passage indicate the time in between the fantasy of the primal scene and the present.

(ii) The child's hatred of the role of the father in disturbing the earlier relation with the mother is signalled by the description of the 'poor player/That struts and frets his hour up on the stage'; and by the phrase 'a tale/Told by an idiot'.

(iii) The 'sound' and 'fury' in the passage are the unnamable things heard.

(iv) The 'brief candle' that must 'out, out' is a phallic symbol.

1. How believable is such an account (5 = very believable; 1 = not believable)?

          5   4   3   2   1

Make a note of any further evidence for this account.

2. Within this critical account, what do you think is being described? Tick as appropriate.

(a) Shakespeare's fantasy about his own early experience.

(b) Macbeth's fantasy about his own early experience.

(c) The critic Norman Holland's fantasy about his own early experience.

(d) A fantasy about early experience shared by both Shakespeare and any reader.

(e) None of these: a representation or allegory of the structure of psychoanalytic theory;

(f) None of these; something else. Specify:

3. Now add to the account described above the following arguments.

(v) The passage is full of mixed imagery (light/darkness, theatre, time, death, etc.); the mixing of imagery indicates how language runs beyond deliberate control by the author and allows psychical material to surface.

(vi) The phrase 'signifying nothing' suggests the connection between early psychical formation and the incapability of language to create full meaning for the self or the world.

Does adding these arguments to the account in 1 alter your response in 2? YES/NO. If 'yes', make a note of the alterations here.

4. Is it possible to devise ways of distinguishing between the following: a specific fantasy being represented; the conventional use of a recurrent fantasy; and the use of conventional themes or imagery which do not have their origins in psychical material?

                    YES/NO

If YES, describe briefly how you might do this.

☛ *Now rejoin text*

2.3.7 DECONSTRUCTION

Deconstruction is one strand within post-structuralism. Historically, it begins in Jacques Derrida's (b. 1930) critique of work by the philosophers of **phenomenology**, Edmund Husserl (1859–1938) and Maurice Merleau-Ponty (1908–61), who argued that humans can achieve moments of full self-presence and self-knowing. Derrida suggests that this idea of being able to reach a moment of self-presence, finding meaning somewhere deep in the self, is consistent with a series of other attempts, in the history of Western thought, to construct centres of meaning by devising systems of **metaphysics**. Metaphysical systems are based on specially valued terms or ultimate sources of meaning (e.g. God, truth, reason, nature, man, speech, etc.); and because they rely on a foundational belief in a source of truth, Derrida describes them as **logocentric** ('logos' means 'reason' in Greek). In order to show that such systems are misguided, Derrida appeals to Saussure for evidence that no linguistic or philosophical term can ever be fully valued in and for itself in the way that metaphysics implies: terms get their value only by *difference* from other terms. Terms like 'God', 'truth', 'reason', and so on get their meaning by virtue of being different from other terms: *God is not the devil*, *truth* is *not falsity*, etc. Developing this point, deconstruction takes the oppositions revealed by structuralism and shows that one pole of any binary opposition is valued more than the other.

Favoured in a culture		Not favoured in a culture
REASON	:	madness
NATURE	:	culture
MAN	:	woman
THEORY	:	practice

Deconstruction claims that in the history of thought and politics, one side of each binary opposition tends to be revered or respected; the other is suppressed and criticised (e.g. reason is thought of as something to be revered; madness is thought of as something to be avoided and controlled).

Deconstruction seeks to subvert the tendency of exalting one term in such oppositions, by showing how the favoured term relies for its meaning on its opposite: if meanings only come into existence through contrasts, you can only believe in 'reason', for example, if you also believe in 'madness'. Deconstruction destabilises the special meaning and value invested in the favoured term in each case, by forcing on people who establish the special value of a term the recognition that it cannot be defined apart from its related, and undesirable, negative pole. Destabilising the 'full meanings' which hold logocentric systems of thought and order in place then makes possible the reinstatement of those things which

have traditionally been subordinated (e.g. madness, culture, woman, practice, etc.); and it is also believed to be capable of shaking people's faith in such systems in general. Instead of such faith, deconstruction advocates an acknowledgement of a **radical freeplay** in language and thought: in place of fixed centres of meaning, there is a play of differences which offers no access to stable identity or certitude.[11]

The use of Saussure in delineating deconstruction involves a radical critique of Saussure's ideas. In his own work, Saussure emphasised two aspects of language:

(a) *value:* terms relate to other terms through systems of contrast within a system; words relate to other words (Saussure's example refers to the money system based on the money unit of the franc: 5 francs equals 5×1 franc) and

(b) *signification:* terms refer out from the system itself into other cultural systems (Saussure's example: 5 francs buys one loaf of bread).

Deconstructionist critiques of Saussure involve rejecting signification (the ability of language to relate outwards, to culture and to things in the world), suggesting instead that language is a *purely* differential system (all attempts to get at meaning only take you to another term in the same, linguistic system; there is never a moment of reference to the world). So while for Saussure language is arbitrary (since it is only social convention that links any group of sounds or letters with particular meanings), deconstructionists stress language's arbitrariness in a much stronger sense; there is no reason for the system of differences to pick out any particular object or meaning for differentiation at all.

As regards the study of written texts, a further important revision of Saussure's ideas is made in deconstruction. Saussure follows the long-standing tradition of seeing writing as merely a convenient reproduction or imitation of the real or authentic condition of human language in speech (where utterance is closest to intention and the self). But Derrida suggests that this is another example of a 'loaded' binary opposition.

Favoured in a culture		Not favoured in a culture
SPEECH	:	writing

Accordingly, he inverts the relationship, to show what is suppressed by it. For him, speech has all the decentred and unstable properties of writing: neither are close to intention, or to the self, since texts have the same capabilities for 'meaning' – and for slippage of meaning – when the speaker or writer is present and alive as they do when he or she is absent or dead.

Deconstructionist work tests to the limits the systems and formalisms through which we construct meanings and values; and it disrupts and throws into question frameworks of meaning and interpretation where these have lost touch with the fragility of the 'language' out of which they are made. In philosophy, this is an important critique of systems of argument, within nineteenth- and twentieth-century traditions of scepticism; and paradoxically, in this context it is *reasonable* to question and investigate the bases of reason. The transplantation of deconstruction from philosophy into literary criticism has opened up new possibilities for showing how New Critical, structuralist and other interpretations which implicitly hold that meanings can be fixed and effective do so only through unstated assumptions and the exclusion and marginalisation of other elements and forces. In this transplantation, deconstruction becomes broader in its scope, so that 'deconstructive' or 'deconstructionist' work may be any work which shows the instability of the formative structures of texts.

☛ *Now do Activity 17 on page 44*

2.3.8 FEMINIST CRITICISM

Feminist criticism cannot be traced to origins in the work of one or more individuals working in a particular period or discipline at a particular time. Rather, it grows out of the historical experience of resistance and self-definition by women in circumstances of social control by men; it is the gradual definition of a critical field often traced to Mary Wollstonecraft's (1759–1797) *Vindication of the Rights of Women* (1792) and incorporating during its history a range of social theories. During its history, feminist criticism has been unified less by a set of goals and methods than by its unity as a movement of resistance to systems of male power, or **patriarchy**; unity of opposition guides its critical concern with, and on behalf of, women in language and literature. Feminist criticism is consequently more a range of interconnected directions of work, seeking to restructure power relations with respect to discourse and social relations, than a single direction to all aspects of which all feminists are committed. There are for example differences within feminism regarding lesbianism and race.

Historically, social inequality between men and women can be traced to unequal power relations in particular societies (e.g. roles and status within families, nurturing responsibilities for children, codes of conduct and public behaviour, legal and economic rights, job opportunities and access to public positions, etc.). But it can also be traced – possibly relatedly – to systems of representation: how women are represented in plays, rituals, photographic images, novels, films, etc. The human species has a biologically fixed, binary sex division between male and female. But superimposed on this are culturally constructed oppositions of **gender**: masculine and feminine, men and women, etc. It is this system of oppositions which the various strands of feminist criticism analyse and seek to change. The binary oppositions of

gender are in virtually all cultures 'loaded' ones (though the precise ways in which they are loaded vary from culture to culture and period to period). In most societies, the privileging within the oppositions is as follows.

Favoured in a culture		Not favoured in a culture
MEN	:	women
MASCULINE	:	feminine
MALE	:	female
etc.		

While 'men', 'masculine', 'male', etc. are taken as privileged, defining terms, 'women', 'feminine', etc. are treated as simply the 'other' of those terms. Specific attributes of women (e.g. bodies, thoughts, beliefs, etc.) are taken merely as negatives to the positive poles of the oppositions, as they are also when linked with other oppositions which involve gender sub-divisions, such as public/private, active/passive or nature/culture. The unity in opposition of feminism comes from its commitment to destabilise these established oppositions, and through doing so to change and improve the social conditions and opportunities of women; it might be argued that feminist literary theorists are unified around a claim that gender (along with race, class, etc.) is a key determinant of how texts are written and read.

Issues to do with gender cut across literary studies in a range of ways; and feminist criticism can be seen as an interconnecting range of types of work across these issues.

1. The historical issue of who is free to write, in what idioms, and who is able to get published or to be studied, has a continuing gender dimension and politics. These features of social and economic history affect the construction of the corpus or canon of texts that is studied; but a politics of gender is rarely recognised as being a major determinant of that construction and selection. Feminist criticism challenges distortions in the social relationships through which texts are produced, published, represented and studied. It points to an omission of women in the constructed literary canon (e.g. the minor role in accounts of nineteenth-century fiction given to Emily and Charlotte Brontë, Mrs Gaskell and George Eliot, or the lack of critical attention to work by Gertrude Stein, Dorothy Richardson, Virginia Woolf and H.D. (Hilda Doolittle) in accounts of twentieth-century modernism). Feminist critical work seeks to rectify this omission by bringing together new and previously unregarded writings by women, to create a history and new canon with claims on critical attention and study. Such work accordingly leads to a range of different forms of activity: to publishing initiatives (to create a corpus of writing by women which has been 'lost' or neglected); to syllabus changes (to make sure those authors are studied); and to

Activity 17   *Deconstructing a text of your choice*
(40 mins)

1. Choose as the object of your deconstruction a critical article about a work of literature. Write the name of the article here.

....

2. Why did you choose this critical article in particular? Here are some possible reasons: tick the reason which applies to you, or add your own.
(a) The article has an incoherent or inconsistent argument.
(b) The article is oppressive (be specific).
(c) You have chosen the article at random because it will exemplify the general claim that all texts can be deconstructed.

(d) ....

....

3. Find an opposition in the article (this might, for example, be male/female, nature/culture, speech/writing, city/country, rich/poor, etc.). You might find it useful to look back at the section on structuralism for the notion of 'opposition'. Write one half of the opposition at the top of the left column, and the other half at the top of the right column.

4. Now decide whether one half or 'term' of the opposition is privileged or favoured in the article. Ways in which one term might be favoured are:

the author might explicitly say that it is good or important;
the author might appear to talk exclusively about it.

Ways in which the other term might be disfavoured are:

the term might only be discussed in a footnote, or an appendix, or be otherwise 'hidden';
the term might be held to be an exception or peculiar case.

In the table, write P in the space above the term you think is privileged; write not-P above the other term (which you think is not privileged). Write in the column under the privileged (P) term exactly how it is privileged or favoured in the text; write in the column under the other, non privileged (not-P) term exactly how you think it is hidden or disfavoured in the text.
5. Compare the two terms. Make a note of any resemblance between them you can identify. Resemblances might exist in terms of:

coming from same etymological root;
both relating in some way to a single, common word;
if technical, both originating in work of same person;
using same type of imagery or figurative language;
having same body of underlying assumptions.

6. Can you see any way in which the obscuring of the second term is necessary in order for the view being expressed to appear coherent? (For example, are characteristics or properties of the second term which are non-privileged also inherent in some way in the first term?)

7. Examine the notes you have made in response to 5 and 6. Consider whether resemblances between the contrastive terms of the opposition serve to reinforce or undermine the contrast. Delete as applicable.
                    Reinforce/Undermine
8. How (if at all) has your deconstruction activity affected your initial view of the text?

☞ *Now rejoin text on page 43*

revision as regards the conventions of critical judgement which determine which writers will be deemed to be good. On this issue, feminist criticism contests the restriction and denial of women's opportunities and lost achievements in literature brought about by the historically subordinate position of women in society. In promoting women's writing, such criticism is concerned with the restrictions on *women as writers and producers of literature*.

2. In many texts, women are represented in ways restricted by conventional stereotypes. Women are widely represented as objects, to be discussed, exchanged and evaluated by men. In such representations, women are regularly attributed particular sorts of characters (silly, trivial, domestic, etc.), and are also represented in forms of sexual display or seduction geared towards the **voyeuristic pleasures** of men. Feminist criticism contests such representations. It offers critiques of existing repertoires of images, by exposing the conventions of turning people into objects, or **reification**, on which they rely (e.g. analysing and challenging male pornography in magazines, TV, advertisements, novels, or criticising stereotypes of 'helpless' or subordinate women in fiction and drama). In doing so, it challenges men on the ways in which they choose to see and think of women, investigates recurrent images or symbols through which women are represented in writing *by* women, and promotes new kinds of alternative images. In such work, feminist criticism is concerned with *women as the content of literature*.

3. In societies whose images of women are largely voyeuristic stereotypes, the implied addressee of images of women is a 'male' construct: to read such texts, women readers or viewers have either to adopt a way of reading or perceiving which accepts these dominant constructs of ideals and norms, or alternatively to adopt the position of **resisting** readers. More generally, too, within a system of predominantly male-written public texts, there is a historically constructed convention that the implied reader (or 'general reader') for a text is male. Feminist criticism shows how such addressees are typically constructed as men, and how men are taken as the 'unmarked' or 'default' form in ways which deny a position and voice to women (as with the use of 'he' in a text to mean 'anyone', or the use of co-referring forms such as 'women . . . *they*'). As a radical correction, feminist criticism analyses the different systems of address available in writing addressed to women, and investigates new forms of address to be directed more appropriately at mixed-gender readerships. In exploring such issues, feminist criticism is concerned with *women as implied readers of literature*.

4. The way men and women use language is itself an issue of gender politics: whether men and women write and speak in the same way, and if not, why not. Feminist critical activity examines differences between the language usage of men and of women (as well as myths about such usage). In literary writing in particular, patterns of discourse are used deliberately to represent states of mind, thoughts and sensations, creating distinctive writing styles (e.g. the styles of Gertrude Stein and Dorothy Richardson). Feminist criticism opposes the undervaluing of such writing styles, and the attribution of stylistic innovation only to male writers (James Joyce, Stephen Mallarmé, etc.). In exploring such issues, feminist criticism is concerned with investigating the possibility of specific *women's discourse styles*.

5. But in feminist criticism it is not only states of mind and thoughts which are taken to differ between men and women, and to be reflected in gender representations. The experience and possibilities of living as a woman in a woman's body – unlike the experience of being in a man's body – has historically only rarely been represented in public forms of writing. The current in feminist criticism called **gynocriticism** seeks to show how women feel in and about women's bodies, and to celebrate aspects of those bodies which have been excluded by convention from public discourse (e.g. childbirth, menstruation, menopause). This type of criticism concerns itself with the **wild zone** of women's experience: an area outside patriarchal restrictions where women express themselves on subjects which cannot be represented in 'male' discourse. This wild zone is considered to be simultaneously an affirmation of women's experience and a subversion of 'male' values. In such criticism, the concern is with representing *experiences which can only be represented in a form of discourse outside and beyond 'male' discourse*.

6. Not all kinds of awareness of the body are conscious. Much twentieth-century thought, influenced by psychoanalysis, suggests that a history of the body is expressed through psychical formations which are beyond access to consciousness, except in the form of symptoms, slips, etc. (see Section 2.3.6 above on psychoanalytic criticism). Feminist criticism working within a psychoanalytic framework charts the representation of specific psychical positions of women in the language of particular texts. Within a Lacanian framework, as a person enters the symbolic realm (simultaneously of language and gender), he or she is formed as a subject; and later use of discourse carries the traces of this entry. Psychoanalysis proposes accounts of the different constructions of men and women in this process. In much feminist criticism, the gender asymmetries of this process are examined critically, with regard to issues such as how far the body itself is destiny; and about the appropriateness or inappropriateness of male-centred concepts such as **penis envy** or **castration complex**. A simultaneously 'sexual' and 'textual' politics is created, involving a potential typology of texts according to the **subject positions** they make available to readers on the basis of the different patterns of psychical formation they represent. One influential counter-tradition to the concern with modalities of entry into the symbolic realm is associated with the

work of the French critic Julia Kristeva (b. 1941). Rather than exploring the structures of pleasure, trauma and psychical formation which are linked to entry into the symbolic, Kristeva investigates the dispersed drives and pleasures which *precede* entry into the symbolic realm. Whereas in a Lacanian framework such pleasures would be imaginary and regressive, in Kristeva's framework they are held to offer an access to the body which is denied later. Kristeva seeks to discover and celebrate what is beyond the formation and control of ordered language; what she calls a **semiotic discourse**, a play of sensations, drives and rhythms most closely approximated to by literary avant-garde writings (especially the work of the French symbolist poet, Stephen Mallarmé). In relation to such semiotic discourse, Kristeva suggests that women have a special access to poetic productivity. Feminist criticism in this area is concerned with issues of the representation in writing of *feminine psychical formation*. 7. Alongside these various types of work on texts and bodies of texts, feminist criticism is also concerned with institutional issues to do with the conduct of academic research, seminar interaction and presentation. In these areas, the sexual politics of feminist criticism means challenging and seeking to change dominating and competitive interactional dynamics set by men; and showing ways in which alternative and neglected possibilities associated with women can be introduced instead. Beyond academic institutions, such work includes setting up publishing companies and journals controlled by women (e.g. Virago, Only Women, *Spare Rib*, *Manushi*, *Ms*, *Feminist Review*). In this area, feminist criticism is involved in a *critique of academic procedures*, waged through institutional struggles and presentation of alternative models.

The various approaches may be summarised as follows.

Feminist issue	Main features	Sample theoretical work
1. corpus of women's writing	establish corpus and structures of contemporary publishing	Elaine Showalter, *A Literature of Their Own* (1977) Ellen Moers, *Literary Women* (1978)
2. images of women	contest existing gender imagery; promote alternatives	Josephine Donovan, *Feminist Literary Criticism* (1975) Kate Millett, *Sexual Politics* (1970)
3. implied reader	challenge convention of male as assumed reader; analyse techniques through which established	Judith Fetterley, *The Resisting Reader* (1978)

Feminist issue	Main features	Sample theoretical work
4. use of language	explore and celebrate gender differences in ways of writing	Hélène Cixous, 'The Laugh of the Medusa' (1975)
5. gyno-criticism	how women represent what it feels like to be a woman in a woman's body	Elaine Showalter, 'Feminist Criticism in the Wilderness' (1981)
6. psycho-analytic criticism	analyse psychical formations specific to women's writing; demonstrate pleasures of language in what Kristeva calls the semiotic	Rosalind Coward, *Female Desire* (1984) Julia Kristeva, *Revolution of Poetic Language* (1974) Luce Irigary, *The Sex Which Is Not One* (1977)
7. institutional critique	challenge masculinist forms of interaction in institutions and academic study	Michele Barrett, *Women's Oppression Today* (1980)

This grid lays out something of the range of directions within feminist criticism; in practice, most feminist critics find it important to combine a range of these strategies.[12]

  Now do Activity 18 on page 47

2.4 Comparing theories

Our descriptions of theoretical work in the preceding sections give very simplified histories and outlines of some of the strands in modern critical work. Our intention in presenting them is to show how critical frameworks operate beyond the particular texts in which they originate; how they may be applied as systems or frameworks by people other than the person who first thought of them – including potentially by *you* if you choose to work in any of the particular idioms.

You may have found our descriptions simplistic. If this is the case, we suggest that you use our accounts as a basis for listing inadequacies which can then form the substance of better, working accounts of your own. Alternatively, you may have found our descriptions too difficult and technical. If this is so, it may be helpful for us to repeat here that what follows in the rest of the book will not necessarily be unintelligible because of this: we have tried to avoid *presuming* detailed understanding of the approaches listed above.

Whether you found our descriptions simplistic or difficult, it is likely that you will have recognised in them terms and ideas you have read, thought, or been taught. Our descriptions should therefore be useful in identifying

Activity 18 *Gender and reading*

(60 mins)

I fear a Man of frugal Speech –
I fear a silent Man –
Haranguer – I can overtake –
Or Babbler – entertain –

But He who weigheth – While the Rest –
Expend their furthest pound –
Of this Man – I am wary
I fear that He is Grand –

(Emily Dickinson (1830–86), written 1862)

1. Make a note of any features of the poem that you judge to have particular significance or effect because you know that the author was a woman. Pay attention to aspects of the poem's subject matter, choice of language, use of capitalisation and punctuation, etc.

3. How far do the differences you have noted in 2 derive from the features you have identified while doing task 1? How far are they the result of the reader being *addressed* in a particular way?

2. Using the descriptions of gender issues above, make a list of differences in interpretation that you might make, (a) reading as a woman and (b) reading as a man.

Now rejoin text on page 46

where some aspects of your ideas come from, and what established directions they have affinities with. This chapter has aimed to distinguish between being interested in theoretical work as history (or as a new canon of texts for you to read) and being interested in theories as systems for practical application and use. We have another aim besides this (which we return to at the end of Chapter 8): to show how the various critical directions are not necessarily all compatible with one another, and to suggest that developing ideas and arguments in literary studies involves thinking through questions of consistency and compatibility between the various ideas you are using.

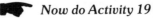   **Now do Activity 19**

Activity 19   *Comparing critical approaches by devising a grid*
(60 mins)

(the length of time is flexible depending on how many approaches you compare)

The various approaches outlined above can be described in the form of a *matrix analysis* which answers the questions below. (The information given in this chapter should be sufficient to enable you to fill in the boxes.)

The questions
A. Does the approach require specialist skills in the analysis of language?
B. Does the approach make use of contextual material (e.g. biography, history) to aid examination of particular texts?
C. Is the approach committed to making value judgements about texts?
D. Are underlying assumptions of the approach explicitly investigated within it?
E. Are all texts equally amenable to analysis using the approach?
F. Does the approach seek to bring about institutional and/or social change?
G. Is the approach generalisable from the works in which it originates?
H. Can the approach be simply explained or taught?
J. Is it indispensable to study works by the originator(s) of the theory?

1. Find a large piece of paper. Draw a grid on it, with the questions (A–J) listed down the left-hand side. Put the names of the various 'theory types' described in this chapter (or particular ones you are interested in among the ones we have described) along the top.
2. Fill in each box with a brief note or comment on how the approach deals with or responds to each particular question. (Each column 'down' will then represent a description of an approach; each column 'across' will represent a set of contrasts with respect to how the approaches deal with particular issues.) If you can't think of a suitable comment for any box, leave a blank and consult some of the books referred to in the further reading, or in the section on 'finding things out' below, in Chapter 4.
3. Now add some further columns along the top (or make a new grid on a separate sheet of paper). Fill in the boxes in the same way, for some approaches which have not been described in this chapter. To do this, you will either need to confine yourself to describing approaches you are already familiar with, or to consult critical works and/or reference texts. You might find it interesting to try to fill in the grid for the approaches associated with works by the following critics and thinkers.

Julia Kristeva	Georg Lukács	Cleanth Brooks
Northrop Frye	Christopher Caudwell	Elaine Showalter
Raymond Williams	Theodor Adorno	Carl Jung

4. When you have finished, examine the boxes that you had particular difficulty filling in. Try to decide why these difficulties arose. Was it because the particular criteria in the A–J list had no relevance to the approach? Was it because the approach is not clear on this point? Was it because no general approach emerges from the text(s) you are considering?
5. Devise ways of improving the grid, by refining, extending or altering the questions in what is currently the A–J list. Does this enable you to resolve the difficulties you had in filling in some of the boxes? If not, why not?

3 The 'objects' of your study: 'texts'

In Chapter 1, the phrase 'English literature' was *analysed* by separating it into some of the specific questions which make it up. Then, in Chapter 2, we explored some existing answers to those questions, answers which have been used to define literary studies in various different periods and places. Together, these two chapters attempt to get at many of the apparently contradictory definitions and blurred boundaries that the term 'literary studies' tends to conceal. But in doing these things we were not trying to empty the phrase 'literary studies' of meaning altogether. Instead, our aim was to force open the question of where the things you might find out or say about 'texts' fit in with the history and present forms of work in this area.

Problems do not end with the word 'literature', however. While querying this term, we have been happy to refer instead to individual **texts**. But in doing so, we appear to assume that what a text is is somehow less problematical than what 'literature' is. But the word 'text', like most words, is open to a range of different understandings and interpretations; and we need to explore what exactly we will be looking at if we decide that, rather than studying a body of 'literature', we are just studying a selected assortment of 'texts'.

3.1 What is a text?

Like many words, the word 'text' does not have a single, fixed meaning which you can just pick out of a dictionary. Any definition of 'text' which you find in a dictionary will be a simplification, to help you understand the word in a particular context. Like most other words, the word 'text' has changed its meaning over the period in which it has been part of the language. At any one time, too, it can mean different things to different people. More particularly, the word has various technical meanings for people working in specific disciplines. So if we are to use the word, especially as a way of getting round problems with other words (such as 'literature'), we need to think about the range of meanings which it can be used to convey.

To find out about the history of meanings for a word, the standard reference source is the complete *Oxford English Dictionary* (the *OED*), also called the *New English Dictionary on Historical Principles*.

Look up the word 'text' in the *OED*.

In many 'defining' dictionaries, when you look up a word you get something like the following: information about the word (its pronunciation, its etymology, etc.) followed by one or more definitions of its meaning(s). In the *OED*, as we saw with the word 'canon' above (p. 9), you get all this plus details of the changing senses of the word over the period in which it has been in use, with examples of those senses. The value of this is that it then becomes possible to work out which possible meanings the word might have in any particular text you find it in. Most words have many differing senses at any one time, and these senses sometimes compete with one another and lead to the construction of different – often conflicting – ideas or points of view. Whenever we use a word, its meaning will depend on the particular sense we are adopting and the context in which it occurs. This can in some cases lead to serious misunderstandings.

For a discussion of this phenomenon, in relation to 'keywords' through which we define our ideas about knowledge, society and social relationships, you might read the introduction to Raymond Williams, *Keywords*. What follows here is an indication of some uses of, and possible meanings for, the single word 'text'. We use Shakespeare's play *The Tempest* as an example. For each meaning we have left space for you to describe a different example.

Meaning 1

The text of Shakespeare's *The Tempest* is the original document written with his own hand by Shakespeare. In this sense of the word there is only one text of *The Tempest*, now probably no longer existing. The technical word **autograph** is sometimes used as an alternative name for this sense of text.

Now name another text in this sense and describe why you think it is an autograph.

Meaning 2

A text of Shakespeare's *The Tempest* is any version of the play: any individual copy or performance of the play. In this sense of the word 'text', there are many texts of *The Tempest*, one of which is at the moment on my bookshelf. We will call any one of these texts a **text-token**. The autograph of the text is one of its text-tokens, and we could say that all text-tokens are physical derivatives from an autograph. A text in this sense is any one of many different physically existing individual forms.

Now name a text in this sense and describe why you think it is a text-token.

Meaning 3

A text of Shakespeare's *The Tempest* is what all the versions of the play have in common. This kind of text is not a physical object at all but is a socially agreed 'construct' or *idea* of the shared properties of all those particular, physical text-tokens which we call *The Tempest*. (It is this sense of 'texts' that gives us the 'texts' people normally study when they study literary texts.) We can call this kind of text a **text-type** (using 'type' in a philosophical sense which we will discuss further in Section 3.2). While there are many different text-tokens called *The Tempest*, there is presumably only one text-type.

Now name a text in this sense and describe why you think it is a text-type.

Meaning 4

'Text' is also a theoretical term used in post-structuralism. Theoretical terms are dependent on often complicated theoretical assumptions, and this makes it hard for us in a short paragraph to fix a definition. But Barthes, in 'From Work to Text', provides a lengthy 'metaphorical definition' of the term, and you should read this short essay if you want to understand this particular meaning of 'text'.[1] For Barthes, 'text' is not the same as text-tokens (which he calls 'works'); it is more like a text-type. But whereas text-types might be thought to be abstract, outside time and space, Barthes's text exists only while it is being read. For an act of reading *The Tempest* to be a text in the sense used by Barthes, the reader should find that *The Tempest* is constantly becoming harder and more complex to understand, with more and more meanings becoming possible the more deeply it is read.

Try to think of an example of a text in this sense, name it and – using material from Chapter 2 if appropriate – describe why you think it is a 'post-structuralist' text. You may find it useful to read Barthes, 'From Work to Text'.

sonnet by Shakespeare, the government health warning on a British packet of cigarettes, the writing on the screen of a computer. Notice that a text in this sense does not need to be made out of language (e.g. a silent film might not involve any language, spoken or written).
Give another example of a text in this broad sense.

....

Give an example of something which is not a text at all, even in this broad sense.

....

Q: How could we define 'text' so as to exclude the table I'm writing on, your left finger, the wiring of the computer, the radio set which transmits the radio programme, etc.? Is this, for example a good definition: 'A text is something which is intentionally meaningful.' If not, why not?

3.2 Text-types and text-tokens; formal and material properties

Types and tokens

What is Shakespeare's *The Tempest*?

Is it the book with that title sitting on my shelf, about a metre from where I am writing? Or is it pages 2–133 of that book (omitting the critical introduction and notes). Or the first printed edition (1623) of the play by that name? Or the performance of that play by the Royal Shakespeare Company in London on 23 March 1973? Or the manuscript that Shakespeare wrote? Or the film with that title directed by Derek Jarman? Or the prose version of the play, written by Charles Lamb? Or the science fiction film *Forbidden Planet*, loosely based on the play? Which of these is *The Tempest*?

In some sense, it is all of these at the same time. One way of understanding the issue is to say that there is something abstract, *The Tempest*, which is *manifested* or *instantiated* in all these different objects and events. Perhaps it isn't manifested in them all to the same extent. (For example, perhaps it is manifested more strongly in the book on my bookshelf than in *Forbidden Planet*.) This problem of defining *The Tempest* is a bit like the philosophical problem of what a triangle is: some abstract thing which can be realised by a lot of different actual shapes (all with three sides, but nevertheless all different). Philosophers call the abstract thing the 'type' and all its instantiations the 'tokens'. Plato (e.g. in *The Republic*) sets the stage for philosophical debates about the reality of types and tokens, and subsequently there is a rough division between two types of philosophical position; **materialism** says that tokens are more 'real' than types, while **idealism** says that types are more real than tokens. We used the distinction between types and tokens in the

Meaning 5
'Text' is also a technical term in different linguistic theories. Linguists who are interested in how language provides a material for building novels, or conversations, or monologues, or letters, etc. refer to connected stretches of language (usually more than one sentence long) as 'texts'. What we will call 'the linguists' text' can be spoken or written (or in sign language). A conversation between two people drawn from *The Tempest* would be a text in this sense.
Now think of a text in this sense and describe why you think it is a 'linguists' text'.

Meaning 6
Finally we come to what we most commonly mean when we use the word 'text'. Examples of texts in this broad sense are: a poster advertisement, a silent film, a radio programme, the first five lines on the fourth page of any novel you like, the credit sequence which ends a film, a

previous section when we referred to the text-type of *The Tempest* which is realised by a very large number of text-tokens, ranging from the manuscript written by Shakespeare to the most recent performance of the play, and including copies of the play on bookshelves in particular bookshops in Singapore, Seattle, or Sydney.

That, you might think, deals with the matter. But our *relationship* to 'texts' raises additional problems.

Q: If you close your eyes and think of *The Tempest*, is what you create in your mind the type or a token of the text?

Q: When we study *The Tempest* do we study a type or a token?

We have to *use* tokens (only tokens, not types, can be bought, borrowed from the library, copied from, written in, picked up, etc.). But you could argue that in our thought and our study we must be getting at the type – otherwise there would be no connection between what you and I do when we each read *The Tempest* using our own tokens. But is a mental image a physical thing (with the result that what you create in your mind could be actually one more token of *The Tempest* rather than a type)? These are hard questions, but fundamental to literary studies, because they are questions about the central objects of study.

👉 *Now do Activity 20*

Activity 20   *Investigating 'types' and 'tokens'*
(20 mins)

1. Make suggestions under each column (we have given examples to start you off).

What things would you identify as being

part of the TEXT-TYPE, *The Tempest*, independent of any particular token?	part of a TEXT-TOKEN of *The Tempest*, and not part of the type? (choose a particular token)
the play describes a shipwreck as a result of a tempest	this token of the play has a green cover

👉 *Now rejoin text*

We can say that the left-hand column in the activity describes **properties** of a text-type and the right-hand column describes properties of a text-token. We now look more closely at this notion of a 'property', to investigate how particular kinds of property are associated with particular kinds of text.

Properties: formal and material

We can illustrate what the word 'properties' means by an example. The chair I'm sitting on has properties. Some of them are: it is 3 feet tall; it is made of wood and plastic; more pressure is at the moment being put on its back legs than on its front legs; it is six years old; it is being sat on by me; it is Art Deco style; etc.

We can distinguish between different *kinds* of properties. We might, for example, distinguish the permanent properties of this chair (what it's made of, its height) as against its changeable or relational ones (how old it is, who's sitting on it, who owns it). Or we could distinguish between formal and material properties. The material properties of something are its modes of physical existence in a particular space and at a particular time (e.g. the chair's weight, height, metal-and-wood composition, etc.). Its formal properties are in some sense abstracted away from its physicality, though they may be based on it: for example, its straightness, its patterning, its being in Art-Deco style.

Only text-tokens have physical or material properties. Text-types don't.

Material properties are fairly easy to get at. Formal properties are harder to grasp. Nevertheless, it is formal properties such as style, tone, etc. which are often the focus of literary studies. In order to try to understand what formal properties are, we ask:

Do text-types have formal properties?
Do text-tokens have formal properties?

We can explore these questions further by focusing on a particular example. I am currently reading Philip Dick's novel *In Milton Lumky Territory*. I think the text is funny: it *has the property of being funny*. But *what* exactly has that property? Is it the text-type or the text-token, or is it the combination of the text plus me as a reader? It would seem to be the third, since the funniness of the text depends not only on the text but also on who is reading it. But can we, or even should we, say the same about rhyme, or rhythm? Are these properties of the text-type or the text-token, or are they a combination of the text and what the reader brings to it?

Q: Is there a limit to how far we can simply say that properties depend on the perceiver? Can we say that the number of lines on a page or the number of pages in a text is merely a matter of our perception or interpretation?

The answer is that not everyone agrees. A lot of work in philosophy has been about such questions, and there is a long history of argument in a number of divergent 'schools' of thought. Whatever the difficulty or technicality of the questions, however, they can't be thought irrelevant to studying literature. Many of the comments you make about literary texts depend on views you take in relation to this issue; and if you adopt existing theoretical work as a model for your own thinking, you are obliged to presuppose arguments and positions on such questions – perhaps without even investigating them for yourself at all.

3.3 Material properties of texts

Most 'traditional' literary critical questions concern text-types; they focus on what we would probably want to call formal properties. These are questions about a work's themes, the author's intended meaning, the dramatic or narrative function of characters, the effect of the style, etc. For the purpose of these kinds of question, the material or physical attributes of the text *as a token* are generally only of marginal interest.

There are exceptions to this. Editorial work on authors seeks to work through the various existing versions (tokens) of a given text (text-type), in order to decide on an edition which is particularly accurate or authoritative, or else particularly suitable for modern readers. Some interpretations of a text appeal to features of textual layout, such as indentation and paragraphing, as supporting evidence; and these can vary from edition to edition. The problem remains that it is diffcult to decide on a dividing line between features which belong to the text-'token' only, and those which are crucial to the identity of the text as a *type*. It is hardly satisfactory to have a grand theory of the artistic achievement of patterning between Shakespeare's dramatic scenes if it turns out that in the earliest versions (tokens) of the play in question they weren't divided up in the way you imagined, or possibly not even distinguished at all.

The decision to abstract away from the physical or material book or electronic image towards an 'idea' of the text beyond that physical existence can make many new insights possible. But it can also distract you from thinking about aspects of the text's social existence and history.

The specific properties of text-tokens can offer readable signs of connection between a text and its social or historical environment. There are technical and material constraints, or limits on possibility, which circumscribe the form a text could have taken, or the ways in which it might have been distributed, preserved or read. When read later, text-tokens are also subject to changing connotations and associations. As regards the future, too, questions arise about the possible shapes and forms of future text-tokens. New formats and technical possibilities emerge (in the twentieth century, radio, film, television, records and tapes, computerised data storage and retrieval, etc.); and in future there will be others – many as yet completely unforeseen. Some technical properties become quickly established (stereo, compact discs); others are less successful (quadrophonic sound, sensurround cinema). Understanding and learning about the history of text-tokens has an important role to play alongside – and in connection with – investigating the features of text-types.

So we will now explore further the ways in which physical properties of text-tokens are of relevance in the study of literature.

3.3.1 MEDIUM AND TECHNOLOGICAL MODE OF PRODUCTION

The **medium** of a text is the physical substance in which the text exists. There are **oral** texts, which take the form of sound, as in speech or recorded sound (e.g. in radio and records); or the medium can be some form of **written shape**, as in writing and kinds of printing. Images, paintings and photographs (as well as road signs, posters, and diagrams) exist in this written or drawn ('graphic') form. When combined together, the sound medium and the graphic medium can produce a compound 'medium' involving two simultaneous channels (sound and vision) as in television, film, and video, allowing the production of **audio-visual** texts.

In oral texts, meanings are signalled by features of tempo, pauses, and the intonational patterns in speech, as well as by those features of the language system which also occur in writing. Often, such texts are accompanied by indicators of meaning like facial expression and gesture. In completely 'oral societies' (whose language does not have a corresponding written form, and whose communications in language therefore take place exclusively in spoken form), such texts have always been used – and in many parts of the world continue to be used – as the forms of a society's historical record. In technologically developed societies, 'oral' texts like telephone conversations and radio programmes can be transmitted over wide areas, and these oral texts can also be recorded, stored and re-enacted at any later time, for a new audience – even after the original speaker or performer is dead.

Written texts can be produced with very different ideas of audience in mind.

A written text might be:	Example:
written for one's own use	shopping list
written for a specific addressee or audience	letter
written for any person or institution (e.g. a library) willing to buy it	book
written for open access	electoral register
written for restricted access	medical record

Written texts can be transmitted or distributed in different ways: by post, by electronic means (such as fax, telex and electronic mail), and by inter-library loan delivery services.

Now do Activity 21

Activity 21 *Written and spoken texts*
(20 mins)

1. Add to the two lists below: one list gives different sorts of spoken text and the other different sorts of written text.

Spoken texts	*Written texts*
...conversation	...magazine ....
...recited nursery rhyme.....	...diary ....
....	....
....	....
....	....
....	....
....	....
....	....
....	....

2. Write 'T' next to the texts in your lists which you would find taught or analysed in a literature course.
3. Write 'I' next to the texts in your lists which, though they would not be taught, might be *imitated* in texts which are taught in a literature course.
4. Compare the texts you have labelled 'I' and those you have labelled 'T'. How many of the texts you have labelled 'I' are also labelled 'T', and is this the result you would have expected? If so, why? If not, why not?

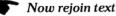 *Now rejoin text*

The question of medium we have introduced here connects with problems of text-types and text-tokens. You can read a text that was devised in the spoken medium (for example, if you read a nursery rhyme or transcript of a speech); you can speak something devised for writing (e.g. by dictating it); you can produce something simultaneously in and for more than one medium (e.g. write a speech for delivery at an event, releasing a written version of it for publicity; the speech is then televised, or recorded on audio – and so instantiated in several different mediums at once). One text-type can be realised simultaneously in a variety of different text-tokens which do not all need to be in the same medium.

> Q: Are *recorded* texts a kind of 'writing'? If so, what properties do they share with texts more commonly thought of as 'writing'? If not, what are the important differences which distinguish them from 'writing'?

The distinctions about medium which have just been made sound like absolute ones ('there is writing . . .'; 'there are audio-visual mediums'). But this is not the case. Definitions of medium depend on the particular **technologies of communication** available to a society at any given time.[2] Oral societies use spoken forms to do many things literate societies do with writing, and use other ways of representing things (e.g. pictures) instead, as well as storing more in human memory. Telephones can take over some of the functions performed in other periods of a society by messengers, talking drums or letters. Someone who wants to tell a story might do it in one society as an oral narrative, in another as a novel or other kind of written narrative, and in yet another by scripting or producing a film, television or video drama.

How many mediums, or *media*, there are depends on historical and technical matters, and is not an absolute or fixed distinction or set of categories.

We cannot, nevertheless, leave it at: 'Someone who wants to tell a story might do it in one society as an oral narrative, in another as a novel or another kind of written narrative, and in yet another by scripting or producing a film, television or video drama.' Stories are formally different in different mediums: oral narratives are likely to be more repetitive than written narratives; and film imposes different constraints on stories than oral narration. Arguments disagreeing with this take forms as simply a convenience for human expression without specific properties of their own. Such arguments propose general, human capacities for communication which are taken to be *beyond the detail of any kind of history of forms of communication*, and which will find one way or another of making themselves felt.

Consider in this context the example of Homer. We cannot be sure whether anyone called Homer, the author or the *Iliad* and the *Odyssey*, ever existed. What we *do* know is that there were epic poet-narrators in an oral tradition in Greece long before the time we first have recorded scripts of the poems now attributed to Homer. We also know that Homer's 'texts' first appear around the time writing gets established in previously oral Greek society. Was Homer, therefore, an individual person who 'wrote' those poems (the celebrated 'father' of Western literature), or is Homer a name given by later people (including ourselves) to a body of traditional, oral texts evolved over many generations of communal improvisation which are simply written down for the first time in

the form we call 'Homer'? (And if so, is it possible that we do this in an unacknowledged wish to *attribute* texts to an individual writer or author?)

Once texts come into existence in the form of books, how do they get produced? In Egypt, Greece and Rome, 'books' take the form of papyrus scrolls, etc. Throughout the early Middle Ages, they exist in the form of manuscripts copied out mostly by monks from an original, written copy. In the late fifteenth century, moveable type is developed – introduced in Britain by William Caxton – and books begin to be produced by mechanical processes. The scale of the book production industry increases in the centuries which follow, though during the Renaissance many of the texts which we now think of as book 'collections' still circulate in manuscript form only. Books then co-exist with chapbooks and pamphlets during the seventeenth and eighteenth centuries, and with daily newspapers from the end of the nineteenth century. During the twentieth century, books begin to be stored in other mediums, especially (by libraries) on microfiche and (like this book) in computer files.

To make sense of this developing industry of book production, we need to think not only of authors, but also of the social contexts in which books are produced: literacy rates and audiences; copyright and censorship; taxes on book production and sale; print-runs, prizes and top twenties, etc. 'Literature' exists within social patterns of writing, printing and reading.

 Now do Activity 22 on page 56

3.3.2 DIFFERENT KINDS OF LAYOUT

Within any book, there is a whole system of internal organisation: conventions of layout which signal the function that any given section or part of the book is likely to serve. Even the overall physical formats in which books are produced are of interest: whether they are hardback or softback, whether they are thick or thin, with pictures or without, since each of these categories can become associated with a social image. For instance, thick volumes and small print can be signs of seriousness, 'bookishness' or pretention; on television, academics are stereotypically seen against a background of filled bookshelves, which symbolise accumulated knowledge. Even the size of a book can be important, if you are trying to find it: libraries often store 'oversize' books on separate shelves, and give them a classification parallel to that of the general holdings.

Collectively, the conventions which make up this system of organisation form a 'grammar', or interrelated set of 'rules' of choice and combination which describe the arrangement of elements out of which apparent organisation is created. The 'rules' can be changed, or 'broken', for ironic, humorous, surrealist or other purposes; but in principle, their underlying grammar could

Activity 22   *Mode of discourse*

(40 mins)

Here are two representations of public speaking by the same senior member of the current (1989) British Government. One is an answer to a question about trade union legislation during a television interview (transcribed by the authors from a videotape); the other is a spoken answer to a question given in advance from an MP on the 'general security situation' in Northern Ireland, made in the House of Commons.

(a) No – uh the – Trade Union Act that – er – I took through – um – which we've put on the statute book which will – enormously improve the requirements for – secrecy – er – for fairness in – er – balloting in union elections – uh – that is now – uh – on the statute book. Uh – in the case of political funds these rules are now being approved – uh – and those are now coming into force progressively for the different unions – er – the other part has n'just come into force and that will come into force – uh – at the beginning of October. (TV interview, 1985)

(b) Since I last answered questions in the House, one soldier has been killed and four civilians have been murdered in sectarian attacks. Three of the civilians were murdered and nine were injured in a brutal and indiscriminate gun attack in a bar close to Belfast city centre. The period has also seen a continuation of particularly vicious punishment attacks.
   The efforts of the security forces are continuing to yield encouraging results. Since the beginning of the year, a total of 140 people have been charged with serious offences, including five with murder and nine with attempted murder. Some 300 weapons, approximately 70,000 rounds of ammunition, and about 4,100 lbs of explosives have been recovered in Northern Ireland. I understand that the Garda Siochana has recovered some 200 weapons, almost 139,000 rounds of ammunition, and 600 lbs of commercial explosives. (reported in *Hansard Parliamentary Debates* i.e. official record of the British Parliament, 1988)

1. List differences in style of speech between the two passages.

2. List differences between the passages as regards how speech is represented in writing (i.e. the system of transcription used).

3. Decide which (or what combination) of the following causes *might* contribute to a satisfactory explanation of the stylistic differences you have noted in 1. The differences are:

(a) a result of the system used for transcribing speech into writing;

(b) a result of the different types of situation in which the utterances take place;

(c) a result of different amounts of preparation made for the two different situations;

(d) a result of having different technical facilities available on the two occasions (e.g. written notes, autocue, etc.);

(e) a result of changes in the speaker's ways of speaking during the period of time between the two quotations;

(f) a result of idiosyncratic and unpredictable variation in the way people speak.

4. Does this activity lead you towards any general observations about how medium might relate to style?

Now rejoin text on page 55

be described. (For example, you might use the simple techniques outlined in Section 2.3.5 on structuralism.)

Conventions governing the layout of texts are socially produced (and they vary from place to place and time to time). Elizabethan scriveners (or compositors), for example, sometimes put extra letters into words – so spelling them differently – as a way of stretching text across to a neat right margin. This produced 'right-hand justification' (a straight right-hand edge), and, since many scriveners were paid by the line, improved earnings.

Conventions of layout can shape social expectations in reading. When you pick up a book, you have certain expectations about what will be in it and where things will be; whether there will be a dedication or an index and where they will be, how the book will be organised (contents alphabetically listed, classified by topic, etc.). This is your knowledge of the 'grammar' of book layout, which guides your experience of the book's overall form and directs how you read through the text. It is not our aim here to build a 'grammar' of book layout (though you might find it an interesting activity to attempt yourself), but you might expect that books will be able to use or exploit at least the following sections or 'slots'.

title page (including such information as author, title, ISBN number)
dedications
acknowledgements
table of contents
preface
chapters making up the body of the text
footnotes
appendices
bibliographies and indices

Some books are made up almost exclusively of just one of the above (e.g. an index or bibliographical reference book, a telephone directory). Within the main body of the text, there may then be tables, diagrams, photographs, and a framework of cross-referencing, etc. Internal structure can be indicated by simple numbering of chapters, by alphabetical convention, or – as with this book – by a more detailed system of 'logical' section numbering, showing relationships between different sections and sub-sections. Two things seem immediately important about matters of internal arrangement.

■ You are likely to have unconsciously 'learned' (without realising it) the conventions of layout customary within your language and culture. This will make you sensitive to variations or stylistic innovations in relation to the conventions, without being particularly aware that you are. One part of *studying* reading is to become consciously aware of the conventions you in fact already know, subliminally or subconsciously.

■ Conventions of layout shape the kinds of reading attention you are likely to give to a particular book. If a book is primarily a catalogue or list (as in a directory), you are most likely to **scan** the text for a particular entry you need. If the book is a continuous, developing narrative or discourse, you are most likely either to **skim** it (reading over the whole text without especially close attention, to get a general flavour) or to **read intensively**, giving attention to each element of the discourse. If the book is laid out as poetry, you are likely to treat it differently again, possibly giving it closer attention, or reacting to it with a particular kind of reverence, scepticism, diffidence or hostility. (We explore these different ways of reading in detail in Chapter 4, pp. 80–82.)

Besides stimulating different kinds or reading, properties of the internal structure of books can also signal different conventions of 'seriousness'. They can even indicate different conventions of 'personality' in a book's composition: narratives and rhetorics seem to imply a personality or speaking voice behind them; but indexes and reference works appear devoid of 'personality' – possibly even being collectively written or produced by machine.

Q: What would the effect be if a novel had an index? Can you think of any such novels? Or if a poem was written with footnotes? Can you think of any such poems?

To examine the features of layout described so far, you need to look at the book 'token' as a whole. (If the features are reproduced in *all* copies of the text, then you might begin to think that the features belong not to text-tokens at all, but to the text-type.) But besides these relatively large-scale features of texts, there are other, more local forms of organisation which are evident on any single page. If you examine a particular printed page, you will notice features of its style which are created by using some or all of the following resources. (There may be other features which create meanings or the effect of a style without specific intention: choice of paper or paper size, smudges and marks, etc.)

capitalisation	lineation	boldface type
italics	underlining	indenting

justification   different type
  (straight edge)   sizes

Again, these resources of the presentation of writing (**graphic or graphological features**) carry different kinds of association, and so carry loosely interpretable messages. Choices about typeface and typesize, for instance, involve stylistic decisions. You don't *have* to read a newspaper headline or article title before reading the smaller text below it. But people generally do. The types of association can be called **connotations**.

☛ *Now do Activity 23*

Activity 23   *Layout and expectation*
(60 mins)

1. On a separate sheet of paper, write out the text below in as many different ways as possible (either in pen or pencil, or by using a typewriter or word-processor). Each different layout should suggest a different idiom, emphasis, style, meaning or context. Use the following resources as appropriate: letter size, letter type, spacing, lineation, punctuation, italics, boldface, capitalisation, underlining. Compare your different versions.

A few feet up on the ridge is a shallow gully gained with a short descent. From the gully a diagonal break leads across to the next ridge on the left at a notch with piled blocks. Now, at last, some sort of upward escape is possible. A few feet up on the left is a ledge which cuts horizontally right and into the depression on the right of

this ridge. From the depression steep grass and scree, trending right but all very variable, lead suddenly out from the face at the summit cairn. A descent is entertaining, especially as the central slope is then quickly passed over, but practical only with the foreknowledge of ascent.

2. Add suitable headlines or titles to each of your layouts, using only words or phrases you can find in the text itself. Compare your different versions.
3. Add numbers, diagrams or sketched illustrations to any of your layouts where they might be appropriate. Compare your different versions.

☛ *Now rejoin text*

3.4 **Effects of physical properties of texts on you as a reader**

The physical properties of a text-token affect how you read. We have suggested, for example, that they can draw your attention to particular pieces of text before other pieces, so structuring the *sequence* in which you process information. They can also emphasise particular elements of the text (e.g. through use of **boldface**, *italics*, CAPITALISATION, or underlining). They can let you know where to find things in the text, or tell you how features of the text are intended to fit together. These signals contribute to your reading alongside your understanding of what individual words mean or what connotations they have for you, how strings of words fit together to form sentences, or how you can connect sentences together which don't seem to be obviously connected, in

ways that make them appear meaningful. (For investigation of these processes, see Chapter 6, pp. 136–7.)

The physical properties which create these effects are in many cases features of text-tokens rather than of text-types. You can tell this by noticing how texts are reproduced, reprinted and re-issued in new editions which differ from first editions. They are modified for new audiences with new expectations, and are reworked to fit with new stylistic conventions. Sometimes the revised editions show more evident care than first editions, sometimes less. Facsimile texts, for example, are deliberately made to look like old texts, though in fact they are new. Black and white films can be old texts which *look* 'old', or they can be new texts which are deliberately made to look 'old', or 'serious', or whatever connotations the producers associate with black and white film.

Physical properties of texts form aspects of their 'styles', and create kinds of meanings and associations, which can be exploited for a wide range of purposes. But these are not always *intended* meanings or effects.

☞ *Now do Activity 24*

Activity 24   *First and later editions* (20 mins)

This activity explores further how first editions and later editions of a text exist in different relationships to their foreseen audience.

Choose two texts, and for each text describe one situation in which you would expect a later edition to be produced with *more* care than early ones, and one situation in which you would expect less care.

Name of text	(a) situation involving more care in later editions	(b) situation involving less care in later editions

2. What general advantages are there in studying an 'original' or facsimile edition; and what advantages are there in studying a modern or modernized edition?

☞ *Now rejoin text*

3.5 Texts, contexts and circumstances

As we have seen, texts carry traces of how they were produced, and these point to aspects of a text's imagined audience and social circulation. Texts can be cheaply or expensively produced; and the resources which create this contrast involve not only a technology and skilled labour of book production but also systems and economies of publishing and distribution. There are strongly contrasting patterns in publishing and book distribution, from limited editions for patrons or collectors and 'vanity' publishing (publishing at the expense of the author) through to much larger print-runs of low unit-cost 'mass' sellers. You can look at any text and ask questions about its production on the basis simply of its surface features (paper, binding, jacket and jacket design, cost, etc.). You won't always get answers, but there is a lot to be learnt simply by asking yourself the questions, and speculating on the basis of available evidence.

Physical properties of texts anchor the text within social circumstances and relations. Text-tokens bear marks of the social formations in which they are produced.

By giving attention to the physical properties of texts, you locate individual human *creativity* in writing within a framework of concrete social forces and relationships. Texts are *social*, as well as *individual* creations. By tracing something of that social existence, you are able to begin to explain why they are the way they are and to expose the myths and mystifications which surround them.

If you read by ignoring this way in which a text hooks into history, and look instead for an essence of the text-type, you may be *adding* to the imaginary and idealised versions of textual history and value, at the expense of *investigating* them.

Authorship: ideas of writers and producers

We suggested above that different kinds of books create the impression, to differing degrees, of a 'personality' of an author (this chapter, p. 57). In many cases, the creation of this impression of a speaking personality, in whose company you spend time when you read, is an important and sought-for effect of the book. But this does not necessarily mean that such works are written by someone *with that 'personality'*. In some cases, a book with personality may be written by a team, committee or editorial group. (Some parts of this book, for instance, speak to you as 'I', 'me' and 'my' – though there are two of us writing it.) The technique of adopting a constructed form of address which does not correlate with actual procedures of writing is common, for instance, in the case of reports and newspaper editorials.

The idea that a text has a particular author remains an important one for literary studies, nevertheless. A class may be built around the works of one particular author (e.g. William Shakespeare or James Joyce). The theme for a book of criticism is often 'the works' of a particular author; and a text may be valued primarily because it was written by an author who is known for *other* books (e.g. the works written in her youth ('juvenilia') of Jane Austen, published in mass, paperback editions). The organisation of books in bookshops and libraries is also often by order of author. But texts in different mediums differ in *the extent to which an author can be identified*.

☛   *Now do Activity 25*

Activity 25   *Deciding on 'authorship'*
(30 mins)

Here is a list of some of the people involved in the making of a 'classic' film, *Citizen Kane* (1941).

cast:	Dorothy Comingore, Joseph Cotton, Agnes Moorhead, Everett Sloane, Orson Welles
director:	Orson Welles
editor:	Robert Wise (and Mark Robson, uncredited)
music:	Bernard Herrman
production company:	RKO
screenplay:	Herman J. Mankiewicz and Orson Welles

1. Is the author the film's producers, its director, its screenwriter, its narrator, main actor, someone else, or some combination of these?

....

2. Many of the same people were then involved in *The Magnificent Ambersons* (1942). This film, however, was cut by the production company, RKO, from 131 to 88 minutes. They also added a finale made without the director's (Welles's) supervision or permission. Given your response relating to *Citizen Kane*, does *this* film have an author, a group of authors, or no author?

....

3. Who is *typically* listed as a film's author?

....

Why?

4. Suggest three other kinds of text (other than films) where the notion of an 'author' is problematic in this way.

(i)   ....

(ii) ....

(iii) ....

Now let's turn once more to a written text. There is probably no more important 'author' for literary studies than Shakespeare (who in some sense symbolically 'stands for' authorship, as a special kind of genius). Significantly, there are special difficulties in the case of Shakespeare as an author: (a) there is a tradition of claiming that Shakespeare's plays were actually written by Sir Francis Bacon; and, (b) there is doubt about exactly who wrote some of the plays generally attributed to Shakespeare and some sections of individual plays generally agreed to have been primarily written by Shakespeare (e.g. *Pericles* or *Henry VIII*). The second part of our 'authorship' activity focuses on some lines from a play generally accepted to be by Shakespeare, *Henry V*, Act 2, Scene 2 (about line 176, depending on edition).

The first edition of this play (called the 'First Quarto', printed in 1600, a year after the play was first written and performed) has these lines:

> Whose ruine you have sought,
> That to our lawes we do deliver you.

The first collected edition of Shakespeare's plays (called the 'First Folio', and printed, seven years after Shakespeare's death, in 1623) has these lines instead:

> Whose ruine you sought, that to her Lawes
> We do deliver you. Get you therefore hence,

The second collected edition of Shakespeare's plays ('Second Folio', 1632) makes another alteration, to give:

> Whose ruine you three sought,
> That to our lawes we do deliver you.

5. Some version of these lines appears in any edition of *Henry V* (e.g. the one which you might use as a 'set text'). In any such edition, who is the real author of these lines? Think about the following possibilities; tick one or more (or add one of your own), and then justify your answer.

(a) Shakespeare, who presumably wrote the (now lost) autograph manuscript of the play.

(b) Actors or others involved in the early performances of the play (the first printed edition ('First Quarto') was probably prepared on the basis of the copy of the play prepared – not necessarily by Shakespeare himself – for the theatre).

(c) The publishers, printers, editors, etc. of the 'First Quarto', 'First Folio' and 'Second Folio' editions.

(d) Later publishers, printers or editors (between 1632 and now).

(e) ....

Make a note to justify your answer here.

6. Now compare your response to 1 and 2 with your response to 5. Is there a *difference in kind* between authorship in different mediums, or is there only a *difference in degree*?

7. How important is it to identify an author? Suggest three reasons for wanting to do so.

(i) ....

(ii) ....

(iii) ....

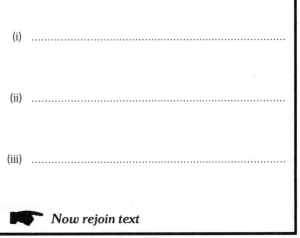 *Now rejoin text*

Even restricting attention to texts which appear to have obvious 'authors', the idea of authorship is a variable one. The impression of an independent creative personality writing in isolation for later publication, for instance, is a relatively recent phenomenon. Historically this notion is largely a product, in Europe, of the emergence of ideas of the 'artist' which developed in the Romantic period, in the context of new ways of thinking about trade and work, which themselves were realised in new ways of trading and working.

Writers occupy different positions in different kinds of society, and in different periods of any given society.

The very different lives of individual writers themselves fit into larger historical patterns. For instance, writers have tended historically to come from changing social groupings, and to have worked in different kinds of profession.

 Now do Activity 26 on page 62

How much you can learn in general from the individual life histories of a few writers depends on how you interpret the information you have available to you. Large-scale comparison suggests that there are historical processes at work.[3] You would be quite right in guessing

that there were no freelance novelists in the fourteenth century, for instance; and that there aren't many courtier-poets now. These guesses simply make use of knowledge about the novel (that the 'novel' form develops after the fourteenth century) and about social structure (systems of royal patronage have altered significantly in most societies over the last four centuries). In the history of writers there are significant *types* of employment: religious service, courtly position, work for a patron, professional employment as a writer. Listing the social class and sex of writers throws up questions: how is the changing position of women reflected in their status as published authors? Why are there no famous working-class Renaissance sonneteers?

> Q: How many examples or case histories do you need to know to begin to generalise? And does the social background or circumstances of a writer finally affect your reading of the texts themselves?

Here are some interesting historical moments to think about.

■ Shakespeare appears to have stopped writing altogether five years before he died, by which time he was wealthy. Did he retire? If so, does this tell us anything about his attitude towards writing and its importance?

Activity 26   *Authors and forms of employment*
(15 mins)

Each author in column A was for a significant period of their life employed as one of column B. The employments in column B have been jumbled so that they are no longer opposite the correct person. Match authors with employments, by writing the number of each employment in front of the chosen author's name (we have done the first one for you). You will probably not know all the answers, but for this activity this does not matter very much. Each time you make a match, make the best guess that you can, given the evidence available to you. For each matching which you had to guess, make a note of why you chose that particular employment for the author.

Column A	Column B
7 Geoffrey Chaucer (1340–1400)	1 doctor
Philip Sidney (1554–1586)	2 soldier
William Shakespeare (1564–1616)	3 broadcasting executive
John Donne (1572–1631)	4 storekeeper
Anna Barbauld (1743–1825)	5 priest
Maria Edgeworth (1768–1849)	6 university professor
William Carlos Williams (1883–1963)	7 controller of customs for wool
T. S. Eliot (1888–1965)	8 professional writer
Amos Tutuola (1920–)	9 property owner
Chinua Achebe (1930–)	10 publisher
Joyce Carol Oates (1938–)	11 schoolteacher

☞   *Now rejoin text on page 61*

■ Before the early eighteenth century in Britain, writers mostly depended on patrons for their living; there were very few professional writers (except playwrights who also worked as actors or theatre managers). In 1709, the first Copyright Act transfers legal rights in a work from the publisher (earlier represented by the Stationers' Company) to the author. In the 1730s, the first generation of professional literary writers emerges, especially associated with a London street called 'Grub Street' (a term later used figuratively to mean poor, commercialised writing).

■ According to Alexander Pope, the poet John Dryden was paid £1,200 in 1697 for his *Virgil*. At that time, an average shopkeeper earned about £50 a year, and a labourer earned about £15 per year.

■ The emergence in the nineteenth century of ideas of the romantic artist working *in isolation from* industry and society is closely linked to the rise of new professions *within* the publishing industry: agents, specialist publishing houses, critics and review journals.

■ T. S. Eliot's and Ezra Pound's modernist poetic works coincide with the expansion of formal studies of literature at the end of the First World War. Is this creation of a new potential audience of scholars connected in any way with the difficult, learned and allusive character of their work?

Writing (and production in other mediums) takes place within patterns of employment, and their related cre-ations of different types of audience. But there are also more specific institutional and legal constraints which surround writing and publication, and which also vary from country to country and period to period. These include:

(a) *Laws* dealing with censorship and copyright, and with libel and defamation. In England, registration by the Stationers' Office in 1558 began as an attempt to control what was published, as well as to give legal and economic rights to publishers; penalties for breach of the relevant laws were imposed by the Star Chamber, which gave or refused permission to all publications until it was abolished in 1641. In 1640, there were twenty-two pamphlets published in England; in 1642, there were 1,966.

(b) *Editorial control*, in forms of corporate writing such as occur in newspapers. (In newspapers and television, there is also the related question of 'independence', or the separation of a newspaper's or broadcaster's editorial stance from its owner's opinions or interest.)

(c) *Conventions of 'balance'*, giving equal amounts of space or airtime to different viewpoints and competing opinions, in countries which have policies aimed at achieving some degree of 'public service' through publishing and broadcasting, monitored by 'autonomous' bodies (e.g. in Britain: the Press Council, the Independent Broadcasting Authority and the Advertising Standards Authority).

In different countries the state owns and controls different amounts of text production. As well as being socially and technologically shaped by the society in which it occurs, human creativity is also legally and institutionally regulated.[4]

3.6 Who reads what?

Some authors prescribed on literature syllabuses went unread in their own times, and some were never published in their own times. Others, such as Shakespeare, became wealthy and famous on the strength of their activities. Some contemporary writers who would shun formal literary critical attention live in the paradoxical situation that they make their living largely out of sales of their works to students.

The particular kind of audience a text reaches is an important question. Historically, kinds of audience vary, and this is partly to do with **access to texts**. What skills does a text require of you if you are to gain access to it (e.g. do you have to be able to read Latin?) and how much does it cost to use (e.g. do you have to buy the book, or buy a television set in order to receive a television programme?)? Can limited-access texts nevertheless be shared by a wide audience (e.g. through libraries, film societies, etc.)?

Consider, for example, the skills required. You can only read a book if you can read (though there are other ways of gaining access to a book – it might be read to you, or you might buy a taped version of it; but notice that these depend on the availability of different mediums). Here, for example, are some estimates of **literacy** at different times and in different places.

In England in 1300 nearly all available reading materials were in Latin, so being literate meant knowing Latin. This skill was more or less confined to the better educated of the clergy (employees of the church), a few merchants and money-lenders, and some barons and kings – at most 3 per cent of the population.

Literacy is easier to assess at some times and places than others. In England after 1753, brides and grooms had to sign or put a mark into a marriage register; this gives us an indication of who was literate (i.e. who could sign their name). So we know, for example, that in rural East Riding in the late 1750s, 64 per cent of men and 39 per cent of women showed evidence of literacy in this way. From an average of 51 per cent overall literacy in the 1750s, by the 1790s the average literacy in the area was 57 per cent.

Compulsory education was introduced into Britain by the Education Act of 1870 (when the national literacy rate, measured by signatures, stood at 80 per cent for men and 73 per cent for women). The first generation of children educated following this Act became adults around the end of the century (by which time the national literacy rate had risen to an estimated 97 per cent). The first national mass daily newspaper, the *Daily Mail*, was founded by Lord Northcliffe at the turn of the century. How reasonable is it to assume that these facts are connected?

In 1942, President Roosevelt reported to the United States Congress that 433,000 men fully fit and eligible for immediate wartime military service had been deferred from call-up because they failed the army's basic literacy requirement.

People do not usually become literate from a desire to read works of literature.[5] In eighteenth-century England, small business people needed to read and write primarily in order to carry out financial transactions in an increasingly complex mercantile world. In Britain now, problems of illiteracy are acute when people are unable to fill in official forms or read official notices. And though literacy brings the possibility of reading works of literature, other social and material factors may intervene to prevent people reading. At the end of the seventeenth century a tax was put on windows, thus making it expensive to let natural light into your home; artificial lighting was expensive – and so one thing that restricted people reading after work was that it was not light enough.

Another social factor which shapes how texts find their audiences is **cost**. Defoe's *Robinson Crusoe* was first published in 1719 at a cost of five shillings, which was half a week's wage for the average labourer. It became more widely available when it was reprinted in cheaper editions and was serialised in a three-times-weekly journal, *Original London Post*. Fielding's *Tom Jones* (1749) would have cost more than a week's wages for a labourer, while it cost as little as the equivalent of two pints of beer to see a play by Shakespeare in 1600. In these ways, the audience for literary works fluctuates with the price of those works – but again notice that medium, and the costs of different mediums, are central to the issue.

Institutional changes, however, can counterbalance cost by enabling wider access to a single expensive text-token. Lending libraries (which you had to pay to join) became very common in England after 1740, and this meant that the audience for novels in particular became much larger. A state subsidy to a theatre company functions in a similar way, and a change in tax laws may make it more acceptable to a private business to sponsor the arts in return for concessions.

Q: The first edition of Samuel Johnson's *Dictionary of the English Language* sold 500 copies in 1755. The first edition of Karl Marx and Frederick Engels' *Communist Manifesto* ran to 1,000 copies. What information would you want to know in order to form an opinion about the possible significance of these facts?

Now do Activity 27 on page 64

Activity 27   *Books and audiences*

(30 mins)

1. Make a rough estimate of the total number of copies sold, since the first edition, for each of the texts below. Don't worry about being too precise; estimate *to the nearest million copies*.

(1) *Authorised Edition of the Bible*
(2) A single edition of *Newsweek* magazine
(3) Alice Walker, *The Color Purple*
(4) Harold Robbins, *The Carpetbaggers*
(5) T. S. Eliot, *The Waste Land*
(6) Charles Dickens, *Bleak House*
(7) A single edition of the journal *Scrutiny*

2. Tick the most accurate description of your estimates.

(a) likely to be accurate
(b) moderately reliable
(c) speculative
(d) total guesswork

3. How likely do you think it is that such information has been collected and is available somewhere (e.g. in libraries, official documents, etc.)? For each text, choose a number on a scale: 5 = very likely; 1 = very unlikely; write the number you choose beside each text in the list above.

4. Would it be useful for information about sales of different books, magazines, etc. to be widely available?
    YES/NO

5. What use would such information be? (Add notes or comments as appropriate.)

(a) It would help readers assess the popularity of texts.
    YES/NO

(b) It would help scholars and students assess the sort of audience texts reach.
    YES/NO

(c) It would help sociologists and others assess the position of texts in relation to different kinds of culture in a society.
    YES/NO

(d) It would help advertisers judge the suitability of texts for placing advertisements in.
    YES/NO

(e) It would help publishers decide whether/how much to pay writers for the next text they produce.
    YES/NO

(f) It would help consumers judge the quality of any text in comparison with other texts.
    YES/NO

Add other suggestions of your own if you think they should be included.

(g) ....

(h) ....

6. Would it be useful to collect information not just about the sales of texts which *have already been published*, but also about the kinds of text that people would *like to see* published?
    YES/NO

7. What use would such information be? (Add notes or comments as appropriate.)

(i) It would make it easier to publish texts that people will genuinely like.
    YES/NO

(j) It would help target advertising and marketing more precisely.
    YES/NO

(k) It would help decide what publications *not* to publish.
    YES/NO

(l) It would help devise formulae for commercially successful writing, to reduce risk when investing in commercial publication.
    YES/NO

Add other suggestions of your own if you think they should be included.

(m) ....

(n) ....

👉 *Now rejoin text*

Seeing texts in their social contexts can only be done by holding apart the distinction between text-types and text-tokens. And thinking about texts in their contexts, unless the texts are contemporary ones, involves thinking historically. But looking at the history of texts doesn't necessarily mean giving up the sort of literary-critical study in which evaluations and critical judgements are important. Placing texts in their social contexts need not be a way of saying that everywhere there are different situations, and you can't compare or judge them. Questions of value and judgement remain.

Your work in this chapter explores whether questions of value and preference are linked, directly or indirectly, to aspects of the larger social contexts for texts. To construct such contexts, you need to work through at least the following **constraints** on the way a text comes to you.

1. Authorship
    (writing constraint)
2. Publication
    (editing and censorship constraint)
3. Distribution
    (publicity, sales and circulation constraint)
4. Potential readership
    (literacy constraint)
5. Reviewing
    (value constraint)
6. Later scholarship and continuing circulation
    (academic study and continuing audience constraint)

We have suggested that investigating connections between the material properties of texts and their social history may help your study in several ways. It can help to explain why editions of texts are the way they are; it can expose myths and mystifications in the history of a particular work or works; and it can contextualise the achievements of individual writers in terms of the technologies, institutions of publishing and distribution, and audiences available to them. Comments on and interpretations of texts often invoke particular properties, without necessarily saying which properties the observations which prompt the comments are based on.

☞ *Now do Activity 28*

Activity 28 explores how far links exist between what you say about a text and your observation of particular properties of it and creation of particular contexts for it. But locating texts in their changing social contexts of production and distribution cannot answer all the questions you are likely to want to ask about them. In most forms of literary studies, in fact, texts are *rarely* looked at in terms of how they were produced, for whom, and what audiences they have subsequently reached or now reach. (Many of the properties of texts that you would need to know about to pursue such study are often thought irrelevant to literary criticism – and only appropriate to consideration by booksellers and other bibliophiles.) Questions about text-tokens and their social circulation – which are often investigated by sociologists of literature – are widely thought to be subservient to other, more important questions. So we should now begin to think about what those other questions are: how you decide which ones to ask, where to look for answers, and what you can do with answers when you have found them out.

Activity 28 *Commenting on* Hamlet
(20 mins)

Q: What do you think about *Hamlet*?

For each answer below decide (a) what it is about the text that the answer is based on, and (b) whether the answer is based on material or formal properties of the type or token. Make a note of any problems that arise. We have given a sample answer.

Response	(a)	(b)
'Attractive cover, and good stiff pages.'	Cover and pages of a copy of the book	Material/token
'Could have sold more, especially in the North.'		

Response	(a)	(b)
'Such a nice boy, shame he was so sad.'		
'Very well acted; adventurous set.'		
'Not much of a substitute for the play.'		
'The best study of neurosis I know.'		

☞ *Now rejoin text*

4 How do you find things out?

As you worked through Chapters 1 and 2, you will have seen that studying literature does not present you with a fixed set of questions to ask, or material to learn. You have to devise questions of your own. In this chapter, we look at how to devise those questions, and how to look for answers to them.

4.1 Novelty and convention

Imagine that you are about to write something. You are aware of ideas around you that what you write expresses *you*: your creativity and originality. But how much of what you write can ever be *completely original*? Or imagine that you are about to read. You set out to read a text largely because you expect to find something new in it. But how *completely new* do you expect the text to be?

To begin to think through these questions, consider this famous line by Shakespeare (Sonnet 18, line 1):

Shall I compare thee to a Summers day?

Before Shakespeare wrote it, this line did not exist. In this sense, it is clearly new and original. But did any parts or aspects of it already exist (e.g. as part of the language of the time) before Shakespeare wrote it?

☞ *Now do Activity 29*

Among other things, it is quite likely that you have put something like 'the individual words' in column A, and 'the combination of the words' in column B. But did the combination 'a Summers day' already exist, as a phrase common in speech, before Shakespeare wrote the line; or was Shakespeare the first to formulate the phrase? This is an interesting question, because phrases have different likelihoods of existing. Established patterns of co-occurrence or combination between words (their **collocation**, or existence together in the same text; see Section 6.3.1) depend on social, conventional aspects of usage, more than on the activity of any individual.

Shakespeare's particular combination of the words 'a Summers day' was quite possibly original. But even here, he was guided by already existing conventions. For example, he *could not* have written:

Shall a day to Summers compare thee I?

or

Shall thee compare I to a Summers day?

But he might have written

to a Summers day shall I compare thee?

or

I shall compare thee to a Summers day.

Activity 29   *Shakespeare's originality*

(20 mins)

To consider how much of this famous line by Shakespeare is 'original', fill in each of the following two columns.

A	B
What parts or aspects of the line already existed, before Shakespeare created it?	What parts or aspects of the line came into existence when, or after, Shakespeare created it?

☞ *Now rejoin text above*

These different possibilities and constraints as regards what Shakespeare might have written show that the language out of which 'original' writing is created already has its own patterns and structures. We will explore some of these in Chapter 6.

For the moment, however, let's turn to another dimension of your choices when filling in the two columns above. You may have put in column B something like: 'the idea of comparing a person to a summer's day'. But,

Q: Do you think this was a conventional comparison at the time, or was Shakespeare the first to think of it?

You could try to answer this question by looking at texts written before Shakespeare's. You might find that in this case not only the language of the text but also the ideas in it are partly unoriginal and already existing. Kinds of convention are incorporated into creative writing as well. Shakespeare chose a kind of poetry, the 'sonnet', which determined in advance how his poems would rhyme, how many lines they would have, to some extent how the meaning of the poems would be constructed, and what the poems could be about. In Chapter 5, we look at how writing works with a range of existing templates: forms and genres which can be repeated, used, or adapted by a writer.

Shakespeare is original and creative; but at the same time he uses ready-made structures and materials and makes use of conventions.

Originality is often considered an important quality in a text. Some people even say that this is what makes a great work of literature truly great. But we should ask ourselves the question: does the fact that Shakespeare's line contains non-original, conventional elements make that line less valuable or beautiful or important? Here are two possible answers to this question.[1]

NO. A great writer is great because he/she transforms existing materials into new work. T. S. Eliot said that the poet 'purified the dialect of the tribe'. His own poem *The Waste Land* contains fragments of popular songs and poetry by Shakespeare, among other borrowed texts.	YES. The function of literature is to make the familiar seem strange. The more rules that are broken, the greater the work. For the Russian Formalists, who held this opinion, the exemplary novel was Sterne's *Tristram Shandy*.

Innovations do of course happen all the time, and they can be credited to specific writers. The kind of sonnet Shakespeare wrote, for example, had a rhyme pattern first used by Henry Howard, Earl of Surrey, over fifty years earlier. Before Surrey, Thomas Wyatt innovated by being the first person to write an English sonnet, though the sonnet structure itself had already been used by Italian poets such as Petrarch. Thus we can trace back a history of conventions and innovations. Usually, innovations are adjustments made to conventions.

Shakespeare may have made innovations with regard to the sonnet form. But could he have changed the individual words from which the sonnet is composed? The most obvious way in which literary texts use already-made material is in the use of language. Generally, writers do not invent their own language. (An exception to this would be the creation of new words – or **neologisms** – by individuals which then get adopted in general usage in the language. The poet and essayist Samuel Taylor Coleridge invented the word 'intensify', for example, though he also invented 'esemplastic' and 'securiorate' which have *not* been used subsequently.) Despite the limitations on inventing a new language, some writers make such radical innovations in language that they might be called language-makers. The activity which follows looks at four sentences drawn from books which are examples of extended innovation of language.

▶ *Now do Activity 30 on page 68*

Work such as you have done in this activity suggests that it is possible to reach more precise answers to the question: do writers create texts out of nothing? On the basis of the activity, you might want to say: no – writers create texts out of what they know, out of the world that surrounds them, which includes language, cultural beliefs and facts, literary conventions, and so on. Even when writers innovate very radically, they still use pre-existing material as the basis for their experiments. Similarly, when we *read* a text, we produce meaning, pleasure, value judgements relating to that text in particular – but also very much in the context of what *we* know, and out of what the world that surrounds *us* is like, which includes language, cultural beliefs and facts, literary conventions, and so on. If the world-for-the-reader is not the same as the world-for-the-author, then the reader may not get out of the text what was put into it. The reader may not reach the understanding of the text which the author intended, but may well understand it in very different ways – pleasurable, valuable, insightful, etc.

People disagree theoretically over the importance of this difference between intended meaning and received meaning. The practical problem for us as readers is that what were pre-existing facts for the writer may have changed. Language changes, for example. Words, and particular combinations of words, come to mean different things. So we may misunderstand a word; we may fail to recognise a literary convention; we may misunderstand the writer's meaning because we don't know the conventional beliefs of his or her time or place; we may miss something that the writer means to tell us by using a plot from another text; or we may fail to recognise that the writer is making an experiment in genre, attempting to create a new form.

These may seem serious – perhaps insuperable – difficulties, as regards reading texts which originate in different social or historical contexts than the reader's

Activity 30   *The language-makers*
(45 mins)

Text 1   from Edmund Spenser, *The Faerie Queene*, (1596)

> Eftsoones himselfe in glitterand armes he dight,
> And his well proved weapons to him hent;
> So taking courteous conge he behight,
> Those gates to be unbar'd, and forth he went.

Text 2   from 'Jabberwocky', in Lewis Carroll, *Through the Looking Glass* (1872)

> 'Twas brillig, and the slithy toves
>   Did gyre and gimble in the wabe;
> All mimsy were the borogoves,
>   And the mome raths outgrabe.

Text 3   from James Joyce, *Finnegans Wake* (1939)

> Eins within a space and a wearywide space it wast ere wohned a Mookse.

Text 4   from Anthony Burgess, *A Clockwork Orange* (1962)

> I get all bezoomny when any veck interferes with a ptitsa singing, as it might be.

1. For each of these four texts, fill in the columns below (an example is given). For text 1 particularly, you may need to use a dictionary, such as the *Oxford English Dictionary*, which gives you historical information about words (such as when they were introduced into the language).

A 'Typical' Which aspects of the text are typical of the language of the time when it was written? Give specific examples.	B 'Not typical' Which aspects of the text are not typical of the language of the time when it was written? Give specific examples.
Text 1 The order of words, e.g. 'he – went'	the order of complement and verb, e.g. 'forth – he went'
Text 2	

Text 3	
Text 4	

2. Are there any similarities between the four texts in the kinds of innovation they make? List the similarities and note which texts you find similarities between.

3. Why should there be specific similarities and specific differences between any of these texts? Choose one similarity, and attempt to explain why texts are similar in this way. Choose one difference and attempt to explain why the texts differ in this way.

Similarity

Difference

☛ *Now rejoin text on page 67*

(which in practice means virtually *all* texts if you take social context in more than vague and general terms). To illustrate something of the scale of these difficulties, think again about the line by Shakespeare.

Shall I compare thee to a Summers day?

The word 'thee' is no longer in common use as an English word. In order to understand the line, we must know that it meant 'you' when Shakespeare wrote. So why didn't Shakespeare write, 'Shall I compare you to a Summers day?'? He *could have*. We must know that the use of 'thee' rather than 'you' was dependent on the relationship between the speaker or writer and the hearer or reader. You possibly know these simple historical facts about English. But how familiar are you with the different meanings of words like 'shall' in Shakespeare's time? 'Shall I' in modern English could be asking a question, or it could be asking permission. Could it have had both these meanings in Shakespeare's time? If we don't know the answer to this, then we will be unable to say whether the form of address the poet adopts is that of a question, a request for permission, or ambiguous between these two kinds of act. As a result, we may misjudge the meaning and function of the poem as Shakespeare conceived it. (We will discuss in Section 4.2 whether it is important to read a text as the author conceived it – an issue which has been important in earlier chapters and which we will return to again.)

One very important – and often neglected – point about questions such as the ones about 'thee' and 'shall' is that they are *very* often easily answerable (the question about 'shall' can be answered by looking the word up in a historical grammar of English, such as E. A. Abbott's *A*

Shakespearian Grammar). The problem for the reader is knowing what questions to ask. The main purpose of this chapter is to show how you can formulate and answer questions for yourself. It seeks to enable you, as a reader, to rediscover obscured facts that surrounded the writer and make up meanings of a text.

4.2 Anticipated audiences

In order to reconstruct intended or original meanings for a text, we need to recover various kinds of fact. Sometimes, however, a text's own author or editors do some of the work for us: a text may be packaged for the reader by the inclusion of supplementary information which is relevant for interpreting it. Texts for study are often packaged in this way. Most modern editions of Shakespeare's plays (either for native speakers of English or for non-native speakers) are combined with a set of explanatory notes. This practice of adding footnotes to Shakespeare has a long history. Shakespeare's complete plays were first published in 1623 (seven years after his death); in the eighteenth century they were first published with explanatory footnotes, and the footnoting of Shakespeare has continued ever since. Even the *first* published editions of texts sometimes include explanatory footnotes. Spenser's *The Shepeardes Calendar* (1579) was first published with 'glosses', footnotes explaining unfamiliar words; Wordsworth and Coleridge's *Lyrical Ballads* (1798) was first published with a footnote on a borrowing from Milton; and T. S. Eliot added to *The Waste Land* (1922) a set of notes explaining allusions and suggesting interpretations. A preface or introduction, whether written by the author or someone else, may also supply information which is useful to the reader in understanding the text.

When an author adds supplementary information to a text, an interesting problem arises: whether the supplementary information actually forms a part of the text or is separate from the text. For example, Coleridge prefaced his poem 'Kubla Khan' with an account of its composition (he had fallen asleep and dreamt the poem, but while subsequently writing it down he was interrupted by 'a person on business from Porlock' and subsequently forgot the rest of the dream and so could not complete the poem). Coleridge's account itself reflects some of the themes of the poem, and it is possible to interpret it as an extension in prose of the poem, rather than as a separate addition to it (the poem is interpretable as being *about* interruption and the failure to remember; it may also be significant that the alliteration in the phrase 'person . . . Porlock' echoes the extensive alliteration of the poem). Similarly, it might be argued that Eliot's additions to *The Waste Land* are as mysterious and allusive (and as much a part of the polyphony of different voices) as the text they purport to explain.

In all cases, we face a general question: what does an author expect her/his readers to know? This question involves a range of more specific issues. What degree of similarity between the worlds of writer and reader can an author expect? What differences of class, gender, social context, and nationality does an author make allowances for, and how far into the future does she/he expect to be read?

➤ *Now do Activity 31 on page 71*

In this chapter, our aim is to help you find out information you don't already have. But first we should consider in more detail whether this is worth doing; does it matter whether the reader recovers the intended meaning or not?

Most reading/watching/listening to texts, where the texts are from some culture geographically, socially, or historically distinct from your own, is done with limited or reduced knowledge of the circumstances in which the texts were produced. In many parts of the world, people read the references to daffodils in Wordsworth's poem 'I wandered lonely as a cloud', but have never seen a daffodil. In many parts of the world people read sentences such as the following, from Elechi Amadi's novel *Concubine* (1965), without having any precise idea of what an 'okwo' or an 'igele' is: 'The okwos tore the air, the drums vibrated under expert hands and the igele beat out the tempo meticulously.' You may watch a television programme such as *Bewitched* made in America in the 1960s but now distributed in many other parts of the world, without being able to pick up on now obscure references to contemporary events and societal attitudes. You may see a film such as *Angel Heart* whose narrative alludes to classical mythology (the story of Orpheus), and fail to notice the allusion.

People differ fundamentally on the question of how important such 'misunderstandings' are. You can take the view that they amount to 'misreadings' of the poem, which defeat the point of reading or watching the text at all. Or, you can take the point of view that such 'misunderstandings' don't really matter, so long as you, personally, make something interesting and relevant to yourself out of the experience of reading the poem, or watching the film or programme. Or you can take the view that it is in the very character of language to force on us such 'misunderstandings'.

Another common view is that differences between the writer (and the writer's context) and the reader (and the reader's context) are not as great or important as they seem to be. Shakespeare's plays, for example, are often claimed to be relevant to our own contemporary concerns – perhaps because the world that surrounds us is like the world that surrounded Shakespeare in certain crucial ways. You can see this view expressed in these words from the back cover of *Shakespeare Our Contemporary* (note the title) by the Polish critic Jan Kott (1965):

> For Jan Kott, a Pole who lived and suffered both the nazi terror and the Stalinist repression, the violence of Shakespeare's world offers many close parallels to our own. He sees Hamlet and Prospero not as romantic characters, but as modern man facing the despair that so many of his contemporaries have known.

Many people build a justification for the study of literature on the idea of such continuities in human experience, across times and cultures. In this view, there is a 'humanity' which is held in common by all human beings, and transcends local, historical detail. This view clearly contrasts with the other, major line of argument in favour of seeing connections between texts from contexts and social situations other than your own: that these other situations, past and present, are different from your own, but co-exist with it, as part of an interconnecting network of social and historical relationships. According to this second line of argument, you need to know about the past, about situations other than your own, and about possibilities for 'meanings' different from those that occur to you, in order to understand your own being and context.

But how do you know *which* questions about the past or about other situations – or about texts more generally – to ask? On the one hand, there is a set of stock, general questions you might ask about a text. What does it mean? Why is it titled as it is? When was it written? Why was it written? etc. Some of these are very large questions, and vague in their present forms; they need to be broken down into smaller and more precise questions if they are to be answered. On the other hand, certain parts of the text will raise more specific questions, while others don't. The word 'shall', for example, raised a specific problem in the Shakespeare line, but the word 'compare' does not. Specific questions that particular parts of the text might

Activity 31   *Expectations of readers*
(30 mins)

Fill in the boxes in the following table, adding A if you think the vertical column describes the actual audience of the text since it was written, and E if you think this was the audience expected by the author. You can do this activity without having read, seen or heard the texts in question. Speculate on the basis of what you *do* know about them. You might find a companion to literature helpful, if you know nothing about the texts at all.

	a specific individual (name him/her)	a specific group of people	a social class	a nation	people who do not generally speak English	students
Milton *Paradise Lost* epic poem England, 1660						
Achebe *Things Fall Apart* novel Nigeria, 1952						
Pepys *Diary* England, 1660s						
Hill Street Blues TV narrative USA, 1980s						
Pope 'Epistle to Arbuthnot' poem England, 1734						
Shakespeare 'Shall I compare thee . . .' sonnet England, 1609						
The Rolling Stones Sticky Fingers LP record England/USA, 1971						
Beowulf oral narrative England, c. 780						
Marilyn French *Her Mother's Daughter* novel USA, 1987						

☛ *Now rejoin text on page 70*

raise are: could a word have an unexpected or hidden meaning? Is a quotation being made? Is a symbol being used? etc.

It would take too long to ask questions about every single word, phrase and line in a text. So we must be selective. We need to look for things in the text which are *likely* to provide interesting questions and answers. To do this, we need to be able to recognise when there might be a quotation (even if we don't recognise the actual quotation), or when there might be a symbol, or when specialised knowledge about the world might be relevant to interpreting the poem.

Learning how to interpret texts means learning what questions to ask, and knowing how to answer the questions.

☛ *Now do Activity 32 on page 73*

4.3 Trying to answer questions you have asked

So far, we have talked about *asking* questions. How do you answer the questions you have asked, and what is the significance of the answers you produce? These are the problems we should now consider.

Sometimes the questions you feel you want to ask are answered later in the text. The process of reading answers the questions. In many novels or short stories which begin with a sentence like, 'It was late by the time she got there', for example, you will learn, simply by reading on, who 'she' is and where 'there' is. The element of 'enigma', or unresolved question, can be an important part of the pleasure or anticipation that reading provides, leaving specific questions to be answered later in the text itself.

Q: Are there any cases of this in the Lowell poem?

Sometimes, on the other hand, there are questions that cannot be answered by anyone other than the author. Writers may include references and allusions that are so personal to them that no other reader can recover what was intended. (Remember that writers have private satisfactions, as readers of their own work.)

Q: Do you think that there are any examples of this in the Lowell poem?

In cases where the question *does* have an answer that can be discovered and where the text itself does not answer the question for you, there are various reference sources that you can use. We will now go through a number of questions, and suggest ways of finding answers. Then we will look at possible significances of those answers.

4.3.1 IS SOMETHING A QUOTATION?

A large number of dictionaries of quotations are available, which list the more commonly used quotations together with their sources. Dictionaries of quotations typically have a list of 'keywords' at the end. If you want to look up 'our coffin's length of soil' you look up the word 'coffin' in this keyword list. If you are lucky, you will find a reference to a relevant quotation in the main listing of the dictionary of quotations. (Another, rather less fruitful, way of looking for a quotation's source is to look up one of the main words in the phrase in question in the *Oxford English Dictionary*. This dictionary gives quotations using the word from a large number of texts, and in some cases, particularly for texts several centuries old, your 'quotation' may actually be there.)

We haven't checked, incidentally, whether 'our coffin's length of soil' is a quotation or not. But we have checked the following line, which is definitely one.

Is Richard now himself again?

Look this line up in a dictionary of quotations (try first under 'Richard'). You will notice that the source is a rather peculiar one. Think about how this peculiarity might fit well into an interpretation of the poem as a whole.

While dictionaries of quotations are an obvious source for finding out whether a particular phrase is a quotation, there are other sources you can use. **Concordances** are useful, for example. A concordance is a list of most of the words used by a particular writer or in a particular work, with short quotations for every use of the word by that writer or in that work. Particularly useful for tracing quotations in English literature are concordances to Shakespeare's works, and to the 1611 Bible. These texts are the source of many quotations used in literature in English (even the titles of many books come from these sources). The following line from the Lowell poem, for example, turns out to involve a direct reference, by way of quotation, to the Bible.

I neither spin nor toil.

Look up the word 'spin' in a concordance to the Bible (1611, 'King James' or Authorised Version). This will give you one or more quotations. In the concordance we consulted, for instance, there are three references cited under 'spin'. Two turn out to be very similar (two versions of the 'consider the lilies' passage, in *Matthew* and *Luke* respectively); the other is significantly different. Your two main choices, therefore, as regards a Biblical origin for the line, are:

(i) And all the women that were wise hearted did spin with their hands, and brought that which they had spun, both of blue, and of purple, and of scarlet, and of fine linen. (*Exodus*, 35, verse 25)

(ii) And why take ye thought for raiment? Consider the lilies of the field, how they grow; they toil not, neither do they spin: And yet I say unto you, That even Solomon in all his glory was not arrayed like one of these. (*Matthew*, 6, verses 28–9)

Activity 32   *Asking questions*
(60 mins)

To get some practice at asking questions about texts, read through the following poem by Robert Lowell.

1. Underline and label parts of the text which you think (a) may be quotations (label with Q), (b) may be symbols (label with S), (c) require some specific facts in order to be interpreted (label with F), (d) involve a word you don't understand (label with W). We have annotated the poem with some suggestions, to start you off.

'Home after Three Months Away'

Gone now the baby's nurse,
a <u>lioness</u> who ruled the roost   ← S
and made the Mother cry.
She used to tie
<u>gobbets</u> of porkrind in bowknots of gauze   ← W
three months they hung like soggy toast
on our eight foot magnolia tree,
and helped the English sparrows
weather <u>a Boston winter</u>.   ← F

Three months, three months!
<u>Is Richard now himself again?</u>   ← Q
Dimpled with exaltation,
my daughter holds her levee in the tub,
Our noses rub,
each of us pats a stringy lock of hair –
they tell me nothing's gone.
Though I am forty-one,
not forty now, the time I put away
was child's play. After thirteen weeks
my child still dabs her cheeks
to start me shaving. When
we dress her in her sky-blue corduroy,
she changes to a boy,
and floats my shaving brush
and washcloth in the flush . . .
Dearest, I cannot loiter here
in lather like a polar bear.

Recuperating, I neither spin nor toil,
Three stories down below,
a choreman tends our coffin's length of soil,
and seven horizontal tulips blow.
Just twelve months ago,

these flowers were pedigreed
imported Dutchmen, now no one need
distinguish them from weed.
Bushed by the late spring snow,
they cannot meet
another year's snowballing enervation.

I keep no rank nor station,
Cured, I am frizzled, stale and small.

2. For each item you have underlined and annotated, think what it was about that part of the text in particular that told you that there was a question to be asked about it. Often it is some *change* in the text that signals a question to be asked. This is particularly true of quotations, which may be in a different style from the rest of the text. Alternatively, you may feel that what drew your attention to a word or phrase was that at that point the text failed to make sense – that you must be missing something.

It is often worth asking questions specifically about:

(a) the title ('why is it called this?')
(b) the names of characters
(c) the first line and first page (often densely packed with clues about the text to come.
(d) the last line and last page (which may obliquely summarise the text)
(e) animals, plants, geographical features ('are they symbols?')
(f) place names, nationalities, dates.

Here are some additional spaces for you to suggest, on the basis of your experience of the poem, other points worth looking for.

(g) ....
(h) ....
(i) ....
(j) ....
(k) ....

 *Now rejoin text on page 72*

The process of deciding whether you are dealing with a 'quotation' of either of these then involves:

(a) judging whether the similarity between the 'source' and the 'quotation' is sufficient to justify calling your 'quotation' a quotation.

(b) judging whether the fact that you've decided it *is* a quotation contributes anything to your reading (you have to decide what function, if any, the quotation serves when it is embedded in its new context).

We have now looked up and considered the word 'spin', and you can make judgements on quotations (i) and (ii) on the basis of the evidence from the Bible which we have presented. A similar process then needs to be carried out if you look up 'toil'. And so on.

4.3.2 IS THERE ANYTHING IN A NAME?

The name of a character in a story may be made up, or chosen because of its connotations, or borrowed from some other story. Because of these possibilities, it is always worth asking:

Q: Why does this character have this name?

Names can be made up in various ways. Here are some examples of made-up names. (They are taken from texts by Charles Dickens, Henry Fielding and Washington Irving.)

(Squire) Allworthy
(Mrs) Sparsit
Blifil
Tom Jones
(Mr) Bounderby
(Uncle) Pumblechook
(Mrs) Jellyby
Rip van Winkle
Ichabod Crane

Q: Do the names tell you what the characters are like, and if so, how? And how could you alter the name 'Pumblechook' to make it into the name of someone 'evil'?

Names are often chosen to identify characters with particular qualities or characteristics ('Squire Allworthy', above, is an example, though you need also to decide, on the basis of the context, whether the names are meant to work literally, or ironically or sarcastically.) In some cases, as in some types of **allegory** (stories whose characters and events serve primarily to represent a moral argument), reference in the name to characteristics can be almost completely unmixed with other dimensions of naming.

'Now Giant Despair had a wife, and her name was Diffidence.' (John Bunyan, *The Pilgrim's Progress*, 1684)

Names can also be chosen, however, for less direct connotations, despite being actual names. The name 'Tom Jones' may be like this. Try looking up 'Tom' in the *Brewers Dictionary of Phrase and Fable* (a useful place to look speculatively for information to help you read literary texts).

Names are also in some cases borrowed from specific, existing texts, and this is where reference books again become particularly useful. *Brewers* is a useful overall reference. Concordances to Shakespeare and the Bible are useful for names borrowed from these texts. Dictiona-

ries of mythology and folklore and classical dictionaries are also helpful.

Here are some names which are allusive.

Michael K. (in Coetzee's *The Life and Times of Michael K.*) alludes to Josef K. (in Kafka's *Trial*))

Ferris Bueller (in Hughes's film *Ferris Bueller's Day Off*) alludes to Beulah (the land of rest in Bunyan's *Pilgrim's Progress*)

Huckleberry Finn (in Twain's *The Adventures of Huckleberry Finn*) alludes to Finn (the mythical Irish folk hero)

In each of these cases, tracing back the allusions in the name provides us with an additional interpretative dimension to our reading of the text in question. We are more likely to see Coetzee's South Africa as Kafkaesque, more likely to interpret *Ferris Bueller's Day Off* as a symbolic film about the opposition between work and play, and more likely to pick up on the mythic connotations of *Huckleberry Finn*.

But how do you know whether a particular name is allusive or not? You can be guided to some extent by the rest of the text. If the text as a whole has a lot of allusions, then the names are likely to be allusive. Otherwise, it is generally worth looking up any name which 'stands out' in relation to the world created by the text. Again, the Bible, Shakespeare, and myths are all much-used sources of names.

 Now do Activity 33 on page 75

When thinking about 'characters' in narratives, consider also the extent to which they are supposed to be functioning as:

1. individuals (idiosyncratic, developing or changing, realistic, explored in specific and detailed ways, etc.);
2. representatives or types (class or regional stereotypes; embodiments of particular moral characteristics, etc.);
3. contrasting types (character types used in thematic or stylistic opposition to one another, cf. blonde and dark-haired women characters in many Hollywood films, rural characters and urban characters, etc.).

In most cases, there will be an element of all three dimensions to a character. The 'individual' level contributes to the realism or naturalism of the text, and to the development of the story; the 'type' level gives general, thematic significance to the text beyond the details of the narrative; and the 'contrasting types' level sets up thematic oppositions within the text through which larger arguments or statements of point of view are worked through, and contributes to a text's **symbolism**.

4.3.3 IS SOMETHING SYMBOLIC?

Symbolism is a very widespread phenomenon. It is found in our social life as well as in the texts we write and read.

Activity 33   *Speculating about the significance of names* (60 mins)

The table below lists some names of characters which can be found in the first few pages of Thomas Pynchon's *The Crying of Lot 49* (1966) (the last four are all part of a law firm). The peculiarity of these names suggests (though it doesn't guarantee) that they may be significant.

For each name, think whether it has some content as described by each column. Put a tick if it does, and add a note to clarify what the reference is. One name might get a tick in more than one column. We have suggested one 'content' of the name 'Pierce Inverarity' (there may be other meanings hidden in this name).

the name . . .	alludes to another name	contains some other word (perhaps slightly changed)	suggests nationality or ethnicity	suggests some meaning by its sound or shape
Pierce Inverarity	√ the philosopher C. S. Peirce			
Mrs Oedipa Maas				
Wendell 'Mucho' Maas				
Metzger				
the law firm of Warpe,				
Wistfull,				
Kubitschek				
and McMingus				

Now rejoin text on page 74

For example, national or religious events often have symbolic elements. The clothes we wear and the food we eat have symbolic importance for us, and so on. Anthropologists are particularly interested in how human society uses symbols, and psychologists are particularly interested in how human individuals think symbolically. (We look at how symbols work in more detail in Chapter 7, p. 160.) Both societies and individuals may use symbols without being aware of them; but some symbols are well-known and are manipulated by people with full knowledge that they are using symbols. A particular symbol may be very widespread. Or it may be very localised. It may mean roughly the same thing in different cultures and in different times, or it might mean completely different things. In Renaissance painting, for instance, a certain shade of blue had a symbolic association with the Virgin Mary. So her cloak was always painted that colour. In Britain the robin is a symbol of Christmas, whereas in the United States it is a symbol of spring. A few common symbols are listed in the table below (can you see a possible meaning for each example?); we have left space for you to insert some examples of your own.

Type of thing which functions as a symbol	Examples
geographical features:	mountain, river, forest, the sea
animals and plants:	flower bud, lion, eagle, mouse
manufactured items:	hammer, gun, pen, book
occupations:	carpenter, magistrate, fisherman
weather:	cloud, storm, rainbow, thunder
seasons:	spring, summer, autumn, winter
colours:	black, white, red, green
....	....
....	....
....	....

As well as objects which are symbolic, things which happen – actions or events – can also be symbolic. Events involving a change of state or a change of location are especially likely to be used symbolically: birth, death, falling into water, travelling (e.g. travelling to the sea). When they are symbolic, these events often occur in particular places in the narrative. Although birth ought normally to come at the beginning and death at the end, narratives sometimes begin with deaths and end with births.

Q: What reason could you give for arguing that a birth at the beginning of a narrative is less symbolic than a birth at the end of a narrative?

One way to find out about the possible meaning or meanings of a particular symbol is to look it up in a dictionary of symbols. Typically, what such a dictionary will give you is information about the use of the symbol in a number of different texts. Often even conventional symbols will have different meanings in different cases. When you discover this, you have to decide which is most relevant to your text.

One thing to bear in mind about symbols is that they do not always have fixed or conventional meanings. The meaning of a symbol can be set by the text which contains it, or it can be peculiar to a single writer. Nevertheless, previous uses of a symbol, in existing texts, or in social or public symbolism, create a background of possible reference which may partly determine what a particular symbol means in any given instance.

 Now do Activity 34 on page 77

4.3.4 WHERE DO STORIES COME FROM?

The same stories are told again and again. The same kinds of things happen in story after story. Sometimes the borrowing of a story or part of a story is significant in itself. Two questions arise, therefore, when we consider a story. First, is the whole plot borrowed from some existing text or tradition? Second, does the plot contain narrative elements which are common to many narratives?

Complete plots which are often borrowed or adapted whole, are:

- the plots of Shakespeare's plays (for example, *West Side Story* (film) borrows from *Romeo and Juliet*; *Gregory's Girl* (film) borrows from *A Midsummer Night's Dream*; *Forbidden Planet* (film) borrows from *The Tempest*; *Ran* (film) borrows from *King Lear*);
- the plots of Greek tragedies, particularly *Oedipus Rex*;
- Homer's *Odyssey* (for example in Ezra Pound's *Cantos* and James Joyce's *Ulysses*);
- stories from the Bible, particularly the stories of Moses, Joseph with the many-coloured coat, the Good Samaritan, Jesus Christ;
- classical texts or myths (for example Xenophon's eye-witness Greek history *Anabasis* is retold as a contemporary American street-gang narrative in the film *The Warriors*);
- stories from mediaeval romances, particularly those associated with King Arthur (the story of Parsival and his hunt for the Grail is particularly commonly used);
- the story of Faust.

Because they are reworked so frequently, it is worth becoming familiar with these stories (by looking them up in a companion to literature or a book which summarises plots, for example).

 Now do Activity 35 on page 77

It is more common for a plot, in a novel or a film, not to imitate another plot completely, but instead to contain certain conventional and commonly used 'bits of story'. These 'bits of story' are called **motifs**. The study of motifs is particularly advanced in the area of folklore because the basic building blocks of most folktales are a set of familiar motifs. A familiar motif, for example, is 'a wedding between the hero and heroine' (usually at the end of the story). Many folktales and fairytales end with this 'bit of story'. Many novels and films also end in the same way.

Just as a character's name may be changed when it is taken from one text to another, and a symbol may be transformed, so a motif may be altered. The motif of the wedding between hero and heroine is often a case of this. The wedding is often transformed in contemporary films (perhaps because the social significance of marriage has changed in many societies); many films end with a man and a woman becoming lovers, which is arguably a version of the same motif. In a similar way, you could say that it is the same motif which is being used, in a slightly altered form, when in many modern American films the film ends with a man, woman and child (who may not

Activity 34   *Symbolic meanings*
(45 mins)

The table below lists some commonly used symbols and symbolic events, with examples from actual texts.
1. Add examples of symbols in other texts that you know.
2. Write in the first column what you think the symbols mean. (You may find it helpful in doing this to look up plot summaries of the texts.) In the second column, give an alternative possible meaning, if you think there is some doubt about what the symbol means.
3. In the third column, make a note of what things you would look for in the text to help you decide which of the two meanings you have proposed is more likely.

	Means	Alternative meaning	What you would look for to help you decide
Falling into water, almost drowning but escaping, e.g. *Huckleberry Finn, Great Expectations*.			
The apparently dead coming back to life *A Winter's Tale, Our Mutual Friend*			

	Means	Alternative meaning	What you would look for to help you decide
A male character with a wounded leg or thigh e.g. the Fisher King (Arthur legends), *Moby Dick*			
A gun e.g. *Hedda Gabler, Herzog*			
A lion e.g. *The Lion, the Witch and the Wardrobe*, Blake's 'The Little Girl Lost'			
A blind character e.g. *Treasure Island, The Waste Land*			

4. Now check your intuitions against conventional meanings for symbols, by looking up the symbols in a dictionary of symbolism.

Now rejoin text on page 76

Activity 35   *Identifying a repeated story*
(10 mins)

1. Fill in the following table with the names of texts you know (books, films or television programmes) whose story seems to have been taken mainly or wholly from an existing text.

	The story which is 'retold'	The story which 'retells'
1. e.g.	*The Seven Samurai* (film)	*The Magnificent Seven* (film)
2.		
3.		
4.		
5.		

Now rejoin text on page 76

have been related at the beginning of the film) being brought together into a kind of family unit.

☞ **Now do Activity 36 on page 79**

The motifs in Activity 36 are all taken from Vladimir Propp's *Morphology of the Folktale* (1928), a book which has had a lot of influence on literary critics interested in narrative, and which we return to in Section 8.4. (The gender-marking in Propp's constant reference to the 'hero' follows simply from the procedures of his work: the motifs were collected from a corpus of already existing folktales.)

Folklorists have identified a large number of motifs, which can be found in motif indexes. A very extensive motif index is Stith Thompson, *Motif Index of Folk Literature*, 6 volumes (1955).

4.3.5 WHAT DO THE WORDS OF A TEXT MEAN?

Even if you are a fluent speaker of English, you are very unlikely to be fluent in all the geographically and historically different varieties of English that exist. So when you read a text written in a variety of English you do not know fully, you are likely to find that you are uncertain of the meaning of individual words.

Sometimes you will be confronted with a word you have never seen before. At other times, particularly when reading texts written in earlier periods, you will be confronted by a familiar word which seems to have an unfamiliar meaning, perhaps slightly different from the meaning you are familiar with. It is often hard to recognise that you are in the second of these situations, though various things may suggest to you that you have failed to understand something (for example, the sentence containing the word may not make complete sense if you assume that the word means what you think it means).

☞ **Now do Activity 37 on page 79**

Assuming that you recognise that you may not understand a word, how do you find out what it means in the text? Again the best reference source available is the *Oxford English Dictionary on Historical Principles*. This dictionary tries to list all the meanings a word has had in its history; it also gives quotations to illustrate each of the nuances of meaning. Necessarily, the information it gives about any word is limited (it is weak on whether the word was restricted to use in particular contexts, such as law courts, street markets, 'polite conversation', etc.). Additional facts about the word can sometimes be worked out by looking at the quotations in the *OED* entries, and thinking about the sources of those quotations. In this way, you might get some clues as to whether a particular word may have been used particularly in poetry, etc.

Try looking up the problematic words from the line quoted in Activity 37. Look up 'battle', for example. Meaning 8 on p. 707 of vol. 1 of the *OED* is: 'A body or line of troops in battle array . . .'; presumably the correct meaning in this line (and not the modern meaning of 'a fight'). A concordance may also be useful: if you want to find out about a word Shakespeare uses, you can look up all the other uses he made of the word.

To find out the meanings of 'grammatical words' – words like pronouns ('his'), auxiliary and modal verbs ('does', 'shall'), and so on – you can use a historical grammar of English, like Strang's *A History of English* or Abbott's *A Shakespearian Grammar*. Dialect dictionaries are also available to give you the meanings of words whose currency is restricted to a particular area or social group, and dialect atlases, or word maps, give pictorial representations of how different word forms and word meanings are distributed over a geographical area.

4.4 Methods of researching

We have looked at some specific questions you might ask about a text. We have also discussed how to find answers to those questions, by using reference sources. As a casual reader, engaging with the occasional question as you read might be enough. But if you are studying a text, the questions you raise are not simply incidental to reading: they are generally part of a larger investigative goal. Usually you study a text in order to reach a view on it in relation to some more general critical, historical or theoretical issue; and in practice this very often means giving a systematic account of your work on it (e.g. in the form of a class presentation, essay, examination answer, publication, lecture, etc.).

> **Your account of or commentary on a text is more than a set of randomly gathered questions and answers; your work develops as part of a larger framework.**

In the rest of this chapter, we look at how you proceed from the local questions and answers we have discussed so far into larger arguments. We examine how you can organise your questioning of a text; and we discuss the forms in which you present your answers.

Methods of researching and methods of presenting are in themselves *ways of thinking*. As you write an essay, you think out what you are doing. One of the best ways to clarify something in your own mind is to try to explain it to someone else. For these reasons thinking is often done in and for a community: as pairwork and groupwork; in research teams and think-tanks. There are various ways of finding things out about a text, in addition to using reference resources.

> You can consult your **intuitions**. By introspection, you come up with ideas about how the text works, and what it means. We consider this process in Section 4.4.1.
> You can **read the text in different ways**, using each way as a means of identifying questions and issues. We consider this process in Section 4.4.2.

Activity 36   *Motifs in texts*
(30 mins)

Here are some commonly used motifs. For each, suggest two texts that you know of in which the motif occurs (perhaps in a transformed version). If you are not sure whether you have really found an example of the motif, add a question mark.

1. One of the members of a family (usually the father) leaves home (often at the beginning of the story).

....

....

2. The hero is ordered not to do something.

....

....

3. Someone gives the hero a gift which has magical powers and enables him to carry out some important action.

....

....

4. The hero is pursued.

....

....

5. The hero, unrecognised, arrives home or in another country.

....

....

6. The hero is married and ascends the throne.

....

....

☞ *Now rejoin text on page 78*

Activity 37   *Words you don't recognise*
(10 mins)

Here is a sentence which contains familiar words which don't necessarily all have familiar meanings. (The sentence is from Shakespeare, *Henry V* (1600), with spelling modernised, as is usual in most modern editions which you might read.)

1. Underline words you think you might not understand.

   The king himself is rode to view his battle.

2. Make a note here of how you decided which word or words to underline.

☞ *Now rejoin text on page 78*

You can **compare** the text with other texts, to bring more clearly into view distinctive things about it which contrast with the other texts you are comparing it with. We consider this process in Section 4.4.3.

You can **alter** aspects of the text in various ways, to see how changing some specific aspect of its form results in changes in its meaning or effects. We consider this process in Section 4.4.4.

You can conduct a simple **survey**, to find out how far other people's judgements about some aspect or features of the text fall into significant patterns.

You can create a simple **experiment**, to test out your own feelings or ideas about some aspect of the text against the reactions of other people. We consider these processes in Section 4.4.5.

Some of these methods are more appropriate to certain kinds of question than others; and in some cases, a combination of more than one of them is appropriate.

4.4.1 USING YOUR INTUITIONS

Your **intuitions** are the judgements you make by introspection (looking inwards at your own thoughts and assumptions). It is possible to work by taking your intuitions as the principal method of your enquiry. In this case, your work will be impressionistic: on the basis of intuitions, you simply assert a view. Alternatively, you can link your intuitions to a process of formulating and answering questions which involves other methods; in this case you explore ways of seeing whether your intuitions can help to explain something: whether they can be shown to be misguided, on the basis of some other kind of evidence; or whether they can serve as catalysts to finding things out.

When we looked at Shakespeare's line, 'Shall I compare thee to a Summers day', we made judgements about what Shakespeare *might* have written and what he would have been *very unlikely to write* on the basis of consulting our intuitions about which combinations of words are possible in English. Even if we haven't heard particular phrases, we have a knowledge of the possibilities of the language, a linguistic **competence**, which enables us to make such judgements. If we simply take those judgements as our 'answers', we have not progressed very far. If, on the other hand, we use those judgements as the basis of an enquiry into how words combine in such a way that certain combinations are possible and others are not, then our intuitions form a useful part of investigation. To take advantage of intuitions, we need to have a specific investigative goal, and know how to link intuitions with other methods so that they form a resource for enquiry rather than a stock of prejudices.

Not all questions allow specific intuitions in the way that our question about how words can and cannot combine in English does. In the case of more open-ended questions (such as whether a text is 'good'), our intuitions are therefore likely to be less useful. But this doesn't mean that we should simply dismiss our intuitions altogether in these cases; they can still form the basis of speculations about the text which enable us to ask questions. Even our most general intuitions (e.g. that something is odd, unusual, peculiar or significant in some way) appeal to 'norms' in texts which are based on accumulated observations over a long period. Our intuitions can therefore be very useful as the input to a process of study. In order to find answers to questions, you need to decide in advance what you are looking for. Similarly, in order to pick out part of a text for close examination, you need to make decisions in advance about what you expect to find in that particular piece of text. Pre-planning in this way is often a matter of intuition and guesswork. Intuitions are what help you to choose to carry out other study activities on a text, which gradually lead towards more precisely defined goals; each time you look at a text you will have a better idea of what you need to look for the *next* time you read it.

4.4.2 DIFFERENT WAYS OF READING

As a 'private' reader, you are likely to read a text uniformly, without any investigative method or direction, and without taking notes. As a student studying a text you are likely to read in a different way. First, you are likely to read different parts of the text in different ways, since reading can be done more or less intensively. **Intensive** or **close reading** is a slow reading of the text, looking at each word and phrase, rereading passages, moving backwards and forwards through the text. Because this kind of reading is very time-consuming you are more likely to read the text as a whole by the faster mode of **extensive reading**. When you look for things in the text, you are then likely either to **skim** (accelerating even the fairly quick reading the 'private' reader may do); or you may **scan** the text, looking through for some particular words, phrases, or characters that you know you are interested in – but not taking in every word.

Different kinds of reading are likely to be usual for different kinds of text. Poems, for example, are less likely to be scanned than novels (partly a result of the difference in length); television programmes, unless videotaped, are difficult to 'read' (i.e. view) closely or to scan: transmitted, broadcast text runs at the speed decided by the broadcaster. Typically you may find that you will need to work on a text by a mixture of skimming and scanning, coupled with local, close reading.

To illustrate how different types of reading can be applied to a text, we explore the processes that might be involved in reading a poem by Aphra Behn, published in 1684. Our aim in reading the poem is not specific to begin with: we assume simply that we need to comment on the poem, perhaps in response to the traditional sort of literary critical question:

Q: 'Comment on the tone, style and content of the following poem.'

Song, Love Arm'd

Love in Fantastic Triumph satt,
Whilst Bleeding Hearts around him flow'd,
For whom Fresh paines he did Create,
And strange Tyranick power he show'd;
From thy Bright Eyes he took his fire,
Which round about, in sport he hurl'd;
But 'twas from mine he took desire,
Enough to undo the Amorous World.

From me he took his sighs and tears,
From thee his Pride and Crueltie;
From me his Languishments and Feares,
And every killing Dart from thee;
Thus thou and I, the God have arm'd,

And set him up a Deity;
But my poor Heart alone is harm'd
Whilst thine the Victor is, and free.

We can work through this poem stage by stage, by choosing a simple aim, carrying out a task based on that aim, gathering the results, and then perhaps working out a new aim on the basis of the results. We might, for example, work through the processes outlined in Table 1 (you should write on the text when instructed to in order to make the best sense of the analysis).

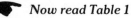 **Now read Table 1**

TABLE 1

Aim	Activity	Result
prepare the text for analysis	number the lines Do this to the text	lines can now be referred to in any notes you make
get an overview of the content	skim the text, make a note of the content as it appears from skimming	'Love is personified as a god. Poet and her lover provide the god with weapons. The weapons enable the god to hurt the poet and to free her lover.'

The process of making a note of the content results in recognising a certain patterning in the poem: the weapons are paired between the two lovers. This can be followed up by carrying out a directed closer reading of the poem.

examine the pairing of weapons from the lover and weapons from the poet	read more closely, make a list	'thy Bright Eyes' – 'fire' 'mine (eyes)' – 'desire' me – 'sighs and tears' thee – 'Pride and Crueltie' me – 'Languishments and Feares' thee – 'every Killing Dart'

This list – and the things you might notice while constructing it – lead to a large number of questions that can now be asked. These might well include:

1. Why does the pairing begin with the order thee–me (lines 5–8) and then go to me–thee (lines 9–12)?
2. In line 7, is 'mine' meant to be 'bright eyes' or just 'eyes'?
3. Is there any significance in the different kinds of phrase which describe the weapons: first two single words (fire, desire), then three pairs of words (sighs and tears, Pride and Crueltie, Languishments and Feares), then a phrase (every Killing Dart)?
4. What does 'Languishments' mean?
5. Why do some of the weapons begin with capital letters (e.g. 'Pride') while others do not (e.g. 'sighs')?

To answer some of these questions, you have to look outside the poem. Question 4, for example, can be answered by looking up the 1684 meaning of 'Languishments' in the *OED*. Question 5 might be answered by finding a book on typographical conventions in late-seventeenth-century poetry. Or it might be answerable by looking more closely at the poem. Other questions require a rereading of the poem (question 1, for example).

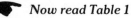 **Now read Table 2 on page 82**

Of course, much more could be done with the poem than we have done so far. There are other questions listed above which we have not looked into yet. And the close reading of lines 11–12 is likely to raise other questions. The general points to note are:

(a) Different kinds of reading get different results. Close reading is not always appropriate; sometimes you need the overview provided by skimming and sometimes scanning for specific items is needed.
(b) Marking the text itself helps you work with it. It is a good idea to develop a clear system of marking (e.g. in this case, marking 'me' words and 'thee' words differently so that a scan of the poem distinguishes them easily).
(c) We could have asked different questions. We could also have started differently. Learning a fixed order of procedures is far less important than developing an awareness of systematic methodology starting with

TABLE 2

answer the question: what determines the order of 'thee' and 'me'?	scanning of the rest of the poem for these two words (and related words like 'thy', etc.) and marking them in the text by putting a box round 'me' words and a circle round 'thee' words Do this to the text above	The overall order is T-M-M-T-M-T-T-M-M-T. A pattern is discernible of two pairs of T-M-M-T combinations, which is disrupted in the middle by the M-T pair of lines 11–12
answer the question: is there any reason for expecting lines 11–12 to disrupt the overall pattern?	close reading of lines 11–12, while scanning the rest of the poem to put the lines in context	Interestingly, lines 11–12 are also unusual in that here the 'mine' and 'thine' are in different places in the lines (the order of pronoun and weapon is different), which is another disruption of pattern. The pattern is also disrupted by the pairing of 'Languishments and Feares' with the structurally dissimilar 'every Killing Dart'.
return to the question: what reason would there be for lines 11–12 to disrupt the pattern of the poem?	close reading of lines 11–12, while scanning the rest of the poem to put the lines in context	Perhaps the fact that line 12 mentions killing: the disruption of the line is related to the line mentioning death?

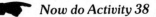 *Now rejoin text on page 81*

the formulation of specific aims for each text you analyse.

4.4.3 COMPARING TEXTS

We have looked at ways of looking outside the text for help. In particular, we looked at reference materials and at our intuitions. But we can also use other literary and non-literary texts as resources to help us notice things and find things out.

Comparison between texts, for example, can be used as a way of setting up contrasts. Instead of having to create questions for ourselves out of nothing, we are led towards questions by observable differences in front of us. But to control the otherwise infinite range of possible contrasts we might set up by comparing one thing with another, we need to compare the text we are interested in with another text which is similar to it in most ways but different in one specific way (or as few ways as possible): ideally, in comparing two texts, there should be one **variable** element; we should try as far as possible to hold everything else **constant**.

But what texts should we use in our comparisons? We list some possibilities here.

Different versions of the same text

You might compare different versions of the same text, including handwritten version(s), the first printed edition, subsequent printed editions, modern edited editions, printed editions with alterations made by the author, etc. Comparing different editions will normally show differences of typography or punctuation which are likely to be of little interest to most people studying literature. But sometimes an author revises a text between printings, and this may give an insight into the author's intentions or way of working which may be significant.

Sources for a text

Writers often take and adapt material from existing texts, just as they adopt and alter stories, motifs and symbols (it is not uncommon for a text to be a translation of a text originally written in another language). One reason for being interested in comparisons of this kind is that they permit a detailed insight into the creative processes of the writer at work. Thinking back to the discussion of originality at the beginning of this chapter, we can see very precisely what Shakespeare took from elsewhere and what Shakespeare added. In some cases, Shakespeare rewrote passages from the historian Ralph Holinshed, for example, and included them in his 'history plays'.

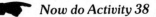 *Now do Activity 38*

Activity 38   *History and drama*
(30 mins)

Here is a passage Shakespeare adapted from Holinshed.

Get ye hence forward, you miserable wretches, to the receiving of your just reward: wherein God's majesty give you grace of his mercy and repentance of your heinous offences.
(from Holinshed's *Chronicles*, published 1587)

. . . Get ye therefore hence,
Poor miserable wretches, to your death;
The taste whereof God of his mercy give
You patience to endure, and true repentance
of all your dear offences.
(from Shakespeare *Henry V*, Act 2, scene 2, written c. 1598)

1. Classify and list the kinds of changes which Shakespeare makes to Holinshed's text.

2. For each change, why do you think it was made?

 Now rejoin text

Texts on the same topic

Comparisons between different versions of the same text and with source texts focus closely on variants on the text in question. But it is equally possible to find significant comparisons with texts that do not have any clear historical link with the text you are primarily interested in. In principle there are very many possible reasons for bringing two otherwise unconnected texts together into a comparison.

It is possible, for instance, to look at several texts dealing with the same subject matter, e.g. five different sorts of text referring to or about the weather (i.e. keep the content constant; take aspects of form as the variable). Such comparison might show up features of the distinctions between poetry and prose; between novel, essay and weather forecast; in different types of poetry; between kinds of metre or layout; or it might indicate contrasts in the varieties of English being used (formal/informal, standard/regional, etc.).

You might want, for example, to find out whether the language of the characters in a particular seventeenth-century play was a realistic imitation of ordinary speech in the seventeenth century. To do this, you would try to find contemporary reports of how people spoke then, so you could compare your passage from the play with a passage found in a seventeenth-century transcript of court proceedings, or in a seventeenth-century record of a conversation between people; or you might look at seventeenth-century diaries or letters to get some sense of how people really used language at that time. This kind of comparison is however very difficult to do, because it is often difficult to interpret the nuances of texts like letters, diaries, and court reports. How accurate a picture do they really give us of how people used language? As an illustration of some possible areas of comparison, consider the two texts in the following activity.

☞ *Now do Activity 39 on page 85*

Comparing texts in this way usually raises certain difficulties. In this activity, for example, can we know how authentic the dialect text is as a record of the speech of rural farmers in Cumberland? We would need to look at other sources as well – contemporary diaries or letters, if we could find them, would give us additional evidence (but we would always have to treat such evidence with care).

4.4.4 ALTERING TEXTS AND MONITORING THE EFFECT

Studying a text is in some ways like **rewriting** it. In some of the activities above, we have glossed (and so rewritten) the content of a poem; we have extracted and written out separately some of its phrases; and we have circled parts of it. Now we will look at some more radical rewritings of the text, which involve changing it into a different text. By altering some aspects of a text you are investigating, you

can see what effects a specific change has, and this may help to draw your attention to the properties which create the effect that is altered by the change. Each act of changing the text creates a contrastive pair between the pre-changed and the post-changed text, and if the particular change you have made does not help in the way you want, you can make other alterations instead. Finally, you may be able to isolate elements which cause particular effects in the poem (once those elements are gone, the effects will not be caused any more). Altering a text produces a 'comparison' activity: a comparison between the original text and the altered text you have produced. One difference between a comparison between two actual texts and a rewriting of the single text is that you can control the potential contrasts more precisely if you are making the changes yourself.

Consider the Aphra Behn poem again. One way of thinking about lines 11–12 which we did not consider in that activity is to rewrite them, and to see whether the rewritten lines have a different effect as part of the poem. The original lines were:

From me his Languishments and Feares,
And every Killing Dart from thee;

We could re-order the parts of the lines as:

From thee his every killing Dart,
And Languishments and Feares from me;

If we try to read the poem replacing the original lines 11–12 with these lines, we can ask whether the poem seems significantly different. Perhaps we could say that a certain finality has gone from the middle of the second stanza. It might be worth asking a group of people to compare the original and rewritten versions of the poem, to see how they differ. These investigations can provide insights into the original poem. One thing to remember, though, is that altering something in a text can result in an unintended alteration somewhere else. So the alteration of phrase order in these lines brings with it a loss of rhyme (by putting 'Dart' in a position where it should rhyme with 'tears'). Instead of making one change which enables us to focus on a particular contrast, we have made two changes; and we need to be able to distinguish the effects of one change from the effects of the other change. With the lines rewritten as they are, it is difficult to be certain whether any change in the poem is the result of the re-ordered phrases or of the disrupted rhyme scheme.

As we said above, in Section 4.4.3, ideally, in comparing two texts, there should be one variable and the rest should be constant. When you rewrite texts, it is important to alter as little as possible beyond the specific alteration which you are looking at. You may also have to overrule some of your resulting intuitions about changed effect (e.g. to ignore the problem with rhymes in the rewritten text).

One way to rewrite a text is to move parts of it around, as above. Or it can mean replacing parts of the text with

Activity 39   *Comparing representations of a dialect*
(30 mins)

In this activity, we compare two different representations of a dialect of English. Wordsworth probably spoke a Southern England dialect of English, but he intended the poems in *Lyrical Ballads* to represent, as he put it, the language of low and rustic men (but 'purified indeed from what appear to be its real defects, from all lasting and rational causes of dislike or disgust'). The following lines are from a poem in the collection 'The Last of the Flock' and are spoken by a shepherd.

> Shame on me, Sir! this lusty lamb,
> He makes my tears to flow,
> To-day I fetched him from the rock;
> He is the last of all my flock.

The text which follows, from a late nineteenth century collection, is an example of Cumberland dialect – the dialect of the 'Lake District' in which many of Wordsworth's poems are set.

> Mey sartey! sec a laugh I gat, to see a bit ov a tarrier meakin watter on yen o' their legs! They're seerly mangrels, hawf-monkey breed; shept for aw t'warl leyke wasps, smaw i' t' middle. To see them paut-pautin aboot puts me i' t' meynd ov oor aul gander; an if they meet a canny lass, they darnt turn about to luik at her.

1. Which words are found in both texts but are written differently?

2. What other differences between the two texts can you find?

3. Try to explain the specific differences in each case.

(Activity 63 in Chapter 6 compares a Wordsworth 'ballad' with an actual ballad.)

 Now rejoin text on page 84

newly written text. So we could also rewrite lines 11–12 as:

From me his Languishments and Feares,
And all the Darts of Death from thee;

Rewriting the lines by replacement like this might enable us to assess the significance of the choice of phrase 'every Killing Dart' in the original.

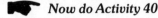 **Now do Activity 40**

Activity 40   *Rewriting a text*

(30 mins)

1. Rewrite lines 5–8 of the poem in order to put the contents of 5–6 after the contents of 7–8.

5...

6...

7...

8...

2. Reread the poem, replacing the original lines 5–8 with your rewritten lines; what is the effect on the poem?

3. How would you explain any difference between the poem with original lines and the poem with rewritten lines?

 Now rejoin text

What kind of things can be moved around and replaced in a text? They have to be part of the surface of the text, that is, words or letters or lines – you can't directly move around meanings or connotations or kinds of resonance. In effect you can move around or replace whatever you could cut out of the text with a pair of scissors. You can then look at the effect of this on meanings or connotations or kinds of resonance.

It is also possible to carry out replacement and movement on plots, but first you have to concretise the plot by writing it down on a piece of paper (by turning it into a short text). This then enables you to move and replace parts of it.

4.4.5 OBSERVING AND EXPERIMENTING

In the last few sections we have been looking at activities which ask and answer questions about texts by going against the ways in which people generally read. We might rewrite a text, or read a text in parallel with another text. In this section we look at some ways borrowed from sociology and psychology of thinking about texts and their contexts, which – although they are alien to many

forms of literary study – nevertheless answer important questions which would otherwise remain unasked.[2]

Consider this critical comment:

'Lawrence was a great writer because he had an exceptionally adjectival style'.

Is it possible to *test* whether this assertion is true or not? Part of the assertion – whether or not Lawrence was a great writer – seems untestable (the claim seems to rely on the commentator's own opinions, and cannot be objectively measured). But if we interpret 'he had an exceptionally adjectival style' to mean that a very high percentage of words in Lawrence's texts are adjectives, then this part of the assertion can be tested. However, in order to test this part of the assertion we have to make certain decisions.

(a) Which words are adjectives? For example, is 'running' in 'the running horse' an adjective? Some people would say 'no', others 'yes' (even 'experts' disagree on this one). What is needed, in order to be able to compare use of adjectives in different texts, is a decision – which may be arbitrary, but must crucially be held to consistently during the analysis of the text.

(b) Which parts of Lawrence's whole collection of texts will we examine in order to test the claim? Claims about the whole of a writer's work are rarely testable over all the texts involved, for practical reasons (not enough time, etc.), and so a representative sample needs to be pre-selected for the test. The question is really two questions: (i) how much text counts as representative (even 1 per cent of his total work is a lot of text to be examined), and (ii) which specific pieces of text are most representative, or should they be selected randomly? The answers to these questions cannot usually be given in advance for every possible case; different answers may apply for different writers and different issues. But since the truth of the claim rests on assumptions about these things, the particular decisions which are made need to be explicit (i.e. made clear in any report or record of your investigation).

(c) How will we decide what a 'very high percentage' of adjectives is? Scalar terms like 'very high' vary in what they mean depending on what they describe. A very high number of deaths on the road in a year might be 3,000, while a very high number of heart attacks for a particular person might be five; thus 3,000 and five are both very high numbers in different contexts. What number of adjectives is a very high number? To answer this question we would have to use comparison with some other texts. We would have to choose some texts not by Lawrence, count the adjectives in these texts and then assume that the number we get is an 'unexceptional' average number. If Lawrence has more adjectives in his texts than the texts not by Lawrence do, he will have a high number of adjectives; if he has many more, he will have a very high number. Notice, though, that it is very difficult to turn 'very high' into an exact numerical prediction.

Once you make these decisions (you could make them fairly randomly, but you do need to make them) and carry out the counting and comparison, you may or may not find some support for the claim that Lawrence has an exceptionally adjectival style. Without such a test you can't say; an answer based on vague intuitions or opinions drawn from your memory of Lawrence's texts is likely to be much less reliable. When you argue the case about greatness, at least those elements which *can* be confirmed will have been. It may be that the original feeling of 'greatness' derives not from 'adjectival style', but from something else. So showing that Lawrence is not unusually adjectival may make possible a new chain of speculation, based on a fresh intuition.

This was an example of a test involving properties of a text. Another reason for interest in measuring comes from references to 'the reader' in criticism of all types. Consider:

'The reader sympathises with Caliban at this point because of the way that Shakespeare has presented Prospero's use of his magic powers.'

Who is this reader who sympathises with Caliban? Is the reader an actual reader or an imaginary reader which one actual reader thinks is implied by patterns in the text? Or are references to 'the reader' simply a way of saying 'the particular reader who is now speaking or writing'. These questions can be explored by a survey; if a survey shows that many or most readers don't 'sympathise with Caliban', the claim may still have rhetorical force, but can be shown to be misleading as a general claim.

There are many questions that you can ask which can be investigated by counting, surveying, writing question-naires and doing experiments: questions about texts themselves, about writers and their work, and about the social contexts of literature. Questions you might ask about a text, or a collection of texts (by a particular writer, or written in a particular year, etc.) include questions of frequency (how many of particular words, motifs, sym-bols, sentence-forms, etc.), and questions about social context (how many copies were sold, etc.). Questions you might ask of a selected sample of readers might include questions of interpretation ('what do you think this line means?'), preference ('do you like Woolf better than Lawrence?'), or actual reading habits ('how many novels written in India have you read?'). The questions and activities themselves are often simple and easy to devise, but there are difficulties both before and after carrying the activities out. The problem for preparing these surveys and experiments lies in finding a way of framing the questions so that your survey gives precisely defined results. When you have got precisely defined results, the problem becomes that of making them mean something for literary criticism, with its concern with difficult and imprecise areas of value, meaning and pleasure.

These difficulties shouldn't deter you completely, however. It is easy, for example, to say that since you can never define your terms fully, surveys will always reflect vagaries or biases of the theoretical constructs behind them. But there are many large patterns that you can *only* see *at all* if you construct surveys and experiments; so even problematic procedures can be helpful, as long as you bear the problems constantly in mind (we come back to this at the end of Chapter 8).

Exploring correlations

Both of the critical comments we looked at ('Lawrence' and 'Caliban') were in fact comments about co-occurrences – how one thing co-exists with something else. Co-occurrences involve correlation between things; but they become more interesting when they suggest **causation**: where one thing does not just co-exist with but causes another thing (in fact, both critical comments above use co-occurrence as a way of suggesting caus-ation).

Claims about co-occurrences and causation pervade literary studies, and run through much Marxist, feminist, and psychoanalytic criticism. For this reason it is useful wherever possible to formulate the claims in a testable way, test them, and report the results of the tests.

An experiment constructed to test a claim needs to be repeatable by anyone else who wishes to test that its results really are accurate. So the experiment has to be reported in as much relevant detail as possible. Experiments which investigate whether there is a systematic co-occurrence between two things use variations on the following basic method. One thing is labelled the **dependent variable**, the other the **independent variable**. Co-occurrence between the two is tested by manipulating the relationship between them, by changing one (the independent variable) and looking to see whether the other also changes (the dependent variable). If a change in one is regularly and consistently accompanied by a change in the other, then there is a co-occurrence between the two. Here is the method, laid out in stages.

(1) Manipulate the independent variable and keep all other factors constant.
(2) Measure the dependent variable with each change.
(3) If changes in the independent variable correspond to significant changes in the dependent variable, then the independent variable *causes* the dependent variable.

As an illustration, consider smoking and cancer. In this case, cancer is the dependent variable (DV), smoking is the independent variable (IV). If you increase the number of people who smoke (i.e. manipulate the numerical value of IV), you might find that the number of cases of cancer also increases (i.e. resulting change in DV). If so, cancer co-occurs with smoking, and, if no other factors are confusing the result, *may* be caused by it.

The crucial thing about an experiment (which is also what makes it difficult to do) is that everything must be constant except the independent variable. To ensure this, you seek to eliminate what are called **confounding variables**: other elements which might be responsible for changes in your results.

Consider how a correlation relevant to literary studies might be examined. Take the assertion:

'In England the metrical pattern of iambic pentameter arises as a result of the emergence of a bourgeois-capitalist society.'

First we need to define the terms. Iambic pentameter is the metrical pattern used by Shakespeare, Milton, and many other poets, and has specific characteristics (see p. 122). A capitalist-bourgeois society is any society with a capitalist mode of production and social relations serving the interests of a bourgeois class, and so can also be defined in specific ways. 'England' also needs definition, since its borders have changed over the centuries. When explicit, working definitions for all relevant terms have been established, we can ask whether in England iambic pentameter first becomes commonly used at the same time as bourgeois-capitalist society first emerges. Notice

that there are some problems of precise testability here, to do with what 'common use' is, etc.; however, a co-occurrence might be suggested. But how could we support the claim of causation in 'arises as a result of . . .'? One way of trying to do this would be to build a kind of 'experiment', dealing with other cases which are 'parallel' according to our definitions. We can look for changes in the variables in different countries in history (in this case we can't actually manipulate the variables for experimental purposes).

'Commonly used metrical structures' is the dependent variable. 'Type of society' is the independent variable. We have considered one co-occurrence, where:

'value' of the dependent variable,
"commonly used metrical   = iambic pentameter
structure"

'value' of the independent variable,
"type of society"   = bourgeois-capitalist
                                society.

We now look at the history of different countries, in each case working out the value of the independent variables at different times (not all societies will have the particular value we are interested in, 'bourgeois-capitalist society'). We look at the values of the dependent variable (i.e. what kinds of metrical structure are commonly used, and when). We would hope to find a co-occurrence between the value 'bourgeois-capitalist society' and the value 'iambic pentameter'; however, if one frequently occurs without the other our claim is seriously weakened. There is a further step which we must take, perhaps the most fruitful step in the exercise, because it may show *other* correlations than the one expected. The step is to investigate *what other, potentially confounding variables have changed*. Given that we are looking at actual historical situations, there are bound to be confounding variables. By identifying these, we can begin to think further about the claimed co-occurrence and possible causation; alternatively, we may decide that there are other patterns of co-occurrence that may be significant, and may account for the causation we are attributing to the element involved in the co-occurrence we identified initially.

In the case we have looked at here, the construction of an experiment helps in part to assess whether the claim is true, but has perhaps greater value in extending the scope of the claim beyond one case (England), and opening up new possibilities and problems. Our particular 'experiment' suffers from two difficulties: first, the impossibility of manipulating the variables (we would have to be able to change a society's economic structure in order to do so – a truly revolutionary stylistic activity); second, the impossibility of ever fully controlling confounding variables, by excluding all factors which might interfere with the particular correlation we are interested in. Because literary study is often concerned with the past, 'experimentation' is often condemned to this less than satisfactory role. However, it is possible to construct experiments relevant to literary studies where variables can be manipulated; for example, by gathering a group of people and setting them an experimental test.

Now do Activity 41 on page 90

4.5 Methods of presenting what you find out

We have been looking at various ways of doing things with texts: ways of asking questions about them, putting them into interesting contexts, and so on. Now we turn to how you might present the results of your investigations.

It may be that you carry out a systematic examination of a text simply for the interest of doing so, for private satisfaction. Most research, however, is directed towards a moment of presenting its results to someone else (a teacher or supervisor, a group of fellow students, a conference audience, or the readers of a journal, book, or thesis). Presentation is not necessarily the conclusion of the research process: in many cases, you learn new things both from the act of presenting your work and from the responses of your audience, which can then be fed back into further research, another presentation, and so on. In this section, we restrict our discussion to different ways of presenting your work in writing.

4.5.1 WRITING ESSAYS

In writing an essay, you need to think about the purposes it is for, and the audience it will address. Together, these enable you to adopt an appropriate format and style.

The kinds of attention and expectation you yourself have when reading texts are likely to be brought to bear by your reader on what you write.

What is the aim of the essay? Not only do you need to know this, but so does your reader. When you think about what your essay is for, you might distinguish between phrases which simply describe a topic or content (what the essay is about) without indicating what you intend to say *about* that topic, and assertions, generally in the form of sentences, which act as claims, arguments or proposals. You can preface your essay with an **abstract** to make the aim clear: a one-paragraph summary of what you will be saying. A table of contents has the same function, but relies on the text being divided into a sequence of identifiable segments. The introduction and conclusion can also be used to express aims ('In this essay I will argue that . . .', 'In this essay I have shown that . . .', etc.)

There are also different ways of structuring the main body of a written report of research results. One possibility is to write the whole thing in continuous prose. Alternatively, you can break up your text into segments, which might have titles or numbers. Segmenting your text in this way exposes its organisation (and it is possible to bring out the organisation of your text in even more detail by having segments inside segments: 1.1, 1.2, 1.2.1, etc., or a system of sub-headings with different typefaces).

Should you divide up your essay into segments?

comprehensibility and clarity	You might consider it important to make what you write as easy to use for the reader as possible. Sections and sub-sections, particularly when they are titled and/or numbered, enable the reader to take the essay in in packaged 'chunks'; they also enable the essay to be scanned more easily. However, some readers may find it difficult to read text that is fragmented in this way, preferring a flow of continuous prose.
connotations of different kinds of textual organisation	It is unconventional to write literary criticism using complexly numbered sub-sections (papers about linguistics on the other hand are rarely continuous unbroken prose). Conventions, of course, can be approached in two directions: they can be respected, or they can be broken. You may choose to use an unconventional structure for some particular effect, to give your essay a particular overall meaning which it will derive from breaking the conventions which we expect it to obey. The connotations of textual organisation can be quite subtle: there appears to be a difference between using roman numerals (I.II. . .) rather than arabic ones (1.2. . .) for your sections, for example.
aims and content of your essay	Your essay may appear to demand particular kinds of structure. For example, if you are writing an impassioned defence or attack, you may feel that continuous prose more appropriately expresses 'passion'. Again, we are partly in the grip of the connotations of different kinds of organisation: numbering paragraphs has a scientific or bureaucratic feel to it, while continuous prose seems more authentic, personal and literary.

Q: How would you describe the structuring of the book that you are now reading? Is it structured uniformly, or in a variety of ways? Why do you think any particular structural choices were made?

Writing procedure

Should you construct a plan of action before you write an

Activity 41   *An experiment in reading*
(60 mins, plus time carrying out experiment)

In this activity we explore one simple experiment, to test the hypothesis that:

> The layout of poetry makes poetry more difficult to read than prose.

How can we test this idea? In its present form, there seems little that can be done. But what if we make the assumption:

> Since mental activity takes energy and time, difficulty will be reflected in the amount of time it takes to carry out a task. (In fact, this assumption lies behind the design of many experiments in psychology, which use timing tasks as a basic procedure.)

If this assumption is wrong, then the results of the experiment will be wrong. But all work makes assumptions; and these simply need to be considered along with the work itself when you decide how seriously to take it. Given the assumption, we can test whether reading poetry takes longer than prose, and suggest that, if it does, then it may be harder to read.

1. Using the discussion on p. 88, decide which variable is which, if we decide that our experiment will seek to correlate the *time* it takes to read something with *different layouts* of the same text.

> Independent variable = ...
> Dependent variable   = ...

After answering this, check on p. 213 whether you are correct. If you made a mistake, read through the section on experiments again. Now consider the following experiment. To test reading times for a piece of text laid out as poetry and one laid out as prose, we can rewrite a piece of poetry as prose, and compare reading times. Take a stanza from the poem 'The Last of his Tribe' by the Australian poet Henry Kendall (1839–82):

> He crouches, and buries his face on his knees,
>   And hides in the dark of his hair;
> For he cannot look up at the storm-smitten trees,
>   Or think of the loneliness there:
>   Of the loss and loneliness there.

2. On separate sheets of paper, write a copy of the stanza in its existing form (i.e. laid out as a particular kind of poetry) and a copy with the text written out as prose.

3. In one or more sessions, give the two texts to different people (ten people is a suitable number). Ask them to read one version of the text at a comfortable speed and then to signal (e.g. by raising their hand) when they reach the end. Then repeat this process with the other version of the text. Keep a precise note of the times taken for each version of the text.

4. Tabulate your results in a suitable form. (Use the suggestions we make in our discussion of tables and graphs below to help you, 4.5.2.) If your table shows that the times taken for reading the 'poetry' layout are generally longer than for reading the 'prose' layout, does this mean that the layout of poetry makes poetry harder to read than prose?

YES/NO/POSSIBLY/NO BETTER OFF THAN BEFORE

5. What aspects of the text itself, other than layout, need to be controlled for in the experiment, in case they distort the result? Do such things as vocabulary, sentence length, idiom, etc. make a difference?

6. Which of these factors are controlled for in a satisfactory way by using two versions of the same text. Which aren't, and why?

7. Would it be better to redesign the experiment so that it uses two different texts, rather than one text rewritten in two different forms? Make a note of points for and against.

For	Against

8. Does it matter in which order you give the prose and poetry versions of the text to your participants? List points for and against.

For	Against

9. Would it be better to redesign the experiment so that it uses two different groups of people, one group reading the texts in one order, the other group reading them in the other order? List points for and against.

For	Against

If your answer suggests that the 'two groups' design would be preferable, make a note here of how you might carry out such an experiment in practice.

10. What other factors, which haven't been considered so far, would be likely to affect the reliability of the experiment in its original and in its redesigned forms?

11. How much do you agree with each of the following comments (5 = agree strongly; 0 = disagree strongly)? Add comments.

(i) The initial idea to be tested is far too general; you have to be more precise in formulating what you hope to test if the experiment is going to achieve anything. 5 4 3 2 1 0

(ii) The size of the sample of people taking part in the experiment needs to be much bigger. 5 4 3 2 1 0

(iii) The size of the sample of people taking part in the experiment is more important than the precise detail of its design. 5 4 3 2 1 0

(iv) Language is so complex that you can't expect to find things out about it with experiments. 5 4 3 2 1 0

Now rejoin text on page 89

essay or paper? Your plan of action might consist of all the titles and numbers of sections and sub-sections (like a table of contents, only in this case you are deciding the outline of contents before writing them). Such a plan can be updated as you write, to take in new ideas; it also allows you to write the essay in pieces – you may, for example, decide to write Section 4 before Section 2 (useful if some parts of the paper seem harder to write than others; you can leave them until you are in the mood, and need not get stuck in the middle of writing the paper). A possible disadvantage of constructing a plan in advance of writing is that it requires you to make decisions you may not yet be ready to make (as there is nothing stopping you revising the plan as you go along, this may not be a serious problem). In effect, writing a plan before writing the essay engages you in a different kind of thinking about your work. If you prefer not to use a plan – for instance, if you write best by producing continuous text 'inspirationally' – it might nevertheless be useful to work out the plan after finishing the essay; if you find it easy to work back from the essay to a plan of its structure, then you know that you have produced an essay with a readily identifiable structure. An essay which is not coherently structured, on the other hand, will often be difficult to turn back into a plan.

4.5.2 USING CHARTS AND TABLES

Prose may not be the best way to present your ideas. Breaking up the prose with numbered sub-sections is itself a mode of argument and presentation; but more radically still for literary studies, charts, tables or diagrams may be more appropriate (e.g. tables can show up systems and contrasts more clearly than essay-writing does).

Consider the work you did in Activity 6 in Chapter 1, involving analysis of a corpus of texts. This work might be best reported in the form of a table, a pie-chart or a graph. Different ways of describing/reporting the analysis have different advantages. Tables are the easiest to write down; pie-charts are useful for representing relative proportions; graphs (which go in one direction rather than in a circle like a pie-chart) are particularly suited to descriptions of historical change.

(a) Tables

Drawing a table is a good way of looking for correlations and regularities. The table which you filled in in Activity 6 showed correlations between genres of text and relative importance of texts; looking at this table will tell you whether Hewitt and Beach assumed certain automatic correlations between genre and value.

Tables ideally show correlations between two lists (correlations between more than two lists ideally require a way of organising information in more than two dimensions; this is best done on a computer). Tables consist of

spaces (each space is the meeting point of a line and a column); the tables which we use in this book (primarily in activities) involve either filling in 'yes' or 'no' or filling in a number or comment.

(b) Pie-charts

If you were to draw the male/female distinction in the form of a table, the contrast in the respective numbers of men and women writers would appear like this.

	number in the canon
male writers	79
female writers	2
total writers	81

But represented in the form of a pie-chart, the disproportion between these figures would be visually much clearer. Female writers would be represented as 2/81 of the area of the circle, male writers as 79/81. Translating this into a pie-chart is easy; you draw a circle, and use a protractor (which marks out degrees of a circle). There are 360 degrees in a circle. Female writers are given a 2/81 'slice of the pie', which is 2/81 × 360, about 9 degrees. Using the protractor, mark off 9 degrees of the circle by drawing lines from the centre to the circumference. This way of representing the proportions is perhaps the most dramatic and effective, if you wish to show this imbalance in the canon.

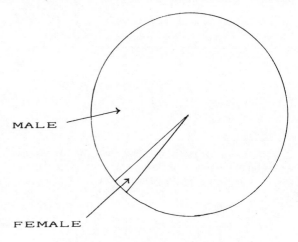

(c) Graphs

If you are interested in whether writers writing at a particular time are more numerous in the canon than writers at a different time, you might represent your findings in the form of a graph. For each writer find the date when he/she was 25, then draw a graph, part of which might be as shown here. You then have to decide whether you want the columns to be twenty-year gaps (as below) or perhaps fifty-year gaps. Twenty-year gaps show a more detailed breakdown, but may not give the clearest image of significant variations. You could also have decided to fix the relevant date as date of birth or date when the writer was 35; in making such decisions, various factors, especially the specific *purpose* of your analysis, have to be taken into account.

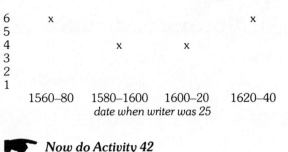

Now do Activity 42

Activity 42   *Taking yourself away from what you write*
(60 mins)

What you write is not in every case primarily an extension or expression of your personality. Many writing tasks involve adapting and applying conventions. The way you write depends on the particular task you are involved in, the idiom you choose, your relationship with the addressee(s), and other factors. But the contribution specific conventions of writing make to creating styles, views, and moods is often obscured by concern with writing as an expression of an authentic or 'real self'. One way to reflect on this is to write deliberately in ways *not all of which you can sincerely believe in at the same time*. This activity explores the element of convention in writing by inviting you to produce contradictory accounts of a single text. The aim of this is to dislodge your commitment to the argument, and so to an 'authentic' mode of criticism, to focus instead on *how* arguments are constructed and presented.

1. Choose a text (a poem, short story, play, TV programme, etc.).
2. Write one paragraph, arguing as clearly and well as you can that the text is bad. Give relevant evidence for this view.
3. Write a second paragraph, arguing as clearly and well as you can that the same text is good. Give relevant evidence for this view.
4. Write a third paragraph, criticising and showing flaws in the argument of each of your first two paragraphs.

5 Sorting texts out

This chapter looks at how we draw on systems of classification when we describe a text, and how these systems form part of the development of critical arguments and theories about literature. In the discussion and activities which follow, we look at reasons why it may be important or useful to draw on and develop classificatory systems, and we consider the difficulties which arise in doing so.

5.1 Classification

We start by thinking in the abstract about what involves classification and what classification involves. Consider the following description.

'*Hamlet* is a tragedy for theatrical performance written during the Elizabethan period, and one of the greatest works by Shakespeare.'

If we say something like this, we have made two kinds of decision. We have decided to say certain kinds of things about the text rather than others, and in doing so have decided that it is *possible* to say the things we say. In this case, we have chosen to say what genre a text is in, what medium it was written for, which period it was written in, how good it is, and who wrote it. We might have chosen otherwise. We might have decided that it is impossible to say how good a text is (and so we would not have said 'one of the greatest works by'). Or we might have decided to add that it is a fictional rather than a non-fictional work. But once we have decided what kinds of classification we want to make, we are in a position to make specific choices *within* each kind of classification. Given that we have decided to classify a text according to genre, for example, we can then choose to say that it is in the genre of tragedy.

The method we follow in classifying a text in this way can be pictured like this:

first select which types of classification to use:

genre	+ medium +	period	+ value +	author	+ *we could add* fictional, etc.
↓	↓	↓	↓	↓	↓

then classify according to each type chosen:

↓	↓	↓	↓	↓	↓
tragedy	theatre	Elizabethan	high	Shakespeare	fiction
or	*or*	*or*	*or*	*or*	*or*
comedy	book	Victorian	low	Dickens	non-fiction
or	*or*	*or*		*or*	
western	film	Contemporary		Ford	

In what follows, we will use the term **paradigm** to mean a type of classification. So when we described *Hamlet*, we used five paradigms: genre, medium, period, value, and author. Each paradigm consists of a number of terms (the vertical columns above, for example). When a classificatory paradigm contains two terms we say that the paradigm is **binary**. This is a particularly common form of paradigm; and we consider some examples of binary paradigms in Section 5.2. Other paradigms are called **many-way** paradigms. We consider examples of these in Section 5.3.

One way of thinking about what we did when we talked about *Hamlet* is to say that we called upon classificatory paradigms which already exist. In this way, paradigms form an already existing resource which we use when we talk about texts.

Drawing on existing paradigms is something we do all the time, not only when we talk about texts but when we talk or think about anything.

The words we use when we talk and think about the world are themselves clustered into paradigms, and when we use words we are (often unconsciously) making classificatory decisions. Different languages have different words in them, and one of the ways in which languages differ from one another is in how their words cluster into paradigms. For example, the Australian language Yidiny[1] has a word *gugu* which can be translated as 'purposeful noise'; this names a paradigm in the language, which includes terms like:

Yidiny word	Translated into English
dalmba	the sound of cutting
mida	the noise of a person clicking the tongue against the roof of the mouth
maral	the noise of hands being clapped together
nyurrugu	the noise of talking heard a long way off when the words cannot quite be made out

The words of Yidiny in this way form a paradigm which can be drawn on by a speaker of the language when that speaker is describing the world. There is no equivalent paradigm in the English vocabulary, though we have just created such a paradigm in English by translating the words into English phrases.

Different paradigms open up the possibility of making different kinds of description of the world.[2]

In the larger, social domain beyond literary studies, classifications are crucial in establishing group and social identifications. A number of individuals are able to convince themselves that they form a coherent group (e.g. a nation, a political party, a subculture, or a theoretical movement) by agreeing to identical (or at least overlapping or interlocking) classificatory decisions. In many cases, the precise content of the classifications is unimportant: it is the *act* of classifying which provides the social bond. In other cases, a social group forms consensus opinions, particularly about value and morality, which arise from shared classificatory decisions in which the content of the classifications is important. In both cases, the classifications are not inert distinctions to be adopted or discarded lightly; they are central to the processes through which social identity is formed, and they connect with the deepest senses of what makes up 'the self'.

In the simplest case, an act of classification begins with a thing which you want to describe, and a choice of paradigm you will use. But how do you decide which term from the paradigm best describes the thing, and what is the basis for your classification? In the case of literary classifications, we have to ask:

Is the basis to be found in the object/text itself?
Or is it to be found in the person making the classification?
Or is it to be found in the relationship between the two?

A major part of the basis for identifying a text as a sonnet, for example, comes from properties of the text itself (the text must have 14 lines). But part of the basis for identifying a text as good or bad comes from the person doing the classifying (from their beliefs about value).

We also need to ask ourselves *why* we should attempt to classify texts into 'tragedy', 'Elizabethan', 'by Shakespeare', and so on at all. One reason is that these paradigms and terms have major, contributory roles in the processes through which texts are created and read. When we read – in the same way as when we do anything else – unconscious and automatic classificatory decisions guide our understanding. If we decide that a particular text is a tragedy, then various significant consequences follow. We might decide to read it or not to read it on the basis of this decision. Or we might have particular expectations about the text, foreseeing a particular plot structure, a particular kind of ending, particular kinds of characters, and so on.

These expectations which routinely follow from our automatic acts of classification can in turn be exploited by a writer. The writer might choose, for instance, to go against some specific convention of tragedy (perhaps the main character will not die at the end), so creating a particular effect in the play. Many texts actually require the reader to be constantly making and revising classificatory decisions as a crucial part of understanding and enjoying them; some examples are T. S. Eliot's *The Waste Land*, James Joyce's *Ulysses*, Margaret Atwood's *Lady Oracle* or Angela Carter's *The Bloody Chamber*, in which the reading process involves finding that the expectations initially formed in reading are being continually manipulated or undermined.

This process is made all the more complicated by the fact that – as we will see in this chapter – classifications connect up with each other in all sorts of complicated ways. Interconnection between classificatory systems is not only an aspect of reading twentieth-century, modernist texts. Consider, for example, a text whose author is unknown. If someone decides that the text is by Shakespeare, then they are likely, as a consequence, to expect that it will be good, and to act accordingly. (The implication might in fact work the other way round: the text might be considered good and hence be expected to be by Shakespeare.) Either way, complex processes of classification involving more than one paradigm (in this case, both 'author' and 'value') enter not only into private acts of reading and interpreting, but also into more public acts of description and criticism, and affect even scholarly judgements about the attribution of texts whose authorship is in doubt. Finally, it is not only authors or critics who exploit systems of classification in an attempt to guide their readers in particular ways. Publishers also do this, in order to sell books. Their catalogues present good examples of complex classificatory systems, where the classifications (e.g. into different series) exist for marketing purposes.

☞ *Now do Activity 43 on page 96*

Activity 43   *Basic classification matrix*
(45 mins)

This activity suggests some binary oppositions by which things (not only texts) are classified.

1. Give examples of objects or texts classified by each term (we have suggested two for you).

2. Think of some *reasons* for carrying out the classification – what function or purpose it might serve (we have suggested two for you).

3. Look at the example objects/texts which you gave for each term, and think how you are able to decide which examples are classified by which terms. More specifically, think whether the classification is guided by the object itself or alternatively by your way of thinking about the object. Write O or P (as instructed). Then make a note of what properties of the object or text tell you that it should be classified by the term you chose (we have suggested two for you).

You may well not agree with our entries. Keep a note of problems you have in filling in the slots.

Terms used to create a particular opposition	1 Examples	2 Examples of reasons for making the distinction	3 Can the distinction be found in the objects themselves (write 'O') or only in the way that they are perceived (write 'P')? What is the basis for the distinction?
a black thing vs. a white thing	coal, night snow, angels		
a TV programme vs. a cinema film		Cinema images are bigger and perhaps affect the viewer differently. TV programmes are cheaper to watch	
a contemporary work vs. a non-contemporary work			P 'contemporary' = written within the last ten years from whenever the classification is made
fiction vs. non-fiction			

Terms used to create a particular opposition	1 Examples	2 Examples of reasons for making the distinction	3 Can the distinction be found in the objects themselves (write 'O') or only in the way that they are perceived (write 'P')? What is the basis for the distinction?
a valuable object or text vs. a worthless object or text			

Make a note of problems and/or unresolved issues here and bear them in mind as you work through the rest of this chapter.

 **Now rejoin text**

5.2 Binary paradigms

Paradigms with two terms in them are called 'binary' paradigms. Some binary paradigms contain two opposed 'poles', and a particular text is located at one pole or the other or at some point in between. These paradigms allow classification in terms of more and less. An example is the 'value' paradigm, with one pole of 'good' and one pole of 'bad', and the possibility of a text falling at some specific point in between the two poles (i.e. closer to good or closer to bad). We could call these **scalar** paradigms. The relationship between the two poles in a scalar paradigm is often privative, where one pole represents the absence of the other pole (one pole could be defined as 'not the other' pole). The 'fiction/non-fiction' paradigm is privative: a text which is fiction is therefore not non-fiction.

Binary paradigms seem to be very important in the way we talk about texts. They are also important in the way we make sense of the world. The structuralist anthropologist Claude Lévi-Strauss in fact proposed that binary oppositions form the basis for much of our thinking, even though many of the oppositions may be hidden from our conscious awareness. He focused particularly on oppositions such as 'cultural' vs. 'natural'. More recently, it has been suggested (particularly by the philosopher Jacques

Derrida) that binary oppositions always involve a value difference between the two parts: one part of the opposition is considered more valuable than the other (the person who employs the opposition 'privileges' one term over the other). As we saw in Chapter 2, these ideas are especially important to structuralist, post-structuralist and deconstructionist thinking.

Here are some examples of binary paradigms whose opposed terms are often used in literary studies. Add two more that you think are just as important, or are used just as much.

fiction/non-fiction
realistic/not realistic
literature/not literature
author male/author female
anonymous/non-anonymous
progressive/reactionary
theoretical/non-theoretical
funny/not funny
sexist/non-sexist

....

....

In this section we explore three binary paradigms in particular. Each is of considerable importance in literary studies. We look at the oppositions: poetry/prose, narrative/non-narrative, and good/bad. It is also worth saying that the activities which follow are based on particular **heuristics**. A heuristic is a systematic method for finding things out. Below, we use a number of different heuristics, each of which can be adapted for use with other paradigms. If you are more interested in the sexist/non-sexist distinction than the poetry/prose distinction, for example, you can change the second poetry-prose activity (Activity 45) in very simple ways by changing the word 'poetry' to the word 'sexist' and the word 'prose' to the word 'non-sexist', throughout. The activity should then function equally well.

5.2.1 IS A TEXT POETRY OR PROSE?

The first activity involves a **rewriting heuristic**. By altering the text itself, its component features can be identified.

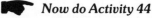 *Now do Activity 44*

Activity 44   *Turning one genre into another*
(60 mins)

1. Choose a poem.
2. Rewrite the poem in order to make it into prose. Keep a note of each feature of the rewriting. These features should then be features which differentiate poetry from prose. Your list should therefore indicate the main contrasting properties of the two genres.

*

3. Choose a short (and, as far as possible, 'self-contained') passage of prose.
4. Rewrite the prose in order to make it into a poem. Keep a note of each feature of the rewriting. These features should then be features which differentiate prose from poetry. Your list should therefore indicate the main contrasting properties of the two genres.

*

5. Now compare your two lists of contrasting properties. How similar are they? How similar would you *expect* them to be?

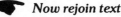 *Now rejoin text*

The second activity involves what we can call a **matrix heuristic**. This particular matrix is intended to first draw out your intuitive use of a particular paradigm (here, poetry vs. prose, though it could be adapted for any binary paradigm) and then to try to work out exactly what details of texts are (possibly unconsciously) guiding you to make these everyday classificatory decisions. The initial 'intuitive' part of the activity is split into two parts – one working from texts to classifications, and the other working from classifications to texts.

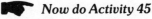 *Now do Activity 45*

Activity 45   *Classifying with a matrix*
(60 mins)

1. In column 1 lines C–I, write the names of any seven texts.
2. Now, for each text, judge which column (2–5) best describes it, and put a tick in that column. It is important to make a decision for each one, even if you are not sure (make a note of any problems you have).
   All the lines should end up looking something like lines A and B, which we have done as an illustration.

1 Name of text	2 is poetry	3 is prose	4 is in between	5 is neither
A Morrison, *Tar Baby*		√		
B Blake, *Vala*			√	
C				
D				
E				
F				
G				
H				
I				

3. Make a note in the box of what factor(s) led to a text getting a tick in column 5 (i.e. what kinds of texts are neither poetry nor prose?)

4. By considering the texts which have a tick in column 2 or column 3, fill in the columns below, being as specific as you can.

What about a text helps you decide whether it is poetry?	What about a text helps you decide whether it is prose?

5. Now look at texts which have a tick in column 4 ('in between'). The prediction would be that for each of these ticks, the text should have a mixture of features from both the left and the right columns in question 5. Is this prediction correct?

YES/NO

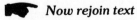 *Now rejoin text*

5.2.2 DOES A TEXT TELL A STORY?

Our investigation of this distinction involves two activities which are similar to the two activities in Section 5.2.1. The first activity tests our intuitive sense of whether a particular text tells a story or not against an existing **definition** of what a story is. This activity is similar to Activity 45 in that it tries to make explicit what underlies our intuitive judgements.

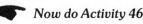 *Now do Activity 46*

Activity 46   *Which texts tell stories?*

(60 mins)

To investigate the kinds of distinction you intuitively make about 'narrative', and the bases on which you make them, work through the following instructions.

1. Use your common-sense intuitions about what a story is, and what kind of text tells a story. Fill in the two broad columns below, being careful to include different kinds of text not just written ones (we have already suggested two). Ignore the narrow columns for the moment. Fill in the columns fairly quickly. You will have a chance to reflect on your intuitive judgements later.

Texts which contain a story		Texts which do not contain a story	
Walker, *The Color Purple*	abcdefg ij	my passport	ab fg

2. You have now classified texts according to a your *intuitions* about 'what a story is'. Now here is a definition of what a story is.

A story typically has:
(a) HAPPENINGS or EVENTS
(b) which are in a SEQUENCE
(c) and there is CAUSE AND EFFECT relationship between them.
(d) A constant 'FRAMING' narrating voice, in which the story is told.
(e) A consistent POINT OF VIEW.
(f) It involves CHARACTERS (usually human).
(g) SIGNIFICANCE: that is, the events are selected in order to convey a point (e.g. ethical or moral).
(h) PATTERNING between characters and events (thematic equivalences and contrasts).
(i) An OPENING: something happens which starts off the sequence of connected events. Often this is a lack or a disruption of some kind.
(j) A CLOSURE: something happens which brings the sequence of events to an end. Often this is a restoration of something or of order in general.

To investigate your classification of the texts you have noted, now carry out the following operations as regards the texts you have named above. If you think a text has one of the features (a–j) listed above, put the associated letter in the column. (To give you an example, we have done this for the first two texts.) Make a note of what leads to your decisions (we would note why we think *The Color Purple* has an opening, etc.). Make a note also of any problems you run into in deciding whether any particular text has a particular story feature.

3. Now we are in a position to ask ourselves: should the definition of 'texts which tell stories', which we offered in the form of listed features (a–j), be changed? Could it be improved? Think about this question by considering whether your intuitive choice of texts which tell stories is adequately reflected in the definition. Delete features from the list above which you now think are inappropriate. Add features below which you think *should* be in the list.

(k) ....

(l) ....

(m) ....

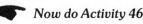 *Now rejoin text*

5.2.3 IS ONE TEXT BETTER OR WORSE THAN ANOTHER?

This activity starts from the assumption that a matrix classification is not appropriate, because the paradigm doesn't work with separate, identifiable 'boxes' or categories. Rather, the paradigm is assumed to be scalar (i.e. texts are somewhere in between two poles). This is reflected in the way the activity is constructed.

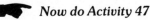 *Now do Activity 47*

Activity 47   *Working with scalar paradigms: value*

(30 mins)

The scalar paradigm containing the poles 'good' and 'bad' can mean different things. A text might be good for a particular purpose (and bad for another). On the other hand, you might want to say that some texts are good (or bad) in some absolute sense. This is a sense in which Shakespeare's plays are often said to be good. Bearing these points in mind, try the following tasks.

(a) Write in column 1 the names of five texts you have read recently.
(b) For each text, *either* fill in headings under columns 2 and 3 (e.g. write 'good for reading on a train', 'bad for moral instruction') *or* put a tick in column 4 if you think the text is good or bad absolutely.

1 Names of some texts you read recently	2 good/bad for . . .	3 good/bad for . . .	4 good/bad (absolutely)
1			
2			
3			
4			
5			

Is the value of a text in each sense derivable from specific properties the text has? If you think so, for each text suggest two properties which determine its value.

Text *(as above)*	Property (a)	Property (b)
1		
2		
3		
4		
5		

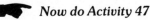 *Now rejoin text*

5.3 'Many-way' paradigms

In this section we look at four **many-way paradigms** (as opposed to binary paradigms). We consider genre (which is perhaps the most fundamental many-way paradigm for literary texts), medium, period, and movement. Genre and medium are related: roughly speaking, genre is a paradigm where texts are differentiated along formal and structural lines, while medium is a paradigm where texts are differentiated along material lines. So, as we suggested in Chapter 3, while medium is a matter of text-tokens, genre is a matter of text-types. Period and movement are also related: periods are often named after large-scale intellectual movements (e.g. the Renaissance and Romanticism).

5.3.1 GENRE

Texts can be classified into types on the basis of their styles, types of content, etc. These types are the **genres** of texts.

There are two fundamentally different ways of thinking about genre. The first is 'reductive': its aim is to find a fixed and small list of possible genres and to classify all texts according to this list. An example of this is Aristotle's three-term genre paradigm[3] which forms the basis for the poetry–fiction–drama distinction in many undergraduate curricula:

genre term	basis for the distinction
poetic/lyric	= a text uttered in the first person throughout
epic/narrative	= a text in which the narrator speaks in the first person, then lets his/her characters speak for themselves
drama	= a text in which the characters do all the talking

This reductive approach to genre which classifies texts according to a small number of fixed and eternal terms is characteristic of criticism and theory from the Renaissance to the eighteenth century. In the eighteenth century, partly as a result of new literary practices, including the publication of genre-mixing texts such as James Thomson's long poem *The Seasons* (1730), a change in the conception of genres took place.

The newer way of thinking about genre allowed for a large variety of different genres, with new genres constantly coming into existence. This way of thinking about genre is now the dominant way (and was the basis for our characterisation of genre at the beginning of this section). Within the framework of this approach, some examples of different genres are given in this table:

comedy	tragedy	picaresque	science fiction
fable	emblem poem	utopian fiction	melodrama
Hammer horror	kitchen sink drama	sonnet	situation comedy
revenge tragedy	Mills & Boon	reggae	broadside ballad
tragi-comedy	letter to the Times	tabloid	epic romance.

This list suggests a number of important points and questions about the 'expansive' conception of genre.

(a) How is it possible to identify the distinctive features of different genres?

In Aristotle's system, genres could be identified consistently by looking for the same kinds of feature in each text you consider (for Aristotle the feature is 'who speaks'). But taking our expansive view of genre, can we still find a consistent way of identifying the constitutive features of any genre?

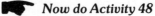 **Now do Activity 48**

Activity 48   *'Features' of different genres* *(30 mins)*

To explore the question whether it is possible to identify distinctive features which make up different genres, work through the following tasks.

1. Fill in the following table, choosing three types of genre and then making as explicit as you can the features of a text which characterise that genre.

Name of genre	Features you would expect to find in a text of this genre

2. Is there any consistent *kind* of feature which you are using to distinguish different genres?   YES/NO
   If 'yes', name it.

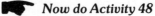 *Now rejoin text*

In this activity, you may have found it quite difficult to find features which unambiguously characterise a particular genre. However, while a failure of precise definition is not unusual when it comes to close inspection of a particular classificatory paradigm, this does not therefore mean that the paradigm should be abandoned. Although notions like 'tragedy' may seem rather vague, they are nevertheless part of the writing and reading process. In reading a text, we are guided by our beliefs and expectations about the text, which include beliefs about the text's genre and the expectations which follow as a consequence. We read or watch a play differently if it is explicitly called 'a tragedy'. Decisions about the genre of a text bring into our mind a cluster of expectations: some vague, some perhaps idiosyncratic. Genres are often characterisable *only* in terms of a set of expectations, which arise as a consequence of reading and developing familiarity with texts in those genres (in a circular fashion).

Q: Is it possible in describing genres ever fully to escape the circularity of formulations such as: 'What do I think the main characteristics of a Western are? Well, let me consider all the Westerns I know and then I'll be able to decide.'?

The question of *change* is especially important. Because genres are characterised by our expectations as readers, which change over time, genres themselves change significantly when our expectations and beliefs about genre characteristics interact with changing knowledge about a changing world. The characteristics of 'tragedy' have changed, for example, so that different kinds of plot and character are characteristic of tragedy at different times.

Q: Classical tragedies are always about the lives and misfortunes of a society's royalty or nobility; modern tragedies are mostly about the 'ordinary' people of a society. Why?

(b) Genre-mixing and its significance

One way in which complex expectations, beliefs, and facts about genres are put to use in literature is in the practice of genre-mixing (as in 'tragi-comedy' in our list). We have already mentioned that eighteenth-century texts which mixed genres were partly responsible for a shift in prevailing conceptions of genre. Genre-mixing is also characteristic of particular literary movements (and other artistic movements, particularly architecture). Many British Romantic texts are instances of genre-mixing. Wordsworth and Coleridge's *Lyrical Ballads*, for example, indicates this in its title (lyric + ballad = lyrical ballad). But genres can be mixed in a number of different

ways. A genre-mixing text might be made up of a combination of pieces of text, each of which is in a specific genre. Or the whole text might be in two (or more) genres simultaneously.

The first technique is often referred to as 'collage', and is particularly characteristic of modernist texts, such as T. S. Eliot's *The Waste Land* (1922),[4] Gertrude Stein's *Four in America* (1947), Flann O'Brien's *At Swim-Two-Birds* (1939), etc. The 'classic' period of modernism in English is between the two world wars (roughly 1920–40), but if we take collage to be a defining feature of modernism, later texts such as the Beatles' record *Sergeant Pepper's Lonely Hearts Club Band* (1967) also qualify as modernist.

A version of the second technique is pastiche. Pastiche is an imitation which signals that it is an imitation rather than the real thing. Genre-mixing constitutes pastiche when a genre is imitated by being merged into a text of a different genre. Pastiche is a characteristic feature (some would say that it is the defining feature) of post-modernist texts (e.g. Joyce Carol Oates's novel *Mysteries of Winterthurn* (1984), Harvey Pekar's comic book *American Splendor* (1980s), the Talking Heads' record *Remain in Light* (1980), etc.).[5] The word 'post-modernism' is used to define a period or epoch in which a society's cultural forms (such as poetry, music or architecture) suggest that there can be no direct, 'real' access to experience or to the expression of experience: everything you want to say or show has to be said or shown in artificial, mediated forms. But instead of suppressing or regretting this need to relate to artificial 'forms' rather than being able to create an unmediated voice capable of expressing real experience, post-modernism exploits and celebrates this condition, immersing us in the vast array of signs and genres which make up the contemporary world.

 Now do Activity 49 on page 104

(c) Proliferation of sub-divisions within any genre you seek to define

In most genre classifications, distinctions multiply. As they do so, hierarchical relations between terms are created: one term of the paradigm acts as a kind of intermediate paradigm for other terms, and so on. Tragedy, Senecan tragedy, bourgeois tragedy, and revenge tragedy are four distinct genre terms but *within* what we might call the **meta**-genre of tragedy.

 *Now do Activity 50 on page 105*

Activity 49   *Genre cocktails*

(30 mins)

To investigate the combinations of distinctive features which make up 'mixed genres', work through the following tasks.

1. Look back to the genres you chose in Activity 48. Invent a mixed genre by combining two (or all three) of these genres. Now write down:

(i) the name of your new, mixed genre:

(ii) the features which you would expect a text to have if it is in that mixed genre (find this out by combining the features of each of the component genres together. You can leave out some if you wish).

2. Imagine a text in this mixed genre. Now write a short, one-paragraph description of that imaginary text, suitable to be an entry in a 'Companion to Literature'.

3. Can you think of an *actual* text which has the combination of features listed in (ii)? Write its name here.

....

 Now rejoin text on page 103

Activity 50   *Is there an infinite number of genres?*

(60 mins)

Is it possible to relate the restrictive notion of genre to the expansive notion of genre? Can all genres, for example, be shown to be sub-types of a fixed and fairly small number of meta-genres? Or is the number of genres infinite? To explore this issue, work through the following tasks.

1. Write down a selection of genre types of your choice.

....
....
....
....
....
....
....
....
....
....

2. Now consider whether these genre types can be grouped together under a few meta-genre headings. Can they be grouped, for example, under Aristotle's three headings? Attempt to formulate some meta-genres and list them below. We give the example of 'tragedy' (but delete it if you don't agree or don't want to use it). Assign a different symbol to each one (e.g. write 't' next to tragedy). If you don't think there are as many 'meta-genres' as the number of spaces we have given you, leave some of the spaces blank.

..tragedy.......= t   ....=   ....=
.................=   ....=   ....=
.................=   ....=   ....=

When you have completed your list of 'meta-genres', try to group the genres you chose in part 1 under the meta-genres you have proposed in part 2. To do this, return to your entries in part 1 and write the relevant symbol you have decided on next to each genre name.

3. Now consider your results. Do all the genres you thought of fit into the genre groups you named?
YES/NO

4. If your answer to (3) is 'no', why *don't* all the genres fit into a set of genre groups? If your answer is 'yes', why *do* all the genres fit into a set of genre groups? Make a note of your thoughts on this issue here.

5. Finally, try to decide whether you would have arrived at the same decisions if you had initially chosen a different selection of genres in part 1.   YES/NO

👉 *Now rejoin text*

5.3.2 MEDIUM

We turn now from genre, which was a matter of text-types, to medium, which is a matter of text-tokens.

Examples of some different mediums in which texts can be found are given in this table:

projected film	photograph
live television	live radio
pre-recorded video cassette	pre-recorded audio cassette
record	word-processed text in a computer
theatre	printed
manuscript	spoken (not broadcast or recorded)

Q: Consider the plural of the word 'medium'. Two different plurals are in use: 'mediums' and 'media'. Are the two completely interchangeable? Is one 'right' and the other 'wrong'? Do they mean different things?

Now here are some reasons for distinguishing between texts in different mediums. Under each reason, describe two types of text which illustrate the distinction. We have done the first as an illustration.

1. **Value:** Texts in some mediums are typically valued more highly than texts in other mediums.
   '*Theatre texts* are typically valued more highly than *television texts*, even though they have many features in common: drama, dialogue, spectacle, music and sound effects, etc.'

2. **Cost of production:** Texts are cheaper to produce in some mediums than in others.

3. **Permanence:** Texts in some mediums are more permanent than texts in others.

4. **Availability:** Texts in some mediums are more easily and widely available than texts in others.

5. **Necessary equipment:** Texts in some mediums require the purchase of special equipment in order to gain access to them, while texts in others are immediately accessible.

At the most basic level, two texts are in different mediums when they exist in different physical or material forms. If you look up the noun 'medium' in a dictionary (as you may have done in answering the question above), you will find that the word has a cluster of meanings concerning how a medium enables something to happen. We explored some of the historical background to issues of 'medium' in Chapter 3. The medium of a text is the material form the text assumes, when you convert a text-type into a text-token. Given this sense of the word, it is clear that a text which is realised as broadcast television is in a different medium from a text which is realised as a printed book.

There is a problem with this description, nevertheless. Intuitively, the difference between a manuscript text and a printed version of the same text is a difference in medium, despite their having very similar material forms (both are made of paper and ink). But this problem can be resolved, if we consider another aspect of the medium in which a text exists: that a text can pass through a series of different material forms, and that we should therefore refer not to a *single* medium for a text, but to the medium of a text at a particular stage or in a particular one of its tokens. The text may be created in one medium, stored in another, and read (or viewed or heard) in another. A television programme may exist, for example, first as magnetic patterns on a tape, then as waves broadcast in the air, then as sounds and images on a television screen, then perhaps as magnetic information on tape again if recorded by the viewer. So we see why the manuscript letter and printed book can be considered as being in the same medium yet also in different mediums: it is because at some stage in their existence a material or physical difference between them is created. The same argument might be used to say that a theatrical performance and a conversation are in different mediums. However, as well as these texts having different material forms or origins (often arising from different technologies), the different mediums are often 'socially different' as well. In the case of the distinction between theatrical performance and conversation, we might argue that the distinction in medium is partly related to further differences: differences in social function, in performer–audience relation, in physical location, and so on.[6]

> **Now do Activity 51 on page 107**

In doing Activity 51, you may well have had more trouble completing column 4 than in filling in the other columns. It *may* be that this is because 'reasons for connections between medium and genre' are not *absolute* or *general* reasons at all, but local and particular historical reasons. Technologies and audiences change, and genres change with them. Classification by medium intersects with questions about how texts fit into their specific contexts.

Connections between the medium of a text and the technology, audience and other social and historical contexts which surround it suggest that the classifications you make by identifying distinctive features need always finally to connect back with specific historical situations and developments.

Activity 51   *Medium and genre*
(30 mins)

To explore how far particular mediums are associated with particular genres, try the following activity. Name three genres in column 1. Then list one or more mediums in which this genre is found in column 2. In column 3, list some mediums in which the genre is *never* found. For each genre, try to explain why it is associated with some mediums and not others. In particular, consider whether the association arises by historical accident or because there is some link between the formal and material properties of the text and aspects of its social or historical context.

Column 1 Genre	2 Mediums in which genre is found	3 Mediums in which genre is not found	4 Possible reasons for connection with one medium but not others

Now rejoin text on page 106

5.3.3 PERIOD

Texts written in a particular country are often classified according to the paradigm of period. They are sorted into groups which fall into a historical sequence. In Britain, we have 'Elizabethan' texts (texts written between 1558 and 1603), 'Jacobean texts' (texts written between 1603 and 1625), and so on. Here are some reasons for dividing up literary history into periods, and some ways in which periods are used.

(i) For educational reasons: to divide up and structure a curriculum (e.g. a class is called 'Romantic and Victorian literature').

(ii) For marketing reasons: to constitute anthologies (e.g. *The Penguin Book of Elizabethan Verse*).

(iii) For institutional reasons: an example would be when an academic job is specified in terms of period (e.g. an advertisement for 'Assistant Professor in Renaissance. Emphasis: Spenser, drama, sixteenth century').

(iv) As a hypothesis about the ways in which texts relate to their time. By naming a period of literary history after a king or queen, the hypothesis is that the monarch's reign encloses a reasonably distinct and unified literary practice; so that, for example, many British texts written between 1837 and 1901 (Victoria's reign) will have particular features in common. We will see in Chapter 8 how ways of thinking (which are reflected in texts) may be typical of a particular period.

**Different people organise the history of British litera-
ture into different sets of periods. One reason for
disagreement in this area is that there are many
different ways in which a period can be characterised.**

Thus:

(a) A period might simply be characterised by dates (e.g.
by the beginning and end of a century). This kind of
periodisation is reflected in the formation of anthologies like *The Oxford Book of Seventeenth-Century
Verse.*

(b) A period might be delimited by the beginning and
end of a particular monarch's reign; e.g. 'Victorian'
texts are texts written between the beginning of
Queen Victoria's reign (1837) and its end (1901).
Monarchs after whom literary periods are often
named are:

Elizabeth I	1558–1603	(the Elizabethan period)
James I	1603–25	(the Jacobean period)
Charles I	1625–49	(the Carolingian period)

(combined, Jacobean and Carolingian are often
called Stuart)

Commonwealth	1649–60	(no monarch during this period; sometimes called the 'Puritan Interregnum')
Victoria	1837–1901	(1837–1870 = 'early Victorian'; 1870–1901 = 'late Victorian')
Edward VII	1901–1910	(the Edwardian period is often considered to last to 1914)
George V	1910–36	(the Georgian period)

Notice that British periods are typically named after
monarchs only between 1558 and 1649 and between
1837 and 1936.

Q: Why do you think only these periods are typically
named after monarchs?

(c) A period may be named after a significant historical
event which happens at its beginning. Examples are:

Reformation	sixteenth century	In England the Reformation begins with the Act of Supremacy (1534)
Restoration	1660–1700	Monarchy restored in 1660 after the kingless Commonwealth period

(d) A period might be named after the language in which
texts are written. Relevant periods in the history of
English are usually dated as:

Old English	450–1066
Middle English	1066–1500
Early Modern English	1500–1700
Modern English	1700–now

(e) A period may be named after an influential writer.
Writers who have had periods named after them (e.g.
'The Age of Chaucer', etc.) are:

Chaucer	late fourteenth century
Spenser	late sixteenth century
Shakespeare	late sixteenth–early seventeenth centuries
Milton	mid-seventeenth century
Pope	early eighteenth century
Johnson	late eighteenth century

The naming of periods in this way is meant to indicate
the influence of a particular writer on the texts of a
particular period. It is also dependent on the evaluation of particular writers. A great writer will have an
age named after him – though rarely does a great
writer have a period named after *her*. It is interesting
that the *Pelican Guide to English Literature*, written
in the late 1950s and 'Leavisite' in the way it
conceives of literary history as a history of great
writers, divides up the periods of literary history into
seven volumes named like this:

The Age of Chaucer	*The Age of Shakespeare*
From Donne to Marvell	*From Dryden to Johnson*
From Blake to Byron	*From Dickens to Hardy*
The Modern Age	

(f) A period may be named after a large-scale intellectual
or artistic movement. These movements are often
European or worldwide, and start and end at different
times in different countries. Some movements which
have given their names to periods of literature in
English are:

The Renaissance	sixteenth–late seventeenth centuries
Neoclassicism	1660–1800
Romanticism	1789–1830s
Realism	nineteenth century
Modernism	twentieth century
Post-modernism	c. 1945–now

While many people would agree with the naming
of these periods, there is typically disagreement
about precisely when periods begin and end. Does
the Renaissance, for example, really last up to
Milton? Does Romanticism begin with the French
Revolution (1789) or with the publication of *Lyrical
Ballads* (1798)? Are we still in the modernist period
(the *Penguin Guide to Modernism*, for example,
covers the period 1890–1930)? And how is it

possible to justify a decision *either* way on any of these questions? Disagreements in this area stem from the fact that deciding whether a particular text is Realist or Modernist, or Neoclassical or Romantic, depends on the definition of these terms you adopt. Large-scale movements are not defined by clear-cut manifestos. Rather, they are a loose collection of ideas and practices. The looseness of the definition means that deciding whether a particular text is part of the movement may often be very much a matter of interpretation.

A fundamental question with all this now arises. Are periods real *things*, somehow an inherent part of history (rather in the way that the liver is an inherent part of the human body)? Or are periods a variable product of how we *think* about history? Most people would say that periods are convenient ways of thinking about literary history. However, there is a tradition – associated particularly with the German philosopher Georg Wilhelm Friedrich Hegel (1770–1831) – of thinking of periods as real entities, objectively distinct from us as observers and classifiers, and which are the building blocks of history. Some work on periodisation in literary studies has been done in the Hegelian tradition; word of this kind is interested in how the 'spirit of the age' is realised in the texts written during a period. Some Marxist criticism is similar, in relating texts to modes of production (distinguishing feudal writing from capitalist writing, for example); Michel Foucault (see also Section 8.3) has examined how history is divided up into periods called 'epistemes' which cause certain kinds of literary texts to be produced; and Fredric Jameson, in *The Political Unconscious*, shows how periods can be thought of as 'minds', with the writings during a period being its 'dreams'.[7]

These different opinions about periods parallel different opinions about genre: differences between people who think that paradigms of genre are a classificatory and interpretive guide, and people who think that the paradigms reflect a pre-existing and constant division of genres which is true of all literature. In philosophical terms, the differences can be characterised by the (binary) distinction between the terms.

realist (periods and/or genres are objectively there in the world independent of us);
and
nominalist (periods and/or genres are simply ways of describing the world and do not reflect its real structure).

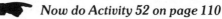 *Now do Activity 52 on page 110*

5.3.4 MOVEMENT

While the period paradigm is typically a way of dividing up literary history in terms of the *context* of texts, the movement paradigm is a way of dividing up literary history in terms of what you might call the *content* or style of the texts produced at a particular time, or in a particular place, or by a particular group of people.

Periods are often identified only after they have finished, but movements are normally identified while they are taking place by writers themselves, who form themselves into more or less coherent groups (a movement may even be identified by a manifesto before any texts are actually written in the form the movement advocates). Movements are defined by a particular set of ideas and practices of writing. But they are also defined by a particular form of social activity (i.e. writing as someone who is part of a named group or circle, and possibly guided by a manifesto).

Two kinds of movement can be distinguished. First, there are long-lasting, vaguely defined movements (which we could call *meta*-movements) like the Renaissance and modernism, as listed in the previous section. Second, there are generally smaller movements, often involving a named and specific group of people. We list some of these here.

Dates	Name of movement	Some of the writers involved
C14	English Chaucerians	Lydgate, Occleve, Burgh
C15	Scottish Chaucerians	James I, Henryson, Dunbar
early–mid-C17	Metaphysical poets	Donne, Marvell, Vaughan
mid-C17	Platonists	More, Welworth
mid-C17	The tribe of Ben	Herrick, Carew
later C18	Bluestockings	Carter, More, Montagu, Chapone
mid–late C19	Pre-Raphaelites	Rossetti(s), Morris, Swinburne
late C19–early C20	Irish literary revival	O'Grady, Yeats, Synge, Lady Gregory
late C19–mid-C20	Naturalism	Gissing, Dreiser, Norris, Crane
1890s	English Decadents	Wilde, Symons, Dowson
early C20	Georgian poets	Brooke, Masefield, de la Mare
1910s	Imagists	Hulme, Pound, Amy Lowell
1910s	Vorticists	Pound, Lewis
early–mid-C20	Bloomsbury Group	Forster, Woolfs
1950s & 1960s	Theatre of the absurd	Beckett, Pinter, Albee
1950s & 1960s	Black Mountain poets	Olson, Creeley
late 1950s	Beat writers	Ginsberg, Burroughs, Kerouac

Activity 52   *Making history*

(60 mins)

The division of literary history into periods can be a way of representing important moments in the development of a tradition or culture. You can name an age after its most important writer (having first decided who is the most important writer), or you can name it after a significant historical event (but which event is significant?), or after the kinds of literature produced. Similarly, where you draw the boundaries of a particular period involves making a decision about important cultural events (e.g. the death of a writer, the accession of a queen, the invention of printing, etc.). This activity gives you the opportunity to draw the boundaries which help divide up into parts a tradition or a culture.

1. Choose a textual tradition which is still developing, and which you have some familiarity with. You could choose 'Writing in English' or 'American literature' or 'Nigerian literature' or 'Rock music' or 'Indian television', etc.

Its name: ....

The date (roughly) it begins: ....

2. Divide the tradition up into between four and ten periods, and name each period. You could name a period after one or more authors, historical events, a reign, or you could simply use dates, or name it after a century or a decade, etc. You will probably need to use reference books (such as a companion to literature). Call your periods things like 'The period of . . .', or 'The age of . . .' or 'The century of . . .' or 'The decade of . . .' (or even 'The year of . . .', if the period is this short). Write your sequence of periods here.

Now rejoin text on page 109

The movements in this list were held together historically in different ways. Some are particular groups or circles of people, who met to discuss their work (e.g. the Bluestockings, the Bloomsbury group). Some published one or more manifestos (e.g. the vorticists, in the magazine *Blast*). Some were identified as movements by a work of criticism (Esslin's *The Theatre of the Absurd* was important in defining the movement; and the term 'metaphysical' was first used, by Dryden in 1697, to define a particular movement after it had ended, and was intended as a term of abuse). Some movements imitate an adopted 'parent' (e.g. 'the tribe of Ben' were followers of Ben Jonson). Some movements are unified by an anthology (the Georgian poets are particularly associated with four anthologies published between 1912 and 1922), or by a magazine (the magazine *Blast* functioned to unify the British futurists and vorticists).

Now do Activity 53 on page 111

5.4 Connections between classifications

So far in this chapter, we have distinguished between binary paradigms and many-way paradigms. We have also noted, though, that one of the characteristics of many-way paradigms is that they contain sub-paradigms within them. 'Tragedy', for example (a term of the genre paradigm) sets up a paradigm of its own, consisting of 'bourgeois tragedy', 'Senecan tragedy', etc.; and 'modernism' (a term of the movement paradigm) sets up a paradigm which contains other terms from the movement paradigm: 'imagism', 'the Bloomsbury Group', etc. These are cases where a term in a many-way paradigm

Activity 53   *Theory and practice in a movement*
(60 mins)

According to Ezra Pound, in 1912 he, H.D. (Hilda Doolittle) and Richard Aldington agreed on three principles for writing poetry which gave them 'the right to a group name'. In 1913, Pound published a statement of these principles, with additional notes and guidelines. The views he outlined have subsequently been taken as a defining document of *vers libre* (free verse), and, more particularly, of one of the modernist movements, **imagism**. Here, in the form of a list (1–14), are Pound's main statements.

Three principles
(1) Direct treatment of the 'thing', whether subjective or objective.
(2) To use absolutely no word that does not contribute to the presentation.
(3) As regards rhythm: to compose in the sequence of the musical phrase, not in sequence of a metronome.

A few don'ts
(4) Use no superfluous word, no adjective which does not reveal something.
(5) Go in fear of abstractions.
(6) Don't allow 'influence' to mean merely that you mop up the particular decorative vocabulary of some one or two poets whom you happen to admire.
(7) Use either no ornament or good ornament.
(8) Don't imagine that a thing will 'go' in verse just because it's too dull to go in prose.
(9) Don't be 'viewy' – leave that to the writers of pretty little philosophic essays.
(10) Don't be descriptive; remember that the painter can describe a landscape much better than you can.

Credo
(11) I believe in an 'absolute rhythm', a rhythm, that is, in poetry which corresponds exactly to the emotion or shade of emotion to be expressed.
(12) I believe that the proper and perfect symbol is the natural object.
(13) I believe in technique as the test of a man's sincerity.
(14) I think there is a 'fluid' as well as a 'solid' content, that some poems may have form as a tree has form, some as water poured into a vase.

Now here is a poem by H.D., widely used in anthologies to represent the work of the imagist movement.

Oread
Whirl up, sea –
Whirl up your pointed pines,
Splash your great pines
On our rocks,
Hurl your green over us,
Cover us with your pools of fir.

1. Make a list of features of the poem which seem to you to exemplify the stated goals of the movement outlined above.

2. Make a list of features of the poem which seem not to correspond with, or to conflict with, the stated goals of the movement outlined above.

3. Which of the following statements seems the most appropriate way of accounting for your answers in 2?

(a) No manifesto or statement of a movement legislates for all aspects of a text; so it doesn't matter that there are features in H.D.'s poem which are outside or conflict with Pound's pronouncements.

(b) Whatever its qualities, the poem is not an 'imagist' poem, because it contains elements which seriously conflict with the dictates of imagism.

(c) You would need to know more about the historical role of Pound's statements in their context to reach any kind of view about this.

(d) It is difficult to assess the relationship between the statements of intent and actual realisations of a movement *retrospectively*, especially if you don't know the precise context of the poem (including what styles of writing it was intended to contrast with).

Add an alternative statement if you wish.

(e) ....
....
....

4. Give reasons for choosing the answer you have chosen in 3:

 Now rejoin text on page 110

---

defines a many-way paradigm of its own. There are also cases where a pair of terms within a many-way paradigm enter into a binary paradigm. 'Tragedy' and 'comedy', in the many-way, genre paradigm, are arguably opposed terms in a binary paradigm; and the same might be said about 'Romanticism' and 'Neoclassicism' in the movement (or period) paradigm.

 Now do Activity 54

Activity 54   *Do genres come in couples?*
(30 mins)

To test out the different kinds of relationship which can exist between categories, work through the following tasks.

1. Write in the space below the names of about twenty different genres.

2. Now draw lines between any pairs of terms which you think are in binary opposition (e.g. you might draw a line between 'tragedy' and 'comedy').

3. If you were successful in carrying out 2 but not completely so, suggest a reason why some genres should be arrangeable into binary oppositions, but not others.

4. You may have found that you were unsuccessful, being unable to pair off the genres when you tried to answer 2. Recall Lévi-Strauss's claim (see p. 34) that binary oppositions can function as the basic units of thought and shape our classifications. If you found that genres did not pair into binary oppositions, does this suggest that genre classification does not derive from the basic thinking processes of humans? Comment here.

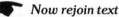 *Now rejoin text*

We conclude this chapter by looking at connections between the ways in which you identify different sorts of texts and what happens, moment by moment, as you read. So far, we have been considering properties of different types of text without considering precisely *how* you recognise them, as you read, watch or listen. How do you know an 'ending', a 'funny section', a 'Neoclassical passage', etc. when you see one?

The activity which follows provides a first opportunity to trace how local features of a text (such as words, phrases and particular juxtapositions) set in motion different types of expectation about what sort of text it is you are reading, and what you expect will follow. We then proceed, in Chapter 6, to look more closely at how what you read on the page is 'translated' into different types of thought, expectation and interpretation.

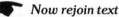 *Now do Activity 55*

Activity 55   *Reading, expectation and genre*
(30 mins)

The extract which follows is from page 17 of *Monty Python's Big Red Bok* (1971), a comic collection produced by a British television/film comedy team. The following note is at the top of the page.

> In many books, page 17 is a sad anti-climax after the exciting events described on pages 15 and 16. We hope to avoid this pitfall by making our page 17 into one of the most exciting and action-packed page 17s that you've ever read.

At the bottom of the page, there is a further note.

> How about that for a page 17? Wake up Dickens! Wake up Graham Greene! Let's show the World that British literature gets on with it!

In between these notes is a box containing a passage (of which the following is the first half):

of her dress as it rode up over her thighs, her slender body thrust forward by the enormous power of the 6,000 h.p. engines, as Horst hurled the car into a shrieking, sickening slide across the wet tarmac. The lion tore savagely at his bronzed thighs as the car soared into the air, turned, twisted, and plunged down the treacherous ski slope, that no man had ever survived. Tenderly Eunice caressed him as the fighters screeched out of the darkness, flames ripping towards him. The sea was coming nearer and nearer, and though neither had eaten for eight weeks, the stark terror of what they saw gave them the last drop of energy to push their bodies to the limits, Eunice groaned, the dark figure of Shahn-el-Shid, dagger raised, hurled himself from the sheer wall of the palace. Horst reversed, swerved, coughed and threw himself into the gorge.

This activity is concerned with what type of text this 'page 17' text represents.

1. On a separate sheet of paper, make one or more lists of words, phrases or events which lead you to attribute the text to a particular classificatory category. Each list should represent evidence for one category. (Your lists might be for, for example, genre, period, etc., and should be as specific as possible.)

2. Is the passage 'unified' in any way?   YES/NO

(a) If YES, what elements *provide* the unity?
(b) If NO, what elements *prevent* the appearance of unity?

Note: If a combination of YES and NO, fill in both (a) and (b).

3. Circle the term in the following list which describes the effect of the passage as a whole most accurately.

(a) exciting   (b) satirical   (c) comical but not satirical

(d) absurd   (e) avant-garde   (f) ....
(fill in own term)

Make a note of what leads you to choose the particular term you have chosen, rather than any of the other terms.

⑥ Language in texts

In this chapter we concentrate on close analysis of the language of texts written in English. In particular we look at ways in which the English language enables texts to have structure and meaning. We might usefully distinguish two roles which the English language plays in a text.

(a) It is one of the materials from which the text is made.
(b) It provides part of the knowledge and abilities we bring to a text when we read it; it is these abilities which enable us to make sense of the text.

The fact that language plays these two different roles raises a general problem, which we will need to consider. Are the patterns in language which we identify (such as alliteration, repetition of words and phrases, rhyme, cohesion, etc.) *in the text*, independent of us as readers, or are they something we *create* in the text as we read. We will tackle this problem in Chapter 7. In the present chapter we will consider some of the many different kinds of structure in language which organise texts.

6.1 The sound structure of spoken English

English is an example of a language which can be expressed in both mediums of sound and writing (some languages, such as British Sign Language, do not use sound, while others have never been written down). If we analyse a piece of spoken English, we can identify three distinct 'layers' in the flow of sound. The first layer is the sequence of sound segments, or **phones**. A word is made of a sequence of phones, one after another, in much the same way that a written word is made of a sequence of letters. In English, the phones in a word form clusters called **syllables**. A syllable normally consists of one vowel, with one or more consonants before it and one or more consonants after it. Below is a transcription of the English word 'alphabetic', represented as a sequence of letters, phones, and syllables (the Greek letter σ here stands for 'syllable').

Note that though sometimes a single letter stands for a single phone (e.g. here the letter 'a' stands for a single sound which we write 'æ', and the letter 'b' for the sound 'b'), at other times, two letters stand for a single sound (e.g. 'p' and 'h' together stand for one sound, written 'f').

The letters of English do not stand very accurately or consistently for the sounds of English; for example the letter 'a' can stand for different sounds (compare the 'a' in 'father' with the 'a' in 'at') and so can the letter 'c' (in 'ceiling' and in 'alphabetic'). For this reason a slightly different 'alphabet' is used for sounds than for written letters, particularly for vowels.

as a sequence of ten letters:　　a l p h a b e t i c

as a sequence of nine phones:　　æ l f ə b ɛ t ɪ k

as a sequence of four syllables:　 ′ σ ′　σ ′ σ ′ σ 　′

The second layer in the flow of sound is the **stress** pattern of words and sentences. When people speak English, they make some syllables louder and longer than others. These differences in loudness and length are called differences in stress. A word has a typical stress pattern which rarely changes (in the word 'alphabetic', for example, it is usually the third syllable [bɛ] which is stressed most). Recognising the stresses in words and sentences is difficult, and we will spend some time on this in Section 6.1.2. The third layer is the **intonational** contour of the speech flow. When people speak English, their voices rise, fall, and pause. The 'contours' – so-called because pictures of intonational structure look like mountain ranges, or very angular graphs – are what we call the intonation of speech. We consider intonation in Section 6.1.3.

These three layers are resources of the English language which are used in literary texts designed to be read aloud.

Texts acquire patterning and structure by making use of the resources of sound structure; and sound structure in turn can lead to particular meanings and kinds of meaning.

Even when texts are not read aloud, the process of representing them mentally as we read probably involves giving a 'sound shape' to them, and so brings partly into effect these sound patterns.

6.1.1 REPETITION OF SOUNDS

Rhyme and alliteration are two ways in which sounds (phones) are repeated in texts. Different kinds of repetition of phones are classified according to where in a word they take place. Here are some examples.

Repetition of phones where in the word the repeated sounds are	name of repetition	example
beginning of word	alliteration	*kill*, *call*
middle of word	assonance involves vowels	*while*, *pine*
end of word	rhyme involves the final stressed vowel in the word plus all the consonants and vowels which follow it	*sun*, *fun*
	consonance involves consonants only	*pit*, *cat*,

Different definitions

If you look in different dictionaries or books defining literary terms, you will find a *variety* of definitions of 'alliteration', 'consonance', etc. We will briefly consider why this is, and what kinds of difference there are between the various definitions.

One kind of difference between the various definitions involves the *amount* of repetition. **Consonance**, for example, is defined by the linguist Geoffrey Leech as repetition of the final consonants in the word, while the critic M. H. Abrams defines it as repetition of the whole sequence of consonants in a word, including the first and middle consonants (e.g. 'pitter/patter'). Thus Leech allows more repetitions to count as consonance than Abrams does; Abrams's definition is stricter. Another kind of difference involves which phones count as 'the same' for the purpose of identifying a *repetition* of phones. Many cases which would automatically be accepted as alliteration actually involve slightly different sounds (although the alphabetic letter is the same). The [p] phone at the beginning of 'pardon', for example, is followed by a big puff of breath from the mouth, while the [p] sound at the beginning of 'picked' is followed by a smaller puff of breath (the puff of breath is called 'aspiration' of the sound). The two sounds are certainly different, but who would deny that 'pardon' alliterates with 'picked'? On the other hand, many people now would say that the [č] phone at the beginning of 'church' is not the same sound as the [k] phone at the beginning of 'come'. But in the poetry written in England 1,000 years ago, these two words *were* considered to alliterate. In this way, we can see that definitions of alliteration differ according to which sounds are considered to be 'the same'.

▶ *Now do Activity 56 on page 117*

So when and how do people choose *between* the competing definitions? Two different factors enter into the choice.

(a) A particular definition may be adopted by a group of writers as a guiding principle for their work. Definition 5, for example, is part of the definition of alliteration which was used in poetry written in England 1,000 years ago (Old English poetry). Such poetry used alliteration rather than rhyme as its basic structuring device (a convention which was displaced largely as a result of French influence during the Norman colonisation of Britain). The convention for writing this Old English poetry can be formulated as a rule, like this: 'each "line" of poetry consists of two parts, with one or two stressed syllables in the first part alliterating with one stressed syllable in the second part'

e.g. *hatan heolfre*. | *Horn stundum sang.*

Because definition 5 was in use, however, it enabled the following line of poetry to fit with the rule:

e.g. *ealdres or-wena*, | *ierringa slog.*

But this raises the question,

Q: Why do you think this particular definition of 'alliteration' was used in writing this kind of poetry?

(b) An attempt to define a particular repetition of sounds (phone repetition) such as alliteration tries to express the fact that people particularly notice specific types of phone repetition (put more technically, some phone repetitions are **perceptually salient**). One way of regarding a particular pattern of sound as perceptually salient is when it appears as a structuring principle in conventional sayings (like proverbs, folk songs, nursery rhymes, etc.). Some patterns we seem to notice more than other patterns. Therefore a definition of alliteration should perhaps match well with our intuitions about noticeable repetition of sounds at the beginning of words; and we can compare definitions by checking which one best characterises the patterns which are widely found. Definitions 1–3 and 5, for example, all *fail* to identify as alliterative the phrase 'reading, writing and arithmetic', despite the fact that these skills are sometimes called 'the three Rs' (suggesting a 'folk-wisdom' belief that the phrase is alliterative). Definition 4 matches better with tradition in this case, because in 'arithmetic', while the first syllable [a] does not begin with 'r', the first *stressed* syllable [rith] does begin with 'r'.

It is common for one kind of sound pattern to be associated with a particular kind of poetry (as in (a)

Activity 56   *Defining alliteration*
(45 mins)

A. Here are some different definitions of alliteration. Add one more definition to the list, as the sixth.
1. The first consonant must be the same.
2. All consonants before the first vowel (i.e. the first **consonant cluster**) must be the same.
3. The first sound must be the same.
4. The first sound in the stressed syllable of the word must be the same.
5. The first sound must be the same, 'ch' alliterates with 'k' (as in 'cat'), and all vowels are considered to be the same.

6. ....

Notice that the different definitions result in different pairs of words alliterating with each other. Definition 1, for example, means that 'cat' alliterates with 'king', but that 'cat' does not alliterate with 'church'. The implications of the first four definitions are shown for you on the chart below.

B. Fill in the last two lines of the chart below to show the implications of definitions 5 and 6.

	cat/ king	cat/ queen	cat/ church	eel/ ear	ear/oil	print/ prank	print/ plant	cat/ acclaim
1	✓	✓				✓	✓	
2	✓					✓		
3	✓	✓	✓	✓		✓	✓	
4	✓	✓			✓	✓	✓	✓
5								
6								

Answers on p. 213.

 Now rejoin text on page 116

---

above). This tendency can be seen very clearly in the case of rhyme, where there are different conventions about which lines rhyme with which other lines. Sonnets, which contain 14 lines, are good examples of this. One convenient way of representing which lines rhyme with which other lines is to use a letter for each different rhyming pair or group: if the first line rhymes with the third line and the second line rhymes with the fourth, we can describe the four lines as 'ABAB'. Using this simple formalism, we can present different ways in which lines rhyme in sonnets.

Sonnet rhyme patterns

pattern 1 (often called
  'Shakespearean sonnet
  pattern')   ABABCDCDEFEFGG
pattern 2 (often called
  'Spenserian sonnet
  pattern')   ABABBCBCCDCDEE
pattern 3 (often called
  'Petrarchan sonnet
  pattern')   a: ABBAABBACDECDE
               b: ABBAABBACDCCDC

These patterns were used by Shakespeare (1564–1616), Spenser (1552–99), and the Italian poet Petrarch (1304–74) respectively. The different patterns have different associations for some writers. Pattern 1, for example, is also called 'English', while pattern 3 is also called 'Italian'. Milton used an adapted form of pattern 3.

Now do Activity 57 on page 118

Purposes of sound segment repetition

Activity 57 raises issues about why particular kinds of sound pattern are used. Some possible reasons for the presence in a text of sound segment repetitions are:

1 to give pleasure to the reader;
2 to give coherence to the poem;
3 to demonstrate skill;
4 to fit into a particular poetic tradition;
5 to qualify as poetry (in certain periods poems have had to rhyme to be considered poems at all);
6 to draw attention to the contrast or similarity in meaning of two words which involve the sound segment repetition;

Activity 57   *Rhymes in a sonnet*

(30 mins)

1. Find two sonnets by the same poet, written after 1780. (If you are stuck for texts, use sonnets by Wordsworth.)
2. Write out the rhyme patterns of both the sonnets. Compare the two rhyme patterns: are they the same or different?

3. If they are the same, why do you think the poet used this particular rhyme pattern? (It might for example be relevant that some other poet had used it.)
4. If they are different, does the difference between the patterns indicate any particular contrast between the two sonnets?

 Now rejoin text on page 117

7 to create a particular effect which results from the salience of the word(s) involved in the sound segment repetition.

Add some further possible reasons of your own here.

8 ....

9 ....

Two examples of reason 4 are: the use of alliteration in Old English poetry, and sonnet patterns. Are *all* poems an example of reason 5?

> Q: Can you think of any kinds of poetry that do *not* have *any* sound segment repetition in them at all?

Reasons 6 and 7 can be characterised together as ways of drawing on associations or meanings of the words which are involved in rhymes. Many comic effects are produced in this way.

 Now do Activity 58 on page 119

Besides the various uses of sound repetition we have indicated, there is another possible use, one you may already have noted as an addition to the 'list of possible reasons'. This is **sound symbolism**, which appears to be noticeable when individual sounds become salient, particularly in alliteration. A lot of [k] sounds in a text, for example, may be taken to symbolise conflict (especially if the text is about a battle or argument), as though actual conflicts involve a lot of k type sounds. But is sound symbolism something which is in the text – a kind of meaning which is just as real as the meaning of the words in the text, or is it something which is put there by a reader?

 Now do Activity 59 on page 120

6.1.2 STRESS PATTERNS IN ENGLISH SPEECH AND
       METRICAL PATTERNS IN ENGLISH POETRY

In this section we discuss different metrical patterns in English poetry. But before we do this, we need to make sure that you can hear and work out stress patterns for yourself. One of the peculiarities of stress patterns is that as a speaker of English you are perfectly capable of pronouncing them, and you notice if someone pronounces them differently (the words will sound strange). Also, you may well be able to judge someone's accent of English according to how you hear them stress words. Despite this clear familiarity with stress patterns, you may still be unable to reflect on this automatic knowledge, or write any of it down explicitly on paper. It is a bit like being able to swim without knowing exactly what muscular movements your body makes when you do. Many things we know are like this: we know how to do them without knowing exactly what we are doing.

Activity 58   *Effects of rhyme in a poem*
(60 mins)

Consider this passage from a poem.

> In France, for instance, he would write a chanson;
>   In England, a six canto quarto tale;
> In Spain, he'd make a ballad or romance on
>   The last war – much the same in Portugal;
> In Germany, the pegasus he'd prance on
>   Would be old Goethe's – (see what says De Stael);
> In Italy, he'd ape the 'Trecentisti';
> In Greece, he'd sing some sort of hymn like this t'ye:
>
> (from Byron, *Don Juan*, c. 1820)

To investigate the effects of rhyme patterns, carry out the following tasks related to the passage.
1. Write down the rhyme pattern of this poem (using the AB.... system; then check at the back of the book (p. 213) that you are right).

2. There are eight rhyming words (or word combinations) in this stanza. Does something about each word/word combination (e.g. its meaning or other associations, conventions of use, etc.) have a particular effect as a result of the word being involved in a rhyme? For each word or word combination, write down as precisely as possible what the effect is, and what it is about the word which gives rise to the effect. (We have listed below at least the last three syllables of each line, as these seem to be the ones relevant to the rhyme.)

effect	what is it about the words which creates the effect?
1 a chanson	
2 quarto tale	
3 romance on	
4 Portugal	
5 she'd prance on	
6 says De Stael	
7 'Trecentisti'	
8 like this t'ye	

Now rejoin text on page 118

The stress pattern in a word

Words are made up of syllables. Syllables are groups of phones, with usually a single vowel as the basic component of the syllable. Some consonants can also act as syllables without a vowel. Here is an example, with [1] as the basis of a syllable.

syllables:	σ	₁ σ
phones:	t r ʌ b	l
alphabetic letters:	t r o u	b l e

In an English word, some syllables carry stress (remember, stress = an additional loudness, or length, or voice height on a particular syllable); other syllables do not. When more than one syllable in a single word carries stress, one syllable is nevertheless always more strongly stressed than the others. This is the main stress of the word. In 'trouble' it is the first syllable which has the main stress.

Now do Activity 60 on page 121

The stress patterns in a sentence

In a sentence some words will be stressed, but other words will not carry a stress at all (e.g. often the short grammatical words like 'in', 'and', 'the', etc.). Of the words which *are* stressed, some will be particularly strongly stressed (called the **nuclear** stresses). This imposes a further level of patterning which incorporates the stress patterns of individual words.

Try saying the following sentence, putting *equal* stress on all the words.

```
1 2   3   4    5    6     7   8  9   10   11   12
```
'I have just read this book which I don't like very much.'

Activity 59   *Looking for sound symbolism*
(45 mins)

Consider the following extract from John Pepper Clarke's poem 'Ivbie' (1962).

Is it not late, so awfully
Late, fingering sun-dried husks and
Shells on whose live-sap suckling,
We stifled our initial pangs?

As a way of considering how sound symbolism works, and the kinds of difficulty which arise when you seek to justify a 'sound-symbolist' interpretation, work through the following tasks and questions.

1. Is any one letter or sound in the text more frequent than we would expect it to be? If so, name it here:..........

2. A study of American English written texts conducted in 1969 found an average order of frequency of letters as follows (most frequent first): e, t, a, i, n, o, s, h, r, d, l, u, c, m, f, w, y, g, p, b, v, k, q, j, x, z. (Clarke is Nigerian, incidentally.) Does this information about frequency support what you have just written in answer to question (1)?   YES/NO   *Why?*

3. What other information would be useful in justifying your claim about the frequency of the sound you have identified? Using your work from Chapter 4 especially, suggest anything you would want to do to build a better supporting framework of comparison for your observation.

4. If you think that the sound symbolises something, describe what it symbolises.

Explain how you know what it symbolises.

5. Does this letter/sound always symbolise the same thing, in every text in which it stands out because of its frequency?   YES/NO
If not, what else might it signify?

What other factors contribute to determining what it symbolises in each case?

☞ *Now rejoin text on page 118*

Activity 60   *Identifying stress*
(45 mins)

The stressed syllable in a word is the loudest and/or longest and/or highest when you say it normally. To get practice at identifying stress, carry out the following tasks.
1. Write σ above each syllable in the words in the following table.

2. Now write ' above the stressed syllable in each of the words. (We have done the first two as illustrations). Make notes in the margin of any problems or ideas which occur to you as you do this.

σ σ	σ σ				
perform	mention	pretext	distrust	develop	mathematics
argument	number	prefer	incorporate	derail	protest
laboratory	act	masculine	monster	monstrosity	blackbird

3. Now check whether you have marked the stress correctly. Do this by reading each word aloud, making the labelled sound longer and louder than the others. If the word sounds strange or comical when you pronounce it like this, try stressing another syllable and then reading aloud again. Another way of checking whether you are identifying stress correctly is to look in a dictionary; most dictionaries indicate the stressed syllable in a word (usually by putting ' *before* the stressed syllable – but you can check the notation by looking at the key to the dictionary). Remember, though, that in a few cases a dictionary may be referring to a variety of English different from your own.
4. Can you give any of the words alternative stressings, with a different meaning? What difference in meaning is indicated by a difference of stress in these cases?

5. Do you think there is any regional difference in the way any of these words are stressed (e.g. a difference between British and Indian English, between Nigerian and American English, between Scottish and English English, etc.)? For which words is this the case, and what are the differences?

Suggested answers based on the authors' dialect are given on p. 213.

Now rejoin text on page 119

Now read the sentence in a way that is comfortable for you; put a line through all the words which do not have stress, and underline the word or words which have the strongest stress.

One answer might be: words 2, 5, 7, 8, 11 and 12 carry no stress at all, and 3, 6, 10 carry strong stress, with 10 the strongest. But it all depends on how you pronounce the sentence; you may have found different results when you read it. In any given sentence, there are often different ways of stressing the words, which depend on how the speaker thinks the information should be presented (strong stress means emphasis, for example). These patterns combine with movements in the height of the voice ('pitch') to produce the third layer of patterning in sound, intonation, which we consider in Section 6.1.3. They also make it possible for poetry to contain metrical patterns, as we will now see.

Metre

If you look at patterns of 'stress flow' in ordinary spoken English, you see a kind of pulsing of stress. A stressed word is followed by an unstressed one, which is followed by a stressed one, and so on. Typically in spoken English, the pulses have the same time between them. (For this reason, English is said to be an 'isochronous' language: the time lapses between stress peaks are equal. To test this suggestion out, beat an even, medium-tempo beat with your hand, and try to read this paragraph comfortably along with the beat.) Metre in English poetry takes advantage of the pulsing of stress in English speech. Many metres ('accentual syllabic' ones, see p. 000) also take advantage of the fact that English speech is a sequence of syllables.[1]

We could say that a particular **metre** is a guideline as to the structure of a line of poetry (or song); when a poem is in a particular metre, its lines all conform to the basic guideline set by that metre. A metre always includes provision for how many stresses there can be in the line, and usually also includes a statement of where those stresses should be (often in terms of which syllables the stresses are on). For example, the metre of **iambic pentameter**, which was much used by Chaucer, Shakespeare and Milton among others, says that lines should have the structure:

iambic pentameter = five stresses & on syllables 2, 4, 6, 8, 10.

('An iambic pentameter line will contain five stresses, which will occur on the second, fourth, sixth, eighth and tenth syllables.') The following lines (from an anonymous poem, 1656) are in iambic pentameter:

You that prophane our windows with a tongue
Set like some clock on purpose to go wrong

If we were to stress these lines exactly according to the

iambic pentameter pattern we would get something which sounds very odd. Try pronouncing the lines stressed like this:

$$\overset{,}{\sigma}\ \overset{,}{\sigma}\ \overset{,}{\sigma}\ \overset{,}{\sigma}\ \overset{,}{\sigma}\ \sigma\ \overset{,}{\sigma}\ \overset{,}{\sigma}\ \sigma$$

You that prophane our windows with a tongue

$$\overset{,}{\sigma}\ \sigma\ \sigma\ \overset{,}{\sigma}\ \overset{,}{\sigma}\ \sigma\ \overset{,}{\sigma}\ \overset{,}{\sigma}\ \sigma$$

Set like some clock on purpose to go wrong

This sounds like someone declaiming a form of verse; but it doesn't sound at all like meaningful speech. A pronunciation of the lines which seems more in keeping with speech patterns requires slightly different stresses. Try pronouncing the line now stressed like this:

You that prophane our windows with a tongue

Set like some clock on purpose to go wrong

We have stressed the first syllable instead of the second syllable in each line, and left out a stress on a 'small' word late in each line. Metres are often adapted in this way in actual practice; this is why we called them guidelines rather than rules. There is a compromise between the stress pattern demanded by the metrical guideline and the stress pattern demanded by the conventions of English speech. Not all deviations from a metre seem to be acceptable, however, and a poet might choose to stretch the possibilities of English word order rather than stretch too far the possibilities of the metre. Describing a metre involves distinguishing accurately between the many possible alterations to the basic pattern which are used and seem acceptable, and those which are for whatever reason not tolerated.

☛ *Now do Activity 61 on page 123*

☛ *Now do Activity 61 on page 123*

The way that we have expressed 'iambic pentameter' is this:

iambic pentameter = five stresses & on syllables 2, 4, 6, 8, 10.

A different way of expressing this is to use the traditional notion of a 'foot':

iambic pentameter = five feet & each foot contains two syllables with stress on the second one.

This has the same result. In both cases a line like the following will be created, if the guideline is followed accurately.

$$\overset{,}{\sigma}\ \overset{,}{\sigma}\ \overset{,}{\sigma}\ \overset{,}{\sigma}\ \overset{,}{\sigma}$$
$$\sigma\ \sigma\ \sigma\ \sigma\ \sigma\ \sigma\ \sigma\ \sigma\ \sigma$$

foot foot foot foot foot

Activity 61   *Metre and the choice and order of words*
(45 mins)

Consider these iambic pentameter lines by Christina Rossetti from 'Monna Innominata' (1881).

Many in aftertimes will say of you

'He loved her' – while of me what will they say?

1. Write σ above each syllable and ′ above the stressed syllables in the above lines as you would pronounce them.
2. Write down words or phrases in the lines which seem unusual (e.g. which you would not use).

3. The line contains some unusual orderings of words (unlike the word order of ordinary speech). Which words or phrases are in an unexpected position?

4. Rewrite the lines to replace all the unusual words/phrases with more usual words/phrases, and change the order of words to give a normal word order; the lines should now be like ordinary speech.

Version 2 ....

....

5. Are the rewritten lines still in iambic pentameter?   YES/NO
6. Was the choice of unusual words and the unusual word order *forced* by the need to fit an iambic pentameter pattern? In order to answer this question, try rewriting the line in two more ways, in between the normal order (version 2) and the actual order (version 1), using original words or replaced words, and original word order or replacement word order, and trying to write iambic pentameter lines (remember, some deviations from the strict rules seem to be acceptable, while others do not).

Version 3 ....

....

Version 4 ....

....

☛ *Now rejoin text on page 122*

The typical kinds of foot found in English metres have traditional names as given in the table below:

example of each kind of foot

iambic   σ σ   σ   σ   σ σ   σ σ   σ σ
          when good king Arthur ruled this land

trochaic σ σ   σ σ   σ σ   σ   σ σ
          how I wonder what you are

anapestic σ σ σ   σ σ   σ σ σ σ σ   σ σ σ   σ
          he sighed in his singing and after each groan

dactylic σ σ σ   σ σ σ   σ σ σ   σ σ σ   σ
          ladybird, ladybird, fly away home

Notice that a line may contain an incomplete foot (e.g. in the examples above, the end of the trochaic line and dactylic line, and the beginning of the anapestic line).

Q: A line involving an incomplete foot like 'how I wonder what you are' presents a problem. Is it a trochaic line (as illustrated above) or an iambic line, with the pattern:

′ | ′ | ′ | ′

σ σ σ σ   σ σ σ

how I wonder what you are

What evidence from the line would you use, and would it be useful to know more of the poem?

One way of answering this question is to look at the other lines in the poem; all the lines in a poem will tend to use the same foot type, and looking further in the poem may help clear up these irregularities. Metres have particular numbers of feet in the lines, and are named accordingly (note however that some poems may alternate between different numbers of feet in a line, e.g. tetrameter followed by trimeter is quite common). We list here three of those most commonly found in English verse.

number of feet in line   *example of each length of line*

′   ′   ′

trimeter   3 feet   come all you sailors bold

′   ′   ′   ′

tetrameter   4 feet   in all affairs of church or state

pentameter   5 feet

′   ′   ′   ′   ′

much mischief by these hailstones there was done

(Note: all the examples in fact involve iambic feet, but this is not necessarily the case.)

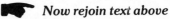 *Now do Activity 62*

The notion of a 'foot' is useful in metres where the number of syllables is rule-governed. These metres are called **accentual-syllabic** metres. Iambic pentameter metre requires ten syllables in the line, for example. But not all poetry written in English is governed by metres which involve syllable-counting. An alternative metrical pattern, **strong stress** metre, does not involve equal numbers of syllables between lines; it is only the number of stresses in the line which is regular, and the number of syllables is less relevant (lines in strong stress metre thus correspond well with isochronous English speech). 'Folk' poetry in English, which is often oral rather than written, is sometimes like this (e.g. ballads, songs, nursery rhymes). The following lines from an anonymous ballad of 1844 provide an example. Note that the lines do not always have the same number of syllables; there are normally eleven, but there is an extra syllable in the middle of line 2 and at the end of line 3, with the final line being very different.

′   ′   ′   ′

σ σ σ   σ σ σ σ σ σ σ σ

A dialogue I'll tell you as true as my life,

Activity 62   *A progress test on metre*
(20 mins)

To test your understanding of the terms we have just introduced, work through the following exercise.
1. How many syllables would there be in an anapestic tetrameter line?
2. How many *stressed* syllables would there be in a trochaic trimeter line?
3. Write σ above each syllable in each line below. Then indicate with ′ which syllables are stressed. Then name the metre of each line.

(i) Lo! Death has reared himself a throne

Metre: ....

(ii) An abridgement of all that was pleasant in man

Metre: ....

(iii) Hail to thee blithe spirit

Metre: ....

Answers can be found on p. 213.

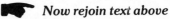 *Now rejoin text above*

σ   σ σ σ σ   σ σ σ σ   σ σ   σ

Between a coal-owner and a poor pitman's wife,

σ   σ σ σ σ σ σ σ σ   σ σ   σ

As she was a travelling all on the highway,

σ σ σ σ   σ σ σ   σ   σ σ σ

She met a coal-owner and this she did say,

σ σ σ   σ   σ   σ σ σ

Derry down, down, down derry down.

Alternative stressings of some lines seem possible.

➤ Now do Activity 63 on page 126

6.1.3 INTONATION

Intonation is in a sense the melody of speech. Melody in music involves the height or pitch of sounds; when you whistle a tune, the main thing you are doing is varying the pitch of your whistle, with successive notes being at different pitches. Every sound has a pitch and so the sounds in a spoken sentence all have a pitch. But the pitch does not usually remain the same for every sound; rather it goes up and down. This rising and falling of pitch is called the **intonation** pattern of speech. Every person has a **pitch band**; that is, a range between a personal highest sound and a personal lowest sound (this range is determined by the length of the vocal cavity in the mouth and throat; typically men have longer vocal cavities and thus a lower pitch band than women). Intonation is related to the major (nuclear) stresses in a sentence, and like stress it can be controlled by the speaker in order to present the information contained in the sentence in a particular way – a question will have a different intonation pattern from a statement, and different emphases in a sentence can be created by different intonation patterns. Intonation is a property of sound, not of writing; but it seems likely that even when you read a written text silently you sound out the intonation in your head, which involves making decisions about what the text means.

When you speak, your words cluster into groups which form continuous stretches of sound, separated by pauses during which you can draw breath. Each group, or 'chunk of information', is called a **tone group**, and can be made up of just a word or short phrase or might be much longer. The division of the stream of speech into such tone groups varies between speech styles and different speakers: the exact way a sentence will be divided up by any speaker depends on how that speaker chooses to present the information contained by the sentence. The presentation of information is determined partly by what the speaker thinks the person he/she is speaking to already knows; the ordering and presentation of new as opposed to already known information is managed partly by intonation and the division into tone groups. A speaker's intonation also depends on how the speaker feels about what he/she is saying: intonation also indicates types of attitude and emotion. Intonational tendencies also vary between dialects.

In each tone group there is a **nucleus** or **tonic syllable**. This is the most heavily stressed word in the group, and can involve a falling pitch, a rising pitch, or a combination of those two directions: a falling–rising or a rising–falling movement (and there are other, less common possibilities). In addition, the pitch movement can be slight or can be accentuated. In a falling pitch movement, for example, the pitch can fall from the middle of a speaker's pitch band to the bottom, or from the top to the bottom. This complicated system of movements – dependent on norms in the way the speaker usually speaks and on the particular situation – creates a network of possibilities for meanings which convey subtle shades of attitude and feeling.[2]

Exactly where you decide to place the nucleus in a sentence has a major effect on what that sentence is likely to be taken to mean. Consider this sentence from one of Keats's letters (to George and Tom Keats, January 1818).

1 2   3   4 5 6   7   8   9 10 11
There is nothing stable in the world; uproar's your only music.

If, in the way that you did in Section 6.1.2, you read through this quotation comfortably, you will put particularly strong stress on certain words. Each one of these will be a nucleus (so as well as receiving particular stress each will also involve movements of pitch). How many tone groups do you divide this quotation into? Possibly two (1: there . . . world, 2: uproar . . . music); or possibly four (1: there . . . stable, 2: in . . . world, 3: uproar's, 4: your . . . music). On each nucleus (two or four in the sentence), which direction does the pitch go? Try reading the sentence aloud, and making your voice go up on each nucleus, and then try making your voice go down on each nucleus. What is the effect in each case? Try putting the nucleus on 'world', and rising in pitch as you say it; if you do a rising pitch somewhere low down in your pitch range, it will sound as if you've stopped in the middle of a sentence (such pitch movements tend to signal that something is unfinished); if you perform a pitch movement ending high in your pitch range, the sentence is likely to sound like a question.

Read the two halves of the sentence separately, and test out what happens when you move the nucleus around. With the first sentence, put nuclear stress on 'in', then put it on 'world', etc. In each case, try to think what the sentence would mean or imply if it was said to you in that particular way (you can focus on this by trying to identify *contrasts* in meaning which appear to result from

Activity 63   *Analysing a metrical imitation*
(45 mins)

Here is an example of a verse in strong stress metre.

And there she's lean'd her back to a thorn

O and alas-a-day, O and alas-a-day

And there she has her baby born.

Ten thousand times good-night and be wi' thee.

Show the metrical pattern of this extract.
1. Write σ above each syllable.
2. Write ' above each stressed syllable.
If you find that there are uneven numbers of syllables in between stresses then this is an example of strong stress metre.

William Wordsworth copied this poem into his notebooks (he found it in a collection of ballads). For his collection with Coleridge called *Lyrical Ballads* (1798), Wordsworth wrote an imitation ballad called 'The Thorn', which was probably influenced in its content by the anonymous ballad cited here. Here are four lines from 'The Thorn'.

A woman in a scarlet cloak,

And to herself she cries,

'Oh misery! oh misery!

'Oh woe is me! oh misery!'

Now carry out the same operations as you did on the ballad above, viz.
3. Write σ above each syllable.
4. Write ' above each stressed syllable.

                                        *

5. Is Wordsworth's poem in the same metre as the anonymous ballad?   YES/NO
6. Make a brief note of similarities and differences between the two verses (including particularly their metres).

Suggested answers based on the authors' dialect are on p. 213.

    Now rejoin text on page 125

the changing sound of the sentence). Now do the same with the second sentence. Put the stress on 'music', and, again, try making your pitch movement go up in one reading, and down in another. Exaggerate the pitch movements of your voice in some readings, and make a note of what connotations and associations those changes have for you (they may be associated with particular regional or class accents, or with individual speakers you know, etc.).

 Now do Activity 64

Activity 64   *Intonation and reading poetry (30 mins)*

When you read a poem, you are partly guided by the metre as to where special emphasis will fall, though there is still scope for reading in different ways.

Consider these lines from Rossetti again, first presented in Activity 61.

Many in aftertimes will say of you
'He loved her' – while of me what will they say?

1. Try reading aloud the first line in three different ways, placing a nucleus (a) on 'many' then (b) on 'aftertimes', then (c) on 'say'. What effects do these changes have on the meaning of the line?

2. Try reading aloud the second line in three different ways, placing the nucleus (a) on 'loved', then (b) on 'her', then (c) on 'will'. What effects do these changes have on the meaning of the line?

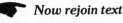 **Now rejoin text**

6.2 The syntactic structure of English

In the previous section we looked at English texts from the point of view of one particular medium in which they can be produced: the medium of sound. In this section we look more generally at ways in which English texts are put together according to rules and conventions of the English language. Specifically, we are interested in how learning about aspects of language structure enables us to think about effects created by the language of texts.

As we did when we were thinking about sound, we can isolate different levels of structure in a text in English. It is possible – and conventionally done – to distinguish discourse structure; sentence and phrase structure; and word structure. In each case we can look at the rules and conventions which help us to distinguish 'normal' from 'abnormal' structures. We can also see how particular structures in a text give it particular meanings. We look at discourse structure in Section 6.3; we will not look at word structure, which has rarely been particularly important in literary texts. In this section we look at some topics in sentence structure (or **syntax**).

6.2.1 HOW SENTENCES INTERPRET EVENTS

Sentences typically describe happenings, events, actions, states of affairs, and so on. In reality, things often happen because someone makes them happen. But sentences can be constructed either to reveal or to hide who or what makes something happen. Let's say, for example, that a child throws a ball and (accidentally) breaks a window with it. We can describe the first of these events as either 'the child threw a ball' or 'a ball was thrown'. If we choose the second form, we are in effect hiding the identity of the person who threw the ball. Alternatively, we can describe the next event as 'the child broke the window' or 'the window broke'. If we choose the second of these, we are describing the event almost as though there was no cause for the window breaking. None of our descriptions can be said to be actually 'untrue', with regard to the events we have described. But they present those events in different ways.

The person who (or thing which) deliberately makes something happen is called the **agent** in a sentence. Different kinds of sentence treat the agent differently, and thus emphasise or de-emphasise the element of deliberate action and causation. In **active** sentences, the agent is normally at the front of the sentence (before the verb), while in **passive** sentences the agent is normally either after the verb or is omitted completely. Here are some examples.

active sentence   Truck drivers tighten blockade
                   agent   verb

passive sentence   Blockade tightened by truck drivers
  or   verb   *agent*
passive sentence   Blockade tightened
                            verb   *(no agent)*

Active sentences and passive sentences are two alternative ways of presenting agency in a sentence. Another alternative involves two particular types of verbs: **causative** and **inchoative** verbs. Causative verbs express the fact that something changes in some way because someone makes it change. Inchoative verbs express the change in the state of something as though it takes place without anyone making it happen. The verb 'melt' is a good example of a verb which can be used either as a causative or as an inchoative.

causative   I   melted the ice
                  agent verb
inchoative   The ice melted
                       verb   *(no agent)*

The possibility of 'repackaging' information to give it a particular slant, without actually telling a lie, has been much discussed by people interested in **media bias**: the way in which news reports, advertising and so on are scripted so as to give a particular, allegedly 'biased' view of events. (Critical Discourse Analysis, which we explore in Section 9.6, is concerned partly with these questions.)

 Now do Activity 65 on page 129

6.2.2 LINGUISTIC AMBIGUITY

We say that a piece of language is ambiguous when it might mean more than one thing. Words are often a source of ambiguity, though they are rarely ambiguous in the context of a particular sentence or utterance. (The word 'bank', for example, could mean a river bank, or a place where money is kept. In *isolation*, therefore, it is ambiguous, but in context these two alternative meanings will only very rarely be equally possible.)

As an illustration of the systematic use of an ambiguous word, consider the word 'love' in Shakespeare's sonnets. Some possible meanings are: (a) the act of loving, (b) the beloved person, (c) love personified as the god of love. Sonnet 40 plays on (a) and (b) when it begins:

> Take all my loves, my love, yea take them all,
> What hast thou then more than thou hadst before?

and continues in a similar way. Such usages are a common stylistic feature of certain kinds of poetry, including Elizabethan sonnets and lyrics.

Another way in which ambiguity occurs in language is when a sentence can mean different things depending on alternative ways in which the words are grouped. In English sentences, words are clustered into phrases, and these phrases can be contained in other phrases. In this way, a sentence is like a big box, with smaller boxes in it, and smaller boxes in each box, until finally you reach the words. Phrases are often named after the category of the most important word in the phrase (noun, verb, etc.). For example, in 'The child threw the book at the window', the phrases are:

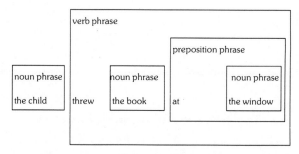

The grouping of words is one way in which the sentence gets a meaning. The groupings are not only clusterings of words, but also distinguish entities and objects in the world (e.g. the grouping 'the child' refers to a particular object). When a sentence can be analysed as having two alternative groupings of words it is ambiguous. Consider the following example, from John Milton.

Activity 65   *Verbs, agency and bias*
(60 mins)

To investigate whether the use of active and passive constructions – and deleting agents – creates particular kinds of 'bias' effect, work through the following tasks.

1. Find five newspaper headlines with the following kinds of structure, and write each one on the appropriate line and under the appropriate column, in the table below.

(a) an active sentence
(b) a passive sentence with an agent
(c) a passive sentence without an agent
(d) a causative verb (active)
(e) an inchoative verb

Active	Passive with agent	Passive without agent
(a)		
	(b)	
		(c)

causative (active)	inchoative
(d)	
	(e)

2. Now rewrite each sentence so that there is an alternative, 'transformed' version of it in the other columns on its line (e.g. rewrite your active sentence (a) as a passive with agent and a passive without agent).

3. In each case, consider this question: does the *rewritten* version of the headline seem to carry a different political or ideological stance towards the happening described? Write Y or N next to each rewritten headline.

4. This activity deals with sentences in isolation. But perhaps bias is also a matter of sentences in their context. To investigate this possibility, consider how far aspects of the text which precedes and follows it might affect the apparent ideological 'loading' of a sentence. For example, is *consistency* of use of a construction significant? Would there be more 'bias' effect if one type of construction is used with far more frequency than another? (To investigate this question, you will need to look at a variety of newspapers, and carry out an analysis of their headlines, using techniques developed from earlier stages of this book, especially Chapter 4).

☛ *Now rejoin text on page 128*

Example: the purpose of an epic

John Milton apparently conceived the idea of writing an epic poem in the late 1630s, when he was about 30 and before he had become blind. At first he considered subjects from British history (such as the life of King Arthur) and from Biblical scriptures. But when *Paradise Lost* was published in 1667, it had a still grander purpose: 'to justify the ways of God to men' (Book 1, line 26). Alongside the acclaim that the poem has received on account of its poetic achievements, the religious seriousness and elevation of this purpose have also been highly praised. But what exactly does the phrase 'justify the ways of God to man' *mean*?

The problem is that the phrase has two alternative groupings, which we illustrate below, in (i) and (ii).

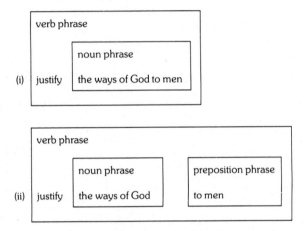

Structure (i) names what must be justified, as 'the ways of God to men'. Structure (ii) names not only what must be justified ('the ways of God'), but also the people to whom the justification is expressed ('to men'). The sentences can be glossed as:

(i) Justify the particular ways in which God treats men, i.e. justify the ways of God *towards* men.

(ii) Address a justification to men of the ways of God in general.

Q: Do you think the ambiguity in the phrase when written without brackets is best accounted for as:

(a) the result of a change in conventions of word grouping in English between the seventeenth century and now?

(b) a shortcoming in Milton's phrasing, which leaves an uncomfortable vagueness at the heart of the poem?

(c) a deliberate ambiguity that makes the aim of the poem more intriguing?

(d) other explanation: ....

....

6.2.3 THE ORDER OF WORDS

It is not clear that there is any sequential ordering between the participants in an action (or event, or state) in *reality*. In the action corresponding to the sentence, 'The child threw the book through the window', for example, there is no real-world ordering: first the child, then the book, then the window, with one coming before the other. However, when the action is put into words, the participants are put into order (in English writing, elements are ordered left–right on the page; in speech, ordered before–after in time).

English sentences have a normal word order; often one noun phrase comes first (the subject), followed by the verb and then the rest of the sentence. But in some cases, this normal word order is disrupted. Usually the disruption arises from a change in the order of the verb and the things which follow it, either by putting the verb at the end of the sentence, or by putting one phrase which would normally follow the verb at the front of the sentence instead. Examples of this which can be found in ordinary speech are:

topicalisation This book I like a lot!
    where 'this book' would normally follow the verb 'like'.
question Who did you see?
    where the person seen would normally be named after 'see'.

In texts written in older forms of English (particularly before about 1700) it is easy to find examples of disruption to what we called the normal order. This is particularly because word order was less rigidly fixed then than it is now – there was greater freedom to move words about without oddness. For example, Walter Ralegh's poem 'To His Son' (written at some point between 1593 and 1616) begins:

Three things there be that prosper up apace

Here the phrase 'three things' is moved to the front of the sentence from the position after 'be' (=are) where we would perhaps expect it to be, as in, 'There are three things that prosper up apace.' In the fourth line of the poem, Ralegh has:

And when they meet, they one another mar

Here the verb 'mar' is moved to the end of the sentence from where we would expect it to be, after 'they', as in, 'they mar one another'. Creating unusual word orders is a standard literary effect, and it can be quite difficult with a text written in an earlier period to be certain whether a word order which seems unusual to us has gained its effect from change in the language over time, or whether a literary effect would have been perceived by its contemporary readers. Although Elizabethan English allowed for freer word order than modern English does, it is still possible that Ralegh's poem might have seemed unusual and 'literary' in its ordering of words to its contemporary readers. To consider that possibility further, we would need to develop *ways of finding out* whether Ralegh's contemporaries would have considered his word orders normal or unusual.

Especially confusingly, the two reasons for unusual word order can come together when a poet deliberately imitates an out-of-date **archaic** language pattern. In this case, the literary effect may come from the fact that at some point in the past (long before the poem was written) the language pattern was quite normal.

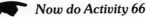 *Now do Activity 66*

Activity 66   *Analysing an archaic word order*

(30 mins)

The following text is the first four lines of Edgar Allen Poe's 'Lenore', published in 1831. Like many other writers writing in English in the early nineteenth century, Poe used archaic words and word orders in his poetry (you could check the archaic nature of his poetic language by comparing this text with a randomly chosen part of one of his short stories).

Ah, broken is the golden bowl! – the spirit flown forever!

Let the bell toll! – A saintly soul floats on the Stygian river: –

And, Guy De Vere, hast *thou* no tear? – weep now or never more!

See! on yon drear and rigid bier low lies thy love, Lenore!

1. Underline the words or phrases which seem to you to have been moved from their normal position and draw arrows to show how they have been moved.
2. Free word order, examples of which you have identified in 1, is one element of archaism. Extend your description of the archaisms in the poem by listing archaisms in the poem's use of words here.

3. What other elements in the text fit in with (or help explain, or support) the poet's use of archaic word order and archaic words? (You might consider the allusions/ quotations in the text, which you could investigate using the techniques described in Chapter 4.)

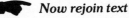 *Now rejoin text*

6.2.4 DESCRIBING SPEECH AND THOUGHT

Every sentence has a specific 'author': the person who speaks or writes it. Nevertheless, it is possible in one sentence to represent another sentence which has been said, or written, or even just thought, by someone else. There are two familiar ways in which this is done.

Direct representation of speech/writing/thought
SENTENCE 1 WRITTEN BY MARY: Peter said 'I am happy'
– where *I am happy* is what Peter said, 'I' refers to Peter rather than the actual speaker/writer (Mary), and it is Peter who is happy, not the speaker/writer (Mary).

Indirect representation of speech/writing/thought
SENTENCE 2 WRITTEN BY MARY: Peter said that he
was happy

– where again *I am happy* is what Peter said, but the
whole sentence is from the point of view of the
speaker/writer (Mary).

The differences can be tabulated as follows.

Direct	Indirect
Words are quoted exactly as they were said/written/thought.	Some words remain the same, while other words are changed. Changes apply particularly to pronouns and words indicating time and place. (These are **deictic** words, whose reference 'shifts', or is dependent on the context in which they are used.)
	Indirect sentences are sometimes introduced by 'that', 'whether', 'if', etc.
Question marks and exclamation marks are used.	Question marks and exclamation marks are not used.
The represented sentences are marked as separate from the rest of the text, by inverted commas, etc.	The represented sentences are *not* distinguished from the rest of the text by punctuation, etc.

In a written passage which involves direct or indirect
speech we usually distinguish (at least) two points of view.
There is the point of view of the author/narrator, and the
point of view of a character whose speech/writing/
thought is being represented. It is the character's point of
view which is represented by direct or indirect speech;
and the distinction between what the narrator says and
what the character says is clear because both direct and
indirect speech are easily identifiable in the text. In novels
in particular, however, a text will sometimes be written in
a way that makes it unclear whether a character's
speech/writing/thought is being represented or not. This
happens to a reader when there are reasons for thinking
that a particular piece of text might be represented as
speech/writing/thought *but* there is no consistent use of
markers of either direct or indirect speech. Some different
ways in which this might happen are:

(a) There are no markers of either direct or indirect
speech.
'He heard his wife in the kitchen and he was aware of
the child beside him, and that brought him his
happiness.' (last line of Philip Dick's novel *In Milton
Lumky Territory*)
    A possible interpretation is that this is not just a

description of his state of mind and perceptions by the
author, but is the character's own consciousness of
his own state of mind and perception. There are
however no overt indications that this is a direct or
indirect representation of thought.

(b) There are occasional markers of direct speech, but
not consistently.
'Between *them* it was more the intimacy of sisters.'
(from the first page of Jane Austen's *Emma*)
    Italicisation is sometimes a formal marker of direct
speech (it indicates emphatic speech); however the
rest of the text is not structured like direct speech.
Nevertheless there are reasons for thinking that this
sentence expresses Emma's own speech rather than
the narrator's.
    Sometimes a marker of direct speech/thought is
contained in a sentence which cannot be interpreted
as fully in direct speech/thought. For example,
'Peter was now happy.'
Here, 'now' is a marker of (Peter's) direct thought or
speech because it refers to the present (few narrative
styles are able to do this, though some – such as radio
reporting of a sports game – can). However, the 'was'
of the same sentence is not compatible with the 'now'
and so appears to be coming from a different voice
(e.g. the narrator).

These possibilities (sometimes called **free indirect
speech**) are often exploited by novelists.[3] They have the
result of making different perspectives and points of view
– of the author/narrator and of characters – seem less
separate from one another. Two possible reasons for
using these devices are:

(a) the devices appear to provide a more immediate
access to a character's consciousness than is possible
with either direct or indirect speech;
(b) they make descriptions in the book seem less reliable
– more subjective than objective.

☞ *Now do Activity 67 on page 133*

6.2.5 PROSE STYLES

The sorts of structure we have described so far can
combine together in many different ways. As they do this,
they produce different large-scale stylistic effects. Users of
English are able to recognise a very wide range of (often
subtly) different styles in both writing and speech; and it is
this recognition which enables parodies and pastiches to
work, alongside serious use of the styles. Styles are
identified (we might say they carry 'trademarks' or
'fingerprints') in different ways. The style of Margaret
Thatcher, for example, is identified largely through accent
and intonation; horse-racing commentary is signalled by
a combination of accelerating tempo and rising pitch; the
style of the tabloid press is identified through a combi-

Activity 67   *Identifying points of view*
(60 mins)

Here is another passage from Jane Austen's *Emma* (1816).

> . . . but scarcely had she begun, scarcely had they passed the sweep-gate and joined the other carriage, than she found her subject cut up – her hand seized – her attention demanded, and Mr Elton actually making violent love to her: availing himself of the precious opportunity, declaring sentiments which must be already well known, hoping – fearing – adoring – ready to die if she refused him; but flattering himself that his ardent attachment and unequalled love and unexampled passion could not fail of having some effect, and in short, very much resolved on being seriously accepted as soon as possible. It really was so. Without scruple – without apology – without much apparent diffidence, Mr Elton, the lover of Harriet, was professing himself *her* lover. She tried to stop him; but vainly; he would go on and say it all. Angry as she was, the thought of the moment made her resolve to restrain herself when she did speak. She felt that half this folly must be drunkenness, and therefore could hope that it might belong only to the passing hour. Accordingly, with a mixture of the serious and the playful, which she hoped would best suit his half and half state, she replied.
>
> 'I am very much astonished, Mr Elton. This to *me*! You forget yourself – you take me for your friend – any message to Miss Smith I shall be happy to deliver; but no more of this to *me*, if you please!'

1. In this passage, since there are two characters, there are three potential points of view: that of (a) the narrator, (b) Mr Elton, (c) Emma (the 'she' of the passage). Using different coloured pens for each point of view (or different types of underlining: single, double, and zigzag), underline each point of view as it is represented in the text. (Note: *all* the text should end up underlined in at least one type of underlining.) Where you are unable to decide between different points of view, underline the problematic piece of text twice or three times in the different colours.

2. How do you know whose point of view you are presented with at each stage of the passage? Look, among other things, at typographical/punctuation devices.

👉 *Now rejoin text on page 132*

nation of vocabulary, sentence length and graphic layout on the page; Euphuistic style (named after *Euphues* (1578) by John Lyly) is identified by vocabulary and particular sorts of sentence structure. In this section we look at two historically influential styles which are trademarked largely through sentence structure; and through the two activities, we suggest general procedures for examining other styles that are not discussed.

We begin with 'Ciceronian' style. Cicero lived in Rome (106–43 BC), and wrote prose and made speeches in Latin, as well as being a theorist of writing and speaking. Mediaeval Latin texts commonly imitate Ciceronian style, and Ciceronian style is also characteristic of many sixteenth-century English texts. Ciceronian style has the following characteristics.

1. Sentences are long. There are many smaller sentences (particularly relative clauses, e.g. 'who . . .', 'which . . .', 'that . . .', etc.) inside the long main sentence.
2. Sentences are **periodic**. This means using a mass of modifiers (additional, 'descriptive' words and phrases and clauses) built around a central point, or building up to a final point (other terms for this way of writing are 'circular' and 'rounded'). A typical example is the placing of modifiers before the things they modify, including the placing of subordinate sentences at the beginning of the main sentence. (One purpose of the periodic sentence is to keep the reader in suspense: only at the end of the main sentence does its meaning become clear.)
3. Sentences have a balance of elements. In particular, there are contrasting terms (often opposites), and repeated grammatical patterns.
4. The end of sentences is marked by putting the relevant piece of prose into a poetry-like metrical rhythm. This last part of the sentence is called the **copia**; and 'copious style' refers to the practice of using an especially rhythmic phrase to end sentences.

Here is an example of a sixteenth-century Ciceronian sentence from Philip Sidney, *The Defence of Poesie* (1595).

> For if *Oratio*, next to *Ratio*, Speech next to Reason, be the greatest gift bestowed upon *Mortalitie*, that cannot bee praiselesse, which doth most polish that blessing of speech; which considereth each word not onely as a man may say by his forcible qualitie, but by his best measured quantity: carrying even in themselves a *Harmonie*, without [=unless] perchance number, measure, order, proportion, be in our time growne odious.

Notice the following features.

1. The overall sentence is long, with many subordinate clauses.
2. There are many examples of delayed information (periodicity): (a) 'if . . . *Mortalitie*' precedes its consequence 'that . . . quantity'; (b) 'that cannot bee praiselesse' precedes things which cannot be praiseless:

'which . . . speech' and 'which . . . quantity'; (c) in the second 'which' clause, 'not onely . . . qualitie' precedes 'but . . . quantity'; (d) in 'without . . . odious', 'odious' is placed at the end (i.e. 'in our time' is moved to before the verb).
3. There are instances of balance: (a) '*Oratio*' is balanced by '*Ratio*' (in both sound and meaning); (b) 'Speech' is balanced by 'Reason'; (c) 'which doth most polish' is balanced by 'which considereth each word'.
4. There is a copia. The sentence concludes with an afterthought, which is more metrical than the rest of the passage, especially the last phrase, 'be in our time growne odious'.

The second style we consider is the anti-Ciceronian style. This takes its name from the fact that its practitioners deliberately wrote in a manner different from the Ciceronians. Another name for this style is 'Senecan' (because it is thought to resemble the style of the Latin writer Seneca). Possible reasons for the development of this alternative style include (a) recognition that linguistic differences between English and Latin present difficulties to Ciceronianism, (b) patriotism and the wish to produce a distinctive, national style of writing, and (c) antischolasticism. Features of anti-Ciceronian style include:

1. Sentences need not be long. If they are, they are composed of a number of short sentences in sequence, often connected only by punctuation marks (especially colons and semi-colons', sometimes by 'and', 'or', etc.)
2. Instead of delaying the completion of the main idea until the end of the sentence (cf. Ciceronian style), the main idea is often stated in the first sub-sentence, as a kind of summary of what is to come. One purpose of this style was to imitate the sequential development of thought, rather than – as in the Ciceronian style – to present the completed thought as a complex package to be deciphered and appreciated.
3. Often the sub-parts of the sentence are unbalanced with respect to each other: parallelism between words and phrases is avoided.

Now do Activity 68 on page 135

The distinction between these two kinds of style – roughly between an informal, conversational (anti-Ciceronian) style and a formal, balanced (Ciceronian) style – has been important for later prose writers. It has affected both their actual practice and how they have thought about their practice. But writers are not always consistent: Bacon, for example, claimed to be opposed to the Ciceronian style, yet often used it nevertheless. We have chosen to discuss these two styles in particular because they underlie a contrast which is still an issue in contemporary writing: the contrast between worked-for rhetorical elegance and (equally worked-for) conversational spontaneity.

Now do Activity 69 on page 136

Activity 68   *Analysing the prose style of a passage*
(45 mins)

The two-sentence passage which follows is an example of anti-Ciceronian style.

> *What is Truth*; said jesting Pilate; And would not stay for an Answer. Certainly there be, that delight in Giddinesse, And count it a Bondage, to fix a Beleefe; Affecting Free-will in Thinking, as well as in Acting.
> (Francis Bacon, 'On Truth', *Essays*, 1625)

Using the list of typical stylistic features provided above, work through the following tasks.

1. Make a list of anti-Ciceronian elements.

Suggested answers are given on p. 214.

2. Are there nevertheless also some Ciceronian elements in the passage?   YES/NO
If 'yes', make a list of them here.

3. Rewrite the passage, to make it more obviously and fully in the Ciceronian style.

4. Now compare the original and your rewritten version. It has been said about the anti-Ciceronians, 'Their purpose was to portray not a thought but a mind thinking.' Do you think your two passages differ in this way?   YES/NO

5. Finally, consider the decision you have made in answering 4. Is this a question that can be answered on anything more than an impressionistic basis? If you are happy with the contrast between a 'thoughts' style and a 'thinking-in-process' style, do you consider these terms preferable alternatives to 'Ciceronian' and 'anti-Ciceronian'?

 Now rejoin text on page 134

Activity 69   *Identifying a prose style*
(20 mins)

The following comment (from *The Lives of the Most Famous English Poets*, 1781) was made by Samuel Johnson, in praise of Dryden's Prefaces.

> They have not the formality of a settled style, in which the first half of the sentence betrays the other. The clauses are never balanced, nor the periods modelled: every word seems to drop by chance, though it falls into its proper place.

To conclude your work in this section on contrasting prose styles, answer the following questions.

1. Is Johnson representing Dryden as a Ciceronian or an anti-Ciceronian?
   Ciceronian/anti-Ciceronian (delete as applicable)
2. Is Johnson's own style in this passage Ciceronian or anti-Ciceronian?
   Ciceronian/anti-Ciceronian (delete as applicable)

☛ *Now rejoin text*

6.3 The structures of discourse

In the last section, we looked at two different sorts of prose style. Prose styles of this sort involve patterns of sentence structure; when repeated consistently enough, the patterns create distinctive overall styles of discourse. In this section, we look at other patterns which similarly function to create specific text styles. In particular, we look at kinds of connection which are made between the sentences of a text to produce forms of bonding or connectedness, and we consider some of the effects that use of different discourse styles can have.

6.3.1 COHERENCE AND COHESION IN A TEXT

We suggested in Section 6.2.2 that words in an English sentence tend to come in particular orders, which can be varied for particular effects. In paragraphs and texts as a whole, the units (often in the form of sentences) are steps in an act of communication or persuasion. These units of discourse are unlike the units which combine in sentences because there is no particular order in which they can be predicted to occur (though there are to some extent usual orders of information as regards how specific types of communicative act are performed). Randomly re-ordering the sentences in a paragraph may produce an odd effect, but nothing like as bad as randomly re-ordering the words in a sentence. The central element which gives structure to discourses is that they have **coherence**: some form of connectedness at the level of ideas or social action which holds the discourse together. In general, sentences do not connect together randomly; they combine together in forms of discourse that people use in a meaningful way. Like all other properties of language structure, the means of creating such coherence can be exploited and 'bent' to create ironic or comic effects, and so an understanding of coherence can lead to a better understanding of these effects.

Some of the connectedness of a text comes from its being perceived to have a topic or subject matter. But how do you know what a text is about? You partly understand this because of a commonness in a discourse of words relating to the same topic (e.g. haystack, field, tractor, silo, etc.). These are **collocations** of words, since clusters of words have a particular likelihood of occurring in the same kinds of text. Words which are generally used less frequently (e.g. technical terms) have a stronger tendency to suggest specific contexts of use than ones that are used frequently; and collocations reflect *socially constructed* clusters which change between people, periods and societies, rather than fixed or 'natural' connections between things in reality. In this way, vocabulary creates links between the forms of the text and the ideas or thoughts it is about: its subject matter is reflected in the patterns of words it is made of.

Besides subject matter and vocabulary, however, there are other forms of connection between sentences, which indicate relations of sequence, causality (one thing leads to another), exemplification (giving an example), implication (suggesting something), and so on. And besides these forms, there are others which do not in themselves direct the discourse, but simply indicate that sentences are to be taken together, and help avoid duplicating material from one sentence to the next. A text which you read helps you to produce connections between its sentences by using direction signals. Together these signals act as markers of **cohesion** in a text: its property of being held together not just because of relationships between ideas or because of purposeful action behind it, but through visible connecting forms and structures in the language itself. These markers can be of a number of types.

1. Words and phrases in the text **co-refer** (i.e. refer to the same entities, so providing continuity).

(a) Pronouns, such as 'he', 'she', 'they', 'it' either refer back to people or things previously mentioned in the text, or else refer to people or things taken as recognisable in the situation,

> e.g. John walked to the shop. *He* bought a paper. A dog approached *him* on *his* way back.

(b) Use of words like 'the', 'this', and 'that' (very often in definite expressions such as 'the X' or 'this X') point to earlier mentions of things (or to things which are assumed to be visible in the context),

> e.g. Whymper made his first ascent of the Matterhorn that year. *The climb* was long and dangerous.

2. Verbs which have already been used are often repeated in condensed, **substitute forms** (generally as a form of the verb 'do' or by the word 'so'), or are left out altogether.

> All buses go to the station.
> At least, most do.
> > = *go to the station*
> He didn't succeed.
> He might have done, if he'd gone earlier.
> > = *succeeded*
> They thought the bus had gone.
> If so, they would have to walk.
> > = *the bus had gone*

3. There are **connective** words and phrases, whose purpose is primarily to signal directions:

consequence: as a result, because of this, so, there-
                fore . . .
ordering: and, firstly, finally . . .
continuation: and, furthermore . . .
simultaneity: meanwhile, at the same time . . .
concession: granted, yet . . .
opposition: on the contrary, nevertheless, despite
                this . . .
etc.

Together, these various elements create what is often called the **texture** of a text: its property of visibly holding together as a connected entity, rather than appearing to be a random or accidental sequence of sentences. Different sorts of text create different types of cohesion and texture. Conversations typically draw heavily on material which is taken as 'given' or 'shared', because it can be retrieved from the immediately surrounding situation. Essays and literary texts, on the other hand, depend less on situational references of this kind; their referring expressions (such as pronouns and definite expressions, as above) tend to be **anaphoric**, referring to things which have already been mentioned in the text itself, rather than **exophoric**, referring to things outside the text in the situation (though it is a common tendency of literary works to create imaginary situations through particular uses of exophoric discourse features).[4]

> *Now do Activity 70 on page 138*

In many cases, besides taking account of the explicit connections created by cohesive markers to help you follow the development of a text, you also have to work out connections between sentences for yourself. Adjacent sentences (i.e. next to each other) do not always have cohesive ties between them, and you have to decide for yourself whether to treat them as connected. To do this you have to think about what the discourse is trying to do (i.e. to impute a purpose), and see sentences as acts rather than simply as forms. Coherence may be created at the level of connections between the acts or functions of sentences (as steps in a communicative process), rather than between words. This type of coherence depends on inferences that you make in reading or listening; and we will investigate how such inferences work in Chapter 7.

6.3.2 RHETORIC

The modern study of how discourse is constructed, and how it can achieve different kinds of effect, has antecedents in **rhetoric**, the classical study of forms of persuasion. The study of rhetoric began in classical Greece in the fifth century BC, and became central to a controversy over whether you can use language to establish anything you like as true (a belief referred to as **eristics**, related to the views of a group of philosophers called the Sophists), or whether rhetoric is (as was later suggested by Aristotle) an instrument of expression compatible with the logical establishment of truth. For some Greek philosophers, such as Isocrates, rhetoric was advocated as a necessary part of civilisation and democracy (playing an essential role in participatory administration and the resolution of problems through negotiation). Nevertheless (or, as many people think, *therefore*) political rhetoric declined during the period of Macedonian domination of Greece, to be later revived in the period of the Roman Republic (where it is especially associated with the legal process, and with Cicero and Quintilian). Rhetoric declined again during the Roman Imperial period, and was held in mixed opinion in subsequent Christian European traditions, partly as a consequence of mixed attitudes to the problem of reconciling Christian piety with admiration for pagan, classical doctrines. With the revival of classical education in Europe during the early Middle Ages, rhetoric was re-established, and was further studied and practised during the Renaissance, with a burst of rhetoric guides in the sixteenth and seventeenth centuries (rhetoric was thought of during these centuries as a necessary accomplishment for a gentleman, and it may be that some Elizabethan texts began as people practising their rheto-

Activity 70   *Looking for connectedness in a passage*
(60 mins)

Consider the following passage from Mulk Raj Anand, *Untouchable* (1935), p. 175.

> The fires of sunset were blazing on the distant horizon. As Bakha looked at the magnificent orb of terrible brightness glowing on the margin of the sky, he felt a burning sensation within him. His face, which had paled and contracted with thoughts a moment ago, reddened in a curious conflict of despair. He didn't know what to do, where to go. He seemed to have been smothered by the misery, the anguish of the morning's memories. He stood for a while where he had landed from the tree, his head bent, as if he were tired and broken. Then the last words of the Mahatma's speech seemed to resound in his ears: 'May God give you the strength to work out your soul's salvation to the end.' 'What did that mean?' Bakha asked himself. The Mahatma's face appeared before him, enigmatic, ubiquitous. There was no answer to be found in it. Yet there was a queer kind of strength to be derived from it.

1. Make three lists of words and phrases which collocate with one another. For each list, suggest a heading which describes its general 'focus' (we have started two lists for you as examples – continue them).

(list a) 'fire': fires, blazing, glowing

(list b) 'despair':

(list c) ....:

2. Work carefully through the passage, sentence by sentence. For each sentence, underline all words that have a cohesive link back to what has gone before. Using the list of connectives above p. 137, make a note in the margin of what sort of connection is being made in each case

3. Now consider the following words. Is there anything unusual or significant about the way they are being used? (Consider the other words in the passage they collocate with, and what sort of words you would *expect* them to collocate with. Compare these collocations with what the words actually *refer to* in the passage.)

'paled'

'burning'

'reddened'

4. Several expressions in the passage begin – like the ones we give below – with the word 'the'; add two more. Then, for each of the examples, try to explain, as precisely as possible, why the word 'the' (rather than 'a', 'some', etc.) is being used.

'the fires of sunset'

'the distant horizon'

....

....

☞ *Now rejoin text on page 137*

---

rical skills). By the mid-seventeenth century, rhetoric was again under attack, as a kind of superficial decoration to expression which was not compatible with the new science and its search for the 'naked' reality of the world. The Romantics, like mediaeval theologians, had mixed attitudes, preferring apparent spontaneity over rhetorical elegance while nevertheless revering writers such as Milton, who was very much influenced by rhetoric.

But what was classical rhetoric like? On the one hand it contained complicated classifications of **tropes** (devices for creating special effects of meaning such as metaphor, metonymy and synecdoche) and of **figures** (devices for playing on patterns of sounds and words). But beyond this, rhetoric also sought to investigate (through handbooks, imitation, etc.) how structures in discourse can serve to create all sorts of psychological effect (changes in feeling, opinions, *etc.*) rather than (as some detractors claimed) just developing devices for stylistic decoration. To give some idea of the basic frameworks of rhetoric, we give some of its classifications in the following table (without their Latin and Greek names).[5]

---

1. *Three types of oratory*
judicial/forensic   = legal (discussions about the past)
deliberative   = political (discussions about future)
epideictic/demonstrative = polemical or praising

2. *Three styles of speaking and writing*
(each style taken to be appropriate to different idioms and genres)
grand
middle
simple

3. *Stages of argument*
introduction
narration
proof (identification of point at issue; arguments for; arguments against)
conclusion

4. *Attempts to convince by . . .*
appealing to a sense of morality
appealing to the feelings
appealing to reason
use of tropes and figures incidental to the main purpose

☞ *Now do Activity 71*

Activity 71   *Rhetoric in modern usage*
(60 mins)

The practice of rhetoric is often thought of as the patterning of discourse for special persuasive or aesthetic effects, using devices such as repeated sounds, phrases, sentence structures, etc. Is there, in modern times, a conflict between the attempt to express personal experience through replicating thought and speech, and the use of formal styles characteristic of rhetoric?

Compare the following two extracts.

(a) I have the feeling that I shall go mad and cannot go on any longer in these terrible times. I hear voices and cannot concentrate on my work. I have fought against it, but cannot fight any longer. I owe all my happiness in life to you. You have been so perfectly good. I

(a)

cannot go on and spoil your life.
　(Virginia Woolf's suicide note, addressed to her husband Leonard, March 1941)

(b) We must all drive ourselves to the utmost limit of our strength. We must preserve and refine our sense of proportion. We must strive to combine the virtues of wisdom and daring. We must move forward together, united and inexorable.
　(Winston Churchill, 'Our greatest glory' speech, 1941)

1. Describe any rhetorical elements you find in each passage

(b)

2. Is one passage more 'rhetorical' than the other.
YES/NO
3. What purposes do the rhetorical effects serve? List
some purposes below, and suggest which effects match
with which purposes.

Woolf (purpose 1):..
(rhetorical effects):

Woolf (purpose 2):..
(rhetorical effects):

Churchill (purpose 1): ....
(rhetorical effects):

Churchill (purpose 2): ....
(rhetorical effects):

4. Are the rhetorical effects used for similar purposes in
both passages?   YES/NO
5. Write down some general observations you think it is
reasonable to make on the basis of this comparison.
Think particularly about:
 (i) possible relationships between style and subject-
     matter;
(ii) possible relationships between style and historical
     period.

6. Using the work you did in Chapter 4, make a note of
further work you would want to do to explore ideas listed
in response to question 5.

7 Interpreting

In Chapter 6 we looked at the language of texts, and how texts acquire structure and meaning by drawing on the structures and meanings of the language they are made from. But those structures and meanings are partly dependent on us, with our knowledge of how meanings can be found in the structures of language, and our ability to produce and interpret texts. In this chapter, we look more closely at meanings, and try to find out exactly how an individual reader arrives at them. We begin by looking at some aspects of what meanings are and how they arise (Sections 7.1 to 7.3). This is followed in the rest of the chapter by an exploration of how readers get meanings out of texts. Section 7.1 shows that there are different ways of thinking about how a form can carry a meaning (e.g. how a word means something). Sections 7.2 and 7.3 then look at two different sorts of meaning which a text can carry. Section 7.2 is concerned with meanings which are **determined** by the text (which we will call 'coded' meanings). Section 7.3 is concerned with meanings which are derived by **inference** from a text, by adding what we know to the text (we call these 'non-coded' meanings). We then look at how humans in particular, with the kind of mind that humans have, find meanings in texts (Sections 7.4 to 7.5). Finally we bring our discussion back more directly to the study of literature (Section 7.6).

7.1 Kinds of meaning

In this section we look at different ways of thinking about the process by which one thing (a **form**) means something else (its **content**). The study of meaning generally is called **semantics**; and one discipline which is concerned with the collection and classification of meanings is **semiotics**. One of the founders of modern semiotics was the philosopher C. S. Peirce (1839–1914). Peirce distinguished three different kinds of relationship between a form and a content. (Add one further example of your own under each of our examples.)

The Peirce classification of meaning

Form	Relationship	Content
an **icon** .... e.g. portrait	is similar to (e.g. similar shape)	what it means person portrayed
....		....
an **index** .... e.g. smoke	is caused by	what it means fire
....		....
a **symbol** .... e.g. head-shake (in India) head-shake (in Scotland)	is conventionally (e.g. in a particular culture) linked with	what it means agreement with someone disagreement with someone
....		....

Notice that 'meaning' is taken by Peirce to cover a range of different relationships. You might think of naming as the standard case of meaning, such as when the name 'John' (a form) means a person (its content); this type of meaning is classified by Peirce under 'symbol'. Meaning in this case is a matter of *replacement*: the form stands for, or replaces, the content. Peirce's notion of 'icon' is similarly a case of replacement. In a symbol the form is related to the content only by convention; in an icon the form is related to the content by some inherent property of the form, such that it is similar to the content. The shapes and colours in a picture (=an icon) are similar to the shapes and colours of the thing portrayed; **onomato-poeia** in language is also iconic, where 'miaow' is an iconic form representing the sound made by a cat. Notice however that similarity or resemblance often seems to have a certain conventional element; different cultures use slightly different words to imitate the sound of a cat (Arabic = 'maw-maw'; Japanese = 'niaw'), and different cultures paint portraits in different ways (with perspective, without perspective, etc.).

Icon and symbol are both examples of form standing for or replacing content. But Peirce's third kind of meaning, 'index', involves not replacement but *sequence*. When 'smoke means fire' it is because smoke follows fire and fire precedes smoke. So when you see smoke, you know there is *already* fire.

Q: Is the relation between a photograph and a person photographed best described as 'icon' or 'index', or both at the same time?

Notice that fire also causes and precedes other things than smoke: it precedes 'charcoal', 'heat', 'ashes', etc. And smoke follows from other things than fire: it follows 'heating a dirty electric grill', 'cigarette', 'smoke bomb', etc. Thus the relationship between form (smoke) and content (fire) in an index is rather looser than the relationship in a symbol or an icon; the same form (smoke) can mean a different content (smoke bomb), and the same content (fire) can be represented by a different form (ashes), as in the diagram shown here.

The indeterminacy of form–content relations in indexes

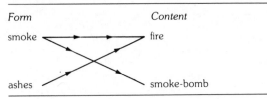

The relationship between form and content in a symbol is *consistent* because it is governed by an agreed **code**. There is no code to govern the relationship between form and content in an index and so the relationship between form and content in an index is to some extent *inconsistent*.[1]

One tradition of thinking in this area, developing from an article entitled 'Meaning' (1957) by the philosopher H. P. Grice, suggests that this distinction between a meaning relationship governed by a code and a meaning relationship not governed by a code is very important in language. While some form–content relationships in language are coded, others are not. An example of a coded relationship would be the use of the name 'John Perkins' (=the form) to mean a particular person (=the content); the relationship between the name and the person is fixed and socially agreed (and in fact taken as legally defining in a document like a passport). The

relationship can be changed of course (someone's name can be changed), but it will always count as a coded relationship. We will look at other coded form-meaning relationships in Section 7.2. An example of a *non*-coded relationship is as follows. If you and I are in a room, I am standing by a closed window, and you say to me, 'It's hot in here' (=the form), one of the contents associated with that form could be stated something like 'open the window' (=the content). You didn't actually say 'open the window' but I can infer that it was what you meant. It is this non-coded type of meaning which is invoked in the phrase, 'I hear what you say but I don't know what you mean'; that is, the hearer can (unconsciously) work out some of the contents (the coded ones) but not all of them (the non-coded ones). This kind of relationship between form and meaning is not conventionally fixed in advance; it has to be worked out by speakers and hearers depending on what each of them knows and where they are. Many aspects of our use of language are like this; we look at them in Section 7.3. To summarise:

Coded	Non-coded
relationship between form and content is fixed by a convention ('the code')	relationship between form and content is not fixed by convention, but must be worked out by applying general knowledge
there are many different codes	
could be called a 'replacement' relationship; by agreement form stands in the place of content	could be called a 'sequential' relationship; content follows after form
Peirce's symbol, icon	Peirce's index

 Now do Activity 72 on page 143

Meaning is an important issue in literary studies: much of what we do is find contents for forms (forms = text-tokens in this case). Some of these contents can be found by applying codes to the forms, and decoding meanings from them; other contents have to be reached by applying our own individual knowledge in the context in which we are reading the text (and so different people in different contexts will find different meanings). Notice that there is a 'grey area' in between the coded and the non-coded. Symbols which are 'public property' (many people use them or understand them in the same way), like the use of the apple to symbolise temptation and sin, are not fully coded but not fully uncoded either; the relationship has something conventional about it (=coded) but still allows for individual interpretation (=non-coded).

Activity 72   *Distinguishing coded from non-coded meanings*
(20 mins)

Here are some different form-content relationships. For each one, decide whether it is coded or non-coded. If you have any problems in deciding, make a note of them next to the relevant example.

Form	Content	
(a) the words: 'William Shakespeare'	a specific (now dead) person	CODED/NON-CODED
(b) the words: 'William Shakespeare'	a way of saying 'the greatest English writer'	CODED/NON-CODED
(c) the words: 'how are you?'	a greeting	CODED/NON-CODED
(d) the words: 'how are you?'	a request for specific information	CODED/NON-CODED
(e) the words: 'I'm hot'	a statement by Charles Dickens that his internal body temperature is 101°F	CODED/NON-CODED
(f) the object: an apple	a way of saying 'temptation and sin'	CODED/NON-CODED
(g) the play: *Henry V* (by Shakespeare)	the tale of a prince who, at the spur of England's need, rose to the heights of manliness and kingship	CODED/NON-CODED

Answers on p. 214.

☛ *Now rejoin text on page 142*

Works of literature in their 'raw' form are text-tokens: bundles of pages with printed marks on them. What makes *Wuthering Heights* importantly different from *Moby Dick* is not physical differences between the two (such as their relative weights or size, which in a publisher's 'series' edition are in any case reduced as much as possible), but the fact that we create different meanings from each book when we read it. We might say that we *extract* these meanings from the marks on the page. But this in itself is not an adequate characterisation of the process.

Meaning is not *contained* in the marks, like cigarettes in a packet (we do not just look at the page and let meaning stream in through our eyes). Rather, we create meanings by applying to the printed forms an additional element: *what we know*.

'What we know' is (a) a number of specific codes, and (b) other things – our memories, beliefs, and knowledge of the world in general. The word 'knowledge' in this sense includes abilities and even reflex actions, as well as vaguely held beliefs and distant memories. In Section 7.2 we look at how we use specific codes to make sense of texts, and in Section 7.3 we look at how we use other kinds of knowledge to make sense of texts.

In the rest of this chapter we work through some more detailed arguments and procedures to investigate these questions, ending up by raising questions which are central to literary studies. Why do people find different meanings in texts and judge their value differently? And, why do people enjoy reading literary texts?

Q: Do you have answers to these questions already? Do you think there *are* answers to them?

7.2 How we use codes to interpret texts

We begin with the marks on the page. When you look at a page you can interpret the marks as corresponding to sounds. But your ability to do this depends on your ability to use a particular code. We will invent a name for this code – 'the English pronunciation code'; what it does is match a range of marks (=the forms) with a range of sounds (=the contents). Codes are the 'property' of particular groups of people at a particular time, and can mutate bit-by-bit, still performing the same function but performing it slightly differently, over different geographical or social areas, or – as the activity which follows shows – over different historical periods.

 Now do Activity 73 on page 145

How English language forms encode meanings

Reading a text involves applying a number of codes, some of which require other codes to have already been applied (e.g. code 2 relies on code 1, codes 3 and 4 rely on code 2, etc.).

Form	Content
code 1 marks on the page	English letters or English sounds
code 2 sequence of English letters	individual words, phrases, sentences worked out
code 3 word	meaning of word
code 4 sentence	the event described by the sentence

The difference between different codes, and what they do, is the domain of linguistics; for example, it might be that what we have called 'code 2' may actually be a collection of separate codes.

Below, for example, is a linguistic code in action. Match up each form with a content. The first one is done for you.

Form (sentence)	Content (an event, indicated here by a picture)

1 The cat ate the fish. ⟵————————————⟶

2 The cat was eaten by the fish.

3 The fish ate the cat.

Activity 73   *Spelling codes*

(45 mins)

This activity uses a photocopy of part of a text printed in English in 1556 (the translation into English of Thomas More's *Utopia*).

1. Try to read the text aloud (if you find it impossible, we have provided a translation on p. 214).

> **with contagious tiſca-**
> **ſes, ſuche as be wonte bp infection to**
> **crepe from one to an other, mpght be**
> **lapde a part farre from the cõpanp of ÿ**
> **reſidue.**

Reading this text turns out not to be very easy. The 'English pronunciation code' has changed in certain ways over the centuries, as is clear when you try to read the text aloud. But some aspects remain the same. For example **b** in this text is much like the modern b, and both stand for the same sound. On the other hand, the tilde ~ over 'o' in **õ** stands in this text for an [m] sound *after* the [o], so that the word is pronounced [company]. This is a form–content pair which is no longer part of the modern English pronunciation code (optional use of the tilde was one of the aids to the sixteenth-century printer we referred to in Chapter 3, which enabled the printer to make the right and left margins straight).

2. Now, match each form (in the left column) with a content (from the right column), according to this 'English pronunciation code'. The first items in each column form a pair, as an illustration for you. (The others are *not* matched.)

Form		Content (example words from modern English)
A **ꝟ**	⟷	[f] sound as in '*f*un'
B **ſ**		[s] sound as in '*s*illy'
C **ꝗ**		[th] sound as in '*th*is'
D **tꝝ**		[y] sound as in '*y*ellow'
E **ꝩ**		
F **ꝑ**		

There is a good chance that you got A, C, D, and F right. The modern English pronunciation code should lead you to match A with [f], C with [s], D with [th] and F with [y]. But did you get B and E right? If you matched B with [f] and E with [y] you were making use of the modern version of the 'English pronunciation code'; if you matched B with [s] and E with [th] you were making use of the 1556 version of the 'English pronunciation code'.

3. The Morse code, which matches sequences of short and long (=forms) to letters (=contents), is a standard example of a code. Consider similarities and differences between the Morse code and the English pronunciation code, and try to answer the following questions.

(a) Are the two codes *learned* in the same way?
(b) Do the two codes *change* in the same way?

(c) Are the two codes *applied* (to translate form into content) in the same way?

Now rejoin text on page 144

Every person who abides by the conventions of English (=speaks the language) is likely to decide that sentences 2 and 3 refer to the lower of the two events, unlike sentence 1. We have a knowledge which enables us to decide this, which is one part of our general 'knowledge of English', and which we could name 'the sentence–event code' (this is a made-up name, not a standard technical term). Our knowledge of English will be made up of a number of codes. Specifically what it does is use information about the left–right ordering of words in order to associate the sentence with an event.

This decoding takes place in our head: we turn a form into a content. But what is the nature of that content? Is it a picture (as above), or some other non-linguistic representation of an event, or is it just a more detailed description *in language* of that event? We will explore the third possibility here – that is, that the decoding takes one piece of language and decodes it into another piece of language. For, example, instead of the diagram above we could use the one below, which takes the meaning of the sentence to be an **annotated** version of the sentence (annotating = underlining, writing underneath, etc.; generally adding information).

The sentence–event code (examples)

Form (sentences)	Content (sentences *annotated* to indicate an event)
1 The cat ate the fish. ←——————→	*The cat* ate *the fish.* ↑ ↑ actor object of action
2 The cat was eaten by the fish. ←——————→	*The cat* was eaten by *the fish.* ↑ ↑ object of action actor
3 The fish ate the cat. ←——————→	*The fish* ate *the cat.* ↑ ↑ actor object of action

---

The arrow which links form and content is two-way because content is turned into form by the speaker and back from form into content by the hearer.

Speaker	Sounds	Hearer
encodes and speaks		hears and decodes
content	→ form →	content

☞ *Now do Activity 74 on page 147*

We have now looked at one code which annotates a sentence, turning form into content. There are many others; we now give a further example.

Form	Content (partially explained)
Susan promised Mary to go.	Susan will go.
Susan persuaded Mary to go.	Mary will go.

Here, the subject of the second verb in the sentence, 'go', is missing, and we have to interpret who the subject of 'go' is; the code looks at the first verb and makes a decision on that basis. We could represent the code as annotating the sentence, as follows.

The subject-interpretation code (examples)

Form	Content
Susan promised Mary to go.	Susan promised Mary SUSAN to go.
Susan persuaded Mary to go.	Susan persuaded Mary MARY to go.

Finally, we suggest you try working out one further code for yourself.

☞ *Now do Activity 75 on page 147*

Activity 74   *Applying the sentence-event code*
(20 mins)

1. Now try out an application of the 'sentence–event code for yourself. Below are some sentences. Apply the code to them and so annotate them (the first one is done for you). Use these annotations: actor, object-of-action, receiver.

(a) M<u>ary</u> patted <u>the cat</u>.

     ↑   ↑

    actor   object-of-action

(b) It was <u>the cat</u> that patted <u>Mary</u>.

(c) <u>Mary</u> gave the <u>cat</u> to <u>Peter</u> yesterday.

(d) It was <u>Mary</u> who gave <u>the cat</u> to <u>Peter</u> yesterday.

(e) <u>Mary</u> gave <u>Peter</u> <u>the cat</u> yesterday.

2. Suggest how we might annotate 'yesterday':
....
3. Why do you think 'it' in (b) and (d) does not get underlined?

4. The three terms suggested as annotations will not be all you need if you are going to apply this code to all the sentences of English. Here are some more sentences; invent new annotations if you think they are necessary, to indicate the underlined phrases.

(f) <u>The wind</u> blew hard.

(g) <u>John</u> was happy.

Suggested answers are on p. 214.

 Now rejoin text on page 146

Activity 75   *Exploring a code*
(20 mins)

The sentences in the table below say very different things about John; in one case he is pleased, and in the other case he is the person who is doing the pleasing.
1. Work out a way of annotating the sentences so that the distinction is made clear, and write each annotated sentence under 'content'. If you think this is a code which we have not already discussed, make up a name for it, and write it at the top (if we have already discussed it, write the name already used).

'..code'

Form	Content
John is eager to please.	

Form	Content
John is easy to please.	

2. Can you think of any other English sentences which are like these?

Suggested answers are on p. 214.

 Now rejoin text

Forms of language which involve both a coded and a non-coded content

Some words and phrases are not fully interpretable by applying a code to them. The example of 'yesterday' which came up in Activity 74 is like this. The word 'yesterday' can be decoded as 'the day before today'. But in order to know which day 'today' is, we need to consult our general (non-conventional and non-coded) knowledge. The meaning of 'yesterday' is therefore partly coded and partly non-coded. Words like 'yesterday' are called **deictic** expressions; we saw an example of their use in Section 6.2.4. Deictic expressions refer to:

a time   e.g. 'yesterday', 'then', 'in half an hour'.
a place   e.g. 'here', 'five miles away', 'in the next
               street'.
a person/thing e.g. 'it', 'she', 'those men', 'I'.

We might want to argue that the use of 'the' is also deictic; when we say 'the elephants' we mean a particular, recognisable group of elephants – recognisable either because they have already been specified in the text which has gone before, or because they are taken to be readily identifiable in the situation or context in which we are referring to them (see above, Activity 70).

The non-coded part of the interpretation of deictic forms involves working out exactly *which* time, place, or person is being 'pointed to' (the word 'deixis' comes from the Greek word meaning 'pointing'). But the question arises: would it be possible to express the meaning of a specific deictic form in a given sentence as an annotation of the form? To try to reach a decision on this issue, we must first consider the coded parts of the meaning of deictics. If Mary Smith said, at 5 p.m. on 6 June 1989, in Presto Supermarket in Glasgow, the sentence, 'I will come back here tomorrow', the decoding of the deictics would be as in the following diagram:

Form₁   I will come back here tomorrow.

decode

Meaning₁ *I*   *will come back* *here*   *tomorrow*
          the speaker   to the place where on the day after the
                                          the sentence is said sentence is said

---

By combining meaning₁ with information about who the speaker is, and where and when the sentence is spoken, we can now interpret the sentence. We can represent this process as another form–meaning relation, this time taking the output of the first process (meaning₁) as the input (the form₂) of the second process (another example of the sequential *ordering* of different processes of matching forms and meaning). Thus:

Form₂   *I*   *will come back* *here*   tomorrow
         the speaker   to the place where on the day after the
                                         the sentence is said sentence is said

Interpretation   (add information about who the speaker is, when and where
                       the sentence is spoken)

Meaning₂ *I*   *will come back* *here*   *tomorrow.*
          Mary Smith   to Presto Supermarket on 7 June 1989

Notice here, though, that the information we add in this case is not part of the codes of the language. It is what we know *in general* (e.g. because we can see a clock, remember the date, know the speaker, and so on). These things are part of our general knowledge, not a code which we apply as part of our ability to use the English language. To interpret a deictic expression we need to combine our knowledge of a code (which tells us that 'here' refers to a place, for example) with our general knowledge of the world (which tells us which place 'here' refers to).

 Now do Activity 76 on page 149

To sum up what we have said in this section, one way of modelling how sentences are interpreted is by a process of taking a form and annotating, or 'rewriting', it to produce its different kinds of meaning. These meanings combine together to produce a composite, 'overall' meaning for the sentence. Sometimes the sentence is annotated by applying a code, sometimes by adding general knowledge. Sometimes (e.g. in the interpretation

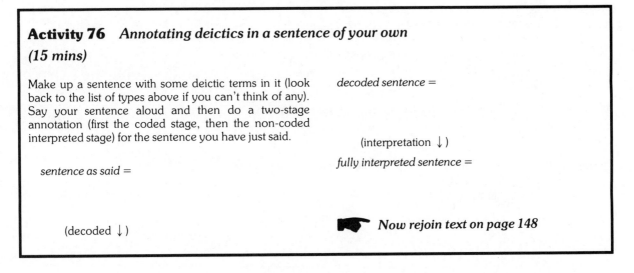

Activity 76 *Annotating deictics in a sentence of your own*
(15 mins)

Make up a sentence with some deictic terms in it (look back to the list of types above if you can't think of any). Say your sentence aloud and then do a two-stage annotation (first the coded stage, then the non-coded interpreted stage) for the sentence you have just said.

sentence as said =

(decoded ↓)

decoded sentence =

(interpretation ↓)
fully interpreted sentence =

☞ *Now rejoin text on page 148*

of deictic expressions) the code is applied first, to produce an annotated sentence which then becomes the input to another process. The operations which lead to the meaning of a sentence are sequential and cumulative. In the next section we look in more detail at the interpreted part of a sentence meaning.

7.3 How inferences create meanings

Not all meanings are coded into a sentence. In Section 7.1 we saw the example of someone saying something and meaning something else; we now look at that example in more detail. Imagine that you and Mary are both in a room. You are standing by a closed window. Mary says, 'It's hot in here.' Using the processes discussed in Section 7.2 you will be able to produce an annotated version of this sentence, probably something like this:

I₁   *It*   's hot in *here*.
     ↑   ↑
     the temperature   this room

But it is quite possible that the sentence is being used to mean more than this. Mary may intend you to understand not only the meaning conveyed by your annotated version I₁, but also that she wants you to open the window. Instead of being indirect and saying, 'It's hot in here', she might have said more directly, 'Please open the window'. If you think this is the case, you might decide that the meaning of the sentence is actually:

C₁ Mary would like me to open the window.

This meaning cannot be derived by a code from the sentence I₁. Sentence I₁ does not mention the window; and in any case it is in the form of a statement rather than a request. We cannot get from I₁ to C₁ simply by filling in information, as we do with deictics. So how *do* we get from the form to the meaning? Here is one way of doing it, by adding intermediate sentences, which take us by a sequence of thoughts to the conclusion.

I₁   It   's hot in here.
     the temperature   this room

C₂ Mary thinks it is hot in this room.
B₁ *If* Mary thinks it is hot in this room *then* she would like the room to be cooler.
C₃ Mary would like the room to be cooler.
B₂ *If* I opened the window *then* the room might be cooler.
C₁ Mary would like me to open the window.

We derived C₁ from I₁ as follows. First, from I₁ we derived the statement C₂ (this might be a coded process, as it looks as though it is predictable). We then introduced a hypothesis B₁. We combined the hypothesis B₁ with the statement C₂; and, by treating these two statements as two premises in a logical deduction, we derived C₃ as a conclusion. We then introduced another hypothesis, B₂. By combining it with C₃, we derived C₁ as a conclusion. The result is a model of how humans think (simplified to the extent that there may well be a greater number of intermediate, analogous steps). Our model treats thinking as a simple deductive process, with one of the basic principles being a logical rule called **modus ponens**.[2]

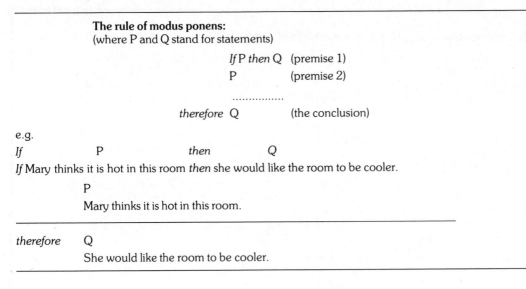

The rule of modus ponens:
(where P and Q stand for statements)

If P *then* Q   (premise 1)
P   (premise 2)

....

therefore Q   (the conclusion)

e.g.

| *If* | P | *then* | Q |

If Mary thinks it is hot in this room *then* she would like the room to be cooler.

P

Mary thinks it is hot in this room.

therefore   Q

She would like the room to be cooler.

The basic idea of the model presented here is that we combine an interpretation of what we read or hear with other ideas and beliefs that we already have, as well as with knowledge of what we can perceive around us at the time. What is significant about the model is that although there may be many individual steps, they are merely repeats of the same, single rule.

For the purposes of the system we are working out, our ideas, beliefs and so on are in many cases stated as hypotheses with the structure of implication, 'If . . . then. . . .' It is this structure which enables us to carry out the rule of modus ponens. The statements and hypotheses which we introduce in order to get from one statement to another statement are called assumptions, or **bridging inferences**. The term 'bridging inference' is used because combining them with what you read or hear creates 'bridges' between statements: to get across the apparent gap between statement I_1 and statement C_1 we have to use two 'bridges', B_1 and B_2.

Having outlined these basic features of our description, we should explain why we are labelling the sentences with different letters: **I**, **B** and **C**. A sentence labelled I is the input (i.e. an annotated version of what is read or heard); a sentence labelled B is a bridging inference; a sentence labelled C is a conclusion.

But notice something very important about our system. If we had introduced different bridging inferences we might have ended up with a concluding statement very different from C_1. For instance, we might instead have introduced bridging inferences B_3 and B_4 as below, which lead to 'meaning' C_4 instead of meaning C_1.

I_1 It   's hot in here.
        the temperature   this room

C_2 Mary thinks it is hot in this room.
B_3 It is not hot in the room
B_4 *If* Mary thinks it is hot in this room *and* it is not hot in the room *then* Mary is probably feverish.

C_4 Mary is probably feverish.

☞   *Now do Activity 77 on page 151*

The relationship between form and meaning in these interpretations of 'It's hot in here' is not a coded one. The meaning that is derived from the form depends on the particular bridging inferences you introduce; and this is likely to vary from person to person. The sequences illustrated above (as well as the one you worked out for yourself in the activity) can be called 'chains of inference'. In principle, they can always be extended; and in this respect they are unlike the decoding of a sentence or the assignment of reference to a deictic (which are processes which can in principle be completed). To demonstrate this potential endlessness of inferential chains, we now illustrate how easily a further bridging inference can be added to the conclusion of our first, 'completed' chain.

C_1 Mary would like me to open the window.
B_5 Mary knows that I am afraid of opening windows.
B_6 *If* Mary knows that I am afraid of opening windows *and* Mary wants me to open the window *then* Mary wants to make me afraid.
C_5 Mary wants to make me afraid.
B_7 *If* Mary wants to make me afraid *then* Mary must hate me.
C_6 Mary must hate me.

☞   *Now do Activity 78 on page 151*

Activity 77   *Being explicit about 'bridging inferences'*
(45 mins)

1. In this activity, you experiment with the simple model of inference we have just outlined. Starting from the same sentence I_1 and the first conclusion C_2, introduce different bridging inferences from the ones we have introduced above, to derive a different 'meaning'. Use the labelling system (B = bridging inference, C = conclusion) to identify the steps of your inferential route.

I_1 It   's hot in here.
   the temperature   this room

C_2 Mary thinks it is hot in this room.

can be managed by taking the social relationships to lead to using particular bridging inferences. Try working out a chain of inferences from the same sentence but this time including the bridging inference, 'Mary is a policewoman'; show how this bridging inference can help lead to a different conclusion.

I_1 It   's hot in here.
   the temperature   this room

C_2 Mary thinks it is hot in this room.

B_{10} Mary is a policewoman.

2. Different social relationships between people can lead to different conclusions being reached; in this model, this

 Now rejoin text on page 150

Activity 78   *Extending an inferential chain*
(15 mins)

Starting with the statement C_6, continue the chain of inference a few steps further, by introducing additional bridging inferences and deriving a new, 'concluding' statement by way of interpretation. You might begin with a bridging inference which starts as:

B_8 If Mary hates me then. . . .

Now rejoin text

Notice that what Mary intended to say doesn't necessarily matter: where non-coded relations are involved there is no automatic guarantee that the meanings which you 'get out of' a form were the same ones that were 'put into' the form.

In some cases, on the other hand, inferential paths become so firmly established that it is no longer clear whether the bridging inferences actually need to be introduced at all, or whether the 'indirect' expression has become a conventional idiom. For instance, to trace a route from 'Do you have a light' to the concluding meaning, 'I would like a light if you have one', you need to construct a short inferential chain (to confirm this, construct a route on a separate piece of paper). But the chain in question has arguably been repeated so often that the question has simply acquired the properties of a request. This was also the case for 'How are you?' in Activity 72. Here we seem to have an example of a non-coded form–meaning pair becoming (by extensive use) a coded form–meaning pair.

Superficially this account might also be true of the relationship between an apple (=the form) and 'sin/ temptation' (=the content). We said earlier that this seems to be partly coded (a conventional link between the two) while still allowing for individual interpretation. However, it is possible that public symbols of this kind do not arise by 'fossilisation' of a non-coded relation. Rather, they may be created deliberately as form–meaning pairs which express public meanings (in this case the symbol is part of an attempt to hold a society together morally and religiously) while at the same time allowing for individual meanings. This combination of the public and the individual is characteristic of many forms of symbolism (e.g. religious symbolism).[3]

Chains of inference can in principle go on for ever, producing more and more meanings. Mary's one sentence might mean any number of different things, according to the range of the bridging inferences which are introduced. If we want our model to be a realistic model of how people think, we must therefore somehow account for the fact that in practice chains of inference do not go on for ever: they are generally curtailed at some (usually fairly early) point. We will consider this further in the next section. We also consider why inferences ever need to be made at all. Wouldn't it have been simpler for everyone if Mary had said what she meant more directly in the first place?

7.4 How the brain enables us to interpret

In Sections 7.2 and 7.3 we presented a way of describing how certain aspects of the meaning of a sentence can be made explicit. This involved describing a number of codes which **annotate** sentences. We showed how information partly drawn from the sentence itself and partly drawn from what the hearer knows is added as a set of implications to the coded meanings in acts of inference. In this section we discuss how close our description might be to the actual processes by which understanding is performed in a person's brain. To do this, we attempt to present a realistic model of how people's brains work in such a way as to enable them to understand language.

Physically, a human brain is made up of above a hundred billion cells, called neurons, each neuron being connected with hundreds of other neurons. A brain is working when there is a flow of electrical charges called nerve impulses across its nets of neurons. We can think of thoughts as being 'written' on the brain in the form of patterns of these electrical charges. It may seem strange to say that thoughts are expressed physically in the brain as patterns of electrical charges, but this is really no stranger than saying that thoughts are expressed physically on a page as patterns of ink or in air as patterns of sound waves. Very many different kinds of information are 'carried' by ink (e.g. calculations, statements, drawings, etc.), or by sound waves (e.g. language, music, noises), so there seems no reason in principle to think that for thoughts to be 'written' as patterns of nerve impulses necessarily *limits* the range of different kinds of information that can be stored or processed.

What we are interested in here is how information is taken into the brain (e.g. how marks on a page are understood as sentences), and how information is passed around in the brain, combining old and new information in acts of thinking. We begin by making a distinction (drawn from the work of the philosopher Jerry Fodor[4]) between the **input systems** and the **central system**. The central system is where things are remembered, and where thought happens. It is here that the kind of processes described in Section 7.3 take place. The input systems have basically a translating function, acting as 'mediators' between the outside world and the realm of thought, and translating the world into a form in which it can be thought and remembered.

One input system which is clearly relevant is the visual system. This consists of the eyes, as well as the 'primary visual cortex' at the back of the brain, and other anatomically identifiable areas of the brain. This input system takes sensory perceptions and 'translates' them into the kinds of image or representation that can be processed by the central system. Another relevant input system is the language-processing system. This takes information which has been processed by the visual system or auditory system (for speech) and shapes it into meaningful sentences. At present this system is less well understood than the visual system, and is less easy to identify anatomically, since there are no separate physical 'organs' of language in the obvious way that the eyes are 'organs' of vision (although it has been clear for over a hundred years that language-processing makes use of at least two specific areas on the left side of the brain, an idea which can be confirmed by analysing the damage to the language-processing abilities which results from damage to these specific areas). What the language-processing system actually does remains controversial. But one hypothesis is that it works rather like the system we described in Section 7.2, consisting of a collection of decoding devices which produce as an end result an annotated sentence (i.e. a thought). Combined together, the visual input system and the language-processing input system translate marks on a page into a thought which can be picked up by the central system. In this form it can be stored and remembered; and the many and various effects of that thought on other thoughts can be worked out, possibly by a logical combination/deduction system like the one described in Section 7.3.

When people read a text, their eyes pause, then move suddenly, then pause (and so on). When the eyes stop they take in about three short words (in normal typeface). The eyes may move backwards and forwards in the text, suggesting that readers unconsciously look back to double-check their understanding of what went before. A fluent reader may recognise the marks on the page as complete words (without having to spell or sound out the individual letters), partly because one of the elements of fluent reading is that expectations are set up regarding what will come next, and those expectations determine to some extent which words are 'seen'. For this reason, mis-spelled words may not be recognised as such, and completely unexpected or unknown words may be incorrectly read as some more expected word. The practice of looking ahead, in which the input system translates and decodes not only according to what it 'sees' but also according to what it expects to see, seems to be characteristic of the language-processor in general. While some of these expectations are part of the code (e.g. only some word sequences are permitted by the code), others probably come from the central system. For example, in a sentence like,

The nurse showed the doctor the patent,

the language-processor in your brain is likely to have developed a higher expectation of the sentence ending with the word 'patient' than the word 'patent', and may as a consequence misread the last word. Expectations in the language-processor arise from general knowledge stored in the central system which associates the word 'nurse' (and 'doctor') with the word 'patient'. This suggests that while a sentence may be decoded by the language-processor in the brain along lines similar to those described in Section 7.2, the 'thinking' stage which comes next (as in Section 7.3) helps to guide what the language-processing stage will end up with. This is clearly true of some of the processes we discussed in Section 7.2. We saw, for example, how the assignment of reference to deictic expressions relies on general non-linguistic knowledge (i.e. knowledge which is stored in the central system, not in the specialised language-processor).

Ambiguity

In Chapter 6, we saw how a written sentence can be structurally ambiguous. In the framework we have now developed, we can put this another way, by saying that it might be annotated in two quite different ways. For example:

Visiting relatives can be boring.

Part of this sentence might be annotated by the processor (in working out what the sentence means) as:

Visiting relatives   can be boring.
         ↑
              object of action (i.e. the people who are visited)

or as

Visiting relatives   can be boring.
   ↑
       actors (i.e. the people who visit)

There are two possibilities as regards how the processor works. It might produce both annotations, and present them to the central system which would then decide which was the appropriate one. Or it might decide to produce one annotation rather than the other. It seems that the processor actually works in the second way: that is, the processor itself resolves the ambiguity.

Apparently not all ambiguous words are treated in the same way, however. In addition to a sentence-processing system, there must also be a system which associates words as they come in with words the hearer knows (i.e. words listed in some kind of mental dictionary). These 'word-finding' mechanisms match a word form with its meaning. Unlike the sentence-processor, however, the word-finding mechanisms do not appear to resolve ambiguities; rather, they present to the language-processor all the meanings associated with a word form, suggesting both that ambiguities arise and are resolved in different ways, and that this is likely to be linked to specific cognitive processes.[5]

Input systems appear to operate inside our heads without our being aware of them. We do not have any access to them through conscious thought, and we are not able to control them. The operations of the language processor, for example, are hidden away from us.

☞ *Now do Activity 79 on page 154*

What does this mean for reading? One interpretation would be that our reading of a text is outside our control: an automatic process which takes place as a kind of reflex action in the brain when it is exposed to written English. But such an interpretation would be inappropriate. This is because, in addition to the language-processor and other input systems, we also have the central system. The

Activity 79   *Trying to interfere with what you hear*

(1 min)

To test out the independence of your language-processor from your conscious control, try the following activity. Get someone to say a sentence in English to you and try (by an act of thought alone) to *hear* – not imagine but actually hear – them saying *something completely differ-* *ent.* If you succeed, you are in effect interfering with the decoding processes carried out by the language processor.

☞ *Now rejoin text on page 153*

operations of this central system *are* accessible to and controllable by consciousness (though probably not completely so, as we will see when we consider other kinds of mental process, including psychical processes). If this were not the case, the fundamental problem in literary studies of **why different people produce different interpretations of a text** could not exist. And since it seems that the questions most relevant to literary studies are likely to have answers related more to the central system than to the input systems, we now consider the central system more directly.

In Section 7.3 we saw how new thoughts can be created by combining an input thought (an annotated sentence processed by the language-processor) with thoughts which are already stored. As a model of how thinking takes place in the brain, this suggests that thinking is structured by logical procedures (such as modus ponens), and that **thoughts, memories, beliefs, desires, etc. are held and moved about in the brain as sentences** ('written' in nerve impulse patterns). This is a particular hypothesis about how thinking works, with which many people who work on these issues would not agree. But because it is an explicit model we will use it as a basis for thinking about some of the fundamental issues relevant to literary studies.

There is reason to think that the central system is divided into two separate sub-systems. In one sub-system – a sort of mental scratch pad – active thinking takes place. In the other, much larger sub-system, thoughts are stored (i.e. this second sub-system is our long-term memory, where practically everything we know is kept). The active-thinking sub-system is where the deductions (as described in Section 7.3) are carried out. Sentences which have just been read are sent to this sub-system by the language-processor, and sentences from memory are 'accessed' out of the memory sub-system into this thinking sub-system. We could draw an analogy with a library: the shelves where the books are stored form one sub-system (memory, with books being like sentences stored in memory), and the desk where you consult individual books forms the other sub-system (active-thinking subsystem). The active-thinking sub-system may

be the only part of our brain which is routinely 'observed' by consciousness: when we remember something, we call up a memory into the thinking sub-system and so present it to consciousness.

The memory stores thought representations in the form of clusters or 'chunks' of sentences (with the result that memory is often compared to an encyclopaedia: both are made up of a collection of thoroughly cross-referenced entries). One name for the 'chunks' is **frames**, suggesting that they are made up of interconnected networks of information. In other cases, memory seems to involve stereotypical patterns or 'templates' of sequences of events or actions. One name for these is **scripts**. A typical memory 'chunk' might consist of a collection of sentences which describe stereotypical information about hospitals, the weather, or a particular experience. It also seems likely that some chunks are more accessible than others. Some kinds of information can be brought out of memory and into the thinking system more easily than other kinds. Moreover, the accessibility of different chunks can be altered, depending, for example, on what the person has recently been doing or thinking about.[6]

We can now try to answer one of the questions asked at the end of Section 7.3. Why don't people always speak and write literally? (After all, if we used only the coded aspects of language, communication would be quicker because it would never require bridging inferences.) There are several possible answers to this question. First, while time would be saved because bridging inferences would not be needed, it would often take much more time to say or listen to completely coded texts. Compare, for example, sentence (1), which requires inferencing, with sentence (2), which requires less inferencing; what (2) gains in literalness is lost by the length of the sentence.

(1) I will come back here tomorrow.
(2) Mary Smith will come back to Presto Supermarket on 7 July 1989.

The second reason for not always being literal is that it is not always relevant to be literal. If I ask you the time, you may say 'two-thirty' instead of the literally true 'two-thirty-two and twenty-nine seconds p.m.'. By being able to take what I hear or read non-literally I can save time and effort. A third reason is also important for us, given our interest in literary texts, which are typically very non-literal and so require a great deal of inferencing. Because the activity of inferencing involves bringing into consciousness other meanings, and involves the creation of (in principle an infinite number of) new meanings, it may be that non-literal texts are capable of being *much more meaningful* than literal texts. A fourth reason is also important for literary study. When we draw inferences by bringing up bridging assumptions from memory, it is possible that we pull up other related memories at the same time (because we access memory in chunks rather than individual sentences); this is perhaps what **evocation** is – the re-moulding of memory on the edges of consciousness. It may be that we gain **pleasure** from interpreting non-literal texts.

Now we can turn to two fundamental questions we raised earlier. First, what makes people *start* accessing memories, and processing the input they receive from speech and writing? And once they start processing, what makes them *stop*? After all, we suggested in Section 7.3 that in principle the adding of new bridging inferences to get new conclusions could go on for ever: we could probably derive an infinite number of sentences from any single sentence. Yet in practice this is clearly not what happens. We rarely search for more and more implications of a sentence, despite the logical possibility of this happening. (The occasions when we do, as in the intensive reading of literary texts, especially poetry, contrast with the usual speed and casualness with which we read and hear.) It has been argued by Deirdre Wilson and Dan Sperber (see note 2, page 216) that our mental behaviour follows from an **economy of processing**. Their account is roughly this:

Thinking as physical action:

Thinking is constrained by having to take place in the brain, with an expense of effort. In order to produce new sentences by adding bridging inferences, the brain must expend energy in extracting the bridging inferences from memory. It may be that the brain expends this effort only if the consequences of carrying out the effort are worthwhile. Processing begins as a way of seeking out **relevance** to the person processing, and it stops when further processing no longer increases the relevance of the input. An input may be relevant because it makes sense, provides useful information, is funny (or pleasurable in some other way), etc., but often decoded texts need to have bridging inferences added to them in order to make them relevant. The mental effort required for a thought process (such as a particular deduction) must be balanced by the usefulness or interest of the results of that thought process to the person carrying it out. Clearly there is a practical problem: how can mental effort (measured presumably

in energy expended) be compared with usefulness of a thought (how would this be measured?). In summary, the idea that how relevant a thought is depends in part on the effort involved in getting at it means that **thinking is constrained as a result of being a physical action**.

The notion of relevance we have outlined appears a suggestive generalisation when related to the kinds of inferential process we have described above. It gives us, for example, a way of explaining why some memories should be more easily remembered than others: we can say that they require less mental effort to get them into the thinking space. If this is the case, then in any particular interpretive act, some memories (bits of knowledge) will be more likely to be used as bridging inferences than others, because they require less effort. This would explain why a reader's interpretation of a text is particularly likely to be guided by what has gone on previously in the text. It would also suggest that when people write or speak they foresee (perhaps unconsciously) the expectations which readers and hearers will bring to their text; they would have to do this in order to make sure that their readers will be led by the need to gain relevance to the meanings and other effects which the writer intends.

Now do Activity 80 on page 156

Exploiting this idea that inferencing is governed by relevance, Sperber and Wilson introduce the **Principle of Relevance**, which states that *every* utterance carries a (tacit) guarantee of relevance: a guarantee that what has been said is relevant enough to be worth the hearer paying attention to it. The relevance of the utterance would come from its having adequate effects for the hearer without requiring unnecessary effort. What the hearer has to do for any utterance is to find an interpretation which is relevant enough (or which the speaker might have thought would be so). In this way, the Principle of Relevance directs the hearer to seek out intended meanings.

7.5 Brain, body and symbols

So far, we have discussed only meanings which appear to be intended or in some way foreseen. Both codes and inferential work relate to thoughts or representations which you seek to recover on the presumption that the text guarantees some degree of relevance by virtue of its signalled intention to communicate. But not all meanings are necessarily like this. In some cases, the meanings which are derivable from sentences may be *unintended*. Very often, as we have seen, this is because of differences of context and background knowledge between you and the author of the text. But in some cases, the unintended meanings are the result of processes of different kinds, which we now explore.

Activity 80   *Testing the idea of relevance*
(60 mins)

The following is the first sentence from Angela Carter's novel *The Magic Toyshop* (1967).

The summer she was fifteen, Melanie discovered she was made of flesh and blood.

1. Here are some (probably partial) interpretations of this sentence, which have been arrived at by applying different bridging inferences to it. Add one of your own, as (d), if you think the sentence has a significantly different meaning than any of those given in (a) to (c).

(a) Before she was fifteen Melanie thought she was made of something other than flesh and blood.
(b) Before she was fifteen Melanie never thought about what she was made of.
(c) When she was fifteen Melanie discovered her sexuality.

(d)

2. Choose the interpretation from the list which comes closest to what you think the sentence means. Label this 'Interpretation-Y', by writing the letter Y beside it. Now pick any one of the other interpretations and label this 'Interpretation-N' by writing the letter N beside it.
3. Using the procedures you followed in Activities 77 and 78, construct a sequence of bridging inferences which lead from the given sentence to Interpretation-Y. Be as specific and detailed as you can (you may need to do this on a separate sheet of paper).

4. Now construct a sequence of bridging inferences which lead from the given sentence to Interpretation-N

5. In 2, you chose a particular interpretation for the sentence, which you labelled Y. Consider the possibility that either or both of the following considerations led you to that interpretation, rather than to any of the others.

'It's most likely I was led to the particular sentence I labelled Y . . .

(a) '. . . because the inferential route from the given sentence to Y is shorter than the route to N (and so requires less energy).'

Is your list of bridging inferences for Y shorter than that for N: YES/NO

(b) '. . . because Y is more relevant to me (i.e. it yields more contextual effects, or assumptions which have consequences in the context in which I am processing them).'

Is Y more relevant than N in this sense?   YES/NO

6. Try to describe some of the contextual effects of Y (eg. perhaps (c) connects with some of the assumptions you hold about what the first sentence of a novel is likely to do, such as establishing a theme).

7. Try to describe some of the contextual effects of N:

8. Now consider how you might go on to process the next sentence in the novel:

> O, my America, my new found land.

Is the way in which you process this second sentence affected by the inferential processes you described in 3, and the contextual effects you described in 6? If so, try to describe how.

9. Now consider some more theoretical possibilities which arise in relation to your decisions in 5.

(a) If you decided that N was *shorter and more relevant* than Y, this would appear to disconfirm the idea of an economy of processing, which we outlined on p. 155.

(b) If you decided that N was *longer and more relevant* than Y, then the prediction would be that the amount of extra relevance is not worth the amount of extra work in processing.

(c) If you decided that Y was *longer and more relevant* than N, then the prediction would be that the amount of extra relevance <u>is</u> worth the amount of extra work in processing.

Notice, however, that (b) and (c) involve the idea of an 'amount' of relevance and an 'amount' of work, which are balanced against each other in the economy of processing. Make a note here of any problems that arise in trying to determine how such 'balancing' might take place.

10. Finally, what difficulties does this activity expose in our outline of procedures for working through a 'relevance' account of interpretation? What would be needed to make such an account more explicit or more satisfactory?

Now rejoin text on page 155

7.5.1 ERRORS

To begin, consider this quotation attributed to the Reverend William Spooner, Dean of New College, Oxford (1844–1930).

I_1: You have hissed all my mystery lectures.

Reverend Spooner was a teacher of history, among other things; and it is likely that what he intended was the sentence:

C_1: You have missed all my history lectures.

To recover this probably intended sentence as a conclusion from the input, you transpose the [h] and [m] segments at the beginning of the words 'missed' and 'history'. Spooner was noted for making such sound transpositions, and the term **spoonerism** is given to this common kind of slip of the tongue. The process by which you get from I_1 to C_1 is the kind of inferential process described in Section 7.3; however, it differs somewhat in that the move from I_1 to C_1 is motivated by a similarity between parts of the two sentences, specifically, a similarity in sound. Inferential processes which are motivated by similarity in this way can be described by the following diagram.

Actual text: ...*hissed – mystery*.........................

Interpreted text: ...*missed – history*..........................

Kind of similarity between actual and interpreted: *first letters inverted*

Details of the similarity: ...*h is changed to m and m is changed to h*..

The kind of similarity is 'exchange of sounds'; the kind of similarity marks this out as a spoonerism. Notice that in order to 'get' the sentence as a spoonerism, you have to bear in mind both the actual and the interpreted texts, simultaneously.

But on what basis do you recover the meaning C_1? One way of accounting for the way sentences of this type are interpreted is to say that the error itself has nothing to do with the 'meaning' at all. All that happens is that in producing the sentence, those parts of the speaker's language-processor responsible for ordering segments (here, phones) have made an 'error' (not surprising, given the number of operations required to make even the simplest sentence). When you read or hear a sentence of this type, you maximise its relevance by processing it along with assumptions that sentences can include errors, that the transposed sounds are likely to be an error, and that the sentence will make better sense if you ignore the error it contains altogether. But this is not the only possibility. You could say, for example, that one part of the meaning derivable from the sentence is:

C_2: You have expressed dislike for my lectures because of their lack of clarity.

Is this part of the meaning of the sentence? If so, by what processes do such meanings get produced and read?

To explore these questions, consider another example, a speech by Mrs Malaprop in Sheridan's play *The Rivals* (Act I, scene ii).

I_2 But mind Lucy – if you betray what you are intrusted with – (unless it be other people's secrets to me) you forfeit my malevolence for ever: and your being a simpleton shall be no excuse for your locality.

In this example, slips also appear to have been made. It is generally 'benevolence' rather than 'malevolence' which is publicly acknowledged to its recipient and which can be forfeited; and it is 'loquacity' (the tendency to talk too much), rather than 'locality', which fits in with the prevailing topic. We would derive:

C_3: But mind Lucy – if ever you betray what you are intrusted with – (unless it be other people's secrets to me) you forfeit my benevolence for ever: and your

being a simpleton shall be no excuse for your loquacity.

The kind of error illustrated here is called a **malapropism** (named after the character in the play who makes them). The same kind of diagram as above can be used to describe malapropisms, which are based on a different *kind* of similarity from the spoonerism. Fill it in.

Actual text: ....malevolence....locality...................

Interpreted text: ....

Kind of similarity between actual and interpreted: ....

....

Details of the similarity: ....

....

We would derive C_3 if we simply carry out the process of compensating for unintended 'errors' as above. But, you might say, this is not the only meaning of the sentence. Another part of that meaning is:

C_4: Mrs Malaprop tries to use long words, but gets them wrong, and so reveals her pretentiousness and ignorance.

It is not difficult for us to account for this meaning using the framework we have developed. We construct an inferential chain which takes recognition of the error as its starting point, and includes at least the following bridging assumptions.

B_1 The words in question are unlikely to be known very well.

B_2 Errors are likely if you try to use words that you don't know very well.

B_3 Choosing to use words you don't know very well can be a sign of pretentiousness, etc.

But this might not satisfy you. You could insist that there is a further aspect of the meaning which has still not been accounted for.

C_5: Mrs Malaprop is really malevolent, not benevolent.

If you derive this meaning, you are claiming that malapropisms can create a kind of meaning that we haven't accounted for at all. Such meanings arise because the particular words selected by mistake reveal unintended, hidden thoughts. If this is so, we need to consider how such meanings can come about, and why.

☞ *Now do Activity 81 on page 159*

How can the apparently random 'machine errors' be connected with the expression of unintended meanings? To consider this question, we need to think again about

Activity 81   *Comparing intended and unintended words*
(40 mins)

In the following malapropisms we have italicised the actual text and bracketed an interpreted text which was probably intended. Make a list of similarities between the words used and the target (intended) words in each case; use your work from Chapter 6 to guide you in picking out properties which the words have in common (pay particular attention to number of syllables, repetition of phones, and stress patterns).

(a) 'Is this place of abomination consecrated ground?'
    'I don't know nothink of *consequential* ground,' says Jo, still staring.

                    [consecrated]

similarities

(b) As cruel as an *allegory* on the banks of the Nile.
                    [alligator]

similarities

(c) *Naughty-story* car-park.
    [multi-storey]

similarities

(d) *Mussolini* pudding.
    [semolina]

similarities

 Now rejoin text on page 158

how language relates to the body and to the forces which stimulate and regulate language use.

The coded aspects of language appear to be independent of the conscious person who uses them; the operations of the decoder in your brain are as far outside your conscious control as the operation of your liver is. The inferential work you do, however, connects language to an economy of the body (a tendency to conserve energy weighed against a concern to maximise relevance). We now consider the possibility that other areas of language performance and processing relate to a bodily economy of energy, too.

When we acquire our first language, we are not fully formed beings learning a system: we *grow into* that system. Acquiring language is not just a matter of developing a system for representing and expressing meanings which are already in existence: as we learn to define ourselves and things around us with it, language also defines us. Entering culture by learning to use the distinctions of a language which exists before you are born is part of a broader process of developing systems of **symbolisation**.

For human beings as opposed to other animals, forms of symbolisation appear to have a special significance. And it is possible that this special role of symbolisation can tell us something about how meanings other than those we intend arise. Two connected evolutionary facts give symbolisation its special significance to us. First, we have developed a higher processing power than our evolutionary ancestors by evolving a biologically bigger brain. Second, human infants have the longest period of (and greatest) dependence on a parent among all animal species. What connects these two facts is that the evolutionary enlargement of the brain in humans seems to have been accomplished only at the cost of being born with a soft skull. In the early stages of this evolutionary development, the large hard skull associated with an evolutionarily growing brain resulted in very high infant mortality among Neanderthal pre-humans. Large soft skulls increased the percentage of successful births, and so soft skulls became the norm. The soft skull was made possible, in evolutionary terms, by a tendency towards earlier, 'premature' birth. But one result of such 'prematurity' is the exceptionally long period of dependence and learning in humans. Our capability for action and self-protection, and our awareness of self and external world, are acquired through a process of learning which involves interaction with a parent or parents, simple acts of simulation and experimentation, and 'modelled' representations of events and states. Collectively, these processes are usually called **play**, and it is through them that 'symbolisation' develops.

7.5.2 SYMBOLS AND SYMBOLISATION

But what exactly are the 'symbols' which are involved in 'symbolisation'? Do they operate in the same way for everyone? And what connection is there between symbolisation in infancy and unintended meanings in texts?

Symbolisation is the process by which formative or defining experiences are connected with ways of representing them. One way of thinking about symbols is to claim that symbolic forms are connected with meanings in a 'code' relationship. If this is so, it should be possible to develop a dictionary of such symbols (including cross-cultural **archetypes**), listing their meanings as in a dictionary of words; whenever you see the symbol you should be able to read off the meaning by using the code to annotate the form. Complex versions of this idea of symbolisation can be found in the work of the psychoanalysts Carl Jung, Wilhelm Stekel, and others. But there is a second possibility, which we develop here. This is that symbols acquire their meanings as part of a larger system which is formed out of unique experiences you undergo as an individual. Your formative experiences take advantage of surrounding symbolising forms, which subsequently retain a special charge (or **cathexis**) connecting them with the experience. If this is so, symbolisation is not a code at all in the sense in which we have used the term above: the relation of form and meaning will not be predictable or generally shared (though you might expect some degree of overlap between symbolic values or meanings, especially for terms like 'mother', 'father', and parts of the body, because of patterns of family bonding and the connection between identifying yourself as a person and exploring your existence as a sexed being). Complex versions of this view can be found in the work of Freud, Lacan, and others – though Freud did produce rough lists of symbols of the 'dictionary' type as well.

The psychoanalytic study of **fetishism** provides an illustration of this way of thinking about symbols. The fetishist notices an incidental object at a moment of decisive sexual experience or trauma (e.g. the moment of discovering that there is more than one sex). From then on, that incidental object – which in itself has no role in the experience – becomes a precondition of sexual pleasures premised on the original experience. For the fetishist, the object acquires a symbolic 'meaning': the fetish object stands in place of an 'underlying' meaning which it replaces. In this way, fetishism shows a possible connection between symbol and meaning by way of a non-coded relation that can only be discovered by searching back for the link between symbol and meaning in the individual life history of the fetishist. It would be no good looking up the fetish *object* in a dictionary of symbols.

Fetishes work with objects. But the process of symbolisation of which they are characteristic may also happen with words. The words which are used in infant play and other formative experiences may also acquire cathexes alongside their other dimensions of meaningfulness. In this respect, many more words than those we generally recognise as being metaphorical or figurative might stand (like fetish objects) for meanings other than their own. However, if we are to consider this possibility seriously we need to examine more closely how language works to represent meanings other than those which are immediately and literally evident.

7.5.3 METAPHOR

So far, we have seen how spoonerisms involve one *sound* standing for another. You can recover the displaced sound easily, because it has simply been transposed elsewhere in the sentence. We have also seen how malapropisms involve one *word* standing in place of another. You can recover the displaced word easily, because of similarities in form, rather than in meaning, between the two. Like a malapropism, a metaphor also involves one word standing in place of another. But while in malapropisms the actual and the intended word are similar in form, in a metaphor the actual and the intended word are similar in meaning.

Consider the following lines from Swinburne's 'Before a Crucifix'.

I_1 Change in a trice
     The lilies and languors of virtue
     For the raptures and roses of vice.

The decoding processes will (among other things) derive from these lines two statements (which are in some sense annotations of the lines).

I_2 Virtue has (or is made of) lilies and languors.
I_3 Vice has (or is made of) raptures and roses.

But what do Swinburne's lines mean, even in these decoded forms? To investigate this, consider the line describing 'virtue' (I_2). This line is not literally true; there are nevertheless various ways of making sense of it. We might, for example, assume that it is a lie, and then go on to investigate why Swinburne might be trying to fool us. If I_1 was produced by a teacher in a class on botany, this particular route might be an appropriate one to follow. However, in poetry we are more likely to interpret a line which is not literally true as true at some other level, so we might assume that the line is metaphorical. To interpret a metaphor you attempt to replace the problem words with words which enable the sentence to make sense and be true; the convention called 'metaphorical interpretation' says that the replacing words must be associated in meaning with the replaced words. We might, for example, interpret, and fill in the diagram as follows.

Actual text (VEHICLE): ....lilies and languors ....

Interpreted text: ....beauty and tranquillity ...

Kind of similarity between actual and interpreted:.....similar in meaning...

Details of the similarity (GROUND):......lilies are beautiful, and someone who is languid is also tranquil (hence languors = tranquillity) ....

We have added to the diagram the terms vehicle and ground, which are often used for the actual text and the details of the similarity in a metaphor. A third term, **tenor**, refers to 'the thing under discussion'; in this line it is 'virtue'.

Metaphors differ from spoonerisms and malapropisms because it is often not obvious exactly what the interpreted text is; several possibilities might be called to mind in the process of interpreting a metaphor (and it is this complexity and quantity of ideas called up which may make metaphors pleasurable). For example, if we were to look at a range of words associated with lilies and languors we might find the following.

lily	*languor*
perennial plant of genus Lilium	laziness
plant with scaly bulb and typically	dreamy relax-
pendulous flowers	ation
coloured flower	oppressive still-
attractive, gentle plant	ness
image of natural purity	tranquillity
image of beauty	etc.
etc.	

Why didn't we replace 'lilies' with 'plant with scaly bulb . . .'? The reason is that the sentence would be slightly nonsensical under this interpretation. The choice of an association for 'lily' is guided by associations of the tenor, such as:

virtue – virtue is good – other things which are good are: beauty, ...

And so the choice for 'lily' of 'beauty' is guided in this way. The metaphor is interpreted by finding compatibilities between the associations of the actual words in the text in order to find the 'hidden' words. However, because the associations of words are at least partly non-coded, and derived by idiosyncratic bridging inferences, it is possible to interpret a metaphor in different ways.

☞ *Now do Activity 82 on page 162*

In principle you can account for all metaphors in the way we have just accounted for the lines from Swinburne. But given our discussion in earlier sections of this chapter, two problems arise.

Problem 1
    The list of word meanings we produced for 'lilies' included a range of associations, connotations and conventional symbolism, in addition to those properties which would determine the particular sorts of flower that are called 'lilies'. As a result, the 'ground' of comparison you make in analysing a metaphor involving 'lilies' is very open-ended indeed. If we include associations and connotations as parts of the meanings of words in analysing metaphors, we are introducing a large, individual

---

Activity 82   *Analysing a metaphor*
(30 mins)

1. Analyse the metaphor in 'raptures and roses of vice', by drawing a diagram as on p. 161, and filling in the parts. In order to reach your interpretation, make a list of associations for the vehicle(s) and for the tenor, and draw on compatibilities between these.

2. To what extent is the interpretation of each metaphor influenced by the interpretation of the other in these lines (i.e. how does *context* help in interpretation)?

☞ *Now rejoin text on page 161*

---

dimension to metaphoric interpretation: can a metaphor, therefore, mean anything to anyone?

Problem 2

Our procedure for interpreting a metaphor doesn't explain the process in anything like psychologically realistic terms. To do this, we would have to specify: (i) how you decide that greater relevance is created by processing the phrase further than an annotated, 'literal' form; (ii) how you add bridging inferences which work through possible resemblances until you reach an interpretation. Such an account could clearly be constructed on the lines we describe in Section 7.3, and it would begin to explain why interpreting a metaphor is not in all cases a simple and decisive process, but an open-ended and individual one which runs beyond shared meanings.

But even if we construct a psychologically plausible model of interpreting our 'lilies' metaphor, we still have difficulties. Is it only inferential activity which produces connections as the ground of the metaphor, or can what we have called 'symbolic' activity do the same thing? Given that the ground need not be a single likeness or similarity, the relationship of tenor and vehicle might be **overdetermined**. By overdetermined, what is meant is that a number of different connections or 'meanings' converge on the same one form.[7] It is versions of the idea of overdetermination in metaphor, for instance, which literary critics use to explain how poetic images can be almost infinitely rich in meanings and associations: how metaphors can be richer than literal expression.

Overdetermination would exist in the 'lilies' metaphor if a number of different sorts of resemblance or connection between 'lilies' and 'virtue' converged in a single reading. 'Lilies' might not only have properties of peacefulness and tranquillity, as suggested above, but might also suggest other things by alluding to the Bible, as we saw in Chapter 4 ('consider the lilies; they work not, neither do they spin'); there might be similarities and associations to do with a lily's shape, colour, or texture, or by virtue of recollections of experiences of the reader in which lilies have played some part, or by virtue of cathexes involving 'lilies' of which the reader has no

recollection. Many of the connections are unlikely to be accessible to conscious attention, and will only operate 'subliminally'.

But to distinguish resemblances which are simply possible in principle from those which are actually activated, we need to know what *drives* our interpretations of metaphor. We have already suggested that the Principle of Relevance, guided by a commitment of energy which sustains processing until the rewards are too paltry to make further inferential activity worthwhile, is responsible for much of the process. But it is possible that there is another economic principle also involved: a drive (or compulsion) towards enabling submerged thoughts to return: a drive called (in psychoanalysis) **desire**. Psychoanalytic work suggests that thoughts to do with the formation of sexed identity are **repressed** to preserve the apparent selfhood and identity which those formative experiences make possible. But the force of desire seeks the return of those repressed thoughts in a **parapraxis** (i.e. as a slip, misreading, pun, etc.).

How could this happen? Psychoanalytic answers to this question suggest that the drive towards the return of repressed thoughts exploits similarities in the forms as well as in the meanings of words. Where forms overlap, combine, resemble one another, etc., unintended meanings escape. If this is the case, some instances of spoonerisms may be transpositions of sounds which expose, in the new words produced by the error, meanings that have been suppressed; and some malapropisms may be 'Freudian slips': mistakes in word selection which create apparently unintended meanings (which 'tell the truth' about the speaker) conveyed by the words they mistakenly introduce.

This might explain how repressed material returns when you speak or write. But if desire is constantly seeking outlets for repressed material, by exploiting linguistic forms, we would also expect repressed material to surface in acts of reading. It is possible that desire is *constantly* at work as we read, especially in the network of connections and associations we employ to process figurative levels of discourse. The search for resemblances to carry out metaphoric interpretation is always mixed with a **metonymic** dimension. Whereas metaphor is a **trope**, or transference of meaning, based on 'resemblance' between the actual words and the interpreted words (i.e. the ground should be one of similarity), metonymy describes transferences of meaning which call on almost any associative relation between actual words and interpreted words (cause for effect, part for whole, one thing associated with another, etc.). An example is calling a king 'the crown' (because a king wears a crown). Because any two things can be 'next to' each other, anything can in principle stand as a metonym for something else. In this way, the operation of metonymy overruns even the weak formal constraint imposed on metaphor (in a metaphor 'resemblance' is needed), and enables thoughts to be driven by desire into the working memory, where they can be expressed or used as the tools of thought.[8]

    Now do Activity 83

7.6 Some relevant questions about interpretation

In the last two sections, we have looked in some detail at processes through which different kinds of meanings are created. In particular, we have examined how meanings are produced by operations of the brain regulated in turn by an economy of the body governing the expenditure of energy. We conclude this chapter by relating these issues more concretely to specific questions in literary study. In particular, we ask why interpretations overlap and why they differ; how the processes of interpretation we have described relate to the literary critical controversy over intention; how it might be that we get pleasure from texts; and how texts are judged according to their value. In the case of each issue, we attempt to show that apparently local questions about how you read ('interpretation' in the sense of a mental act) may help develop views on the

---

Activity 83   *Metaphors and metonyms* *(60 mins)*

Using the distinctions we have made in this section, analyse the following examples of figurative language, and identify in them either metaphors or metonyms. Draw a diagram for each one, paying particular attention to the kind of similarity between the actual text and the interpreted text. We have done the first one for you as an example.

(a) The kettle is boiling

Metonym

Actual text: .....kettle.....

Interpreted text: .....water.....

Kind of similarity between actual and interpreted: ...one contains the other...
Details of the similarity: ...kettle contains water and causes it to boil...

(b) Have you read Faulkner?

(c) Life's but a walking shadow.
           (Shakespeare, *Macbeth*, Act V, scene v)

(d) The frost performs its secret ministry
       Unhelped by any wind.
             (Coleridge, 'Frost at Midnight')

(e) O for a beaker full of the warm South....
             (Keats, 'Ode to a Nightingale')

☛ *Now rejoin text on page 163*

large issues of 'interpretation' (in the literary critical sense).

So far in this chapter 'interpretation' has meant mental activity: processing a written page and combining the new information which results with information already stored in memory, to create new mental effects and continuously reach local interpretive conclusions. But in literary studies, 'interpretation', usually means something different. Interpretation is not an act which takes place, but a consolidated, written report on acts that have previously taken place, directed towards some overall general thematic or theoretical goal, and presented to a public.

The distinction might be tabulated like this.

Interpretation as brain behaviour	Interpretation as public, critical essay
Non-explicit	Explicit
Potentially incomplete	Complete
All deductive processes occur spontaneously, instantaneously, and continuously	Deductive processes are deliberate, planned and evaluated, and reported selectively

As an illustration of the significance of these differences, consider the non-explicitness of brain behaviour. What this means is that we may not be conscious of all the effects involving rearrangement of memory, or we may be only semi-conscious of them (they are evoked); we are unlikely to be conscious of all the deductions we are making or what bridging inferences we are introducing. This is not to say that the process is less full or thorough than a published criticism. It merely means that different levels of operational precision are characteristic of each activity: only in linguistic theory, not in literary criticism, is an attempt made to specify all the stages of an interpretation (and then it is to discover how interpretation works in general, not what happens in any particular case).

☛ *Now do Activity 84 on page 165*

7.6.1 INTERPRETIVE CONSENSUS AND DIVERGENCE

It should be clear from your work in Section 7.3 why interpretations differ; that is, why different people can in principle understand very different things from a text. The first stage of reading – the decoding stage – will produce the same results for all readers who share the same codes. But readers may be using different codes and so will decode differently, coming to different initial understandings of the text. This is the case, for example, when modern readers and sixteenth-century readers are likely to be using a different spelling-pronunciation code, and so will read the 'ye/the' word differently (as we saw in Activity 73). On the whole, decoding differences are likely to be relatively minor (substantial differences will relate

Activity 84   *Two types of 'interpretation'*
(60 mins)

On a separate sheet, write for each of the contrasts in the table on p. 164, a brief commentary, explicating the difference. Make a note of issues it raises as regards what literary criticism does, should do, or cannot do.

Now rejoin text on page 164

mainly to the meanings of words, which tend to change a lot, and to differences across dialects). Such differences will not account for many divergent interpretations, though it is easy to underestimate historical difficulties to do with changes in the code (as we have seen above, and will see in Chapter 9).

It is in the second, non-coded stage of reading that divergences are likely to occur, because where a text requires bridging inferences in order to make sense of it, different people may bring very different bridging inferences to that text (e.g. one reader might see a particular text as sexist or racist by applying a particular set of bridging inferences to it, while another reader might not apply those bridging inferences and so would not see the text as sexist or racist). The kinds of texts which require an especially high degree of bridging inferences are, for example, non-literal, metaphorical, symbolic, or ironic texts. Small examples of this kind of text are jokes and advertisements. Large-scale and extremely complex examples are literary texts; and it is literary texts which will demand bridging inferences to the greatest extent. So it is also literary texts which are likely to end up being interpreted in the most different ways. Also, the decontextualisation of literary texts means that there will be fewer assumptions that can be taken as shared by virtue of the context; so more reliance will be placed on personal assumptions, and on the network of assumptions the text itself sets up as it goes along. Hence the greater divergence in readings.

But readings do not always diverge; readers will agree on many things. If the brain is such that interpretations are likely to diverge, how can we explain the existence of an **interpretive consensus**? One possibility is that different people might be coming to the same conclusions *accidentally* by following different routes (via different bridging inferences). But this would not explain the commonness of the phenomenon. An alternative explanation is that the different people must be bringing the same bridging inferences to a text. Remember (Section 7.3) that bridging inferences are fragments of knowledge or belief which have been brought out of memory. This means that the different people who come to the same interpretation must have fragments of knowledge or belief in common. We will use the term **assumptions** to include both knowledge and beliefs. In a conversational situation, these assumptions come partly from features of the situation itself which are obvious to everybody (where is 'here', who is 'I', etc.). For readers of a text, the preceding text creates a common context for all readers in the same way: what has happened in the text before the reader got to this sentence will give rise to overlapping assumptions for each reader. The text will have prepared the different people to bring similar bridging inferences to the sentence.

Where people share similar assumptions and so come to similar interpretations, we say that the people form an **interpretive community**. An interpretive community will be held together (perhaps without the individuals involved being aware of it) by the fact that people share similar assumptions (and hence bridging inferences); in certain cases, we call the similar assumptions (i.e. the set of statements, bridging inferences, etc.) an **ideology**. Activity 85 attempts to isolate specifically the kinds of assumptions which are ideological.

Now do Activity 85 on page 166

7.6.2 THE MEANING OF A TEXT AND THE INTENTIONS OF ITS AUTHOR

Two (different) claims about meaning which are common in literary criticism are:

(a) the meaning of a text = the meaning intended by its author.
(b) the meaning of a text = the meaning derived from it by a (skilled) reader such as a critic.

In this chapter we have seen another way to look at meaning. Meaning is always meaning-for-someone: meaning is something which arises in the bodies of thinking animals (most of all, humans). Recall our discussion in Chapter 3 of types and tokens; we have taken a

Activity 85   *Separating ideological and non-ideological assumptions (40 mins)*

The word 'ideology' is very commonly used for some kinds of shared assumptions, but only very rarely used to describe other kinds of shared assumptions. The two columns below seek to separate selected kinds of assumptions which are generally thought of as ideological from kinds which aren't. We have provided a few possible examples. (You may not agree with them.)

1. Add three more entries to each column.

Shared assumptions which one might claim to be ideological	Shared assumptions which one might claim not to be ideological
Helping the rich helps the poor.	Water is wet.
Women and men should have equal rights.	You exist.
All animals are equal, but some are more equal than others.	Things fall downwards if you drop them.
....	....
....	....
....	....

3. How can the distinction be explained more generally? Do you think ideological assumptions are:

    (a) different in content?   YES/NO
    (b) learned in a different way?   YES/NO
    (c) stored in the brain in a different way? YES/NO
    (d) used socially in a different way?   YES/NO

If you can think of a better general way to characterise ideological assumptions, write it here.

4. If the distinction between the two kinds of assumptions is not a reasonable one, does this mean that everything is ideological or that nothing is? Give a meaning for the word 'ideological' that shows how it is a useful concept distinguishable from simply 'assumptions', 'knowledge', 'ideas', and other similar concepts.

If you think that there is no difference between the two kinds of assumptions, answer question 4; otherwise answer questions 2 and 3.

2. Write in the space provided some of the specific characteristics of the examples of 'ideological' assumptions which make them different in kind from the examples of non-ideological assumptions.

☛ *Now rejoin text on page 165*

very token-oriented view of things, with the result that we can say that meaning can only be some state or behaviour of the brain. The meaning of a text might be a representation 'written on' the electronic patterns of the brain (as a conclusion in an inferential process), or if we think of the evocative and connotative kinds of meaning, meaning could be a name for the re-ordering of 'deep' and 'surface' knowledge which results when we carry out inferencing. Meaning in this approach is a matter of tokens only.

What all this means is that there is no single meaning for a text. Every 'cogniser' of the text – its writer and every reader of it – will have meanings for that text. There might nevertheless be a coincidence between all the individual 'token' meanings of the text (perhaps because everyone decodes a text in an identical way, or perhaps because of bridging inferences in common); but this still remains a coincidence of tokens rather than the emergence of a type which would be *the* meaning of the text.

If we think now about the notion of author's intention, we can see that reading (and hence the production of meanings) is guided not so much by the search for that original intention as by the belief that there *was* an original intention. In order to interpret a text you have to assume that it is intended to communicate, and this assumption then sets in motion your attempt to derive relevance. Instead of recovering original intention, you seek to derive implicational effects which were likely to have been foreseen in constructing the text in a particular way. The less inferential activity you carry out, the more you are likely to attribute your conclusions to the author; the more inferential activity (the greater the range of weakly implied meanings), the more you accept the interpretation as your own product.

 Now do Activity 86

Activity 86   *Recovering intention*
(30 mins)

Benedetto Croce made this comment about reading texts written in earlier periods (quoted in W. K. Wimsatt, 'The Intentional Fallacy')

> Historical interpretation labours . . . to reintegrate in us the psychological conditions which have changed in the course of history. It . . . enables us to see a work of art (a physical object) as its author saw it in the moment of production.

Make a note of the main points you can think of which support this statement. Then make another list of points which stand against it.

For	Against

 Now rejoin text

7.6.3 PLEASURE

Although pleasure is an acknowledged end of reading literature, we don't know much about exactly how it is gained in reading. Consider these possibilities.

1. Pleasure is associated for the brain with a particular thought. Using that thought as a bridging inference, or coming to that thought as a conclusion, or simply stating that thought in the thinking space, all give rise to pleasure. Some thoughts are like erogenous zones: when you make contact with them, you get pleasure.
2. Particular sequences or structures of thoughts are pleasurable. They form fantasies or wish-fulfilment fictions, enabling the thinker to pursue gratification in fictive forms without real-world constraints.
3. Pleasure arises in the brain as a by-product of interpretive activity. Perhaps there is a correlation between the accessibility of a bridging inference and the pleasure which is caused by bringing it into the thinking-space (either drawing up a hard-to-access piece of information stored in memory may be more pleasurable than drawing up an easy-to-access memory, or vice versa). The pleasure may be ex-

tended because entries in memory are associated with each other, and so bringing up one entry will make other entries more accessible.
4. Pleasure may be different in different sorts of texts and there may be a possible genre classification by type of pleasure offered: narrative closure (suspension in enigmas followed by gratification in resolution), inferential work (riddles and puzzles, pleasure in thinking), simulation of primary processes (dreamwork, the processing of repressed material). This classification would make possible a 'politics' of pleasure. Different types of pleasure may correlate with different psychological character types (psychotic, schizophrenic, etc.), such that having those kinds of pleasure makes you temporarily a 'psychotic', a 'schizophrenic', etc. Reading would then be a perverse activity, and the politics of reading would be a sexual-textual politics.
5. Routes to pleasure may depend more on the person getting the pleasure than on the text: put ten different people in front of the same text and they may seek and find different sorts of pleasure – reading in different ways.

☞ **Now do Activity 87**

Activity 87   *Stating your pleasure*

(60 mins)

1. On a separate sheet of paper construct a grid with different types of pleasure listed along one axis, and with a list of texts along the other axis.

2. For each box (the coincidence of a text with a type of pleasure), show, if appropriate, how the text gives rise to that kind of pleasure.

☞ **Now rejoin text**

7.6.4 VALUE

Questions of value are central to traditional definitions of literary criticism, and to the selections of texts made for study. Like pleasure, value is often a taboo subject in a literary studies course. Does a text have a value, though, or can texts be ranked in terms of value? As with the meaning of a text, there are several options: you can say that the text inherits some kind of absolute value either from the (vaguely defined) Tradition, or from its having been assigned that value by a good critic; or you could say

that every value is a value-for-someone, and that there are no absolute values for texts. But just as meaning is to some extent determined by a text, could we say that the value of a text is to some extent also determined by the text (i.e. the text has inherent value in some sense)? The following activity may help you to think about this question.

☞ **Now do Activity 88**

Activity 88   *Value*

(45 mins)

Here is one way of thinking about how a text might have some kind of inherent value.

Look back to Section 7.4 and recall what we said about the balancing of processing effort against rewards (the Principle of Relevance). All texts require some processing effort in order to read them. Perhaps texts can be evaluated depending on whether the work that they make a particular reader's brain do is balanced by the interest, relevance, or usefulness of the interpretations which are come to, and/or by the pleasure and other effects which arise as side-effects of doing that interpretive work. The value of the text will still be relative to its reader, but the text makes a contribution itself to its value (i.e. the value is not entirely given to it by the reader).

1. Find arguments for, and/or against, this suggestion about the value of a text.

2. How does it compare with ideas of value you have encountered elsewhere (e.g. earlier in this book)?

8 Developing theories

In this book we have presented literary studies as being made up of a collection of questions for you to answer, rather than a body of things for you to know. In Chapters 1 and 4 particularly, we have investigated the scope and range of those questions and how you might hope to find answers to them. We now broaden the scope of this investigation. In this chapter we explore the questions and answers in a larger context. We look at how a collection of questions and answers both depends on and adds to a larger viewpoint, or contributes to the development of a theory. We also look at some different kinds of theory and some different reasons for having a theory.

8.1 Kinds of question and answer

To begin, we offer a distinction between two kinds of question and answer. The first kind of question is one which has a single, definite answer. We will call this a *question of fact*; the answer to such a question is a fact about the way things are. The second kind of question is one whose answer depends for its correctness on the people who are thinking about it, or on the circumstances in which they think about it. We will call this sort of question a *context-dependent question*; the answer to such a question is an assumption about the way things are.

Immediately, we need to ask ourselves:

Q: Is this binary opposition justified? Or is the class of factual questions and answers merely a sub-class of context-dependent questions and answers whose dependence on context has not been acknowledged? Are there *in fact* any facts?

Many people have ready-made answers to this question (either that all facts depend on you and your perceptions; or that facts are facts, and people who reject this don't accept the real world). To begin to think the question through for yourself, consider each type of question in more detail.

Questions of fact

Here are some examples of what appear to be this kind of question.

When was Shakespeare born?
What metre is this poem written in?
Was Cooper's *The Last of the Mohicans* first sold as a novel?

Add some more examples of questions of fact here.

....

....

....

....

Even if you decide that something is a question of fact, it may still be impossible to find out the answer. A birth date, for example, may not be discoverable because records were not kept or have been destroyed. This does not mean that no birth date exists: the birth date is the (lost) answer to the question. Or again, the answer to a question of fact might be coded differently in different systems: the same birth date will be stated differently in different calendar systems, but there is still a single correct birth date which can be translated from one system to another. The correctness of an answer to a question of fact should be independent of who asks or answers the question, or on the circumstances in which it is asked or answered. The possibility of actually answering the question, or of being able to judge whether the answer is correct or not, may still be dependent on the circumstances or the people involved, without affecting the fact-based nature of the question and answer in principle.

Context-dependent questions

In this second kind of question, answers depend for their correctness on the people answering them, or on the circumstances in which the question is asked. In this case we are not dealing with an absolute or objective truth.

Rather, we are concerned with relative, personal, subjective, or goal-oriented truths. Questions and answers to this kind of question seem to be very important in the study of literature (though they are less important in other disciplines dealing with language, such as linguistics). Here are some examples of what appear to be this kind of question.

Is Richard Wright a better novelist than James Baldwin?
What does this poem mean?
In what genre is Shakespeare's play *The Winter's Tale*?

Add some more examples of this kind of question.

....

....

....

....

Context-dependent questions may have answers which are relative to a single individual, or to a group of people. Questions of value (e.g. whether a reader likes a particular author) may be exclusively of personal relevance, and the same may apply to questions about certain kinds of meaning. Vague connotations and evocations are likely to be restricted to particular individuals, and so questions like 'What memories does this poem give rise to?' will have different answers for different people. Other context-dependent questions may be formulated in terms which make sense to a particular group of people; these will have a particular answer according to the conventions of interpretation of that group. People who belong to a group which we might call 'Leavisites', for example (see Section 2.3.3), will formulate questions which have a particular significance and importance to them, but may not make sense outside their particular assumptions. A question like 'Can it truly be said that Thomas Hardy is part of the great tradition of the English novel?' depends on a community-specific assumption that there is a great tradition of the English novel. Outside the community in which that assumption is held, it may not be possible to think about the question at all.

➤ *Now do Activity 89 on page 172*

When you worked through Activity 89 you may have found that the possibility of a distinction between facts and assumptions becomes more, rather than less, problematic. Perhaps the attempt to make a distinction is itself based on community-specific assumptions which are untrue. The instances we provided of what we called 'questions of fact' above may be simply context-dependent questions. Or it may be that you can never get at questions about the world at all, because language never enables you to get at the world (all you can talk about is just other examples of language). You might therefore conclude: *no answer* can *ever* be objectively true: *every answer* is only true relative to a particular set of assumptions, which may be consciously or unconsciously shared by a community of people at a particular time and in a particular society.

Q: If this was your conclusion, would it be absolutely true or only relatively true?

Even if you agree that the distinction exists in principle, you still need to think about the classification of particular questions and answers. You might agree, for example, that our first question ('When was Shakespeare born?') is indeed a question of fact, but you could still claim that our second question ('What metre is this poem written in?') is instead a context-dependent question.

8.2 Theoretical frameworks

So far, we have looked at assumptions underlying individual questions. The assumptions generally took the form of statements. But when we look further into any individual statement, additional questions can be found. It can be useful, therefore, to restate statements which make up our assumptions in the form of the implicit questions and answers they contain.

question	+ answer	= statement
When was Shakespeare born?	1564	Shakespeare was born in 1564.
In what genre is Shakespeare's play *The Winter's Tale*?	comedy	Shakespeare's play *The Winter's Tale* is in the genre of comedy.

We will call statements like this (which might be factual or context-dependent) 'assumptions'. (We want to emphasise that any statement might not be true, even the most obvious ones, like 'Shakespeare was born in 1564', and so we use the word 'assumption'.) No single assumption exists in isolation. Individual assumptions are linked in networks. The assumption 'Shakespeare was born in 1564', for example, depends on the assumptions: 'Shakespeare was a person', 'People are born', and, 'It is possible to know the birth date of a person.' Similarly, the assumption '*The Winter's Tale* is a comedy' depends on the assumptions: 'It is possible to name the genre of a text', and, 'One possible genre is "comedy".' In each case,

Activity 89   *Facts and assumptions*

(40 mins)

In this activity we ask you to focus on specific questions, in order to assess whether they are questions of fact or context-dependent questions. The overall goal of the activity is to move towards a decision on the larger question of whether there really is such a thing as a 'question of fact'.

1. Look at each question below and try to demonstrate that it is a context-dependent question (you may not be able to). To help you get started, here are two ways in which you might do this.

   (i) Try to find an assumption (or more than one assumption) which forms the basis for the question, or which is required for the answer. The assumption has to be something which only some people would accept at a particular time and in a particular society. Write the assumption under the question.

  (ii) Try to find in the question a word which has a meaning (relevant to the question) which is restricted to a particular time or group of people. If you find such a word, underline it, and note the meaning and the group, society, or time with which it is particularly associated.

(a)   Is *Frankenstein* too improbable as a fiction to achieve any human relevance?

(b)   Is the first line of *Paradise Lost* in the metre of 'iambic pentameter'?

....

(c)   Is an awareness of 'persona' relevant in understanding Robert Burns's poetry?

....

(d)   In what ways have Scottish writers since the Union of 1707 employed and adapted features of the older Scottish literary tradition?

....

2. Now try to find, and write below, three questions of fact which are *not* dependent on assumptions or meanings which are 'private' to a particular group of people (i.e. which are definitely not context-dependent).

(a)   ....

(b)   ....

(c)   ....

For each of these 'questions of fact', test your answer by examining it for assumptions and community-specific word meanings, as you did in 1 above.

3. On the basis of your answers, consider whether you now think that the distinction between facts and context-dependent questions is a necessary and accurate one.

4. Did your answer to 3 itself involve community-specific assumptions?   YES/NO

👉 *Now rejoin text on page 171*

the connection between the assumptions is one of **presupposition** or **preconstruction**. A particular assumption relies on other assumptions; and those assumptions are the presuppositions which form the basis – and preconditions – of the new, compound assumption that you go on to build.

Assumptions might be facts; others will be context-dependent assumptions which may never have been questioned; and others will be more obviously dependent on a prevailing, socially specific framework of suppositions. When you read critical, theoretical, or historical texts, you find many assumptions simply formulated as statements. Instead of saying, 'We assume that Shakespeare was born in 1564', a text will simply state, 'Shakespeare was born in 1564.' This process of taking certain assumptions as given is inevitable (and, as we have seen in Chapter 7, assumptions called 'bridging inferences' are necessary in enabling you to read at all). To analyse or assess what a critical work is saying, nevertheless, you need to examine the presuppositions which underlie its statements.

8.2.1 PRESUPPOSITIONS

The statement 'Shakespeare was born in 1564' displays an assumption; but the same assumption might be hidden in a reference to 'Shakespeare's birth in 1564', or statements like 'When Shakespeare was born in 1564' embedded in other sentences. There are many words and idioms in English which in themselves have the property of signalling presuppositions. It is always worth looking at words and phrases of this kind particularly carefully when you read an argument; and so we list nine of the main types with their linguistic names here (we will use the symbol » to mean 'presupposes'):[1]

1. Definite expressions
   '*The great tradition* cannot be understood except by. . . .'
   » 'There is a great tradition.'
2. Cleft sentences
   '*It was* Hemingway *who* introduced real conciseness into modern novel-writing.'
   » 'Someone introduced real conciseness into modern novel-writing.'
3. Pseudo-cleft sentences
   '*What* Hemingway achieved *was* the introduction of real conciseness into novel-writing.'
   » 'Hemingway achieved something.'
4. Factive verbs
   'Ezra Pound *regretted* supporting Fascism during the 1930s.'
   » 'Ezra Pound supported Fascism during the 1930s.'
5. Iteratives (markers of repetition)
   'Emily Brontë began the novel *again*.'
   » 'Emily Brontë had begun the novel before.'
6. Implicative verbs
   'Structuralism *managed* to alter our understanding of textuality.'
   » 'Structuralism tried to alter our understanding of textuality.'
7. Counterfactual conditionals
   '*If* the New Critics had believed that language structures consciousness. . . .'
   » 'The New Critics did not believe that language structures consciousness.'

8. Temporal clauses
   '*When Dickens visited the United States*, he was received like a pop star.'
   » 'Dickens visited the United States.'
9. Wh- questions
   '*What* is the principal theme of Chinua Achebe's *Arrow of God*?'
   » 'Chinua Achebe's *Arrow of God* has a principal theme.'

What you should notice in this list (» 'you should notice something in this list') is that the assumptions attached to these words and phrases (» 'there are assumptions attached to these words and phrases') are presupposed, rather than asserted. They are taken as 'given', or already established, rather than being proposed as 'new', and therefore in need of proof or justification. This does not mean that they are true. But it does mean that they act as preconditions for accepting the overall statement as true. And you can negate the sentences (e.g. 'Ezra Pound did not regret, etc.'; 'Emily Brontë did not begin, etc.') without affecting the assumption presupposed. So:

'Ezra Pound did not regret supporting Fascism during the 1930s.'
» 'Ezra Pound supported Fascism during the 1930s.'

The presuppositions are also unaffected when they occur in many other kinds of sentence related to the ones above (e.g. 'It is possible that Emily Brontë began . . ., 'Either Emily Brontë began . . .', 'Because Emily Brontë began . . .', etc.). The presuppositions are attached to the words and phrases which trigger them: you *have to* deal with the presuppositions in order to assess the statements.

☞ *Now do Activity 90 on page 174*

8.2.2 THEORIES

When you read an essay or critical argument, as you have just done in Activity 90, you follow a path through a series of connected assumptions. Together with the forms of implication or derivation which make development in the essay possible, these assumptions make up the argument. When you assess whether that argument is believable, reasonable, useful or whatever, you are either persuaded by its powers of expression (it might appeal to you in all sorts of different ways), or you evaluate it, explicitly or implicitly, as some kind of 'theory'. But in evaluating it as a theory, you inevitably depend on some idea you hold of what a theory is. If we simply say, as we have said here, that a THEORY is a connected sequence of assumptions, is this enough of a definition? To consider this, we need to think about what a 'theory' is in more detail.

The word 'theory' comes into English, from Greek by way of Latin, in the sixteenth century. The classical words which make up the etymology of the modern word

Activity 90   *Identifying presuppositions* *(60 mins)*

For each of the following two passages, make a list on a separate sheet of paper of presuppositions which the passage contains. (Use the list above as a guideline.) In the case of the first passage, keep three separate lists: one each for the two quotations (from Murray and Coleridge), and one for the main argument which incorporates those quotations.

Passage 1
(from the introduction by A. R. Humphreys (1962) to the Everyman edition of Henry Fielding's *Joseph Andrews* and *Shamela*)

In *Unprofessional Essays* (1956). Middleton Murray observes that
'Fielding's kind of moral intensity, not being laboured, does not lead to laborious analysis and critical expatiation. For that reason it can, apparently, pass entirely unrecognized, dismissed as "the genial tolerance of the man-about-town", or as "a simple attitude". Nevertheless, it exists, and is pervasive.'
It is this intensity, of moral grasp and art also, of engrossed and delighted attention to life and cleanness of writing, that makes the novel's great effect, an effect such that no one, Coleridge asserted, could rise from perusing it 'without feeling himself the better man – at least, without an intense conviction that *he* could not be guilty of a base act.' No praise could better testify that Fielding had triumphantly succeeded in doing what he wished to do.

Passage 2
(from P. Brooker, 'Post-structuralism, reading and the crisis of English' (1982), in P. Widdowson (ed.), *Re-reading English*)

Furthermore, if English teaching, as a form of intellectual work engaged in the production of knowledge, is to be recognised as a meaningful site for political change, it will need to co-ordinate radicalised textual deconstruction and a critique of the ideology of 'literature' with an argued challenge and socialist alternative to conventional pedagogy: to the construction, imperatives, validation and assessment of English courses, and to their complicity in the institutional mechanisms of control and authority which serve bourgeois hegemony.

When you have made your lists of presuppositions triggered by particular words and phrases, use the kinds of work you have done in Chapters 6 and 7 to analyse the passages more generally. In particular, look for linguistic forms, or appeals to particular bridging inferences, which suggest specific assumptions about the foreseen readership for the passages and the goals and methods of literary study.

☞ *Now rejoin text on page 173*

'theory' had meanings of contemplation, speculation, and mental 'view'; they derived the sense of abstract thought from metaphors of what you can see: sight leads to vision. But modern senses of 'theory' have more specialised senses than this, many of which have been developed in the history and philosophy of Western science. At the same time, the word 'theory' also enters into a range of different kinds of opposition:

theory versus (or leading to) practice;
theoretical work as opposed to pre- or non- theoretical work;
theoretical discussion as opposed to metatheoretical discussion;
etc.

To specify what a 'theory' is more precisely, we therefore need to consider the range of senses in which the word is used. We can do this by listing the main possibilities. A theory is one or more of these:

1. A description of something.
2. A general statement of rules and principles about something.
3. A system of interconnecting ideas or statements held as an explanation or account of a group of phenomena.
4. A hypothesis (or stated system of ideas) held as an explanation of a group of facts or phenomena and how they are caused which also makes predictions about cases you haven't already examined.
5. An unsupported hypothesis or conjecture that is not yet confirmed by experience or practice.

There are clearly major differences between these senses. Sense 5 is dismissive of 'theory', while the others are not; and senses 2, 3, and 4 are more specific than sense 1, etc. Within each, however, there are more fundamental difficulties of definition:

■ what a 'rule' or a 'statement' is;

- what 'a prediction' is;
- how an 'account' of something is constructed;
- what counts as a cause (a necessary cause? a sufficient cause? a necessary and sufficient cause?); etc.

Beyond all these definitional problems, there is also the consideration that a 'theory' in any of these senses has to make certain basic assumptions to start with. If the theory chooses to make what it presupposes explicit, these assumptions will be its **axioms** (self-evident, undemonstrated assumptions). From these the theory might develop **theorems** (statements not self-evident but demonstrable by argument: things proved); and/or it might explore **problems** (questions that require not only proof, but also that something should be done). But a theory in sense 1 would not have to do any of these things. So what are the qualities that distinguish theoretical work? There seem to be three main stages.

1. **Description.** Work of this type formulates a specialised vocabulary for commentary (a **metalanguage**, or language for citing and talking about texts, interpretations, and issues). It then 'translates' aspects of the text, the reading, or the issue being investigated into the metalanguage, so producing a description. Some degree of generalisation and abstraction away from particular cases may be possible: you can then describe many things using the framework of your first description.

Q: Why should anyone be interested in your description, rather than in making up their own?

2. **Explanation.** Work of this type carries out the operations of description; but it seeks, beyond this, to state general laws or principles based on a speculation about **cause**. An explanation involves some mechanism or process which is claimed to explain why the description is accurate and is formulated in the right way. Although you may be able to describe many things using a description, you need to have reasons for preferring your description to any other if you want your description to be more than an arbitrary paraphrase.

Q: You may decide that your description *should* (or even must) be an arbitrary paraphrase. But what reason would anyone have for being interested in it if it was?

3. **Prediction.** Work of this type carries out the operations of description and explanation, but it also makes predictions, consistent with its general principles, about other cases you haven't come across. Such cases, in this framework, should conform to the general principles extracted as explanation from the description.

☞ *Now do Activity 91*

Activity 91   *What is a theory?*

(45 mins)

1. To explore the criteria of a theory further, decide which of the following you think are theories. Record your decisions by putting ticks where appropriate in the 'Is a theory' and 'Is not a theory' columns. (If you can't decide, put question marks instead.)
2. When you have done this, add numbers in the 'Is a theory' column to indicate which senses of the word 'theory' in the list above (1–5) are applicable.

	Is a theory	Is not a theory
1. A 'No entry' road-sign	·	
2. An assertion that there is a great tradition in English novel-writing		

	Is a theory	Is not a theory
3. *The Book of Genesis* (in the Bible)		
4. An assertion that things fall rather than rise when you drop them		
5. *Hamlet*		
6. A map		
7. An assertion that there are two types of statements: factual and non-factual statements		

☞ *Now rejoin text*

The aspect of theoretical work in science that many people think is either impossible or inappropriate in literary study is that it contains **predictions** and **hypotheses**, as well as assertions. We have seen that an assumption is a statement which is assumed to be true. A hypothesis is a statement which *could be* true, given other assumptions of a theory. A prediction is a statement which *must be* true given other assumptions of a theory. A theory develops by testing whether its hypotheses and predictions are true or not. Hypotheses and predictions act as a guide to future work; they suggest new questions and ideas. Predictions on the basis of a hypothesis are a way of testing whether a collection of assumptions are in fact true. If a set of assumptions leads inevitably to a particular prediction, and that prediction turns out to be incorrect, then this is likely to suggest that those assumptions in turn are incorrect. For this reason, examining predictions is a way of testing a theory. If it is useful to be able to test a theory (for example to distinguish between the infinite number of possible theories you might encounter or develop), it helps if the theory makes a large number of predictions. Theories which are testable in this way are called **falsifiable**. Sometimes the fact that a particular prediction turns out to be incorrect means that one central claim of the theory – or the whole collection of assumptions which underlies that prediction – is also incorrect; and so the theory is shown to be wrong. Sometimes it is only part of the theory (some small group of assumptions which may not be central) which is shown to be incorrect; in such cases the theory can be adjusted without being abandoned. This method as a whole is sometimes referred to as **hypothetico-deductive**; and the idea of falsifiability on which it is based is associated with the philosopher of science Karl Popper.

▶ *Now do Activity 92 on page 177*

The procedures we have been describing in this section probably resemble what you already do when you write essays and textual analyses more than you might at first think. We have simply attempted to make different types of critical argument, and different stages within an argument, more explicit. In writing your own critical arguments, you are likely to . . .

(a) . . . take for granted a set of *assumptions*. These are connected (and form a kind of mini-theory). Examining these assumptions leads you to make . . .

(b) . . . *hypotheses*, or speculative general statements, which suggest . . .

(c) . . . *predictions*, which you explore as you carry out the work.

To illustrate this sort of procedure with a standard type of literary problem, we will now look at a simple example.

Example: Blake and the question mark

William Blake had complete control over the printing of his collection of poems, *Songs of Innocence and Experience* (1794). He engraved the printing plates himself, and then sometimes retouched the printed texts (so that different printings of the first edition of the book are slightly different). We begin with an **observation** which we made on reading a photo-facsimile copy of one of the first editions of the text.

OBSERVATION

Many of the poems in *Songs of Innocence* contain questions without question marks. Look, for example, at the first two lines of the poem 'The Lamb'.

Little Lamb who made thee
Dost thou know who made thee

However, Blake did use question marks in *Songs of Experience*, e.g. in 'The Tyger'.

What the hammer? What the chain.
In what furnace was thy brain?

Since we think that this observation is true we will count it as our 'starter' assumption (1). We can combine it with some further assumptions, about William Blake, which we happen to hold (based on context-dependent knowledge).

(2) Blake was very careful about all aspects of his text.
(3) Blake knew the prevailing conventions for using question marks.
(4) Blake experimented with the layout of texts.

Together, these assumptions lead us to a prediction:

(5) Blake deliberately omitted some question marks in *Songs of Innocence*.

This prediction by itself is difficult to test, since it relies on demonstrating 'intention' in a person who has been dead for over 150 years. So we simply add it as another assumption to the assumptions we already have. The collection of assumptions which we have doesn't tell us why the question marks are missing. If we wish to discover this, we need to construct a hypothesis (which we get from looking at some specific examples of questions without question marks).

(6) Blake omits the question mark after questions which are unproblematic, because the answer is straightforward and easy to find, and causes no problems.

This hypothesis may not be fully testable but it is partly testable. We can test it by looking at every question with a missing question mark, and judging whether or not, in its context, it is an unproblematic question. For example, the question, 'Little lamb who made thee' is easily answered in the context – God did. On the other hand, the question, 'Did he who made the lamb make thee?' in the poem 'The Tyger' is presented by the poem as a problematic question (it isn't clear in the poem what the answer to it is).

Activity 92   *Falsifiable theories*

(40 mins)

1. Look back to the nineteenth-century corpus you have already examined in Chapters 1 and 4 (first presented in Activity 6, p. 10). That corpus is built on a collection of assumptions, not all of which may have been clear to the writer. Make a list of presuppositions which underlie the assumptions made by the writer in constructing this corpus. (Find them by using the techniques outlined in Activity 90 and in the passage about presuppositions above.)

2. Now consider your list of presuppositions. Do these make up a falsifiable theory? Make a note here (if you can) of three predictions which can be made on the basis of the presuppositions you have listed.

Prediction 1:..

Prediction 2:..

Prediction 3:..

3. Can these predictions be tested? For each prediction, what is the result of the tests?

Prediction 1 (result):..

Prediction 2 (result):..

Prediction 3 (result):..

4. On the basis of your answers, can you now say whether the theory is:

(a) falsifiable/non-falsifiable
and
(b) (as far as you can tell) true or false? ....

➤ *Now rejoin text on page 176*

We do the same with all the questions without question marks.

If our hypothesis seems to be satisfactory, we can add it as an assumption. We can then introduce another assumption, and begin to develop our 'theory' further. The assumption we decide to introduce is:

(7) *Songs of Innocence* portray a state of innocence.

We can then add another hypothesis:

(8) Blake considered unproblematic questions to be typical of a state of innocence.

One way of testing whether this hypothesis is true or not is to look for questions which *do* have question marks (i.e. problematic questions) in *Songs of Innocence*. If both the assumption and the hypothesis are true, then there should be no question marks in *Songs of Innocence*. In fact, though, there is one question mark, in a poem called 'Infant Joy' which we reproduce in its entirety below.

> I have no name
> I am but two days old. –
> What shall I call thee?
> I happy am
> Joy is my name, –
> Sweet joy befall thee!
>
> Pretty joy!
> Sweet joy but two days old.
> Sweet joy I call thee:
> Thou dost smile.
> I sing the while
> Sweet joy befall thee.

This fact means that our observations are not fully consistent with our assumptions. A crucial question we must now ask is:

> Is the particular question, 'What shall I call thee?' a problematic one?

If the answer is 'yes' (we would have to construct arguments for this position), then assumption 7 is incorrect as it stands (given the other assumptions, particularly 6 and 8); so it will have to be modified, as:

(7a) *Songs of Innocence* portray a state of innocence, but some poems include elements which are not characteristic of innocence.

We can now, given this new assumption, test it by formulating another hypothesis.

(9) Other poems in *Songs of Innocence* may include elements which are not characteristic of innocence.

(As evidence for this hypothesis, we might cite the 'staining of the water' in the introductory poem, etc.)

But what if we answer 'no' to the above question, and say that 'what shall I call thee' is *not* problematic? In this case, one or more of the assumptions we have already made must be incorrect.

> Q: Which assumptions might be incorrect?
>
> Write probable numbers here: ....

We have now outlined the basic procedure for constructing our argument. Many more questions can be asked, new assumptions can be introduced, and hypotheses and predictions can be constructed and tested. Where we test a prediction and find that it isn't supported by our observations, we have a **counter-example**. We then need to decide whether the counter-example is a genuine **exception** (a case which is not covered by our hypothesis, and for which additional, supplementary arguments need to be made), or whether the counter-example shows that our hypothesis is inaccurate. Work-

ing in this way, we can build and rebuild an account of Blake's work, starting from a very simple observation and some assumptions.

But certain requirements on how you formulate assumptions and hypotheses have to be met if your argument is to develop. The more *precise* your assumptions and hypotheses are, the easier it is to test them and to see what their implications are. We could improve our account of question marks in Blake considerably if we had a clear definition of what a 'problematic' and 'unproblematic' question are. All the assumptions we make have to be *consistent* with one another, and they should be generally compatible with what we take to be true. Using an assumption such as

(10) Blake was generally uninterested in the layout of his poems

to support the claim that Blake was simply careless in punctuating, is inconsistent with what we know of his general working methods. This does not mean that you can't pursue such a line of enquiry. (Very often, investigations set off on completely wrong lines.) But it does mean that your argument is likely to be beset by counter-arguments based on the opposite assumption, and linked to predictions and observations about the rest of Blake's work.

8.3 Interpretive communities

In this section we look more closely at the kinds of assumption you are likely to introduce into the development of a 'theory' (either deliberately, or without being aware of doing so). In particular, we explore the question of whether there is a connection between the context in which you live and work and the assumptions that you take for granted.

Where a group of people share the same assumptions to a substantial extent, we have said, in Chapter 7, that they form an **interpretive community**. They will share the same presuppositions, and be likely to use the same bridging inferences, when they interpret things. Among the assumptions that will be made in an interpretive community are assumptions about goals (what it is worth doing) and assumptions about methods (how to do something that is thought worth doing). There will also be general assumptions about what is true. Some of the assumptions about what is true may actually be mistakes (for example, 'Does the sun go round the earth, or the earth go round the sun?' is a question of fact; there was a time when many people assumed an answer which has now been disproved). Other assumptions taken for granted in a particular interpretive community involve questions which could probably never have a universally true answer. Each interpretive community provides a different answer to these questions (which include many moral questions, religious questions, questions of value, questions of pleasure, and questions of meaning).

Shared answers to these various kinds of question will be what holds an interpretive community together, though they may be unconscious. Members of a community are likely to see their assumptions as obvious or commonsensical, and not worth thinking about. Someone outside the community, on the other hand, may well see the same assumptions as clearly community-specific.

To the outsider, the assumptions which make up an interpretive community's common sense may appear as its 'myths': its way of taking, as given, particular answers to foundational questions.

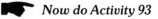 *Now do Activity 93*

Activity 93   *Are you in any interpretive communities?*
(60 mins)

In this activity, we explore whether you share basic assumptions with other people, such that together you form an interpretive community.

1. Think about whether you are part of any groups of people who think as you do about things (i.e. whether you are part of any interpretive communities). You may be part of many different ones. List some of the interpretive communities here.

(a) ....

(b) ....

(c) ....

(d) ....

(e) ....

(f) ....

2. Now write down ten of your basic assumptions. Include some which seem simply common sense, and some which you recognise are not shared by everyone in the world. (You need to think about these carefully, as your own assumptions are not likely to be easy to get at.)

(1) ....

(2) ....

(3) ....

(4) ....

(5) ....

(6) ....

(7) ....

(8) ....

(9) ....

(10) ....

3. For each assumption you have listed, decide whether it is connected with any of the interpretive communities you have identified. If it is, add the letter for that community at the beginning of the assumption.

4. Are any assumptions not associated with the interpretive communities you listed? Can you think of an interpretive community which the assumption is associated with? If you can, add it to your list in 1.

5. Now name one interpretive community which you are *not* a member of.

....

6. List five assumptions which are shared by members of that interpretive community.

(11) ....

(12) ....

(13) ....

7. Was it easier to identify the community you are not part of (and characterise its assumptions) than a community you *are* part of?
YES/NO
If you answered 'yes', try to explain why it was easier.

(14) ....

(15) ....

☞ *Now rejoin text*

The interpretive communities you have listed in Activity 93 can be classified into types (along the lines developed in Chapter 5). Some communities will be likely to relate to social groups, some to subcultural groups, others to institutions, regions, age groups, etc. Some of the communities may be quite small (e.g. it could be argued that 'undergraduate students at Strathclyde University' form an interpretive community); others may be very big (e.g. 'patriarchy'). Much of the way you see yourself in your society relates to what you take to be true, and how you use your assumptions to interpret things. So the interpretive communities you have listed are likely to correlate closely with how you think you fit into the various overlapping and conflicting social groupings around you. Collectively, the assumptions which link you to the interpretive communities to which you belong are your 'ideology' or 'ideologies'; they make up not only the repeated patterns, but also the horizons, of your thought.

As a checklist of 'sites' where interpretive communities can be found, we suggest the following.

- literary and artistic movements (a good example of deliberately constructed interpretive communities)
  e.g. dadaism, surrealism, vorticism, the decadents
- general and widespread intellectual movements
  e.g. the Renaissance, the Enlightenment, feminism
- religions
  e.g. Hinduism, Catholicism, Islam
- historical periods
  e.g. Victorian Britain, post-Independence India, the Great Depression
- groupings of intellectual disciplines
  e.g. natural sciences, social sciences
- specific academic fields
  e.g. linguistics, literary criticism, anthropology
- divisions within a discipline, often following the work of a particular person or procedure
  e.g. New Criticism, structuralism, deconstruction
- divisions within a discipline centred around a particular institution or place
  e.g. Prague Linguistic Circle, Yale School, Glasgow Media Group.

None of these distinctions *necessarily* means a distinction between interpretive communities, though they can act as a rough guide. But interpretive communities also overlap one another. Structuralism and New Criticism have different underlying assumptions and different goals, for example, and so can be said to form different interpretive communities. Yet they are still both part of a larger, more inclusive interpretive community that might be called 'exponents of literary studies'. Beyond this, they are both parts of the interpretive community of 'academic' or 'intellectual' discourse; and beyond this again, they are part of the even larger community which some people argue has underpinned thought in Europe and elsewhere for thousands of years: the community of 'Western metaphysics'. But even this characterisation does not describe the possible relationships adequately. Not only can you be in several interpretive communities at the same time (because of the possibility of one being included within another), but you can also be part of interpretive communities which overlap only partially. Structuralism and Marxism, for example, may be interpretive communities which share some assumptions but have other assumptions which are incompatible. In being part of both, some of your assumptions may contradict others, or else you may be able to change between assumptions.

☞ *Now do Activity 94 on page 181*

Between coming into existence and ceasing to exist, the existence of an interpretive community means that communication inside the community (*intra*-community) is easier than communication outside it, because so much can be taken for granted. As we saw in Chapter 7, assumptions work as bridging inferences, so they enable language to be much more expressive than if total reliance is placed simply on the code. But reliance on shared assumptions also means that communication across the borders of the community (*inter*-community) is more difficult, for the same reason: failure to share certain assumptions may hinder understanding.

The difficulties involved here have been the object of much argument in philosophy and the philosophy of science.[2] The philosopher of history Michel Foucault, for

Activity 94   *How do interpretive communities start?*

(30 mins)

Interpretive communities come into existence and go out of existence. This activity suggests some reasons for this and asks you to think of an interpretive community which is an example of each reason. Try to think of an example of a particular interpretive community that fits each heading. For example, under (a), write the name of an interpretive community which came into existence because new questions couldn't be answered by the old community. Look at the lists above (and material in Chapter 2) for ideas; and look names up in an encyclopaedia or companion to literature if you are not familiar with them. (Don't worry that your answers will involve some degree of simplification and speculation.)

An interpretive community comes into existence because
(a) new questions become urgent which an existing interpretive community is unable to answer.

....

(b) a new generation wants to distinguish itself from the interpretive community associated with the preceding generation: its 'parents'.

....

(c) the new interpretive community is established in an attempt to imitate some other interpretive community.

....

An interpretive community goes out of existence because
(d) the fundamental assumptions of the interpretive community are shown to be incorrect.

....

(e) the members of the community are forced by other people to stop working or to change their work, and so the ideas die out.

....

(f) the implications of the assumptions held by the community come to be considered unacceptable as a result of some kind of social change.

....

 Now rejoin text on page 180

---

example, suggests that there are large-scale interpretive communities, lasting for several hundred years, which he calls **epistemes**. An episteme is like the foundations on which the intellectual buildings of a particular collection of ways of thinking (which may characterise a whole culture) are built (so the historian interested in past ideas is a sort of archaeologist, looking for buried foundation sites). Foucault suggests that interpretive communities are so different from each other in their underlying assumptions that there is little possibility of communication across them. A modern reader cannot really understand a sixteenth-century text, for example, because the 'theories' which the modern reader assumes are so different from the theories about the world which the sixteenth-century reader assumed. The philosopher of science Thomas Kuhn has expressed a view with many similarities to Foucault's. Kuhn argues that scientists working as a group have a particular combination of underlying assumptions which he calls a **paradigm**. They work according to the predictions of this paradigm and interpret the world according to its possibilities. But there comes a time when the paradigm is overwhelmed by new questions which cannot be answered using its assumptions. What happens then is that the scientists adopt a completely new

paradigm (or set of assumptions). Kuhn calls this moment a **paradigm shift**. But it is not possible to understand the new assumptions from the perspective of the old paradigm, or to understand the old assumptions from the perspective of the new paradigm; so the word **incommensurability** is often used to describe the relationship between them.

Since they assume some degree of incommensurability between interpretive communities, both Kuhn and Foucault are pessimistic about the possibility of understanding different interpretive communities or different periods. But there are two varieties of this pessimism. The first suggests that while a single individual *can* put himself or herself into different interpretive communities, by adopting the assumptions of that community, the problem remains that what is 'known' while the person occupies that community cannot be known when he or she switches back (this is something like Kuhn's position). The second, deeper variety of pessimism is that it is not possible to put yourself into a different interpretive community at all: many things just can't be known (this is something like Foucault's position, though not all Foucauldians are pessimistic in this way).

Not everybody agrees with the claim that there is

incommensurability between interpretive communities. In their orthodox forms, some disciplines (such as anthropology and history) take as a basic assumption that it is possible to understand the working of different interpretive communities from a unified perspective – though there are conflicts within many disciplines about exactly how far this is possible. If, on the other hand, you *accept* the idea of incommensurability, then as regards literary study there will be at least three major sorts of problem.

1. It will be difficult in reading to make sense in our own terms of literary texts which originate in a different episteme from ours. We will need to be cautious when reading, for example, an eighteenth-century critical essay, or a theoretical work written by someone on the other side of the world. We will need to be aware not only of how words can mean different things, but also of how fundamentally different assumptions can be hidden behind even familiar words.

2. There will be the danger, in trying to make sense in our own terms of texts from different epistemes, of taking our own assumptions as a 'centre' or 'norm', and reducing reading to an issue of 'self' and 'other'. This 'other' of a culture – the 'beyond' or 'outside' of the particular symbolic systems it adopts – is often described by use of the term **the Other**, and it is likely to be simply stereotyped as the unknown, the remote, the exotic, or the dangerous.

3. We will face difficulties of comparison when reading theoretical and critical work about literary studies. It will be likely, for example, that the insights of poststructuralist criticism, Marxism, cognitive science, and anthropology will be incompatible, if they are based on different paradigms.

  Q: Does the idea of incommensurability reduce theoretical work to a matter of blind faith: 'pick the theoretical paradigm of your choice, because you can't properly compare them'?
  Q: If not, why not?

▶ *Now do Activity 95 on page 183*

8.4 How theories can be useful even if they aren't true

You might argue that only a theory which you consider to be true is of any interest. A false (or more specifically, falsified) theory can therefore only be of interest in showing what you need to avoid when constructing your theory. In this section, however, we explore a different possibility: perhaps you can think a theory is not strictly true and yet still use it.

  This possibility can be associated with the philosophical tradition of **pragmatism**, and particularly with American philosophers such as C. S. Peirce and William James.

Pragmatists think that truth is not primarily an objective fact; rather, it is whatever a group of people decide the truth to be. (Pragmatists differ on whether or not an objective truth is eventually reachable, or whether an objective truth lies behind all the relative truths which are perceived by people.) If you pursue this line of argument, you are likely to be more interested in the acceptability of a theory than in its truthfulness (which may or may not turn out to be an empty notion). You would evaluate a theory on how widely acceptable it is, and perhaps also on how persuasively the theory is presented: the acceptability of a theory might relate to how it enables certain practical goals to be reached. The goals themselves might be local and specific (for example, that the theory enables a certain kind of text analysis to be carried out, which is useful for some other purpose), or they might be larger and more ambitious (for example, that the theory makes large-scale social change possible). In all cases, if you take a pragmatic line of argument, you are not fundamentally concerned with whether or not a theory is true, only with how efficiently it permits a particular goal to be reached.

  Q: Words like 'strategic' and 'tactical' are often used to describe goals of work in literary theory. Does the use of these words suggest anything about whether such work has a commitment (a) to 'truth', or (b) to achieving a chosen purpose? Can the two types of commitment combine?

Sometimes a theory might be *intended to be true*, but might fail in some way and yet remain pragmatically useful. To illustrate this, we will look at a theory which, despite serious problems of testability, can still be useful in producing analyses and helping us to think about texts.

Propp's analysis of the structure of folktale narratives

On the basis of his analysis of a large number of Russian folktales, the Russian formalist Vladimir Propp formulated a theory about how their narratives are constructed.[3] The four basic theoretical principles (i.e. the four underlying hypotheses of the theory) are:

Hypothesis 1. Different sequences of events in different fairytales can be understood as a sequence of the *same* events manifested in different ways. For example, consider:

(a) 'A tsar gives an eagle to a hero. The eagle carries the hero away to another kingdom.'
  And in another folktale:

(b) 'An old man gives Sucenko a horse. The horse carries Sucenko away to another kingdom.'

These two different sequences of events can be understood as being manifestations of the same abstract sequence of events:
'*Somebody gives the hero something, which enables the hero to go to another kingdom.*'

Activity 95   *Thinking yourself into another world*

(60 mins)

1. Here is a description of a woman, from John Donne's 'Second Anniversary' (1612), which draws on one conventional body of assumptions. Read it through and try to decide what it means.

> She whose complexion was even so made
> That which of her ingredients should invade
> The other three, no fear no art could guess:
> So far were all remov'd from more or less.

2. What does the quotation say about the woman? Is it a passage of conventional praise or condemnation?
Underline one:
PRAISE CONDEMNATION NEITHER DON'T KNOW

3. Now look at the quotation again. Add assumption 1.
   1. The word 'complexion' doesn't mean the colour or texture of the face; it means a combination or balance between elements which make up the personality.
Think again about whether the passage involves praise or condemnation.
Underline one:
PRAISE CONDEMNATION NEITHER DON'T KNOW

4. Now add assumptions 2 and 3.
   2. The body is made up of four 'humours' or liquid substances produced by the liver from the food you eat; melancholy, phlegm, blood, and choler.
   3. The balance between these humours leads to human characteristics and predispositions towards particular moods.
Think again about whether the passage involves praise or condemnation.
Underline one:
PRAISE CONDEMNATION NEITHER DON'T KNOW

5. Now add assumptions 4 and 5.
   4. The world is made out of four elements: earth, water, air, and fire.
   5. The humours, the elements, and common qualities are linked in a set of correspondences, viz.

Element	Humour	Common quality
earth	melancholy	cold and dry
water	phlegm	cold and moist
air	blood	hot and moist
fire	choler	hot and dry

Think again about whether the passage involves praise or condemnation.
Underline one:
PRAISE CONDEMNATION NEITHER DON'T KNOW

6. Now add assumptions 6 and 7.
   6. Balance between humours in the body signals a well-balanced personality.
   7. Harmony in personality is a reflection of harmony in the created universe.
Think again about whether the passage involves praise or condemnation.
Underline one:
PRAISE CONDEMNATION NEITHER DON'T KNOW

7. Now add assumption 8.
   8. Human beings form a bridge between God at the top and lowest inanimate objects at the bottom of a vertical chain of being.
Think again about whether the passage involves praise or condemnation.
Underline one:
PRAISE CONDEMNATION NEITHER DON'T KNOW

8. Have these basic elements of historical scholarship resolved difficulties in the passage?
   YES/NO
If 'yes', does this mean that the problem of incommensurability can be solved by research?
   YES/NO

9. Now try to create a mental context for the interpretation of the passage you have made by combining assumptions 1–8; think 'outwards' from the passage itself into surrounding inferences and implications. Think in particular of:

your ideas of anatomy and medicine
your perceptions of beauty
your ideas of morality
what you are likely to mean if you use the words 'angel', 'beast', and 'nature'.

10. We could say that there was an 'order of things' which characterised the transition in Britain from a mediaeval social order into new kinds of Renaissance humanism. How far do you think this activity suggests that it is possible to project yourself from your own assumptions into this episteme?

☛ *Now rejoin text on page 182*

Propp called these abstract events **functions** (the ones we have cited are numbers 14 and 15).

Hypothesis 2. All the fairytales Propp looked at made use of a limited number of abstract event-types or functions. Specifically, only thirty-one functions are used to construct all the stories.

Hypothesis 3. Not all of the thirty-one functions appear in every story. But if two functions appear, they always appear in the same order in the story. (If, for example, the function, 'somebody gives the hero something' (no. 14) and the function, 'The hero is enabled to go to another kingdom' (no. 15) both appear in one story, they will always be ordered as follows: 14 before 15.) This is complicated, however, by the fact that a story can *contain* other stories.

Hypothesis 4. All folktales fit into the same basic pattern; they are all constructed by selection from the same sequence of thirty-one functions.

We now list the thirty-one functions (you will need them for Activity 96.)

The Propp functions

The preparatory part of the tale
Initial situation (simple introduction of family or hero)
 1. One of the members of a family absents himself from home.
 2. An interdiction (command not to do something) is addressed to the hero.
 3. The interdiction is violated.
The VILLAIN enters the tale
 4. The villain makes an attempt at reconnaissance.
 5. The villain receives information about his victim.
 6. The villain attempts to deceive his victim (*often by disguise*) in order to take possession of him or of his belongings.
 7. The victim submits to deception and thereby unwittingly helps his enemy.

The complication of the tale
 8. The villain causes harm or injury to the member of a family.
The tale may also begin with some kind of lack, such as:
8a. One member of a family either lacks something or desires to have something.
(Another way for a tale to begin is by the 'transfer of a middle element to the beginning' – such as the catching and sparing of an animal.) The HERO enters the tale. Types of hero are the seeker or the victimised hero.
 9. Misfortune or lack is made known; the hero is approached with a request or a command; he is allowed to go or he is despatched.
10. The seeker/hero agrees to or decides upon counter-action.
11. The hero leaves home.

The DONOR is introduced (friendly or unfriendly), who will provide the hero with something (usually magical) which will enable the tale to be brought to a conclusion.
12. The hero is tested, interrogated, attacked, etc., which prepares the way for his receiving either a magical thing or helper.
13. The hero reacts (positively or negatively) to the actions of the future donor.
14. The hero acquires the use of a magical thing or power.
The hero now uses the magical thing/power; while in a sense he now does nothing (the donor has done it for him), the hero's intentions nevertheless create 'the axis of the narrative'. For Propp, the hero is defined as the person who receives/uses the magical object/power.

15. The hero is transferred, delivered, or led to the place where the thing which he seeks is to be found (often in some strange or foreign place).
16. The hero and the villain join in direct combat.
17. The hero is branded or recognisably wounded.
18. The villain is defeated.
19. The initial misfortune or lack is reversed. *This is the 'peak' of the narrative.*
20. The hero returns.
21. The hero is pursued.
22. The hero is rescued from pursuit.
Sometimes in a story there is now a new villainy, which starts the plot sequence off again on a 'second move', with a new lack and restoration.
23. The hero, unrecognised, arrives home or in another country.
24. A false hero presents unfounded claims.
25. A difficult task is proposed to the hero.
26. The task is resolved.
27. The hero is recognised.
28. The false hero or villain is exposed.
29. The hero is given a new appearance.
30. The villain is punished.
31. The hero is married and ascends the throne.

Propp's four hypotheses and his list of functions can be tested for accuracy against the particular group of folktales he analysed. They can also be tested against another corpus of folktales that Propp himself did not analyse (or even know of), to see if his predictions are confirmable beyond the original, fixed corpus. But it is also possible to make a larger hypothesis: that Propp's hypotheses and list of functions apply not only to folktales but also to narratives in novels, films, and television programmes. We can now test whether this hypothesis can be confirmed.

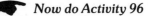 ***Now do Activity 96***

Activity 96   *Testing a simple theory of narrative functions*
(60 mins)

1. In order to test whether Propp's predictions apply in the case of all narratives, think of the plots of four films, television programmes, or novels you have recently watched or read. For each one, decide whether it contains versions of any of the thirty-one functions listed above (check that you understand Propp's hypotheses 1–4 first). List the functions you think are in the texts in the order in which they appear in the narrative.

(3)..   ....

(4)..   ....

Name of film/programme/book	Function numbers (in order of appearance)

2. Are the functions in the order predicted by Propp's theory?
    YES/NO

(1)..   ....

(2)..   ....

Now rejoin text

You may have run into a problem when you tried to do the first part of Activity 96: how do you recognise a function when it occurs as a specific event in an actual text? The functions described above apply clearly to folktales, but how will they be 'translated' or reworked in a realistic narrative? Direct combat (function 16) will be realised differently if it is in a film about modern business rather than in a film about knights or warriors. Similarly, the final function 31, 'the hero is married', may be translated as 'the re-uniting of the family' (without any marriage) or perhaps even as 'the two people become lovers'. The other part of function 31 ('and ascends the throne') may be translated as 'inherits property' or 'is promoted', etc. And what if the hero in a text is a woman? In translating the functions across contexts in this way, you add an amount of interpretation as you apply and test the theory. But how far can a particular function be stretched? Have we already stretched the folktale conclusion function 31 too far by allowing it to be realised as 'the two people become lovers' (a typical film narrative conclusion)? Unfortunately, the theory fails to help us out here. Propp's predictions are not clear enough for the theory to be satisfactorily tested, which seriously weakens the theory as an account of narrative structures.

This does not mean that the theory is therefore useless; it can still come in useful as a way of achieving particular goals. Even if we can't be certain that the theory gives us a true description of the underlying 'skeleton' of a nar-

rative, it can nevertheless be an aid to a particular act of investigation. By applying and interpreting Propp's schema in a particular novel, we can produce interpretations which might otherwise not have occurred to us, and which can then be investigated further.

As an illustration of this, consider Mark Twain's novel *Huckleberry Finn*. At the end of the novel Huck, who has lost his father at the beginning of the narrative (function 1), is potentially reunited with a 'mother', Aunt Sally ('she's going to adopt me and sivilise me'), possibly a form of 31. But instead, Huck intends to avoid this by leaving for 'the Territory', so threatening to re-open the narrative again (function 1). Or, again, we can interpret the events of the last chapters as an instance of functions 23 and 24. Function 23 occurs when Huck, the hero, arrives unrecognised (i.e. he is thought to be Tom) at Aunt Sally's house (which will become his home); function 24 occurs when Tom Sawyer, the false hero, presents unfounded claims (i.e. he claims to be Sid, and pretends to Huck and Jim that Jim is still a slave). Such a matching of the narrative with the function list opens up the possibility of thinking of Tom Sawyer as 'false hero' in the novel, a speculation which is interesting both in terms of Tom's character and in terms of the relation between this novel and Twain's earlier novel, *The Adventures of Tom Sawyer*.

So if you can get good use out of even a theory that you can show to be seriously flawed, how important is the truth of a theory that you are using to achieve a particular goal? Sometimes, a theory is acting simply as a **catalyst**, or inspiration; it provides a random entry point into solving a particular problem or reaching an already established goal. In this case, the truthfulness of the theory is not very important; what is more important is its ability to inspire and interest. Alternatively, a theory may be connected to progress towards your particular goal more specifically. For instance, your main procedure for producing an account of what *Huckleberry Finn* means may be that of applying Propp's schema to the text, in detail and systematically. In this case, the theory is acting as a **heuristic**, or tool for finding things out (see also p. 98). So does the accuracy of a therory affect its usefulness as a heuristic? In the case of Propp's theory, there are reasons to think that its usefulness as a heuristic is related to its being to some extent an accurate theory. The fact that the theory produces satisfactory generalisations about some of the narrative segments of *Huckleberry Finn* does not need to be because Propp's theory is a theory of all narratives. Rather, it may be that Propp's theory is an accurate description of certain standard folktales, and that *Huckleberry Finn* makes use of those folktale narrative elements. Similarly, an account of Hollywood films based on Propp's work might work reasonably well because some screenwriters have *studied*

Propp. In either case, Propp's work is useful in investigating how narratives are constructed, without that usefulness deriving directly from its being a true theory of narrative.

8.5 Putting theories together

Different sorts of activity are called theories. Theories might be based on explicit axioms or on metaphorical or poetic formulations; they might be coherent or self-contradicting. There are a range of possible claims: a theory might simply describe some fragment of reality, or it might explain it and make predictions about the realities of the future. Theories might be used to find out the absolute truth, or some relative truth, or might be used for a particular pragmatic purpose. They may provide inspiration, or act as a heuristic (or some combination of these). Some people use the word 'theory' for any activity which reflects on itself.

Given these different practices called 'theory', is it possible to compare them with each other, or are they so different that there are no grounds for comparison? And can theories be combined, so that their different insights provide a greater joint insight?

☞   *Now do Activity 97*

Activity 97   *Looking back at Chapter 2*
(60 mins)

1. In Chapter 2 we presented 'snapshots' of actual theories, and the chapter ended with an activity in which you were asked to compare theories. But in Chapter 8 we have said that some people think theories cannot be compared. Look back at your comparisons in Activity 19. Are you still happy with them, could you improve them, or do you feel that the exercise now seems impossible because theories cannot be compared?

2. If you think theories cannot be compared, explain why you think this.

3. If you think theories *can* be compared, now carry out the following further comparative activity.

(a) For each of the theories described in Chapter 2, compile a list of presuppositions and basic assumptions.

(b) Decide whether each theory makes predictions, and, if so, what they are.

(c) For each theory, is it committed to finding out 'the truth'?

(d) For each theory, is the reason for having it that it underlies a particular practical application?

If the information in our descriptions in Chapter 2 is not sufficient to enable you to decide these things, consult books listed in the bibliography, and look in other bibliographies and secondary material to find further references.

4. Which theories do you think are compatible with each other? Suggest some possible combinations, chosen from Chapter 2 and other theories which you can think of (e.g. the 'cognitive' theory we presented in Chapter 7).

9 From your study into the world

In this chapter, we look at some of the ways in which the study of literature takes its place in the world beyond or after academic study. It is common for courses in literary studies to set as their horizons the imagined boundaries or limits of the discipline, and to leave connections beyond this to supplementary teaching provided by careers advice or general studies, or to extra-curricular personal ethics and political involvement. In this chapter, however, we draw into literary studies some of these considerations and the interface they signal between literary studies and other areas of work and social life. We begin by interpreting 'taking a place in the world' as meaning simply 'having a job'. We then look at how the kind of job you are being prepared for is bound up with the place of the English language in the world; and we supplement the detailed analyses of English structure (Chapter 6) with an overview of the historical development, geographical spread and range of uses of the language. More generally, we also look in this section at the politics of involvement with English. Extending the political theme, we turn to a second interpretation of 'taking a place in the world', this time meaning 'adopting a (possibly evaluative or critical) relationship to culture and society'. We conclude by looking at how the various demands of the future might shape developments and research in literary studies.

9.1 Studying literature in English and getting a job: some traditional possibilities

We begin by asking how the kind of study you have been following above fits in with your opportunities for employment. We turn later in this chapter to other practical uses of literary study, but first we ask: what kind of job, if any, is your course likely to enable you to do when you finish?

For many academic fields there are – subject always to vacancies existing in the relevant areas of employment – apparently clear answers to questions of this kind. If you study computer science, for example, you might hope to gain employment in the field of computer sales, software-writing or computerised systems management. If you follow a course in marketing, catering, marine engineering, or forestry, you might reasonably think of corresponding fields of potential employment which draw on the skills you develop in those courses. But the situation is much harder when it comes to subjects in the arts and humanities. What future does your work in these areas have?

For a long time people have suggested that the study of literature is good preparation for a variety of kinds of employment (look back to Chapter 2, for example, to our discussion of Arnold's ideas about a generalist education through literary studies). In such assertions, the claim being made is that studying literature has this capacity because it offers specialist preparation in skills of thinking, writing, and criticising. But the extent to which these 'values' have any real currency in the world is unclear. The image may be an accurate one. Equally, however, it is possible that these values may be representations of how things are imagined to be, rather than how they are; we could call such imaginary representations a 'mythological' view of the value of the subject. This would indicate that – as much as any story about gods, tooth fairies, or leprechauns – myths about 'good preparation for employment' can present an account of the ways things work which many people believe, but which are based mainly on unanalysed faith. Myths can serve clear purposes (e.g. justifying current ways of doing things and enabling them to continue, making people feel comfortable or optimistic, etc.), without necessarily representing a real state of affairs, and because of this they can be misleading. Without investigation, you simply can't say whether the traditional employment opportunities for literature students are 'mythical' or whether they actually exist.

To consider this question more concretely, we begin by taking up once more our consideration of literature in English as an academic field from our discussion in Chapter 1, and we list the traditionally cited 'professional' possibilities for literature students.

Teaching: English as a second or foreign language (ESL and EFL)
Teaching: English composition to native speakers;
Teaching: English Literature to native or non-native speakers;
Work in English-medium communications: television, radio, newspapers, journalism, advertising, etc.

The management and presentation of 'information': business administration, publicity and public relations work, etc.

Various kinds of employment which don't directly use or require familiarity with literature at all in societies which nevertheless give special status to the ability to communicate in and understand English.

'Leisure'-use (e.g. to pass time while unemployed or during retirement), taking advantage of the 'humane' benefits of advanced literacy.

In one form or another, these are justifications for studying literature in English produced by careers services and departments of English. The view from inside a profession may be different, though: many professionals working in journalism, television, and radio think of training in English literature as of little or no use as preparation for such work. Many even think that such study clouds the mind as regards acquiring 'real' practical professional skills, and creates its own specialised kind of 'false consciousness' (though professionals in these fields may of course be deriving this belief from their own myths about themselves). To help clarify *your own view* of how a literature in English course prepares you for different kinds of employment, try the following activity.

 Now do Activity 98 on page 189

9.2 Job possibilities as a 'social' question

In Section 9.1 we listed some professional opportunities which literature courses are thought to prepare you for. These were well-established examples from academic 'mythology' in the arts and humanities (and like a myth they *may* be firmly based in fact). The activity showed you your own opinions in the matter. Now we will consider how far it is reasonable to think that such opportunities actually *exist*. The extent to which the idea of these opportunities has any meaning in the social world depends on patterns of employment, which differ from time to time, place to place, government to government, and between different kinds of social situation. Opportunities to 'use' your acquired academic skills are social rather than simply individual. No matter how well prepared you are for work or a career, if there is no vacancy for you in your area or region, or if there are other, non-academic factors which in practice restrict your access (your gender, race or skin colour, class, accent, religious beliefs, politics, etc.), you may in the present form of your society face obstacles that academic preparation does not in itself surmount.

Study exists in much broader contexts of social opportunity (and limits on it). This is one reason why it is necessary constantly to locate the contents of this book in a general map of thought and intellectual enquiry (as in Chapter 8) and in the social map outlined in this chapter.

Only by thinking in terms of these larger contexts is it possible to check the perpetuation of myths about studying literature.

There are many different types of constraint which are likely to affect the 'vocational' usefulness of literary study.

Geography Different places have different roles and uses for the English language and forms of expression in it. These functions and uses have been shaped by specific histories (in many cases histories involving colonialism).

Kinds of institution Different kinds of institution call on different types of training, initiative and ability: multinational corporations, nationally based organisations, public service institutions, small businesses, community services, group collectives, individual entrepreneurism (such as desk-top publishing).

Social policies Different kinds of social policies increase or reduce public sector jobs, encourage or discourage service industry enterprise, etc.

Even ignoring inequalities of opportunity (such as those caused by prejudice over class, race, gender, and religion), conditions of the sort illustrated above ensure that the 'applicability' of a course in 'literature in English' will vary. Opportunities will be different, for example, for a student in New Delhi, Nairobi, Belo Horizonte, Manila, Chicago, and Glasgow in 1989. They will also be different for a student in any one of these places in 1989 and a student in the same place in 1959, 1969, 1979 – and in 1999.

Images of the usefulness of literature courses can't be *timeless* and *universal*. They need to be set in actual, relevant contexts of particular times and places. Even the use to which you put this book will vary fundamentally according to the particular circumstances in which you, as its reader, find yourself.

9.3 The changing situation of English

We have been looking at constraints on professional opportunity. Most of these involve large-scale, structural variations in and across societies, and many are affected in particular ways by the changing history and influence of the English language. Studying English literature often takes much of its justification and importance from its claimed connections (or implied connections) with the study of English language. Often, for instance, it is claimed to be a necessary part of the development of advanced reading and writing skills among native speakers, or of the acquisition of English as a foreign language by non-native speakers. It is even possible that without the current international role of the English language in the world, the study of literature in English would shrink back within the borders of countries where English is the principal, native language. Bearing these claimed connections in mind, we should now consider the situation of the English language more directly.

Activity 98   *Preparing for employment*
(60 mins)

1. For each of the jobs described below (which are regularly cited as making use of qualifications and skills in literature in English), outline in column A the special skills or knowledge you feel you *do* acquire from studying literature which will be directly useful. In column B, outline the *additional* skills or knowledge you think you would still need to acquire, from some other source.

A What you *do* learn	B What you still *need* to learn

Teaching English as a foreign language (Imagine you would be teaching English to a group who don't know any English, but would like to.)

Advertising copywriter (Imagine you would be writing copy, including slogans, to advertise a wide range of commercial products.)

Public relations or information officer/clerk (Imagine you would be preparing documents which seek to represent the activities of your employer/client to a larger public (potential customers, civil or legal authorities, its own staff, etc.)

Teacher of English composition to native speakers (Imagine you would be teaching native speakers to write letters, essays, reports, poems, etc.)

Teacher of literature in English (Imagine you would be teaching students, for whom English may or may not be a first language, a course in literature in English.)

Now look over your two columns.

2. Do any skills repeat themselves in the entries you have made for any of the jobs *in either of your columns*?   YES/NO

If 'YES', name them, and explain why this should be.

Tourism specialist (Imagine you would be describing and marketing a city or region to visitors.)

3. Name the job for which you put the *least* under column B).

....

This is the job you think a literature course offers fullest preparation for.

4. Here are four statements about literature courses. In the light of the two columns you have filled in above, consider how accurate these statements are. Write next to each one 'completely accurate', 'accurate' or 'inaccurate'.

Journalist (Imagine you would be researching and writing articles on a wide range of non-literary topics for a newspaper or magazine.)

  (i) A literature course seeks to prepare you for many different kinds of job, so you would expect additional, more specialist training to be necessary. Nevertheless, such courses give you a valuable 'core' training.

 (ii) The whole point of a course in literature is that it remains separate from – and so enables you to reflect critically on – particular types of social activity, including employment; the course *shouldn't* be directly vocational. Literature course were devised precisely to be separate from employment and practicality: to be disinterested. Generalist education is best, preparing you for life with general problem-solving skills which can then be adapted to specific purposes later.

(iii) There's a problem with literature courses: they don't prepare people adequately for jobs. But they *could* do if they were adapted from their present form – keeping but modifying some elements and adding new ones.

(iv) There's a problem with literature courses: they don't serve any useful function. And it's not easy to see how they could be adapted to make them useful.

☞ *Now rejoin text on page 188*

It is specific forms of interest in the English language which connect the work you do in studying literature with social and professional opportunities beyond your study.

 Now do Activity 99

9.3.1 ENGLISH AS AN INTERNATIONAL LANGUAGE

Some initial sense of **the scale and spread of English** is necessary if you are to understand:

- the range of functions for which the language is used;
- the social and educational controversies surrounding it in terms of standards and variation;
- the literary questions that face writers when they choose which variety of the language (or in many cases which language) to write in.

The massive scale of use of English in the late twentieth century comes largely from the fact that **English increasingly functions as an international language** – almost certainly as the major international language in the world. It is used, that is to say, by very many people for whom it is not a first or native language, even in situations when it is a foreign language for *everyone* involved in the conversation or communication. Many more people speak English on a daily basis today in India than spoke English world-wide at the time of Shakespeare.

Besides English, there are still a number of other important, internationally used languages; and there have been others in the past. Dutch, French, Japanese, Mandarin Chinese, Greek, Spanish, Portuguese, Latin, and Sanskrit are all languages which have had a wide international currency, and are still used in parts of the world outside the countries in which they developed.

 Now do Activity 100 on page 192

The political situations (generally involving forms of control, either through military force or commercial influence) which initially give rise to the extended, transnational use of languages do not remain constant. In large historical terms, therefore, there is no compelling reason to imagine that, because English is currently the major international language, it will necessarily still be so in a hundred years' time (though many people do think this is likely to be the case). English as a means of international communication competes with other languages (such as French, Spanish, Chinese, and Russian), as well as with artificially constructed languages such as Esperanto. Challenging the link between specifically linguistic and more broadly cultural influence, too, there are movements against the impact on other languages of English (for example, in France against 'Franglais' – the use of words borrowed from English to replace French words: 'le weekend', 'le floppy-disk', etc.). In the case of countries which wish to gain access to technological or scientific information in English without compromising indigenous cultural or religious values, there are also attempts to distinguish the communicative from the cultural dimensions of 'English as an international language'. So, sending students to study English in India rather than the United States, for instance, is thought of in some countries (especially in Africa and the Middle East) as a way of avoiding one kind of cultural influence ('cocacolonialism'), and gaining access instead to a form of 'non-aligned English'.

The international circulation and prestige of a language are not a result of special features of that language, but a historical accident of the present or

---

Activity 99   *How much do you know about the English language?*

(10 mins)

In studying English, it is easy to lose sight of many basic social facts about the language as a result of concern with more specific or local questions. To highlight this, in this activity we present you with a list of assertions about English (many take the form of closest estimates on the evidence available). All you have to do is decide whether the assertions are true or not. Delete as applicable.

(1) There are around 750 million regular speakers of English in the world.   True/False

(2) There are around 300 million native speakers of English in the world.   True/False

(3) Three-quarters of the world's mail is written in English.   True/False

(4) The *OED* contains about 500,000 words.   True/False

(5) 500,000 words is about half of the words in the English language, if you take technical terms into account.   True/False

(6) About half of all business deals made in Europe are made in English.   True/False

(7) The official language of international air traffic control is English.   True/False

Answers on p. 214.

 Now rejoin text above

Activity 100   *Languages, countries and international languages*
(60 mins)

Fill in the columns for each language. Consult one of the reference books listed at the back of this book to check and add to your ideas.

Language	Countries in which it is now used on a signfiicant scale	Time-span during which it had/has the largest number of speakers worldwide
French		
Portuguese		
Latin		

Language	Countries in which it is now used on a signfiicant scale	Time-span during which it had/has the largest number of speakers worldwide
Spanish		
Mandarin Chinese		
Russian		
Persian (Farsi)		

☛ *Now rejoin text on page 191*

past prestige, power or influence of those societies which happen to use it.

Q: Is the use of any particular language *regulated by law* in your state or country? (For example, is English a required condition of citizenship?) And is there guaranteed provision of schooling in minority languages?

9.3.2 DIFFERENT KINDS OF USE OF ENGLISH

Above we have listed numbers of users of English. But given complexities in the international use of English, we need to add some detail of the different *types of use* of the language. Here are some more figures.

(i) Some ENL users of English (English as a Native Language, 'first' language, or 'mother tongue'):

USA	250million
UK	55m
Canada	25m
Australia	16m
New Zealand	3m

(ii) Some ESL users of English (English as a Second Language):

(around thirty countries, all multi-ethnic and multi-lingual; English as a form of contact between different groups)

India	28m out of	750m
Bangladesh	3m out of	94m
Philippines	2m out of	50m
Tanzania	0.8m out of	20m
Malaysia	0.6m out of	14m

(iii) Some EFL users of English (English as a Foreign Language):

USSR	2m out of	270m
Indonesia	1.5m out of	150m
China	1m out of	1000m
Egypt	0.5m out of	5m

What is instantly clear from these tables is not only that English is used by very different proportions of speakers in different countries, but that it is used for *a range of different purposes, and in many different contexts:*[1]

■ as a native language (or mother tongue), among monolinguals;

■ as a native language, among bilinguals or multi-linguals;

■ as a specialised, learned medium of communication (e.g. in diplomacy, business, technology, and science);

■ as an 'associate' or 'link' language (facilitating contact between users of different first or native languages).

In the case of English being used as a second or foreign language, these different uses relate to different kinds of motivation, on a scale between **integrative motivation**, where the aim is to be part of a culture or society which uses the language, and **instrumental motivation**, where the aim is simply to acquire the language for specific communicative purposes.

Looked at simply as a phenomenon of the contemporary world, this range of functions, contexts and motivations can be described in many different ways. (Describing this variety in uses of the language is a part of the fields of applied linguistics, sociolinguistics and sociology of language). But when you think about literary and cultural dimensions of the questions raised by this kind of variation, it is clear that the range of functions and contexts results from particular historical developments within English as a language. So we should now consider *how* and *why* English came to be used in these circumstances and in these ways. Facts about types and numbers of users, and of possible kinds of motivation, need to be linked with particular *histories* of countries or regions to develop detailed language 'portraits' of the use of English around the world. And doing so inevitably suggests a far more complicated world situation than any utopian image of 'universal communication'.

9.3.3 HISTORY OF ENGLISH

Looking back historically shows up the scale of changes in the use of English. Even though it may be tempting to look away from complexities of the world situation described above to contemplate an earlier and simple 'golden age' of English, nostalgic views of this kind have little to do with actual history. Consider, for example, the language situation of fourteenth-century Britain.

(a) In England, Parliament and the law were conducted in French during the first half of the century, then in English during the second half. (In 1362, the Statute of Pleadings made English the language of the law courts, even though Latin would continue to be used as the language of legal record . . . and the Statute itself was written in *French*.)

(b) John Gower (1330?–1408), a contemporary and friend of Geoffrey Chaucer, wrote three main poems during the period: one in French, one in Latin, and one in English – though the one in English nevertheless had a Latin title, *Confessio Amantis*.

(c) Virtually all scholarship, religious ceremony, and speculation were conducted in Latin throughout the century. The southern English variety of English was only beginning to be accepted as a 'standard'; and you would be unlikely to understand someone else's variety of English if you travelled a hundred miles in most directions from wherever you lived. Welsh was generally spoken in Wales (though the use of the language was in decline, following the English invasions of Wales); Gaelic was spoken in most of Scotland, with Inglis (later to become Scots) becoming established in the lowland, central, and eastern regions.

Many factors contributed to the changes which took English from this almost minor role in the complicated language situation of mediaeval Britain to give it its current pre-eminence as the major international language in the world in the late twentieth century. These factors include political conquest by the English within the British Isles (of Wales, Scotland, and Ireland), and colonisation by Britain overseas (of America, Australia, India, some of Africa, etc.). More recently, the history involves the legacy of such colonisation: movements of British and other English-speaking people to many parts of the world, and migration of people from colonial and post-colonial countries (such as Pakistan or Jamaica) to colonising and former colonising countries (such as Britain). In the twentieth century especially, the role and status of English are affected by the further rise of the United States as a colonial and commercial power, the development of English-speaking multinational corporations, neocolonial satellite governments and 'client' states, new markets, and data networks and systems across the globe.

Languages are formed and change through *contact* and *conflict*, as well as through internal, purely 'linguistic' forces.

To understand how studying literature in English is connected with this changing history of the English language, it is necessary to trace that history in more detail. But a still very simple sketch can be given, to trace the development of the language from its first emergence in the British Isles, within the context of the other languages of Britain.

1. *Humans invade* 'Britain' (not at that time a separate island), probably using a variety of different languages, from about a quarter of a million years ago. The oldest language for which we have any record is Pictish, spoken by inhabitants of northern Britain. Pictish is still being written (on gravestones) as late as AD 800.

2. *Celts invade*, from the European mainland, 700–600 BC (or possibly as early as 2000 BC), bringing the Celtic language (or perhaps a variety of Celtic languages) that later develop into Irish Gaelic, Scottish Gaelic, Cornish, Cumbric, Manx, Welsh, British (not the same as English) and – by combination with the earlier Pictish – Celtic Pictish. Only the two Gaelics and Welsh survive today.

3. *Romans invade*, 43 BC, bringing Latin. Colonisers and probably the upper-class and urban colonised speak Latin; the lower classes remain Celtic speakers. The Roman armies withdraw from Britain around

AD 410, and about AD 600 Latin dies out as a language in common spoken use, but St Augustine revives Latin in Britain to some extent in AD 597 by using it in Christian ceremonies.

4. *Anglo-Saxons invade*, from north-west Europe, from about AD 400, bringing the earliest form of 'English' to Britain, in one part of the worldwide nomadic movements which brought the 'Dark Ages' to the classical empires of the world. As the Anglo-Saxons conquer an increasing part of England they bring with them the Germanic language known as Old English or Anglo-Saxon (we know of four main dialects of the language).

5. *Vikings invade*, from Norway and Denmark, AD 800–1000, bringing the Germanic language Norse, and colonise (by the 'Danelaw' political settlement) part of England. Speakers of Old English can probably understand speakers of Norse and vice versa. By 1100 Norse is dying out in England, but survives in part of Scotland for a further period of several hundred years, and on the North Scottish islands of Orkney and Shetland develops into the language Norn, which dies out in the nineteenth century.

6. *Normans invade*, from Northern France, AD 1066. The Normans reached France as Norse-speaking invaders, but by 1066 are speakers of Norman French. The language which develops in England is called Anglo-Norman, and is used by the colonisers for law, administration, literature, etc.; Old English – itself rapidly changing and influenced by the colonisers' language – is used by the colonised, with some bilingualism. Norman colonisers are politically cut off from France during the thirteenth century. There is gradual ascendency during the twelfth and thirteenth centuries of new forms of English ('Middle' English), borrowing heavily from Norman French. Norman French survives to some extent today in the British Channel Islands.

7. *'Modern' English arrives* from the fifteenth century onwards. Midlands dialect is gradually adopted as 'standard', e.g. by Caxton and Wycliffe in the fifteenth century for early printing. English spreads in Scotland, particularly during the sixteenth century, partly as a result of the post-Reformation requirement of an English Bible. There are arguments during the late sixteenth century about whether English is a good enough language for literature, compared with Greek, Latin, French, and Italian. Both the Reformation in the sixteenth century and the Civil War in the seventeenth century reduce the influence of Latin.

8. *British invade* many countries (including Ireland) from the seventeenth century onwards. Eighteenth-century dictionaries, grammars, pronunciation manuals, and other teaching materials emphasise the value of 'standard' forms of English. During the nineteenth century the systematic export of English to India, through the formal system of education, begins.

American Independence begins the process of separate definition of the 'American language'. The late nineteenth century sees the rise (especially through public schools, the army and the Civil Service) of 'received pronunciation' as a non-regional 'standard' accent, later called 'Queen's English', 'BBC English', etc. Changes to English in the twentieth century occur in colonial and post-colonial societies.

This short sketch does not capture the complexity of the linguistic history of Britain (e.g. there have been other demographic changes).[2] We could, for example, have described the travelling people (from the fifteenth century onwards) speaking Romani and now Anglo-Romani, Dutch-speaking Flemings (fifteenth century), French-speaking Huguenots (sixteenth century), Spanish- and Portuguese-speaking Jews (seventeenth and eighteenth centuries), and, in the twentieth century, speakers of German, Punjabi, Cantonese, Urdu, Greek, etc. Sometimes languages new to Britain have survived; sometimes they have died out or are dying out, leaving a few traces in the British English vocabulary.

☞ *Now do Activity 101 on page 195*

Why do languages change? Linguists think that there are both internal and external reasons.[3] Languages change 'from the inside' when the systems which underlie them regulate themselves. But change inside the system underlying a language may coincide with (and be caused by) external changes in the linguistic situation: when new languages come into contact with existing languages, or new uses of language become common. Not only do languages change, but often the use of a language changes (children no longer learn it and it dies with its last speaker, or it is imposed by law on a population, etc.). Literature is of interest in this respect as one of the *public forms of language* (along with legal language and the speech of prestigious and powerful social groups) which construct images of a unifying national identity within a society. Equally, however, such images of identity, once constructed, leave contradictions and a residue of unfinished business.

Unresolved issues as regards images of national identity and 'unity' – as well as the established images themselves – are represented and worked through in literature and other uses of language, such as storytelling, jokes, etc.

Many steps in the spread of English have involved either colonisation or the setting up of trade links. In this way cultures come into **contact**. In trading, employment and slavery situations, simplified versions of English have been used to make transactions possible, mixing features of English with those of the traders', employers' or slaves' own first languages. These 'trading varieties' are known as **pidgins** (languages used for localised forms of contact but lacking 'native speakers'). When speakers of different

Activity 101   *Investigating earlier forms of English*
(60 mins)

There is considerable variation in Old English, in Middle English, and in Modern English. Nevertheless, in this activity, we seek to compare the broad differences between these three stages of the language.

(1) Old English (some letters modernised)

Ic this giedd wrece   be me full geomorre,
minre selfre sith.   Ic thæt secgan mæg,
hwæt ic iermtha ge-bad,   siththan ic upp weox,
niewes oththe ealdes,   na ma thonne nu.
    (from the anonymous poem *The Wife's Lament*,
    written down c. AD 950–1000 but may be older)

Word-for-word translation
I this poem recite   about myself very sad,
my own experience.   I this say can,
what I of miseries lived through,   after I up grew,
early or late,   never more than now.

Modern English version
I recite this poem about my very sad self and my own experience. I can say of what miseries I lived through after I grew up, early or late, never more than now.

(2) Middle English

Me thoghte thus: that hyt was May,
And in the dawenynge I lay
(Me Mette thus) in my bed al naked,
And loked forth, for I was waked
With smale foules a gret hep
That had affrayed me out of my slep,
Thorgh noyse and swetnesse of her song.
    (Geoffrey Chaucer, from
    The Book of the Duchess, 1369)

Word-for-word translation
I thought thus: that it was May,
And in the dawn I lay
(I dreamed thus) in my bed completely naked,
And looked forth, for I was woken
by small birds a great heap
that had frightened me out of my sleep
through noise and sweetness of their song.

Modern English version
This is what I thought: that it was Mary and (so I dreamt) I was lying in my bed at dawn and I looked around because I was woken by a large number of small birds that had frightened me out of my sleep through the noise and sweetness of their singing.

1. For each of the passages, try to identify changes in the language between the original and the translations. (This may not be easy, as – without detailed work on Old English and Middle English – you are likely to have serious difficulty following the original texts.) As far as you can, nevertheless, make a list of changes in each of the following areas (keeping your lists for the two texts in separate columns).

Text	(1) Old English text	(2) Middle English text
Spelling changes		
Words no longer used (even if you modify their spelling)		
Words which are used, but no longer mean what they appear to mean in the extract		
Word orders which differ from Modern English		

2. Now try to read the Old English and Middle English passages aloud, guessing by the spelling as best you can how they were pronounced. By trying to read the passages aloud you will get some sense of the *change* between these earlier varieties of English and varieties of English in the twentieth century.

Now rejoin text on page 194

languages who communicate by way of such a pidgin have children, those children acquire the pidgin as their first or native language, not just for specific transactions but for all social purposes. The pidgin in these circumstances *does* have native speakers, and is known as a **creole**. Some people think that Middle English developed in this way as a **language of contact** between Anglo-Norman and Old English. Change of this kind can lead to the gradual establishment of distinct varieties of 'English', different from those with which the pidgins and creoles were originally connected; nativised dialects are formed. (Frequently these varieties 'fossilise' or produce their systematicity at a level of complexity of language rules less than that of the language on which they are based, and often they show features of 'transfer' from aspects of the first or native language of their speakers.) In many cases, the nativised variety gradually gains prestige and recognition, and becomes accepted as a local standard dialect.

9.3.4 VARIETIES AND VARIATION

Language change leads to language variation.[4] Sometimes people try to deny the existence of language change, and claim that they stand outside language variation (e.g. they claim to speak the 'proper' form of the language rather than a dialect), as though they are able to *see* contrasts in meaning and connotation between regional, class, and situational varieties, but are somehow not themselves subject to the distinctions and instability of 'identity' which these entail. But there is no known society where language variation doesn't exist. You will never find a pure, unchanging, and unvarying 'standard' variety to suit all purposes. (If it's formal enough for some situations, it won't be intimate enough for others, and so on.) Your use of English therefore locates you somewhere in a complicated and changing field of variation in the language, which carries with it not only deep-seated meanings about regional and class origin but also your constantly changing perceptions of what kind of situation or relationship you think you're involved in at any given moment.

We can distinguish two principal types of language variation: variation according to *who you are* and variation according to *the situation you find yourself in*.

Variation according to who you are: accent and dialect

People who speak in different **accents** pronounce things differently. People who speak different **dialects** use a slightly different grammar and vocabulary (as well as pronunciation). Everybody has an accent, and everybody speaks a dialect (though an individual may speak, and usually can understand, more than one accent and more than one dialect). Looking at class and regional *variation* in broad social terms, a clear pattern is visible in Britain, which is not, however, paralleled in all other societies which use English.

The higher up the class system you look, the less regional variation you find. The lower down the class system you look, the more regional variation you find.

Variation according to the situation you're in: register

Different situations call for different types of language. Variation of this kind is called **register** variation (or variation in 'style'). Different registers of language are associated with particular types of situations.

The classification of situations might be scalar	
Formality	very formal – fairly formal – fairly informal – very informal
Technicality	very technical *through to* non-technical

Or the classifications can be many-way	
Medium	different kinds of language are considered appropriate to writing, speaking into a telephone answering machine, etc.
Relationship between speakers	different kinds of language are used in relationships according to issues of formality, gender, social position and power, age, etc.

☞ *Now do Activity 102 on page 197*

The various possibilities for register variation combine; you can have an informal technical conversation, a formal non-technical one, an intimate answerphone message, and a technical or non-technical telex. But in any actual situation the linguistic behaviour of the participants is unlikely to be governed by an objective and conscious characterisation of the situation. While there *are* external constraints which define types of situation (e.g. job interviews and courtroom cross-examinations are unlikely to encourage informality), situations are also defined by the participants in them. They are responsive to changes of atmosphere as they develop. Your use of language varies – spontaneously and without consciously monitoring it, although you can also intervene to control variation deliberately – according to an idea of *appropriateness* to your purpose and context.

Moreover, just as you can make your selection of words and grammatical constructions *fit with* your idea of what a situation demands, you can also choose them in deliberate opposition to what you think it demands (to show that you reject an assumed definition of the

Activity 102   *Register variation*

(15 mins)

Here are some different types of situation. In each case, find examples which show up the potential contrasts, and try to find words, phrases or sentences which mean the same (differing only in style or some formal property). We have given a suggestion to start you off.

technical situation: ....sodium chloride ....

non-technical situation: ....salt...........................

formal situation: ....

informal situation:...

situation of writing a business letter:.................................

....

situation of writing a friendly letter: ....

....

legalistic situation: ....

religious situation: ....

situation of talking to a 2-year-old:...............................

....

situation of talking to a 20-year-old:...............................

....

☛ *Now rejoin text on page 196*

---

situation, for instance, or to override an expectation, or to be ironic or funny).

☛ *Now do Activity 103*

Identity and situations

The distinction between who you are and what situation you're in is not a clear-cut one. There are, for instance,

periods of social mobility which alter the meanings and connotations of the language of entire regions and classes. Such large-scale changes change the system of contrast between prestigious and non-prestigious, desirable and undesirable varieties. (Historically, for instance, classes rise and fall, and class values change with them.) Alongside these large-scale changes, there is also – unevenly and changing in accordance with other patterns of social development – individual social mobility. Indi-

---

Activity 103   *Exploring register variation*

(20 mins)

And the last we saw was the bloody car rounding the corner and old sheepsface on it gesticulating and the bloody mongrel after it with his lugs back for all he was bloody well worth to tear him limb from limb. Hundred to five! Jesus, he took the value of it out of him, I promise you.

When, lo, there came about them all a great brightness and they beheld the chariot wherein He stood ascend to heaven. And they beheld Him in the chariot, clothed upon in the glory of the brightness, having raiment as of the sun, fair as the moon and terrible that for awe they durst not look upon Him. And there came a voice out of heaven, calling: *Elijah! Elijah!* And he answered with a main cry: *Abba! Adonai!* And

they beheld Him even Him, ben Bloom Elijah, amid clouds of angels ascend to the glory of the brightness at an angle of fortyfive degrees over Donohue's in Little Green Street like a shot off a shovel.

1. Mark, on this extract from James Joyce's *Ulysses*, where you think significant changes in register occur (if you think the passage contains such changes).
2. Underline the words, constructions, etc. which prompt you to mark the transitions where you have put them.

☛ *Now rejoin text above*

viduals' accents and dialects change, and are modified, to suit personally changed social circumstances. If you have more than one dialect available to you, you can put to use your ability to change between them just as you use your ability to change register. Or, on the other hand, there can be a tendency to use specific parts of your register-spectrum to suit *all* purposes, exchanging the potentially open-ended range of situation varieties into a relatively fixed social 'identity' (for example by never being 'informal' or 'intimate'); problems which people have with writing and speaking can often stem from an inability to adapt their register system.

Your overall language **repertoire** is the range of varieties you are able to use. It derives from the combination of your background and the range of situations you find yourself in coupled with your perception of how you want to appear in those situations and your ability (either spontaneous or acquired) to perform the registers you feel appropriate. As regards listening and reading, your repertoire is far wider than it is in speaking and writing: you are likely to be aware of a broad range of contrasts, and to have complicated (partly individual and partly socially constructed) connotations relating to them.

☛ *Now do Activity 104*

Activity 104   *Linguistic variation and your own situation*
(40 mins)

1. Tick the boxes in the grid below, which seeks to construct an image of the language(s), or particular varieties of language, you use. Judge for yourself what 'standard' means.

The language you use	At home	At work or college	In shops	In books you read	In newspapers you read
A standard form of English					
A standard form with a non-standard accent					
A non-standard form of English					
A language other than English					

2. Make a list of difficulties which arise as you try to fill in this chart. (Try to be as precise as possible about the problems of, for example, defining different *uses* of language which all exist 'at home', or of defining where one variety ends and another begins, or indicating differences between what you hear and what you say, etc.)

☛ *Now rejoin text*

9.4 Literature in the English language

We suggested earlier in this chapter that the significance of studying literature in English is linked to specific contexts of use of the English language. We now need to consider how the fact of language change and consequent variation is relevant in the study of literature.

Awareness of the changing and complicated contexts of use of English is a necessary background to exploring literary works. Literature is made of language; so one important part of studying it involves studying its language. Variation within English functions both as a resource for *selection* (choosing a 'language of literature' out of all the various possibilities that exist for expression) and/or as *potential for contrast* within an individual text (juxtaposing and shifting between different varieties to create particular local effects).

Many current varieties of English began their existence as learned, second-language varieties, only later becoming a native language for anyone; and for this reason these varieties are often called **nativised varieties**. In their early forms, such varieties are generally restricted in prestige by their apparent derivation from and competition with some notion of a 'standard English'. One part of the process through which such varieties gain acceptance, as new regional standards, is that of extension to their functional range: from being used initially merely in servile and administrative registers through to a fuller range of varieties – humorous, intimate, poetic, etc.

As well as serving as a way of representing a culture, the existence of 'literature' in a variety acts as one type of claim to respectability.

Like all other uses of a language, literary use negotiates diversity in the language. But a restriction on using non-prestigious varieties for literary purposes is imposed by ideas of the appropriate language for *high* culture ('the right language for literature', 'literary language' as something that needs to observe conventions of **decorum** or special propriety).

Historically, choosing which language or which *variety* of a language to use in literary writing has always been an important issue. English, for instance, was not widely considered an appropriate language to write literature in during the fifteenth and early sixteenth centuries. Anglo-Saxon literature had been widely displaced by literature in French after the Norman invasion; and Caxton is often remembered as having taken a bold step, during the fifteenth century, in printing such a large proportion of works in English. Spenser, writing at the end of the sixteenth century, felt he needed to invent features of the language to elevate it for literary use.

By the mid-seventeenth century, nevertheless (following the period of work by Shakespeare, Ben Jonson, etc.), English was widely praised as a language with an exceptionally, possibly uniquely, rich literature. This is an important shift in attitudes to English: because people treat books as worthy of respect and somehow definitive of the language they use, books *serve* as a major force in reproducing and validating the language on which they draw.

In this context, it is worth noting that there are at least two meanings for the phrase 'a language'. The first describes the internalised, mental knowledge of speakers of that language; whatever they say or write is 'part of the language'; anything they wouldn't accept as part of the language isn't. This is the sense of 'a language' used by linguists. The second sense describes the accepted *public* forms of a language, as given through published works, textbooks, courses of instruction, etc. This 'language' overlaps with the first but is hardly ever the same as it. It is this second language which is stored in dictionaries like the *OED*.

Because written texts, especially published written texts, draw on particular *parts* of the language in which they are written, they reinforce (or can modify) larger patterns of the language-using culture of which they are a part.

Q: How many novels do you know, or know of, which are written in the dialect, or variety of English, of your own area, region, ethnic group, or class? Most/many/some/not many/none

Before 1400 works written in English are written in many different dialects. Within any single text, however, there is seldom any mixing of dialects (although there are a few examples of a word being borrowed from another dialect in order to maintain a rhyme, for instance). After 1400, however, things begin to change; and by 1450 most texts are written in just one dialect: that of the capital of England, London (which was in fact Chaucer's dialect). It is at about the same time that you first find one dialect embedded in a text principally in another dialect, and being used to create a specific effect relating to dialect: dialectal *difference* arrives on the literary agenda (early examples can be found in Chaucer's *The Reeve's Tale*, and the Wakefield *Second Shepherd's Play*). The particular effect intended by the use of dialect, at least in Chaucer, relies on an assumption that the London dialect is superior and the regional dialects inferior; the regional speakers are intended to be comic. *Stratification* within varieties of a language creates potential for representing different ideas of social prestige, gender types, and seriousness; moreover, stratification will be different depending on social attitudes. Dialect-speaking characters are, before the twentieth century, almost always minor. Their speaking of dialect can mark them out as one or a combination of: comic, stupid, 'naively' wise, likeable, 'low-life' villainous, acting above their station (where they mix dialect and prestige forms unsuccessfully), etc. The narrator's voice in a novel is always in standard English.

In the twentieth century, however, a series of changes seems to have confronted this pattern of relatively clear stratification and connotation.

1. In **literary modernism**, especially poetry, there has been an inclusion of registers and dialects not previously associated with literature. (These varieties have frequently been introduced as elements in juxtapositions or collage, presenting contrasts and contradictions of social 'voice'. The varieties often appear to be used, nevertheless, to 'refine' literary language from an initially uncontrollable linguistic polyphony into a proper, serious voice of the artist – the artist finding a voice after the collapse of an assured, Romantic identity for the writer.)
2. In writing in colonial countries, there has been use of

emerging varieties of English at the same time as colonial struggles, leading to a **post-colonial legacy** of active creative writing in English (cf. the 1930s in India and the 1950s in Africa).

3. **National media such as television** have often started out (e.g. in Britain) with their presenters (experts, newsreaders, etc.) using only prestige accents. The development of regional media has brought regional speech, however; and this has had some influence on nationally broadcast television. Nevertheless, speakers with non-prestige accents are still often (slightly comic, though wise or skilled) 'personalities' rather than relatively anonymous presenters.

Each of these shifts or innovations exerts a force on patterns of usage and prestige of the different varieties of English. Each plays a small role in changing their cultural meanings and values. It is difficult to ascribe clear causes to these changes. But one simple way to think about them is to associate them with 'breaks' or moments of disruption or collapse.

Modernist writing   : Europe breaks down.
New English literatures   : Empire breaks down.
Media and popular culture : Ideas of 'Literature' break
                            down.

Together, these changing forces shift an emphasis from the creation of a selective 'literary language' in English to a new – still unresolved – 'broken English', or range of competing and conflicting varieties in which social relationships and perceptions can be represented.

9.4.1 THE POST-COLONIAL WRITER'S DILEMMA

A further, urgent question has arisen in post-colonial situations. Colonisers often draw national boundaries around a heterogeny of peoples; and many colonial countries (e.g. in Africa) combine speakers of many different languages. The introduced, colonial language may have been the only language in principle common to the country during the colonial period, and as colonisers withdraw, countries and the writers in those countries have often been left with the awkward question: is it inherently 'anti-patriotic' to continue to use an imposed, colonial language?

YES, many say, if that use restricts the development of cultural expression in indigenous languages, and accentuates contrast between an educated cosmopolitan elite and an (often regional) underclass.

NO, others say, who consider that English was used importantly and constructively as the unifying language in many nationalist struggles which have ended regimes of direct colonial power, and who see a necessary, continuing role for English as a contact language in cultures now redefining themselves following the colonial experience.

This issue has been a topic of energetic argument, especially since the 1950s. Consider the three following influential views regarding whether, in countries where English was first imposed by a colonial regime, it should now be used for literary purposes; and, if so, what variety of English should be used.

We cannot write like the English. We should not. We cannot write only as Indians. We have grown to look at the large world around us as part of us. Our method of expression therefore has to be a dialect which will some day prove to be as distinctive and colorful as the Irish and the American. Time alone will justify it. (Raja Rao, preface to *Kanthapura*, 1938)

So my answer to the question. Can an African ever learn English well enough to be able to use it effectively in creative writing? is certainly yes. If on the other hand you ask: Can he ever learn to use it like a native speaker? I should say, I hope not. It is neither necessary nor desirable for him to be able to do so. The price a world language must be prepared to pay is submission to many different kinds of use. The African writer should aim to use English in a way that brings out his message best without altering the language to the extent that its value as a medium of international exchange will be lost. He should aim at fashioning out an English which is at once universal and able to carry his peculiar experience. . . . It will have to be a new English, still in full communion with its ancestral home, but altered to suit its new African surroundings. (Chinua Achebe, 'English and the African Writer', *Transition*, 1965)

The oppressed and the exploited of the earth maintain their defiance: liberty from theft. But the biggest weapon wielded and actually daily unleashed by imperialism against that collective defiance is the cultural bomb. The effect of a cultural bomb is to annihilate a people's belief in their names, in their languages, in their environment, in their heritage of struggle, in their unity, in their capacities and ultimately in themselves. It makes them see their past as one wasteland of non-achievement and it makes them want to distance themselves from that wasteland. It makes them want to identify with that which is furthest removed from themselves; for instance, with other people's languages rather than their own. (Ngugi wa Thiong'o, *Decolonising the Mind*, 1981)

9.4.2 REPRESENTATION OF DIALECT IN POST-COLONIAL SITUATIONS

Not all writing in Anglophone situations involves markers of dialect. In fact, most doesn't. Most literature in English in such post-colonial situations is written in standard English. Its difference from British, American, or Canadian literature in English lies in its representation of different ways of life and different kinds of social experience and relationships: innovating in terms of perception, symbolism and cultural reference, rather than local features of linguistic style.

When such works *do* involve dialect and accent representations, it's easy to assume that these reflect some actual, 'authentic' usage. But is this the case? Or do such representations *construct* images of dialect not for their accurate reflection of usage but for other purposes?

 Now do Activity 105

Activity 105   *Analysing the language of 'New English' literatures*
(60 mins)

1. For each of the following extracts, underline features which appear to belong to a dialect different from your own.

(a) It was the day's ending and Okolo by a window stood. Okolo stood looking at the sun behind the tree tops falling. . . . Okolo at palm trees looked.
      (Gabriel Okara, *The Voice*)

(b) I was a palm-wine drinkard since I was a boy of ten years of age. I had no other work more than to drink palm-wine in my life. In those days we did not know other money, except COWRIES, so that everything was very cheap, and my father was the richest man in our town.
      (Amos Tutuola, *The Palm-Wine Drinkard*, 1952)

(c) I am standing for peace and non-violence.
      Why world is fighting fighting
      Why all people of world
      Are not following Mahatma Gandhi,
      I am simply not understanding.
      Ancient Indian Wisdom is 100% correct.
      I should say even 200% correct.
      But Modern generation is neglecting –
      Too much going for fashion and foreign thing.
      (Nissim Ezekiel, 'The Patriot', *Very Indian Poems in Indian English* from *Latter Day Psalms*, 1982)

2. You are unlikely to know more than one of these varieties. Is it nevertheless possible for you to estimate whether these texts accurately represent a particular dialect of English? Make a note of what you can say about this just by reading the texts.

How would you confirm your speculations, and/or find out more about the accuracy of the varieties?

3. What is the purpose of the use of dialect in each passage? Is it authenticity, or a desire to create a stereotype, or to be funny, etc.?

4. Consider your own response to each text (whether you found it funny, moving, annoying, etc.). How much was your response conditioned by the associations and connotations which each of these dialects has for you?

 Now rejoin text

9.4.3 THE QUESTION OF AUDIENCE FOR THE NEW LITERATURES

Apart from whether the language being used is a 'standard' or 'nativised' dialect, a further major issue arises: that of the scope of the audience being addressed. What audience exists for writing in the non-native varieties of English (the 'New Englishes')? Is this an intranational audience (within one country) or an international audience? The language someone chooses to write in clearly depends on the range of languages available to her or him, the audiences reachable through each, and the connotations of the language in question. To begin consideration of this, let's start by reviewing an African writer's possible linguistic choices.

 Now do Activity 106 on page 202

Activity 106   *Africa: choosing a language to write in* (60 mins)

1. Imagine yourself to be a person (speaking any languages you choose) living in an African country. You are setting out to write a novel, a poem or a short story. Write here:

(a) the country you imagine yourself to be in ....
(b) the kind of text you are going to write: novel/poem/ short story (delete as applicable).

2. But on what basis do you choose which language(s) to use in your text? The vertical side of the table below suggests some of the options. Fill in all the slots in the table, thereby assessing the various alternatives and the consequences of choosing between them. Fill in each vertical column in order, starting with the left column and working across to the right column. (You may need to use reference works, but leave slots empty if you wish.)

Name of language	Likely audience of your text	Advantages	Disadvantages	Political meanings of the choice
The most widely used African language of the country State which				
An African language used widely in Africa State which				
British English				
American English				
An African English				

Another non-African language State which				
A personal idiosyncratic form of English				
A combination of languages State which				

3. When you have filled in the grid, assess each horizontal line. Each line identifies implications you think follow from choosing a particular language or variety. Now consider the rightmost vertical column. This outlines the 'political' alternatives you think a writer faces in the situation you have chosen.

4. Finally, draw a similar grid on a separate sheet of paper to explore the alternatives facing a writer in a different social situaiton. Choose your own situation if appropriate, or consider one of the following: the Philippines, Singapore, Sweden, Mexico, India. (Again, you may need to refer to reference books, or to leave some slots empty.)

Now rejoin text

Activity 106 concerns decisions you might have to make before starting to write. But questions about the circulation and influence of a text do not only concern decision-making by authors before writing; they also arise for readers, when you read texts written in varieties which have different connotations for you than they would have for other kinds of reader. Will an international audience have the same kinds of difficulty understanding a text written in a 'New English' dialect as modern audiences have understanding other kinds of dialect writing, or in reading texts from earlier periods?

Now do Activity 107 on page 204

The divergence in ways of reading we hope to expose in Activity 107 is one between kinds of reading which explore formal potentialities of language irrespective of social context (resemblances between words, rhymes, associations, common etymologies, etc.), and kinds of reading which locate meanings and significances of language primarily in terms of social conditions and contexts. It is not a question of simply deciding which is the better or 'more valid' way of reading, then simply reading in that way. Fundamental issues about how to read are raised by the instability of the relationship between how and why you yourself are reading, and the meanings of the text foreseen in view of the various social contexts in which it was expected to circulate.

9.5 Roles for English studies

We have looked at connections between studying literature in English and the changing circumstances and potentialities of English as an international language. These connections locate much of the intellectual work involved in earlier chapters of this book within a larger context of different types of language use and social opportunity. But questions remain about the broader relationship between studying literature and surrounding social structures. What kinds of social role does studying literature prepare you for within a specific language

Activity 107   *Reading 'New English' texts*
(60 mins)

To explore some of the issues raised by variation in meanings and connotations of language varieties, consider the following first stanza of a poem by the twentieth-century poet Rolando Tinio.

Sa Poetry

Sa poetry, you let things take shape,
Para bang nagpapatulo ng isperma sa tubig.
You start siyempre with memories.
Yung medyo malagkit, kahit mais
Na mais; love lost, dead dreams,   (5)
Rotten silences, and all
manner of mourning basta't murder.
Papatak yan sa papel, ano. Parang pait,
Kakagat ang typewriter keys.
You sit up like the mother of anxieties,   (10)
Worried na worried hanggang magsalakip
Ang odds and ends ng inamag mong pag-ibig.
Jigsaw puzzle. Kung minsan, everything fits,
Kung malas ka, magkakalintik-lintik.
Pero sige ang pasada ng images   (15)
Hanggang makuha perfectly ang trick.

1. Assuming you are not familiar with all the words in this excerpt, make a note of difficulties you encounter in reading and interpreting it.

2. Circle the most appropriate general response to the extract among the four responses which follow.

(a) The text doesn't make sense; it is therefore not worthy of further attention.
(b) It is possible to make some sense out of the text by exploring sound patterns and resemblances between the unknown 'words' and words of English and other languages I know. Such reading would be valuable in exploring the properties of the 'signifier' and the play in language.

(c) The text may or may not mean something, depending on whether the 'words' I don't recognise are part of a social *code* or language which could be interpreted if I knew it. Only knowledge of the text's social and historical context would enable me to decide.
(d) Option (b) and option (c) are not alternatives; they are compatible. (Say how:)

3. Now compare your response to this excerpt with your response to the two following extracts, and choose for each excerpt the most appropriate of the four general responses above.

Now, to compleat anglers, beloved bironthiarn and hushtokan hishtakatsch, join alpha pea and pull loose by dotties and, to be more sparematically logoical, eelpie and paleale by trunkles. (James Joyce, *Finnegans Wake*, 1939)

I get all bezoomny when any veck interferes with a psitsa singing, as it might be. (Anthony Burgess, *A Clockwork Orange*, 1962)

4. Are your responses to the three excerpts the same or different? If they are different, try to describe why this is.

5. Now consider whether it makes any difference to your initial response to know the following context to the poem 'Sa Poetry': Rolando Tinio is a Filipino writer. 'Sa Poetry' was written during the early 1970s, in a variety known as 'Taglish': a code-switching compound between Tagalog (a language spoken in the Philippines) and

English. Such code-switching frequently takes place among bilingual sections of the population; and, for a Tagalog/English bilingual readership, the poem is readily interpretable:

e.g.
1–2 = In poetry, you let things take shape,
      Like letting a candle drip on water.

15–16 = But images continue to flow, until you perfect the trick.
etc.

 Now rejoin text on page 203

situation; and what kinds of aspiration and priorities is it likely to develop in you? This was the question with which this book started; and it is a dimension of all work in studying literature.

Ways of studying English are in all cases kinds of social gesture. This was made clear in Chapter 2, for instance, when the very different aims and methods of various established critical approaches were outlined. The criticism of Arnold, Leavis, and others was shown to be concerned with establishing and preserving cultural values. If your thinking is shaped and influenced by this sort of criticism, its significance beyond the seminar room is to contribute to this larger, 'humanising' social project. Forms of Marxist criticism, by contrast, are concerned to show connections between cultural activity and other, economic and political structures in a society. If your thinking is shaped and influenced by this sort of criticism, its significance beyond the seminar room is to contribute to this larger, 'political' project. We can't say that there is socially 'engaged' literary study and socially 'disengaged' literary study. All approaches to studying literature promote social and cultural values, and seek to oppose or curtail the development of other values.

The problem is that many definitions of literary study are so vague as to keep open almost *all* major lines of direction. If you say, for example, 'studying literature is a way of analysing culture', this could still mean several things. It could mean:

1. learning and 'familiarising' yourself with a selected version of 'the best that is known and thought in the world', so supporting an evaluative idea of knowledge and culture (the 'Arnold/Leavis' tradition);
2. using commentary on literary texts as an opportunity for a critique of hegemonic forms of culture, exposing their ideological function and 'defamiliarising' them (the 'structuralist/Marxist' tradition);
3. investigating cultural forms anthropologically and historically, as a body of social behaviour and cultural reference linked to social patterns of knowledge, leisure, and opportunity (the 'cultural/historical' tradition).

Each of these orientations is shaped by an idea of what 'culture' is. Each leads to a different perspective on present cultural forms, and on the future directions 'culture' should take.

 Now do Activity 108 on page 206

9.6 Study and social change

Studying literature means playing a role either in reproducing or in changing existing conceptions of culture and the study of culture.

How literary studies function in relation to larger patterns in a cultural formation depends not only on the forms of study themselves but also on other larger, external patterns in the social formation.

But how does literary study interact with things going on outside itself? Does it have a role in relation to contemporary creative writing or media production, or in relation to other areas of social action? Or is the familiar anti-intellectual criticism that it is an 'ivory-tower' activity with no significant consequences for other areas of social action justified?

There appear to be three main ways in which literary studies claims to have, in addition to the general functions of education, specific effects in the world beyond its own province.

(a) Literary criticism serves to advocate new writing or media production: it heralds and defends the new, as well as saving the old from being forgotten.
(b) Literary theory demystifies unanalysed images and prejudices, and opens up new opportunities in society for otherwise suppressed meanings and reinterpretations.
(c) Critical discourse analysis exposes the ways texts produce meanings, and how they are frequently complicit with established ideologies; in this way it empowers social polemic and contributes to social change.

Activity 108   *Theoretical perspectives and popular dogmas*
(30 mins)

1. Link each of the five types of critical approach on the left with views you might expect them to correlate with from the right-hand column. (You can use each view more than once if you think it is consistent with more than one of the critical viewpoints. If you think views in the right-hand column are not appropriate to any of the approaches, do not assign them.) If you have trouble deciding what you think any of the critical approaches says, consult Chapter 2. We have made two suggestions to start you off.

Modern forms of popular culture are mostly bad.

Pleasure and value are entirely relative: one person's 'crucial' work is another person's 'rubbish'.

Arnoldian-Leavisite, 'humanising'

Marxist

Soap operas distract their viewers from the important things in life.

The range of texts you study should reflect the balance of different social groups in the make-up of society.

Structuralist

It's regrettable that people nowadays watch television instead of reading.

'Value' is not an issue of any relevance to literary study.

Feminist

Studying 'canonical' works of literature is important.

Capitalism is responsible for a contemporary cultural decline.

Deconstructionist

Popular culture is the real art of the working class.

The world needs to change.

Do you think that any of the critical approaches on the left do not take an identifiable view on particular issues in the right-hand column? If so, should they? If not, describe why you think they don't need to.

Now rejoin text on page 205

From your own experience, or referring to newspapers or books in a library, make a note here of cases of each of these effects of literary study that you are familiar with.

(a) ....

(b) ....

(c) ....

If you have difficulty thinking of examples, how much is this simply because you don't know any, and how much is it because examples don't exist?

9.6.1 CRITICAL DISCOURSE ANALYSIS

In Section 6.3 we looked at discourse analysis as a technique for analysing texts. We now turn to a way of applying these analytical techniques in a manner which might enable social change. *Critical* Discourse Analysis (CDA) is a specialised use of techniques of analysing how language or rhetorics of sounds and images serve to construct social meanings. CDA develops from the basic idea that many of the rhetorics around us serve particular ideological interests, and reflect these in the way they represent events, views, and ideas. By exposing the ways in which the particular 'slant' or 'bias' in a text is produced, it becomes possible to see the political invest-ments in it, and so to be in a position to challenge them. If you were to hear, on the news, for example,

> Enemies of the nation continue to impede economic recovery. Whenever unions go on strike it is the general public which suffers.

you would be likely to make a connection 'enemies of the nation' = 'unions'. But this 'equivalence' is an ideological relationship constructed in the discourse, not an absolute fact. Even if you don't believe the relationship is reasonable, you have to 'make' the connection in order to understand the discourse. Similarly, if you were to hear,

> The *unions* say the strike may lead to a General *Election*; the Prime *Minister* says the country *won't* be held to ransom.
> (italics signal intonational nuclei)

you would be likely to make a similar connection: 'for a strike to lead to a General Election' = 'for a country to be held to ransom'. Again the discourse constructs the idea. CDA analyses newspaper and broadcast discourse, police and medical interviews, essays, journalism, etc. to identify the linguistic bases of bias and ideological dimensions of discourse (see above, Chapter 6, pp. 128–9).

But the question is, *how* does analysing discourse in this way contribute to social change or reform? Does exposing interests and ideas in itself change them? Or is regulation or censorship of publishing and media also desired or required?

👉 *Now do Activity 109 on page 208*

9.7 Studying literature in English: the future

In Chapter 1, we saw that the study of literature in English is, very roughly, now celebrating its centenary. But not everyone is joining in the festivities. And in circumstances of major and rapid changes in educational policy, it is at least possible that literature may turn out to have been just a hundred-year 'blip' on the screen of educational history.

Both inside and outside the academic world, there have been criticisms. There are . . .

- the *vocational critique*, which says that education should prepare you for employment, and that at present literary studies merely offers distractions and develops irrelevant desires and feelings;

- the *necessary skills* critique, which says that literary studies don't prepare you adequately with relevant language skills: of spelling, grammar, and writing, or of linguistic comprehension and analysis;

- the *communications and media* critique, which says that since people now watch television more than they read, the need for literary studies has been replaced by a need for media and communication studies, and for the new field of 'information science'.

It is not possible to predict what will happen to the field you are now studying, except to say that it is likely that it will change, quite significantly, in this generation. But we can get a glimpse of that future by thinking through what 'research' in this area means, since research shows the discipline reaching out from where it is now into new, uncharted regions and possibilities.

Activity 109   *Flow diagrams of Critical Discourse Analysis*
(40 mins)

To explore how CDA might contribute to social change, consider the two flow diagrams below. Each represents a (simplified) explanation of how CDA might achieve a social effect.

Model One	Model Two
Stage 1 See something you don't approve of.	**Stage 1** See something you don't approve of.
↓	↓
Stage 2 Explain to others how effect is produced.	**Stage 2** Explain to authorities how effect is produced.
↓	↓
Stage 3 Change in people's interpretive habits.	**State 3** Regulation of production and/or distribution of original text.
↓	↓
Stage 4 Situation improved. Audience too 'literate' to tolerate original effect.	**Stage 4** Situation improved. Criticised effect gone.

1. Link each of the three arguments below, each of which represents a view of how CDA might achieve its effects, with the models given in the flow diagrams above.

Argument One
CDA works as a kind of education towards social literacy. When you've seen how socially biased meanings are produced, you won't be tricked into believing them, or agreeing with them, again. When everyone has done CDA, we can expect things to begin to change.

Fits with Model One: YES/NO
Model Two: YES/NO
neither: YES/NO

Argument Two
CDA is a means of intervention and so a part of struggle. When you've seen how socially biased meanings are produced, you can mount an institutional struggle to control them, through the law and regulatory bodies (e.g., in Britain, the Press Council, the IBA).

Fits with Model One: YES/NO
Model Two: YES/NO
neither: YES/NO

Argument Three
CDA is a way of acquiring skills in techniques of *producing* biased discourse, so that you can achieve desired social effects for yourself, and promote your own views.

Fits with Model One: YES/NO
Model Two: YES/NO
neither: YES/NO

2. Decide which argument seems closest to how you think CDA might work.

3. Finally, make 'refinements' to the models and arguments presented, if you think they give too simplified a picture of how CDA might work.

☞ *Now rejoin text on page 207*

Research is the future in the making

Constantly you *read* the results of research, as part of your studies (e.g. new editions, literary critical books, reference works). But do you wonder how such research is produced: what its foreseen purposes were, who pays for it, or why it is the way it is? And beyond what you yourself know, do you have a clear idea of what *is* known in the field (by others, by 'experts')?

We don't, for example, know definitively whether Shakespeare actually wrote Shakespeare. And we can't be certain how much of the play *Pericles*, usually attributed to Shakespeare, was written by whoever wrote all the other plays by Shakespeare. Nor do we know how much Shakespeare knew of classical philosophy and rhetoric, or what he means by 'I can tell a hawk from a handsaw' in *Hamlet*. We do not know for sure how many people saw Shakespeare's plays, or how many people read the first editions. Nor do we know exactly how many people could read – and to what levels – at the time of Shakespeare. And this is just Shakespeare. In fact, it's just the beginning of all the things we don't know about Shakespeare – the most celebrated and studied single author who has ever written.

But are all these uncertainties of the same importance; and to what degree do they affect you? After all, so far in this book we have suggested that studying literature in English is largely concerned with interpreting and making sense of texts, rather than researching new facts about them.

With this in mind, it is worth listing the main kinds of research that are currently done in the field of literary studies, before going on to explore differences between them.

Main directions in current literary research

Editorial work
>(producing more accurate and more scholarly editions)

Bibliographical work
>(discovering and cataloguing source materials relating to a given text or author, to serve as reference points for other kinds of scholarship)

Historical and sociological study
>(investigating the social contexts of works of literature; studies of influence, traditions, and reception)

Interpretation and evaluation
>(using existing editions and scholarship on works or authors to 'reread' them, suggesting new meanings, significance or relevance)

Literary theory
>(investigating how literature works: what literature is, how we read it, how criticism works)

Educational research
>(developing new syllabuses and teaching materials)

☛ **Now do Activity 110**

**Activity 110   *Evaluating research projects*
(40 mins)**

Decide what usefulness you think each of the following research projects would be likely to have. Imagine yourself for a moment to be part of a research-grant-awarding panel, and decide which projects you feel are worth supporting. Leaving aside questions of how, or how well, such research would actually be carried out, make a brief note in the space provided of points for and against each, as a *direction for investigation*. (If you are in doubt about any of the terms in the titles, check earlier stages of this book for comment.)

1. The role of music symbolism in Elizabethan and Jacobean plays.

2. A deconstructionist reading of Michael Jackson's *Thriller* video.

3. Unequal reception: a comparison between critical responses to 'male' modernists and 'female' modernists.

7. A psychoanalytic study of the poetry of Ezra Pound.

4. Narrative techniques in TV serialisations of 'canonical' novels.

8. A catalogue of current research on audiences for novels in the early nineteenth century.

5. Sexual abuse: 'Susie Wong' figures in Western fiction.

9. A study of the relation between eighteenth-century theories of government and Samuel Johnson's view of language change in his 'Preface' to *A Dictionary of the English Language*.

6. From blackboard to workbook: new classroom methods in teaching literature.

10. Add the title of a research project of your own here (or make one up which you would like to do):

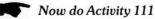 *Now rejoin text*

Research, courses and textbooks

Literary Studies in Action began with an assessment of your expectations regarding the study of literature in English. Many of these may have been confirmed by your experience of the contents of this book; others may not

have been. It is therefore appropriate to end with an activity which focuses on the processes this book has itself involved.

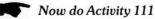 *Now do Activity 111*

Activity 111   *What do you think of* Literary Studies in Action?
(60 mins)

1. Make a note of all the things you feel have not been dealt with in this book.
At all:

2. Make a note of all the things that in your opinion we have given too much prominence to.

To some extent, but not properly:

3. Make a note of topics or parts of the book that you think you will now give particular attention to, and will follow up.

4. Compare your own image of the study of literature with our representation of it in this book. To do this, circle the appropriate number on the scales below (5=very much; 0 = not at all).

Literary Studies in Action is . . .

.....committed to present forms of the
study of literature in English 5 4 3 2 1 0
.....committed to changing present forms
of the study of literature in English 5 4 3 2 1 0
.....simplistic about the main issues of
literary studies 5 4 3 2 1 0

5. Use the improved grid for comparing theories you devised in Activity 19, to analyse the approach to the study of literature in English presented in this book.
6. Re-do the tasks in Activity 17, taking *Literary Studies in Action* as your text.

☛ *Now rejoin text*

9.8 Conclusions

This chapter has tried to look over the battlements of the study of literature in English, into the outside world and into the future. We have done this in the belief that, just as you need to know something of the subject's history and present lines of direction if you are to work effectively within it, so you should also, for the same reasons, form a view of its potentialities and possible future. Doing this should allow you to become interested in the large educational questions which will shape that future, by helping you to follow discussion of those issues in newspapers and on television, as well as in your studies.

As we pointed out at the beginning of this book, *Literary Studies in Action* is not a fully self-contained programme of study. To be effective, it needs you to relate it constantly to your everyday patterns of reading, watching, and listening, as well as to any formal course of study you are taking.

The future of the subject depends on demands made on it, from inside as well as out. The aim of *Literary Studies in Action*'s D-I-Y approach has been to strengthen your voice, by insisting that meanings in and for literary study are something you have to make, rather than something for you to consume.

Throughout this book, we have stressed the interactive and process-based character of studying literature in English, rather than the established idea of a fixed content of knowledge or scholarship that has simply to be learned. As you come to the end of *Literary Studies in Action*, you may nevertheless feel disappointed that we do not often provide answers for you to check your work against. If you are not using the book in the context of a course (or informal study group), it is likely that you will find it difficult to get any feedback on the work you have done.

If you do feel that some specific response to your experience of using this book would be valuable, we, as the book's authors, will be pleased to hear from you with queries, suggestions, or comments. Subject to pressure of our commitments, we will try in all cases to reply to communications, whatever aspect of *Literary Studies in Action* they are about; and we will try to take your suggestions into account in further work we do. Write to us at the Programme in Literary Linguistics, or phone us on 041–553 4150.

Answers to selected activities

41 1. The Independent Variable (IV) is the variable you *manipulate*. In this case, it is 'layout type' which is being deliberately changed or manipulated to test what happens as a consequence of the changes. The Dependent Variable (DV) is the variable whose changes, resulting from changes in the value of IV, you *measure*. In this case, we are measuring 'reading time', so 'reading time' is the Dependent Variable.

56 All except cat/acclaim.

58 ABABABCC.

60 2. (in our dialect, Southern Standard English; your dialect may be different)

```
  ,         ,         ,         ,         ,            ,
σ σ       σ  σ      σ σ      σ σ      σ σ σ      σ σ σ σ
perform   mention   pretext  distrust  develop    mathematics
```

```
,            ,          ,        ,            ,         ,
σ σ σ      σ  σ       σ σ      σ σ σ σ      σ σ       σ σ
argument   number    prefer   incorporate  derail    protest
```

```
  ,              ,         ,          ,              ,         ,
σ σ σ σ  σ     σ  σ σ     σ σ        σ   σ σ σ      σ  σ
laboratory  act  masculine  monster   monstrosity   blackbird
```

4. 'protest' has stress on first syllable if a noun, second syllable if a verb; 'blackbird' with stress on 'black' refers to a particular species, while with stress on 'bird' could refer to any bird which is black.

5. 'laboratory' has stress on the first syllable in standard American English. There may be others; we don't know of any.

62 1 = 12, 2 = 3, 3i = iambic tetrameter, 3ii = anapestic tetrameter, 3iii = trochaic trimeter.

63 1–2. We suggest these stressings for the first verse (which suggest that it is strong stress metre); other stressings are possible, particularly for the fourth line.

```
       ,           ,           ,          ,
σ      σ      σ      σ       σ  σ   σ σ  σ
and there she's lean'd her back to a thorn
```

```
 ,        ,         ,         ,
σ σ     σ σ σ    σ σ σ     σ σ σ  σ
O and alas-a-day O and alas-a-day
```

```
     ,            ,          ,          ,
σ       σ      σ σ    σ   σ σ   σ
And there she has her baby born
```

```
 ,              ,            ,            ,
σ      σ  σ    σ     σ    σ  σ   σ σ  σ
Ten thousand times good night and be wi' thee
```

5. The Wordsworth text appears to be in iambic tetrameter (with a concession to ballad form by having a short second line).

68 1. Some anti-Ciceronian elements are: first sentence is short; second sentence has main thought, 'there be . . . Beleefe', with added thought afterwards, 'Affecting . . . Acting'; there is not much 'balance' – in fact the last part seems deliberately unbalanced: 'in Thinking as well as in Acting' instead of the more balanced 'in Thinking and Acting'.

72 (a) coded; (b) non-coded*; (c) coded; (d) coded (though not literally the meaning, this is a conventional meaning for the phrase in some cultures); (e) non-coded (because who 'I' refers to and how hot 'hot' is are entirely dependent on the situation in which the sentence is heard); (f) non-coded*; (g) non-coded. (*(b) and (f) both involve some element of convention, and so are in some sense coded – see text following activity.)

73 . . . 'with contagious diseases, suche as be wonte [are likely] by infection to crepe [creep] from one to an other [another], myght be layde a part farre [might be laid apart far] from the company of the residue.'

74 1. (b) cat – actor, Mary – object; (c) Mary – actor, cat – object, Peter – receiver; (d) same as c; (e) same as c.
2. Could be 'time of event'.
3. 'it' in these sentences does not refer to anything specific in the world which could be involved in an event.
4. (f) 'the wind' is not an agent; perhaps 'state of the weather' is an appropriate annotation; (g) 'John' might be called 'experiencer'.

75 1. annotated sentences might be: *John* is eager to please

$$\uparrow$$

actor

John is easy to please

$$\uparrow$$

object of action

This might be a version of the 'sentence–event code'. But notice that it differs from it in that it is not the order of words that matters but the nature of the adjective. So it might be a different code – perhaps a 'subject-of-adjective interpretation code'.
2. Similar sentences involve the adjectives 'happy', 'difficult', etc.

99 All the assertions are true, according to McCrum, Cran and McNeil, *The Story of English*. For other comparable estimates, see Crystal (ed.), *The Cambridge Encyclopedia of Language*, Kachru (ed.), *The Other Tongue*, or Pride, *New Englishes*.

References and Further Reading

Chapter 1

1 For further discussion of the idea of a literary 'canon', and of the definition of the content of literature courses, see Eagleton, *Literary Theory: An Introduction*, Chapter 1.

Chapter 2

1 For more about the history of English words, see Williams, *Keywords*, especially the Introduction, and Empson, *The Structure of Complex Words*. On beginnings and origins, see Said, *Beginnings: Intention and Method*.
2 A history of literary studies in the UK up to Richards and Leavis is Mulhern, *The Moment of Scrutiny* (see especially Chapter 1).
3 See Ohmann, *English in America*.
4 Lodge (ed.), *Twentieth Century Literary Criticism: A Reader* contains a representative selection of theoretical work up to the 1960s. For a selection of readings of more recent work, see Lodge (ed.), *Modern Criticism and Theory: A Reader*.
5 A representative selection is Craig (ed.), *Marxists on Literature*. For a recent example of Marxist criticism which looks at both stylistics and the problem of post-colonialism, see Ngara, *Art and Ideology in the African Novel*.
6 Leach, *Lévi-Strauss* provides an introduction to structuralism. Harland, *Superstructuralism* is a history of structuralism into post-structuralism. Culler, *Structuralist Poetics* is an overview of structuralism as it applies to literature.
7 Anderson, *Phonology in the Twentieth Century* gives an account of phonology, with extensive accounts of Saussure and the Prague Circle.
8 An example of one binary opposition studied in depth is provided by Williams, *The Country and the City*.
9 Two representative collections of stylistics are Freeman (ed.), *Linguistics and Literary Style*, and Freeman (ed.), *Essays in Modern Stylistics*.
10 As an introduction to psychoanalysis and psychoanalytic criticism, see Freud, *Introductory Lectures on Psychoanalysis*, Lacan, *The Four Fundamental Concepts of Psycho-analysis*, and Wright, *Psychoanalytic Criticism*. Laplanche and Pontalis, *The Language of Psychoanalysis* is a useful reference work.
11 As an introduction to deconstruction see Derrida, *Of Grammatology*, and Norris, *Deconstruction: Theory and Practice*.
12 Two introductions to feminist literary theory are Greene and Kahn (eds), *Making a Difference*, and Weedon, *Feminist Practice and Poststructuralist Theory*. Two collections are Eagleton (ed.), *Feminist Literary Theory: A Reader*, and Marks and de Courtivron (eds), *New French Feminisms*.

FURTHER READING

Ducrot and Todorov, *Encyclopedic Dictionary of the Sciences of Language* covers many of the theoretical movements discussed here. Cook (ed.) *The Cinema Book* has summaries of many theories, and discussion of their application to films. Lerner (ed.), *Reconstructing Literature* is an anthology of opposition to recent literary theory. Fabb *et al.* (eds), *The Linguistics of Writing* presents a montage of different directions in current work.

Chapter 3

1 Barthes, 'From Work to Text' is anthologised in, e.g., Barthes, *Image-Music-Text*, ed. Heath.
2 For a discussion of oral and literate societies, see Ong, *Orality and Literacy: The Technologizing of the Word*. Williams, *Communications* discusses modern communications and society.
3 For discussion of the historical circumstances of writers in England between the Middle Ages and the twentieth century, see Williams, *The Long Revolution*, Chapter 5, 'The social history of English writers'.
4 For a detailed history and analysis of the current legal situation in Britain, see Robertson and Nichol, *Media Law: The Rights of Journalists, Broadcasters and Publishers*.
5 For a detailed study of the history and politics of literacy, see Levine, *The Social Context of Literacy*. Chapter 3, on the historical contexts of literacy, is particularly useful.

FURTHER READING

For the social background to reading and writing in Britain, see, for example, Lawson and Silver, *A Social History of Education in England*, and Watt, *The Rise of the Novel*.

Chapter 4

1 See, for example, Eliot, 'Tradition and the individual talent', in *Selected Prose*, or Shklovsky, 'Sterne's *Tristram Shandy* and the theory of the novel' in Lemon and Reis (eds), *Russian Formalist Criticism*.
2 For discussion of how to devise experiments, see Miller, *Experimental Design and Statistics*. For detailed study of the

use of statistics in linguistics, with some discussion of experiment and survey design, see Butler, *Statistics in Linguistics*.

Chapter 5

1 From Dixon, *The Languages of Australia*, p. 105.
2 An influential theoretical proposal about this, called the 'Sapir–Whorf hypothesis', suggests that humans are limited by their language in how they are able to think about the world (for discussion, see Hudson, *Sociolinguistics*, Chapter 3). This hypothesis is not generally accepted now: see Rosch, 'Linguistic relativity', and other articles in Johnson-Laird and Wason (eds), *Thinking: Readings in Cognitive Science*.
3 From Abrams, *A Glossary of Literary Terms* (entry on Genre).
4 T. S. Eliot, *The Waste Land* is a 'textbook' example of modernist genre combination; reading it and thinking about it is likely to be as useful a starting place as any.
5 For a collection of articles on post-modernism see Foster (ed.), *Postmodern Culture*. Krauss's article 'Sculpture in the expanded field' is particularly interesting as regards the application of classification to creative work.
6 The formal implications of medium are discussed in Ellis, *Visible Fictions: Cinema, Television, Video*.
7 See Foucault, *The Order of Things*, and Jameson, *The Political Unconscious*, particularly Chapter 1.

Chapter 6

1 For different ways of looking at metre, see Attridge, *The Rhythms of English Poetry*, Hayes, 'Metrics and phonological theory' in Newmeyer (ed.), *Linguistics: The Cambridge Survey*, vol. 2, and Easthope, *Poetry as Discourse*.
2 See Couper-Kuhlen, *An Introduction to English Prosody*.
3 For extensive discussion, focusing particularly on French writers, see Banfield, *Unspeakable Sentences*.
4 See Halliday and Hasan, *Cohesion in English*, and Brown and Yule, *Discourse Analysis*.
5 See Vickers, *Classical Rhetoric in English Poetry*.

FURTHER READING

Leech, *A Linguistic Guide to English Poetry*, Leech and Short, *Style in Fiction*, and Traugott and Pratt, *Linguistics for Students of Literature* provide a more detailed discussion of many of the topics in this chapter. There are many good introductions to linguistic theory; for example, Aitchison, *Teach Yourself Linguistics*, Fromkin and Rodman, *An Introduction to Language*, and Akmajian, Demers and Harnish, *Linguistics*. For a collection of articles surveying current linguistics see Newmeyer (ed.), *Linguistics: The Cambridge Survey*, 4 vols. An introduction/reference is Crystal, *The Cambridge Encyclopedia of Language*; section 12 is on language in literature. Crystal, *A First Dictionary of Linguistics and Phonetics* is a useful reference.

Chapter 7

1 For further discussion of kinds of code, see Barthes, *Elements of Semiology*. For an introduction to semantics see Lyons, *Language, Meaning and Context*.

2 The idea that thoughts are sentences is argued in Fodor, *The Language of Thought*: arguments that it is specifically rules of logic like *modus ponens* which are used to get from sentence to sentence come from Sperber and Wilson, *Relevance: Communication and Cognition*.
3 See Sperber, *Rethinking Symbolism*.
4 See Fodor, *The Modularity of Mind*. A distinction of this kind similar to Fodor's has been explored by Stephen Krashen (see *Second Language Acquisition and Second Language Learning*) to account for problems in second-language-learning; he distinguishes language acquisition (=input systems) from language-learning (=central systems). Parallels between Fodor and Krashen are drawn in Schwartz, 'The epistemological status of second language acquisition'.
5 See Frazier, 'Grammar and language processing', in Newmeyer (ed.), *Linguistics: The Cambridge Survey*, vol. 2. For an introduction to how the brain handles language see Matthei and Roeper, *Understanding and Producing Speech*.
6 For an introduction to schemas, frames, and scripts, and more generally to the role of background knowledge in interpreting discourse, see Brown and Yule, *Discourse Analysis*.
7 For discussion of overdetermination in dreams, see Freud, *The Interpretation of Dreams*. For discussion of overdetermination in metaphors and metonymies in particular, see Metz *Psychoanalysis and Cinema: The Imaginary Signifier*, Part 4. Timpanaro, *The Freudian Slip* gives a Marxist and anti-psychoanalytic account of slips and metaphors.
8 See Lacan, 'Agency of the letter in the unconscious', in *Ecrits: A Selection*.

FURTHER READING

See Stillings *et al.*, *Cognitive Science: An Introduction*, Gregory (ed.), *The Oxford Companion to the Mind*, and Scientific American Book, *The Brain*. Churchland, *Matter and Consciousness* discusses different philosophical approaches to mind and the brain. A detailed account of psychoanalytic approaches to metaphor and metonymy is Metz, *Psychoanalysis and Cinema: The Imaginary Signifier*. Ideas about meaning deriving from linguistics and semiotics have been influential in other disciplines, such as post-modern architectural practice – see, for example, von Moos, *Venturi, Rauch and Scott-Brown: Buildings and Projects* – and law – see, for example, Goodrich, *Legal Discourse: Studies in Linguistics, Rhetoric and Legal Analysis*.

Chapter 8

1 The list is from Levinson, *Pragmatics*, Chapter 4.
2 See, for example, Foucault, *The Archaeology of Knowledge*, Kuhn, *The Structure of Scientific Revolutions*, and for an account of a specific 'way of thinking' see Tillyard, *The Elizabethan World Picture*.
3 Propp, *Morphology of the Folktale*, Chapters 2 and 3. See also Cook, *The Cinema Book*, pp. 234–6 (section on applying Propp to film narratives).

FURTHER READING

Hacking, *Representing and Intervening* gives an overview of different ways of thinking about scientific theories and how they relate to the physical world.

Chapter 9

1 For further information about the scale and kinds of use of English in the world, see Pride, *New Englishes*, Kachru, *The Other Tongue*, Greenbaum, *The English Language Today*, McCrum, Cran and MacNeil, *The Story of English*, and Trudgill and Hannah, *International English*. The figures given in our chapter are estimates; there is sometimes disagreement about population and speaker counts.

2 For detailed accounts of the history of English, see Strang, *A History of English*, Leith, *A Social History of English*, and McCrum, Cran and MacNeil, *The Story of English*. For an account of the other languages of Britain see Price, *The Languages of Britain*. Trudgill (ed.), *Language in the British Isles* and Ferguson and Heath, *Language in the USA* are collections of essays on English and other languages in these countries.

3 Aitchison, *Language Change: Progress or Decay?* is an introduction to how and why languages change.

4 For studies of social variation in English, see Hudson, *Sociolinguistics*, and Montgomery, *An Introduction to Language and Society*. For investigation of regional variation in Britain, see Francis, *Dialectology: An Introduction*.

FURTHER READING

Howatt, *A History of English Language Teaching*, and Stern, *Fundamental Concepts of Language Teaching*. Crystal, *The Cambridge Encyclopedia of Language* is a useful source book and overview.

Bibliography

Abbott, E. A. (1891), *A Shakespearian Grammar: An Attempt to Illustrate Some of the Differences Between Elizabethan and Modern English*, London, Macmillan.

Abrams, M. H. (1981), *A Glossary of Literary Terms*, 4th edn, New York, Holt, Rinehart & Winston.

Aitchison, J. (1978), *Teach Yourself Linguistics*, Sevenoaks, Hodder & Stoughton.

Aitchison, J. (1981), *Language Change: Progress or Decay?* London, Fontana.

Akmajian, A., Demers, R. and Harnish, R. (1984), *Linguistics: An Introduction to Language and Communication*, Cambridge, Mass., MIT Press.

Anand, M. R. (1935), *Untouchable*, New Delhi, Heinemann.

Anderson, S. (1985), *Phonology in the Twentieth Century: Theories of Rules and Theories of Representations*, Chicago. Chicago University Press.

Arnold, M. (1869), *Culture and Anarchy*, London, Smith, Elder & Co.

Arnold, M. (1880), 'The study of poetry' in Ward, *The English Poets*, London, Macmillan.

Attridge, D. (1982), *The Rhythms of English Poetry*, Harlow, Longman.

Banfield, A. (1982), *Unspeakable Sentences: Narration and Representation in the Language of Fiction*, London, Routledge & Kegan Paul.

Barber, C. (1976), *Early Modern English*, London, André Deutsch.

Barthes, R. (1967), *Elements of Semiology*, New York, Hill & Wang (first published in French in 1964).

Barthes, R. (1977), *Image–Music–Text: Essays Selected and Translated by Stephen Heath*, London, Fontana.

Benjamin, W. (1973), 'Theses on the philosophy of history' in H. Arendt (ed.), *Illuminations*, Glasgow, Fontana (Theses . . . first published in German in 1950).

Berger, J. (1972), *Ways of Seeing*, London, BBC Publications and Harmondsworth, Penguin.

Brewer, E. C. (1978), *The Dictionary of Phrase and Fable*, New York, Avenel Books (facsimile of 1894 edition).

Brown, G. and Yule, G. (1983), *Discourse Analysis*, Cambridge, Cambridge University Press.

Butler, C. (1985), *Statistics in Linguistics*, Oxford, Basil Blackwell.

Chomsky, N. and Halle, M. (1968), *The Sound Pattern of English*, New York, Harper & Row.

Churchland, P. M. (1984), *Matter and Consciousness: A Contemporary Introduction to the Philosophy of Mind*, Cambridge, Mass, MIT Press.

Cook, P. (ed.) (1985), *The Cinema Book*, London, British Film Institute.

Couper-Kuhlen, E. (1986), *An Introduction to English Prosody*, London, Edward Arnold.

Coward, R. and Ellis, J. (1977), *Language and Materialism: Developments in Semiology and the Theory of the Subject*, London, Routledge & Kegan Paul.

Craig, D. (ed.) (1975), *Marxists on Literature*, Harmondsworth, Penguin.

Crystal, D. (1980), *A First Dictionary of Linguistics and Phonetics*, London, André Deutsch.

Crystal, D. (1987), *The Cambridge Encyclopedia of Language*, Cambridge, Cambridge University Press.

Culler, J. (1975), *Structuralist Poetics*, London, Routledge & Kegan Paul.

Derrida, J. (1976), *Of Grammatology*, Baltimore, Johns Hopkins University Press (first published in French in 1967).

Dixon, R. M. W. (1980), *The Languages of Australia*, Cambridge, Cambridge University Press.

Ducrot, O. and Todorov, T. (1981), *Encyclopedic Dictionary of the Sciences of Language*, Oxford, Basil Blackwell (first published in French in 1972).

Eagleton, M. (1986), *Feminist Literary Theory: A Reader*, Oxford, Basil Blackwell.

Eagleton, T. (1983), *Literary Theory: An Introduction*, Oxford, Basil Blackwell.

Easthope, A. (1983), *Poetry as Discourse*, London, Methuen.

Eliot, T. S. (1953), *Selected Prose*, ed. J. Hayward, Harmondsworth, Penguin.

Ellis, J. (1982), *Visible Fictions: Cinema, Television, Radio*, London, Routledge & Kegan Paul.

Empson, W. (1977), *The Structure of Complex Words*, 3rd edn, London, Chatto & Windus.

Fabb, N., Attridge, D., Durant, A. and MacCabe, C. (eds) (1987), *The Linguistics of Writing: Arguments Between Language and Literature*, Manchester, Manchester University Press.

Ferguson, C. A. and Heath, S. B. (eds) (1981), *Language in the USA*, Cambridge, Cambridge University Press.

Fiske, J. (1982), *Introduction to Communication Studies*, London, Methuen.

Fodor, J. A. (1975), *The Language of Thought*, Cambridge, Mass., Harvard University Press.

Fodor, J. A. (1983), *The Modularity of Mind*, Cambridge, Mass., MIT Press.

Foster, H. (ed.) (1985), *Postmodern Culture*, London, Pluto Press.

Foucault, M. (1970), *The Order of Things*, London, Tavistock (first published in French in 1966).

Foucault, M. (1972), *The Archaeology of Knowledge*, London, Tavistock (first published in French in 1969).

Francis, W. N. (1983), *Dialectology: An Introduction*, Harlow, Longman.

Freeman, D. C. (1970), *Linguistics and Literary Style*, New York, Holt, Rinehart & Winston.

Freeman, D. C. (ed.) (1981), *Essays in Modern Stylistics*, London, Methuen.

Freud, S. (1973), *Introductory Lectures on Psychoanalysis*, Harmondsworth, Penguin (first published in German in 1917).

Freud, S. (1976), *The Interpretation of Dreams*, Harmondsworth, Penguin (first published in German in 1900).

Fromkin, V. and Rodman, R. (1988), *An Introduction to Language*, 4th edn, New York, Holt, Rinehart & Winston.

Goodrich, P. (1987), *Legal Discourse: Studies in Linguistics, Rhetoric and Legal Analysis*, London, Macmillan.

Greenbaum, S. (ed.) (1985), *The English Language Today*, Oxford, Pergamon Press.

Greene, C. and Kahn, C. (eds) (1985), *Making a Difference: Feminist Literary Criticism*, London, Methuen.

Gregory, R. L. (ed.) (1987), *The Oxford Companion to the Mind*, Oxford, Oxford University Press.

Hacking, I. (1983), *Representing and Intervening: Introductory Topics in the Philosophy of Natural Science*, Cambridge, Cambridge University Press.

Halliday, M. A. K. and Hasan, R. (1976), *Cohesion in English*, Harlow, Longman.

Harland, R. (1987), *Superstructuralism: The Philosophy of Structuralism and Post-Structuralism*, London, Methuen.

Holland, N. (1968), *The Dynamics of Literary Response*, Oxford, Oxford University Press.

Howatt, A. P. R. (1984), *A History of English Language Teaching*, Oxford, Oxford University Press.

Hudson, R. (1980), *Sociolinguistics*, Cambridge, Cambridge University Press.

Jameson, F. (1981), *The Political Unconscious: Narrative as a Socially Symbolic Act*, London, Methuen.

Johnson-Laird, P. N. and Wason, P. C. (eds) (1977), *Thinking: Readings in Cognitive Science*, Cambridge, Cambridge University Press.

Kachru, B. (ed.) (1982), *The Other Tongue: English Across Cultures*, Oxford, Pergamon.

Kott, J. (1967), *Shakespeare our Contemporary*, London, Methuen (first published in Polish in 1964).

Krashen, S. (1981), *Second Language Acquisition and Second Language Learning*, Oxford, Pergamon Press.

Kuhn, T. (1962), *The Structure of Scientific Revolutions*, Chicago, Chicago University Press.

Lacan, J. (1977), *The Four Fundamental Concepts of Psycho-Analysis*, London, Hogarth Press and the Institute of Psychoanalysis (first published in French in 1973).

Lacan, J. (1977), *Ecrits: A Selection*, London, Tavistock (first published in French in 1966).

Laplanche, J. and Pontalis, J.-B. (1973), *The Language of Psychoanalysis*, London, Hogarth Press.

Lawson, J. and Silver, H. (1973), *A Social History of Education in England*, London, Methuen.

Leach, E. (1974), *Lévi-Strauss*, London, Fontana.

Leavis, F. R. (1948), *The Great Tradition: George Eliot, Henry James, Joseph Conrad*, London, Chatto & Windus.

Leech, G. N. (1969), *A Linguistic Guide to English Poetry*, Harlow, Longman.

Leech, G. N. and Short, M. H. (1981), *Style in Fiction*, Harlow, Longman.

Leith, D. (1983), *A Social History of English*, London, Routledge & Kegan Paul.

Lemon, L. T. and Reis, M. J. (eds) (1965), *Russian Formalist Criticism: Four Essays*, Lincoln, University of Nebraska Press.

Lerner, L. (ed.) (1983), *Reconstructing Literature*, Oxford, Basil Blackwell.

Levine, K. (1986), *The Social Context of Literacy*, London, Routledge & Kegan Paul.

Levinson, S. C. (1983), *Pragmatics*, Cambridge, Cambridge University Press.

Lévi-Strauss, C. (1972), *Structural Anthropology*, Harmondsworth, Penguin (first published in French in 1958).

Lodge, D. (1972) (ed.), *Twentieth Century Literary Criticism: A Reader*, Harlow, Longman.

Lodge, D. (1988) (ed.), *Modern Criticism and Theory: A Reader*, Harlow, Longman.

Lyons, J. (1981), *Language, Meaning and Context*, London, Fontana.

McCrum, R., Cran, W. and MacNeil, R. (1986), *The Story of English*, London, Faber & Faber and BBC Publications.

Marks, E. and de Courtivron, I. (eds) (1981), *New French Feminisms*, Hassocks, Sussex, Harvester Press.

Matthei, E. and Roeper, T. (1983), *Understanding and Producing Speech*, London, Fontana.

Metz, C. (1982), *Psychoanalysis and Cinema: The Imaginary Signifier*, London, Macmillan (first published in French in 1977).

Miller, S. (1975), *Experimental Design and Statistics*, London, Methuen.

Montgomery, M. (1986), *An Introduction to Language and Society*, London, Methuen.

Moos, S. von (1987), *Venturi, Rauch and Scott-Brown: Buildings and Projects*, New York, Rizzoli.

Mulhern, F. (1979), *The Moment of Scrutiny*, London, Verso.

Newmeyer, F. J. (ed.) (1988), *Linguistics: The Cambridge Survey*, 4 vols, Cambridge, Cambridge University Press.

Ngara, E. (1985), *Art and Ideology in the African Novel: A Study of the Influence of Marxism on African Writing*, London, Heinemann.

Norris, C. (1982), *Deconstruction: Theory and Practice*, London, Methuen.

Ohmann, R. (1976), *English in America*, Oxford, Oxford University Press.

Ong, W. J. (1982), *Orality and Literacy: The Technologizing of the World*, London, Methuen.

Pratt, M. L. (1977), *Toward a Speech Act Theory of Literary Discourse*, Bloomington, Indiana University Press.

Price, G. (1984), *The Languages of Britain*, London, Edward Arnold.

Pride, J. B. (1982), *New Englishes*, Rowbury, Mass., Newbury House.

Propp, V. (1968), *Morphology of the Folktale*, Austin, University of Texas Press (first published in Russian in 1928).

Robertson, G. and Nichol, G. L. (1985), *Media Law: The Rights of Journalists, Broadcasters and Publishers*, Beverley Hills, Sage.

Said, E. (1985), *Beginnings: Intention and Method*, New York, Columbia University Press.

Schwartz, B. (1986), 'The epistemological status of second language acquisition', *Second Language Research*, vol. 2, no. 2, pp. 120–59.

Scientific American Book (1979), *The Brain*, San Francisco, W. H. Freeman.

Sebeok, T. (ed.) (1960), *Style in Language*, Cambridge, Mass., MIT Press.

Selden, R. (1985), *A Reader's Guide to Contemporary Literary Theory*, Hassocks, Sussex, Harvester Press.

Sperber, D. (1975), *Rethinking Symbolism*, Cambridge, Cambridge University Press.

Sperber, D. and Wilson, D. (1986), *Relevance: Communication and Cognition*, Oxford, Basil Blackwell.

Stern, H. H. (1983), *Fundamental Concepts of Language Teaching*, Oxford, Oxford University Press.

Stillings, N. A., Feinstein, M. H., Garfield, J. L., Rissland, E. L., Rosenbaum, D. A., Weisler, S. E. and Baker-Ward, L. (1987), *Cognitive Science: An Introduction*, Cambridge, Mass., MIT Press.

Strang, B. M. H. (1970), *A History of English*, London, Methuen.

Thompson, S. (1932–6), *Motif Index of Folk Literature*, Helsinki (published as FF Communications 106–9, 116–7).

Thrale, W. F. and Hubbard, A. (1960), *A Handbook to Literature*, New York, The Odyssey Press.

Tillyard, E. M. W. (1943), *The Elizabethan World Picture*, London, Chatto & Windus.

Timpanaro, S. (1976), *The Freudian Slip – Psychoanalysis and Textual Criticism*, London, New Left Books (first published in Italian in 1974).

Traugott, E. and Pratt, M. (1980), *Linguistics for Students of Literature*, New York, Harcourt Brace Jovanovich.

Trudgill, P. (ed.) (1984), *Language in the British Isles*, Cambridge, Cambridge University Press.

Trudgill, P. and Hannah, J. (1982), *International English*, London, Edward Arnold.

Upton, C., Sanderson, S. and Widdowson, J. (1987), *Word Maps: A Dialect Atlas of England*, London, Croom Helm.

Vickers, B. (1970), *Classical Rhetoric in English Poetry*, London, Macmillan.

Watt, I. (1957), *The Rise of the Novel*, Harmondsworth, Penguin.

Weedon, C. (1987), *Feminist Practice and Poststructuralist Theory*, Oxford, Basil Blackwell.

Widdowson, P. (ed.) (1982), *Re-reading English*, London, Methuen.

Williams, R. (1962), *Communications*, Harmondsworth, Penguin.

Williams, R. (1961), *The Long Revolution*, Harmondsworth, Penguin.

Williams R. (1973), *The Country and the City*, London, Chatto & Windus.

Williams, R. (1976), *Keywords: A Vocabulary of Culture and Society*, London, Fontana.

Wimsatt, W. K. (1946), 'The intentional fallacy' in W. K. Wimsatt (1954), *The Verbal Icon*, Kentucky, University of Kentucky Press.

Wright, E. (1984), *Psychoanalytic Criticism*, London, Methuen.

Index